PAPER FLIGHT

Jack Botermans

PAPER FLIGHT

48 MODELS READY FOR TAKE-OFF

An Owl Book

HOLT, RINEHART AND WINSTON
New York

Published in the United States by Holt, Rinehart and Winston,
383 Madison Avenue, New York, New York 10017.

Published simultaneously in Canada by Holt, Rinehart and Winston
of Canada Limited.

Library of Congress Cataloging in Publication Data

Botermans, Jack.
Paper flight.

Translation of: Flieger aus Papier.
"An Owl book."
1. Paper airplanes. I. Title.
TL770.B55713 1984 745.592 83-49043
ISBN 0-03-070506-1

First American Edition

Models conceived and illustrated by Jack Botermans
Text by Bert Jansen, translated by Deborah Ogle
Photography by David van Dijk

Printed in Belgium by Brepols S.A.

10 9 8 7 6 5 4

ISBN 0-03-070506-1

It's always difficult at first . . .

CONTENTS

Introduction 7
Tools and techniques 9

Fantasy flyers 10
Basic model 11
Speedy 12
Manta 15
Wright flyer 16
Wings 20
Rocket 21
Paper plane 22
Bat 24
McDonnell 26
SX 101 (PF) 28
Pterodactyl 30

Genuine reproductions 32
Mirage 34
Tiger Moth 36
Saab 37 Viggen 40
Tupolev (Bear) 42
F-16 45

Experimental models 48
Flying saucer 50
Matchstick rocket 51
Starship 53
Catapult plane 54
Flying fish 58
Flying arrow 60
Paper helicopter 62
Carousel 64

Competition craft 66
Cirrus 75 68
Hunter 70
Sprinter 72
Acrobat 74
Sailplane 76
Sakoda 78
Sherlock special 80
Flying dragon 82
Flying Christmas tree 84
Anti-aircraft device 86
Catapult defense craft 88

Birds 90
Basic crane 91
Crane 92
Heron 94
Eagle 96
Seagull 98
Wild geese 100
Wild duck 103
Swallow 104
White dove 106
Carrier pigeon 108

Insects 110
Dragonfly 112
Moth 114
Flies 116
Butterfly 119

INTRODUCTION

Making paper airplanes: a child's game or the unfulfilled dreams of youth? That was the image for years and the people who took it seriously were often ridiculed. There is the tale of a well-known professor who made a paper airplane out of the program during a boring evening at the theater, involuntarily let it fly, and immediately it attracted more attention than the action on the stage.

The turning point in its recognition as a respectable hobby came about with a competition in the magazine *Scientific American*. The first International Airplane Competition was announced on December 12 1966 with a full-page advertisement in the *New York Times*. The inspiration was the Lockheed-Boeing supersonic aircraft design. The famous Concorde is certainly reminiscent of the old and familiar craft made out of a sheet of paper. The response was enormous and, just as *Scientific American* suspected, there were more talented aircraft enthusiasts around than most people envisaged.

Certainly many thousands of devotees have had a try at some time or another; using paper from school exercise books or pages torn out of glossy magazines, clumsily or carefully folded, countless paper planes have flown through the air to make their first smooth, or sometimes rough, landing. The old schoolboy model was definitely a favorite but it looked rather awkward; another child made a much better one which was graceful and attractive in the air. Another model is the one frequently made during a boring afternoon at the office; an irritating memo from the boss is folded eight times and look at the glorious, satisfying result – a sweeping glide and the illusion, however short-lived, of being in control of the sky. Of course, it never lasts for more than a few seconds and then, fulfilled or not, the day's routine must be resumed.

But the paper plane is not a discovery of the school or business world. Leonardo da Vinci, one of the first in a long line of inventors, experimented with planes made out of parchment. And just think, if the Montgolfier brothers had not casually hung a paper bag up over the wood fire, the discovery of the hot air balloon would have been left to someone else.

Paper has always been a suitable medium for man's dreams of flying like a bird. The dreams continue although the fantasies are perhaps less romantic with the advent of jumbo jets and the Concorde. What happened to those childhood dreams of becoming train drivers and jet pilots? You can buy plastic kits for building replicas of airplanes, but what use is a plane that is too heavy to fly? A noisy radio-controlled model made of balsa wood and glue can fly but, after all those months of working every Sunday afternoon, it could well firmly set itself on a course for self-destruction despite all the clever engineering. This desire to make a precise copy often results in disappointment and disillusionment.

Far more rewarding is the plane that is carefully folded from a piece of paper which glides through the air from the palm of the hand, hovering a while and causing no disturbing noise, and no greasy hands or sticky fingers. Paper planes are harmless and require nothing more than ingenuity, patience and perseverance. They can fly indoors or out in virtually any conditions – even a sultry summer evening can produce good results. A final piece of advice – put your name and address on the model in case of a spectacular maiden flight!

Just at first, folding paper planes may appear easier than it really is. Many prototypes will make an untimely landing in the wastepaper basket, but persevere. Isn't it satisfying to find that complicated F-16s can be made out of a simple piece of paper. And what is there to prevent you from organizing your own air show, designing the models and painting them in your own colors? You won't require lots of tools: two hands, patience and the instructions on page 9.

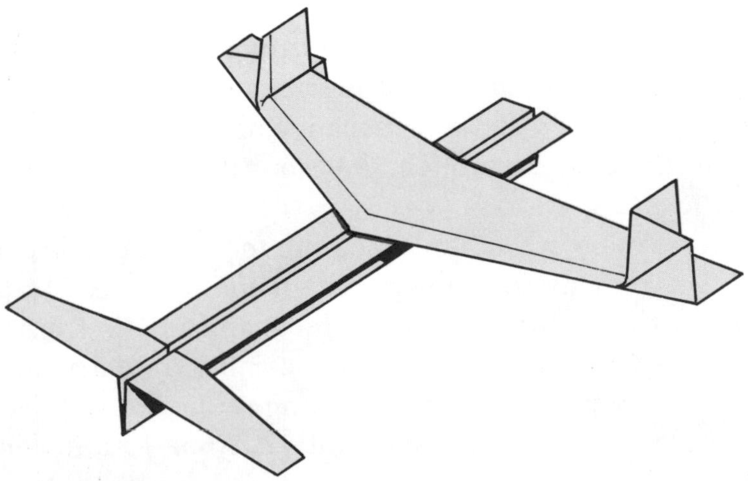

TOOLS AND TECHNIQUES

The principal tools for folding paper models are your own two hands. In some cases additional equipment is required but most things are available in any household. To make successful aircraft involves conscientious practice and detailed study of all the diagrams. If something isn't immediately clear, examine the appropriate diagram carefully, make one or two practice folds and the method will become clear. Patience is absolutely essential.

General

Work on a clean surface. The basic material for paper aircraft is of course paper. The weight of the paper used will depend upon the size of the finished model. Models of 10 to 20cm require 60g paper. The models illustrated in this book never require paper heavier than 80g; average bond typing paper (not copy paper) is approximately this weight. Complex folding patterns require thinner paper, perhaps as fine as cigarette paper, but to do these requires experience. Generally, the larger the model, the thicker the paper but you can always experiment. Before attempting a model, always study the step-by-step diagrams carefully. In fact, the photographs of the models will probably tell you more than any explanation. To make sharp, clean edges you may score the lines; do this by scratching a straight line where the fold should be with the blade of a pair of scissors. This can also be done with a knife but only on thick paper as there is a risk of cutting through the paper. Some folds necessitate a 'double crease', made by folding the paper backwards and forwards on the same line to achieve a flexible 'hinge'. In addition, there is the 'inverted fold' which is explained here with a diagram.

Explanation of the diagrams

Dotted line: fold here or make a double crease by folding backwards and forwards along the dotted line.
Solid line: the position of an existing fold or cut.
Scissors: cut along the line indicated.
Inverted fold: first fold the paper backwards and forwards along the dotted line and then push the top point inwards as the arrow indicates; good sharp folds make it easier.
Thunderbolt arrow: first make an inwards fold, and then an outwards fold.
If you follow the direction of the arrows accurately you can't go wrong.

Tools

The few you use must be good ones. You will need a sharp pair of scissors, preferably small ones, for example haircutting scissors; a pencil (to mark down measurements), not too hard so that you can rub it out; a craft knife (the type which has a continuous blade, the end of which may be broken off when blunt); paints and paintbrushes (poster paints are best for the job as they won't make the model too damp); paper glue; a stapler to fasten parts of the models together (Scotch tape or glue may often replace the stapler); a ruler for measuring and to help to make straight folds.

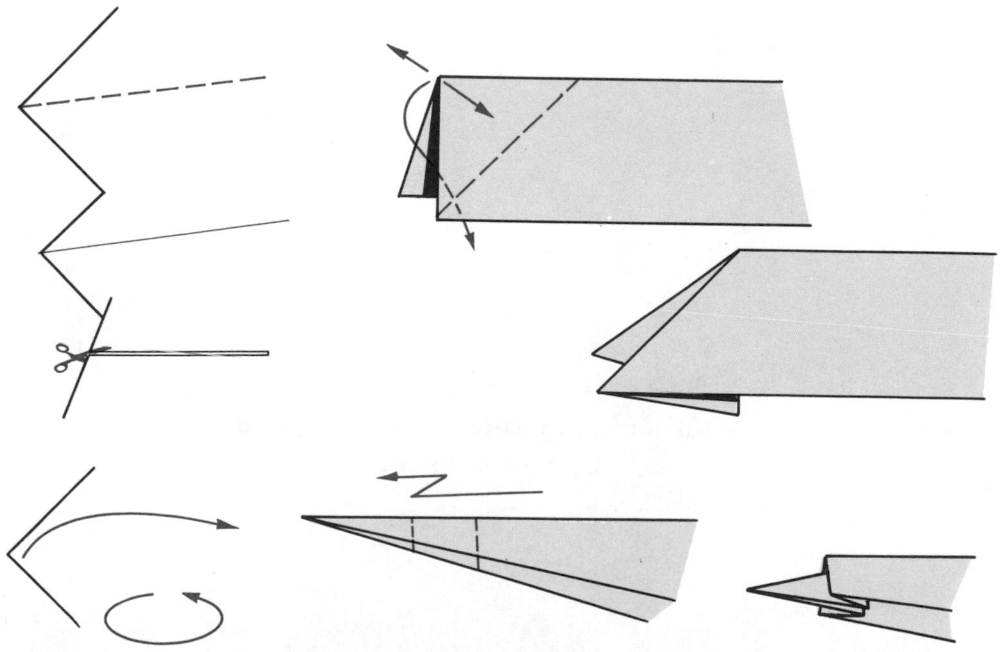

FANTASY FLYERS

This section includes a number of basic models, each one unique and providing plenty of scope for your imagination. These models are imaginary because they bear no resemblance to any recognizable airplane design. Having mastered the techniques used in this section, the designs may be altered to your own specifications. You may decide to build an original Starfighter equipped with delta wings, or even deliver a special message by personal airmail.

The first thing a carpenter learns is how to hit a nail into wood. In the case of a paper aircraft, the first thing to learn is the art of folding paper: how, where and in what way it should be folded is clearly explained with the help of diagrams. These make-believe models are

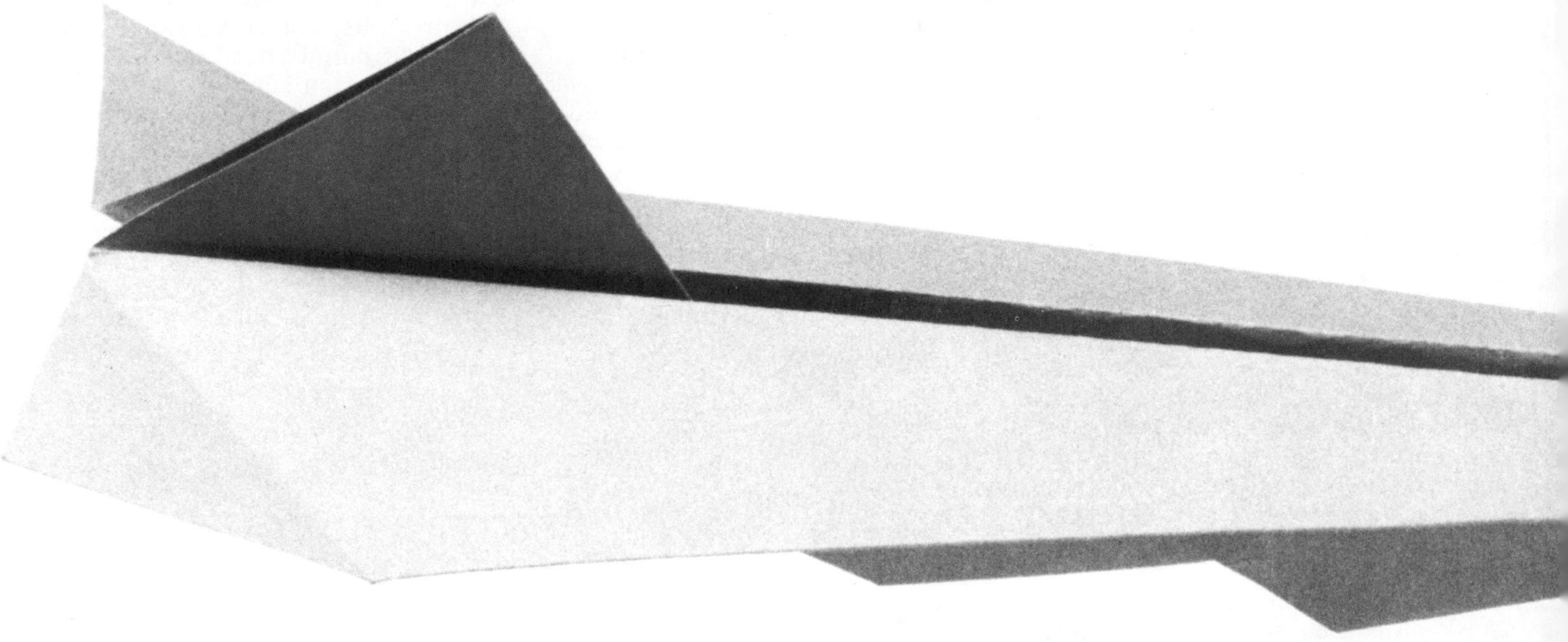

included to explain the working methods and folding skills as thoroughly as possible rather than to demonstrate high-performance flights.

Eleven designs are included in this section – some are easy for developing your command of the techniques and others are more difficult. Try them all and experiment by combining different designs. Make sure you have a plentiful supply of paper . . .

Basic Model

Everyone has made this model at some time. This is the one that has been thrown at many an unsuspecting teacher standing at the blackboard. It is quickly and easily made from a sheet of paper 20 × 30cm (8 × 12in). The one shown here looks rather like a rocket. This is a good time to develop you own ideas and try to improve on this simple design. You may, for example, decide to glue on the wings of the Wright Flyer on page 16. The directions tell you to use a staple but you could glue it, making the model stronger and more solid. The rudders are folded and bent to enable the plane to perform different flight patterns, as the instructions will show.

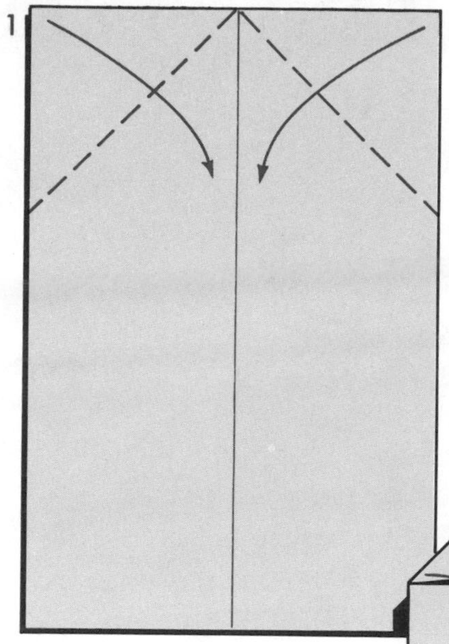

1 Take a sheet of paper 20 × 30cm (8 × 12in) and fold it in half lengthways. Open out flat and fold in the two corners as shown by the dotted line.

2 Fold the two sides along the dotted lines, towards the center fold.

3 Again fold in the two sides towards the center fold.

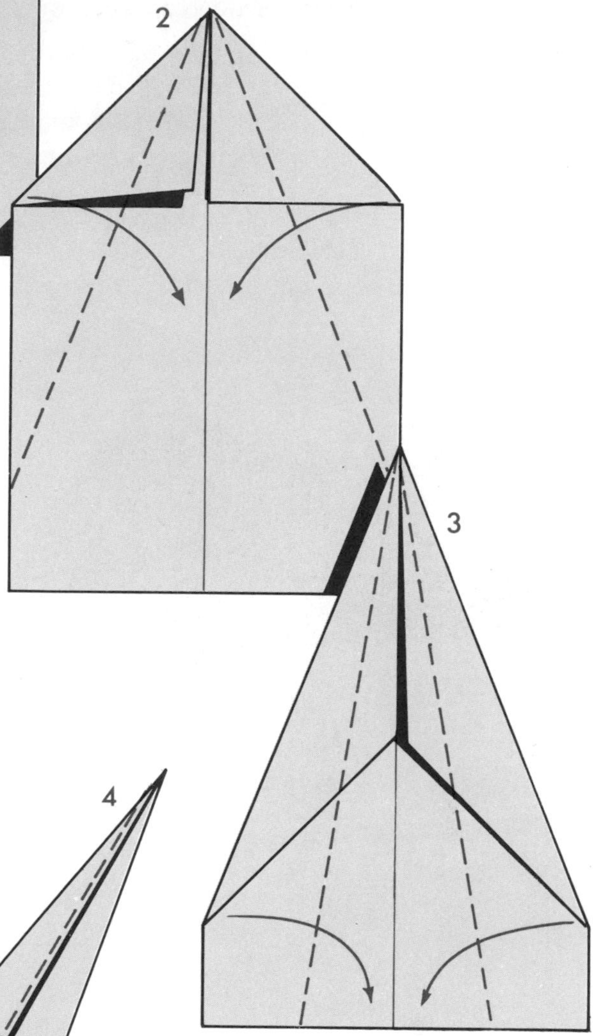

An airplane which has been aimed at many unsuspecting teachers . . .

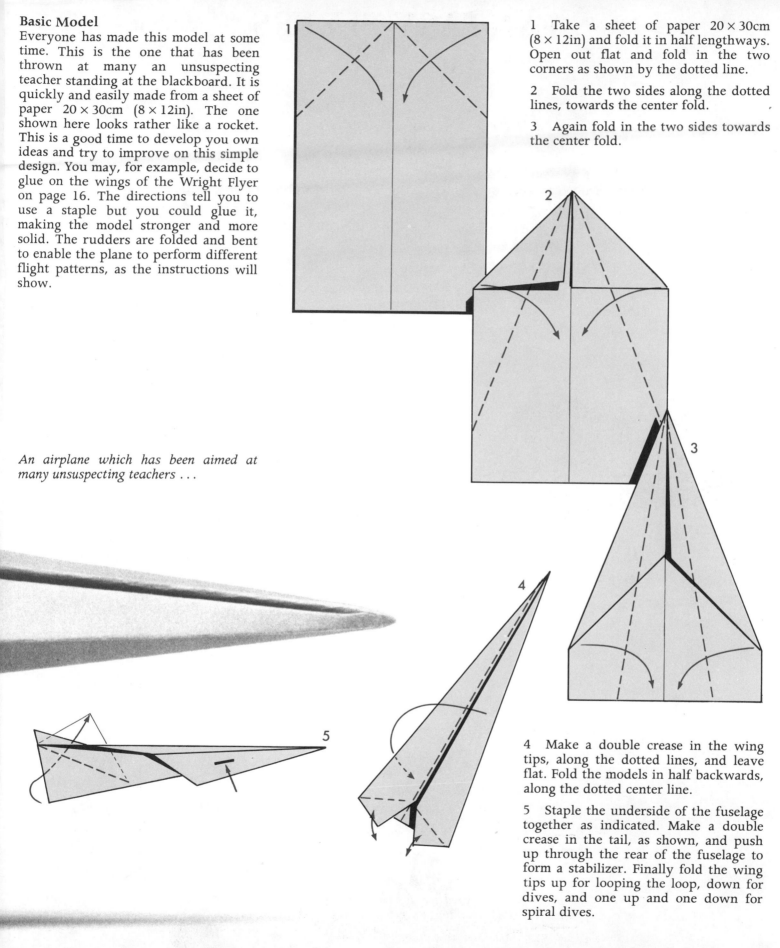

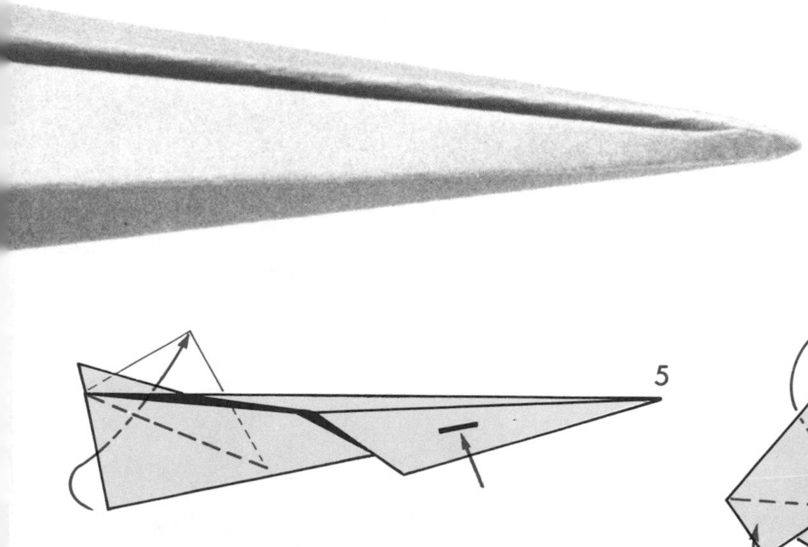

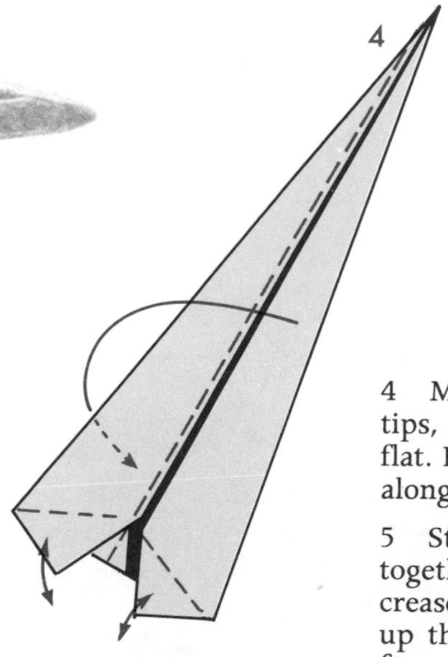

4 Make a double crease in the wing tips, along the dotted lines, and leave flat. Fold the models in half backwards, along the dotted center line.

5 Staple the underside of the fuselage together as indicated. Make a double crease in the tail, as shown, and push up through the rear of the fuselage to form a stabilizer. Finally fold the wing tips up for looping the loop, down for dives, and one up and one down for spiral dives.

Be prepared for unscheduled flights from this small tough aerobat . . .

SPEEDY

This is an original cross between a French Mirage Jet and a Bat. We call it 'Speedy' because it has turned out to be a fast and cunning flyer, always trying out some new trick. This model is an easy one to fold and you can easily make lots of them at once. Why not assemble a whole squadron, give them names or numbers and fly them all together?

1 Take a piece of paper 20 × 30cm (8 × 12in) and fold the two opposite corners together.

2 Fold up the bottom edge, exactly half the distance of 'a'.

3 Fold the paper in half along the dotted line.

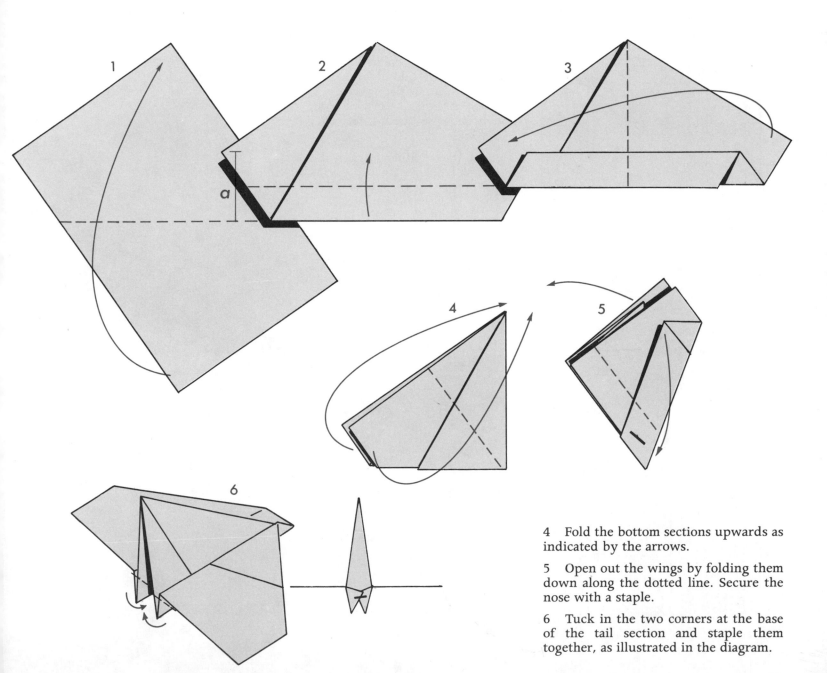

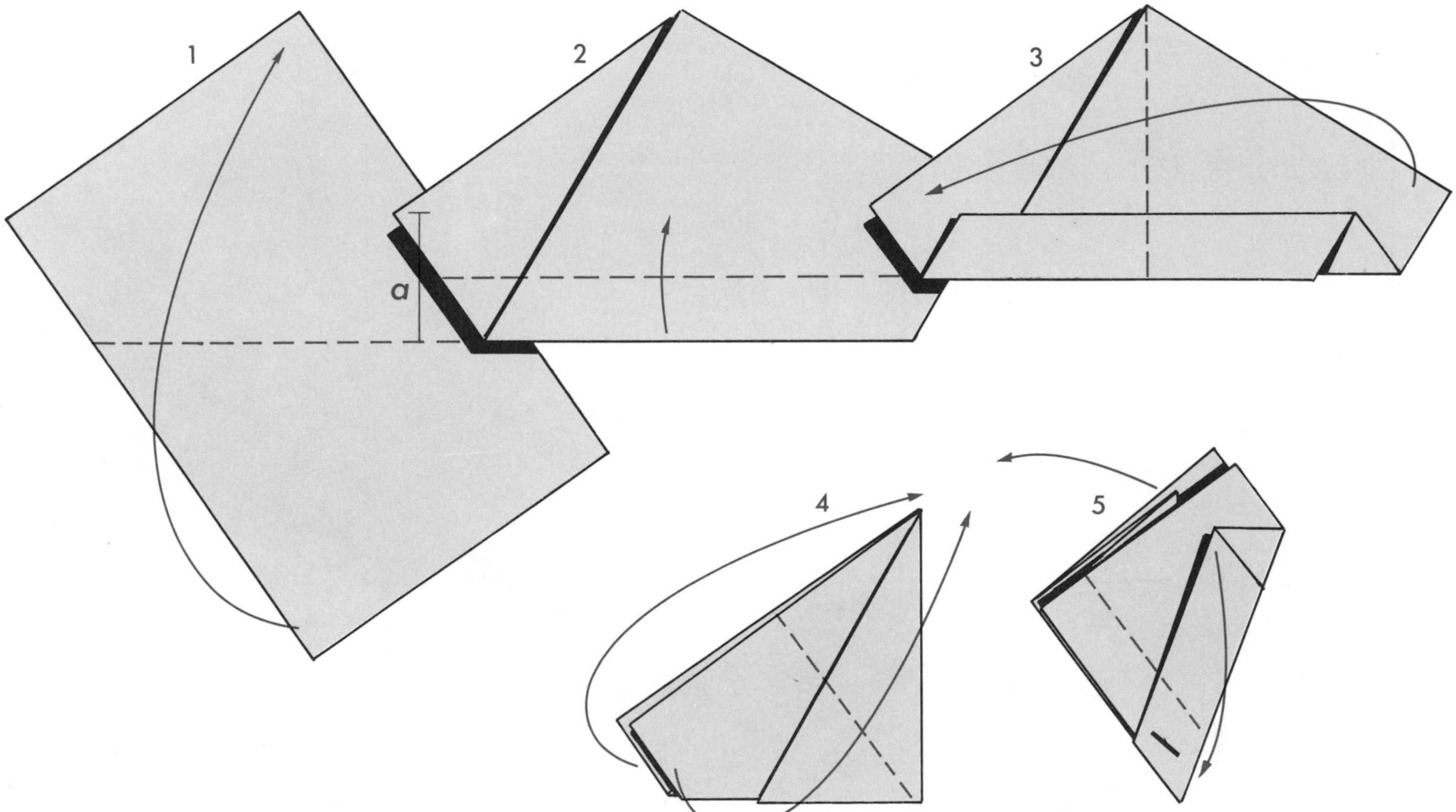

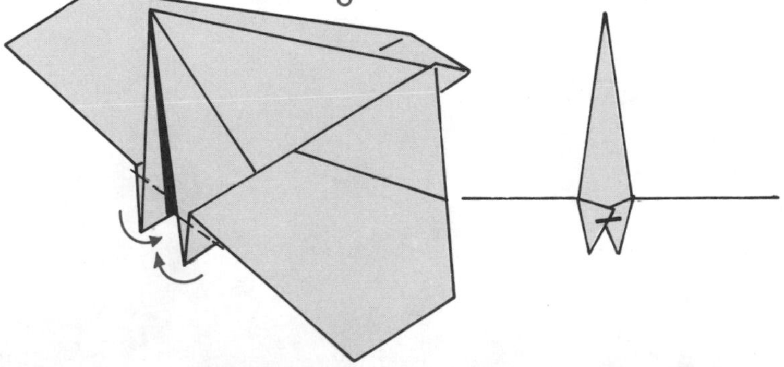

4 Fold the bottom sections upwards as indicated by the arrows.

5 Open out the wings by folding them down along the dotted line. Secure the nose with a staple.

6 Tuck in the two corners at the base of the tail section and staple them together, as illustrated in the diagram.

MANTA

If a car manufacturer can name its product after the magnificent manta ray, there is no reason why we shouldn't follow suit with this Manta.

By and large the paper airplane bears a far greater resemblance to the fish than the car does. The front, in particular, has a similar menacing shape. Certain characteristics of the airplane are also similar: great endurance and stability. The Manta is primarily a glider and not well suited to aerobatics.

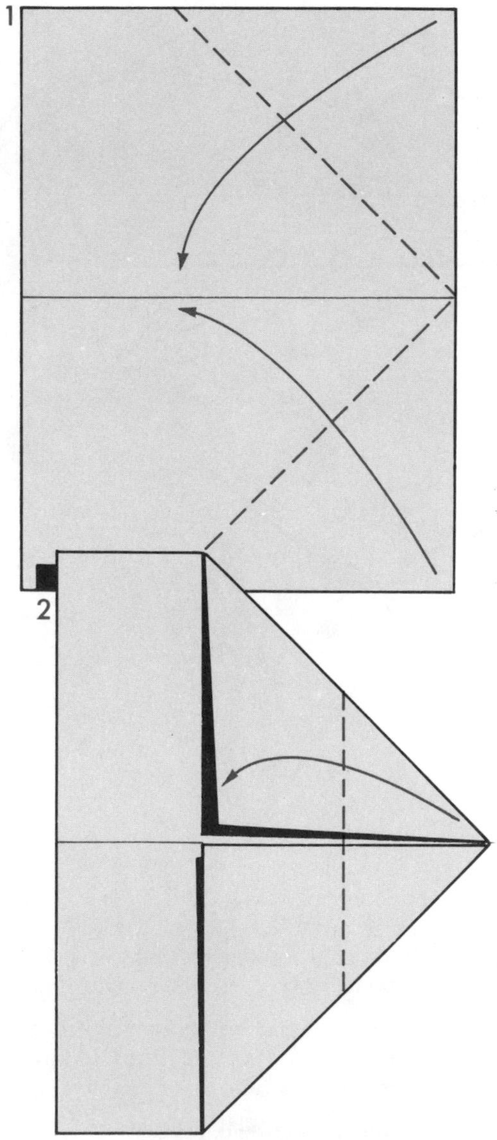

1 Take a sheet of paper 30 × 40cm (12 × 16in) and fold it in half widthways. Open it out flat again and fold in the two righthand corners along the dotted lines so they meet along the center fold.

2 Fold the righthand triangular section in half.

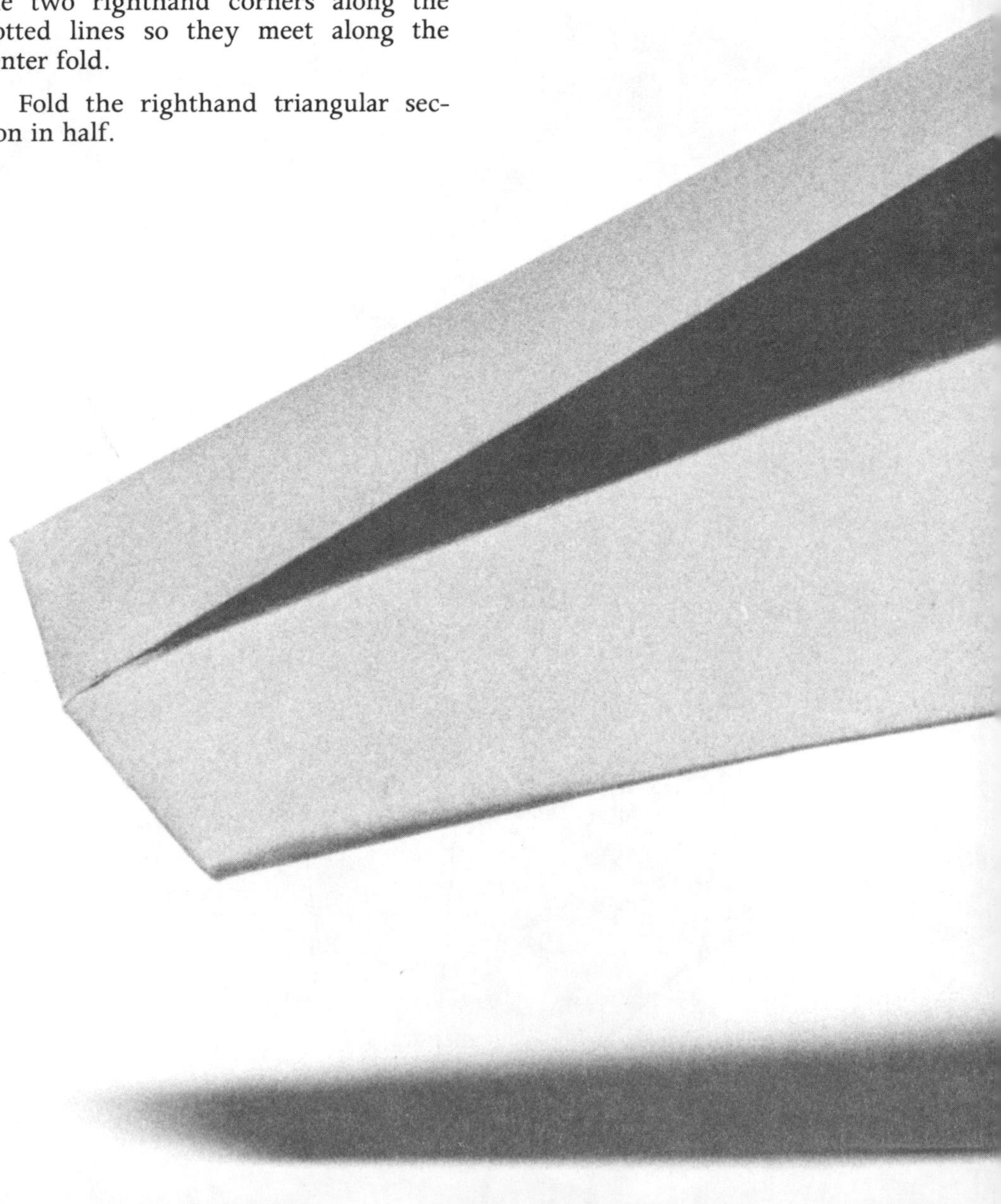

In flight its characteristics are stability and great endurance . . .

3 Now fold the two sides inwards to meet at the center fold.

4 Turn over and fold in half along the dotted line.

5 Everything has been very easy until this point; now it gets a little harder. Following the diagram carefully, push the middle section of the tailpiece up through the center by means of an inverted fold. Make the wings by folding upwards along the dotted lines, one wing to either side.

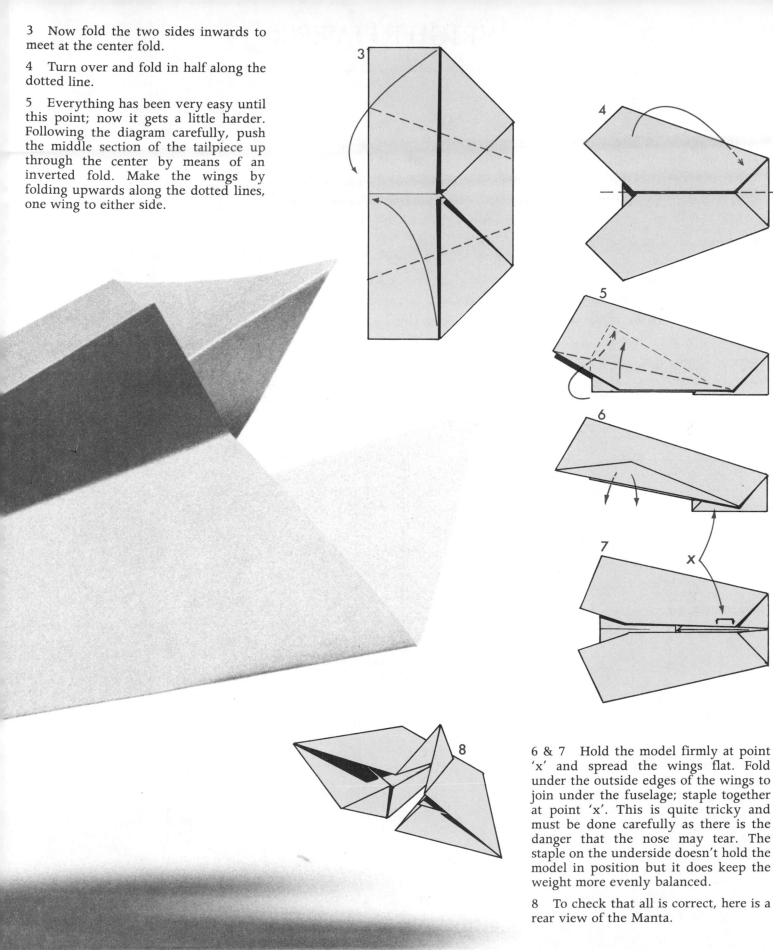

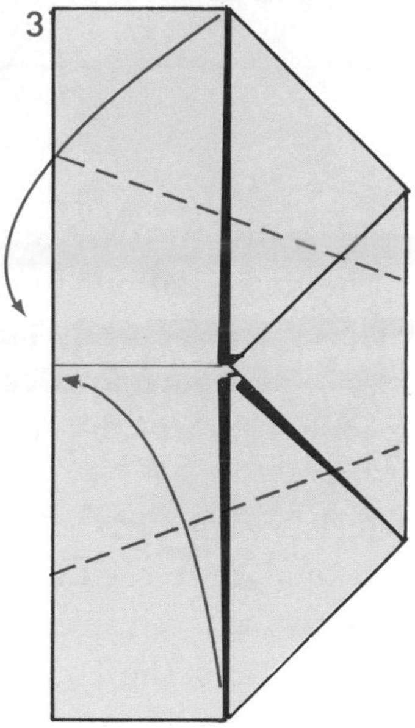

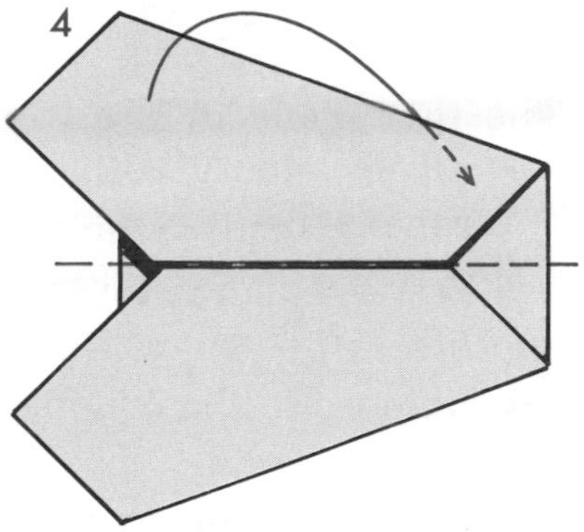

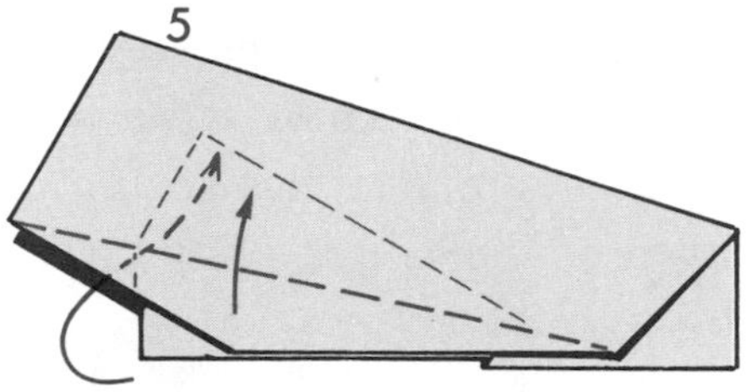

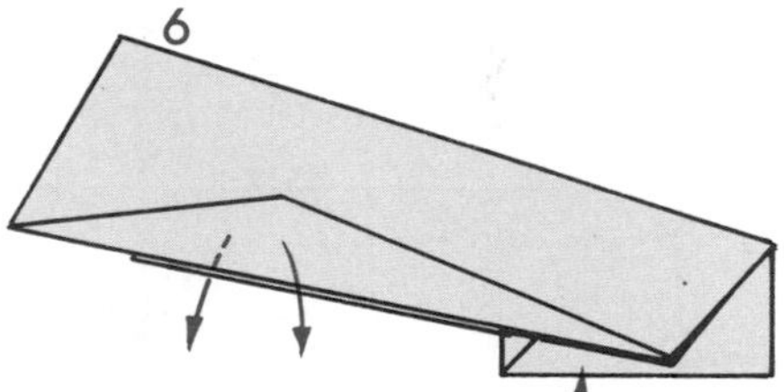

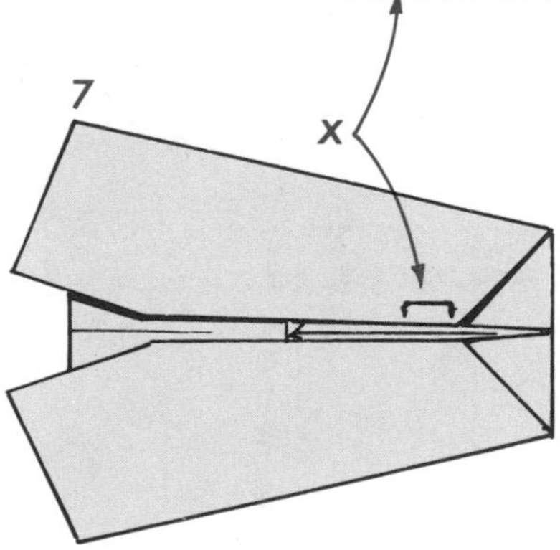

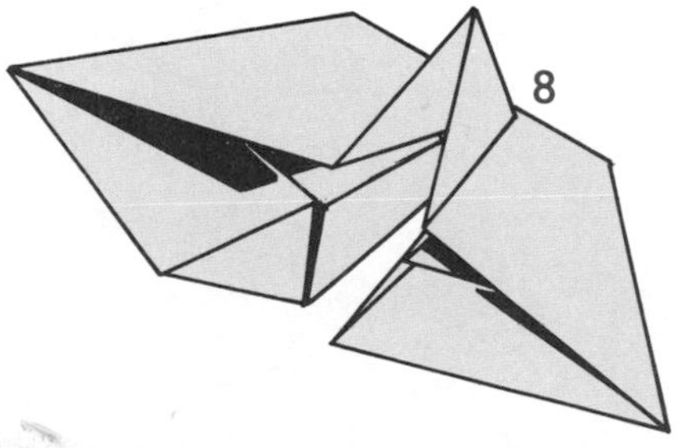

6 & 7 Hold the model firmly at point 'x' and spread the wings flat. Fold under the outside edges of the wings to join under the fuselage; staple together at point 'x'. This is quite tricky and must be done carefully as there is the danger that the nose may tear. The staple on the underside doesn't hold the model in position but it does keep the weight more evenly balanced.

8 To check that all is correct, here is a rear view of the Manta.

WRIGHT FLYER

The first plane in the world that could really fly was built by the Wright brothers, Orville and Wilbur. The design of our model recalls it with the small wing in front and larger one behind. The Wright brothers' airplane was actually a biplane, so you may like to build another wing on top so that your model bears an even greater resemblance to the original.

To demonstrate the flying characteristics of this plane to the greatest advantage, it should be allowed to glide freely away from the hand. The small wings should always be in front; this seems unusual but the early planes were built in this way and the construction of supersonic planes has seen a revival of this type of design. The front edges of the larger wings are curved so that the plane soars further through the air.

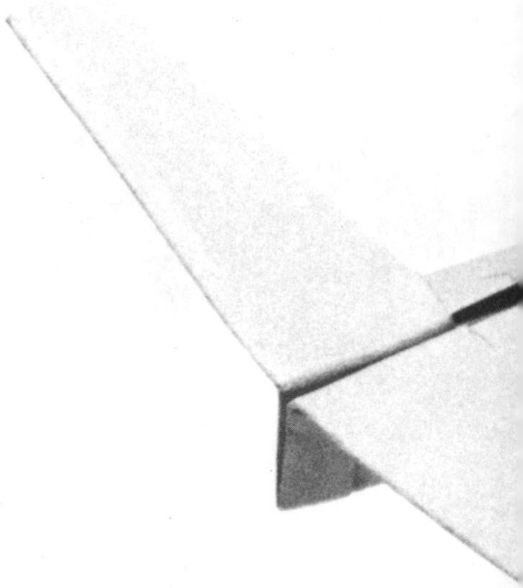

1

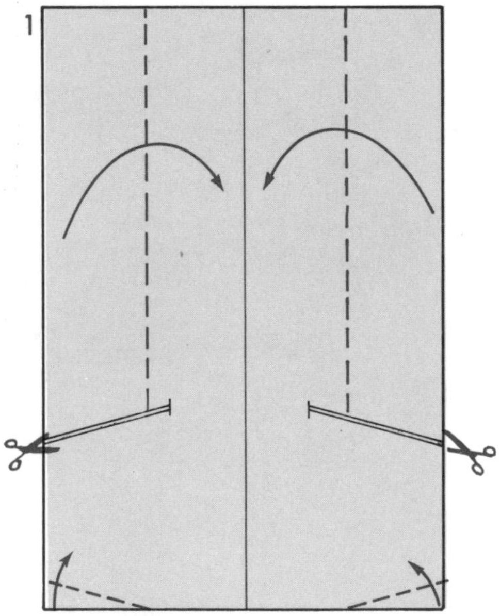

2

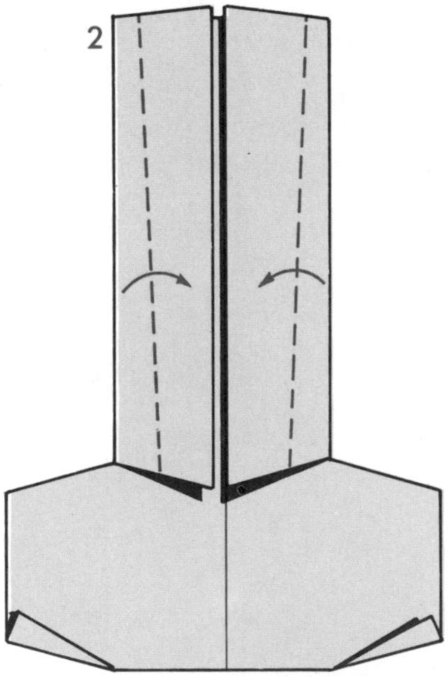

3

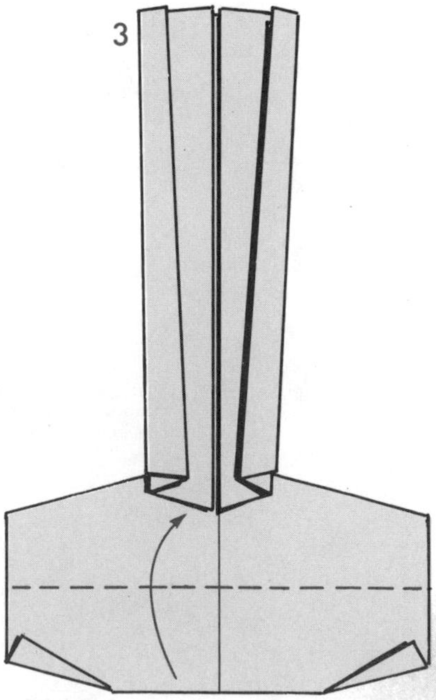

Fuselage

1 Take a piece of paper 20 × 30cm (8 × 12in) and fold it lengthways. Make a short cut on both sides, as illustrated. Fold both the left- and the righthand flaps to the center along the dotted lines, and also fold over the bottom corners along the dotted lines.

2 Fold both sides inwards again, along the dotted lines.

3 Fold up the bottom edge, as illustrated.

The first planes were built like this and the construction of supersonic planes has seen a revival of this design . . .

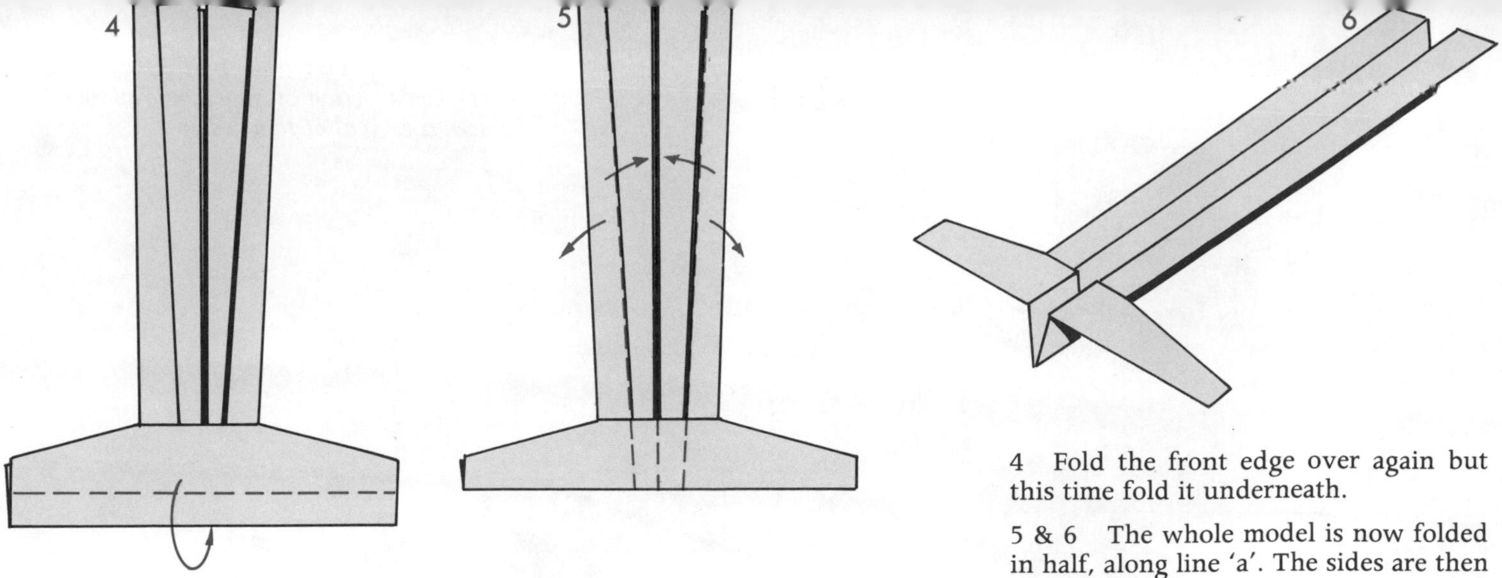

4 Fold the front edge over again but this time fold it underneath.

5 & 6 The whole model is now folded in half, along line 'a'. The sides are then both folded back down as shown in Fig 6. The fuselage is now completed.

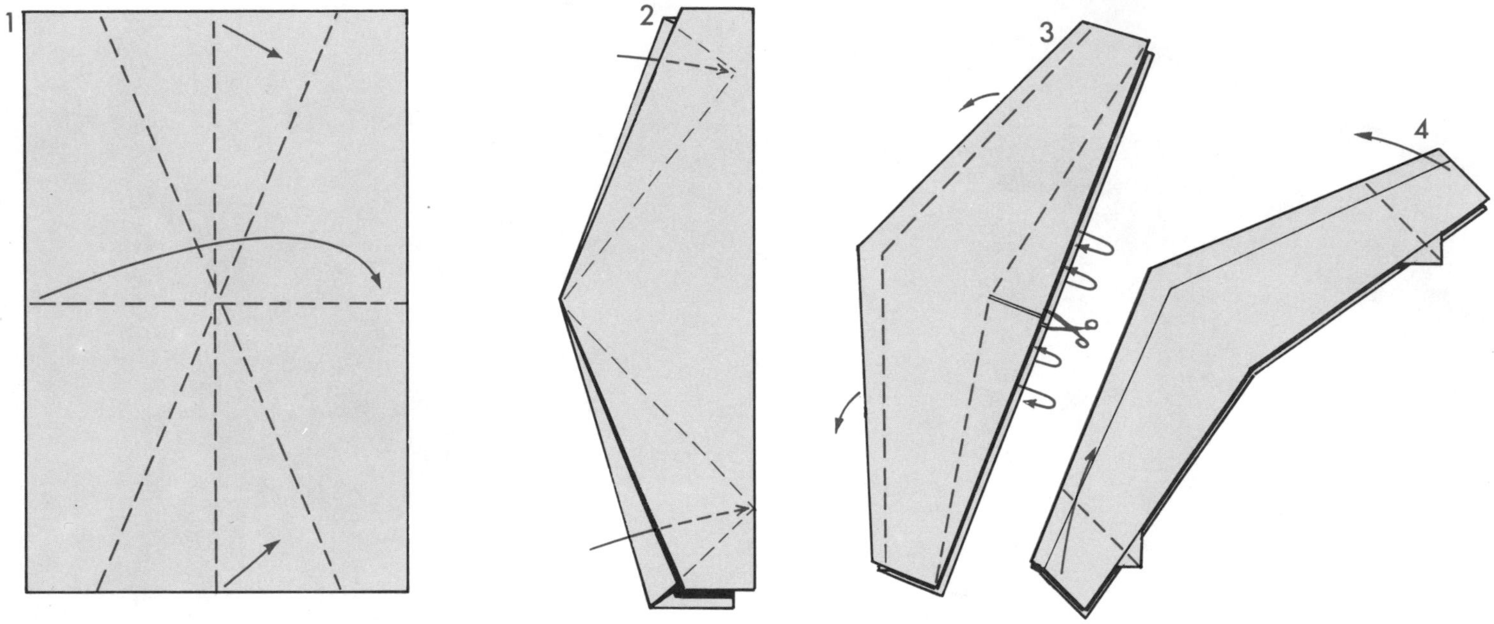

Wings

1 Take a sheet of paper 20 × 30cm (8 × 12in) and fold it in half, first lengthways and then widthways. Flatten it out and fold it again along the diagonals illustrated. (It is advisable to crease it backwards and forwards along each fold a few times.)

2 Fold the paper in half lengthways. At the same time press in the corners of the diagonal folds. If you have done it correctly the wing shape will be evident.

3 Bend the lefthand edge, that is the front edge, of the wings downwards and make a small cut in the center of the back edge, as shown. Fold the four loose flaps inside along the dotted lines.

4 Bend up the uppermost layer of both wing tips so that they stand vertical to the wings and act as stabilizers. Glue the front edges of the wings together.

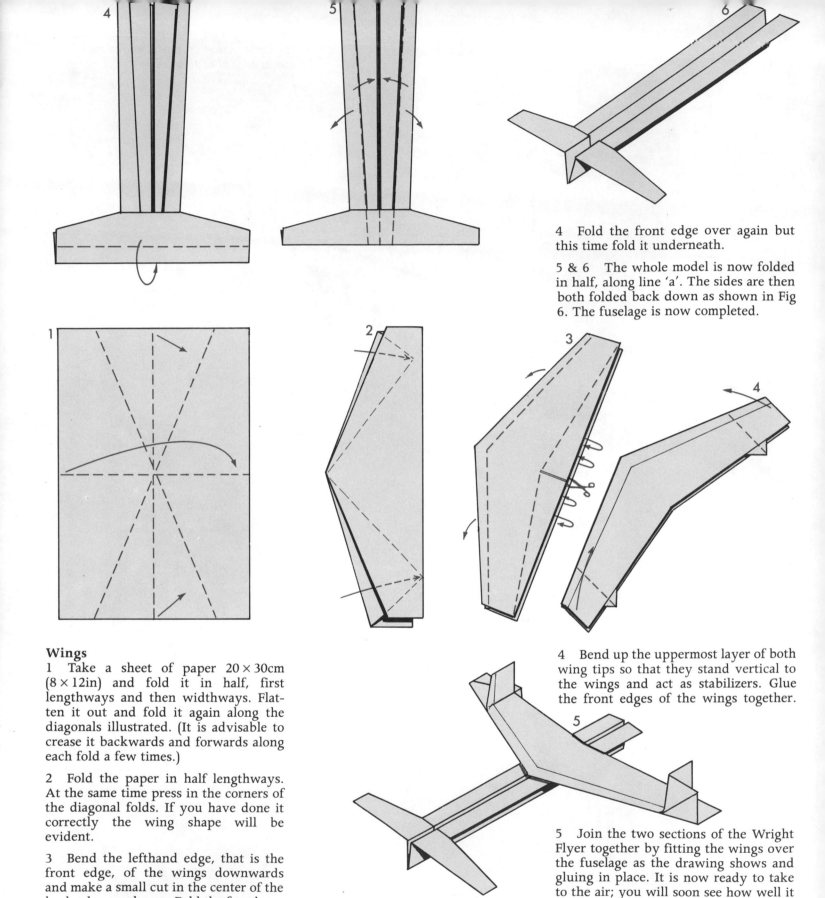

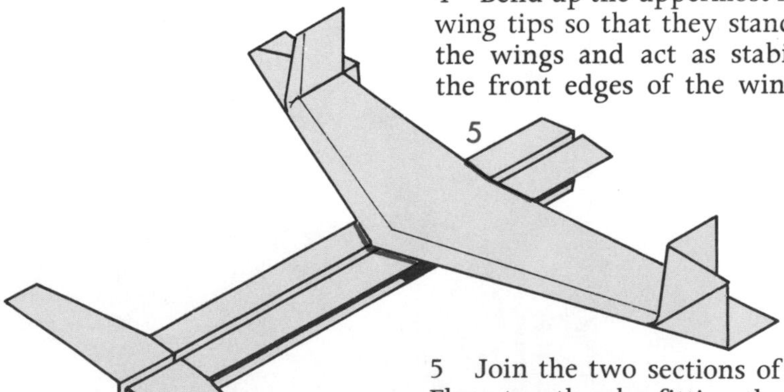

5 Join the two sections of the Wright Flyer together by fitting the wings over the fuselage as the drawing shows and gluing in place. It is now ready to take to the air; you will soon see how well it flies and that the pioneer's theories were well-founded.

ROCKET

Paper planes tend to go their own way. Having launched them, we have to wait and see where they land. They may fly over the neighbour's fence, lodge in an overhanging tree, get stuck out of reach in a hedge, or sometimes even disappear completely. Here the Rocket made a crash-landing on the assembly instructions – it's either a cunning attempt to obliterate the instructions or simply a case of high spirits. But don't worry, over the page you'll find full instructions for assembling the Rocket.

A high performance model which is also good for stunt flying, here the recalcitrant Rocket goes its own way.

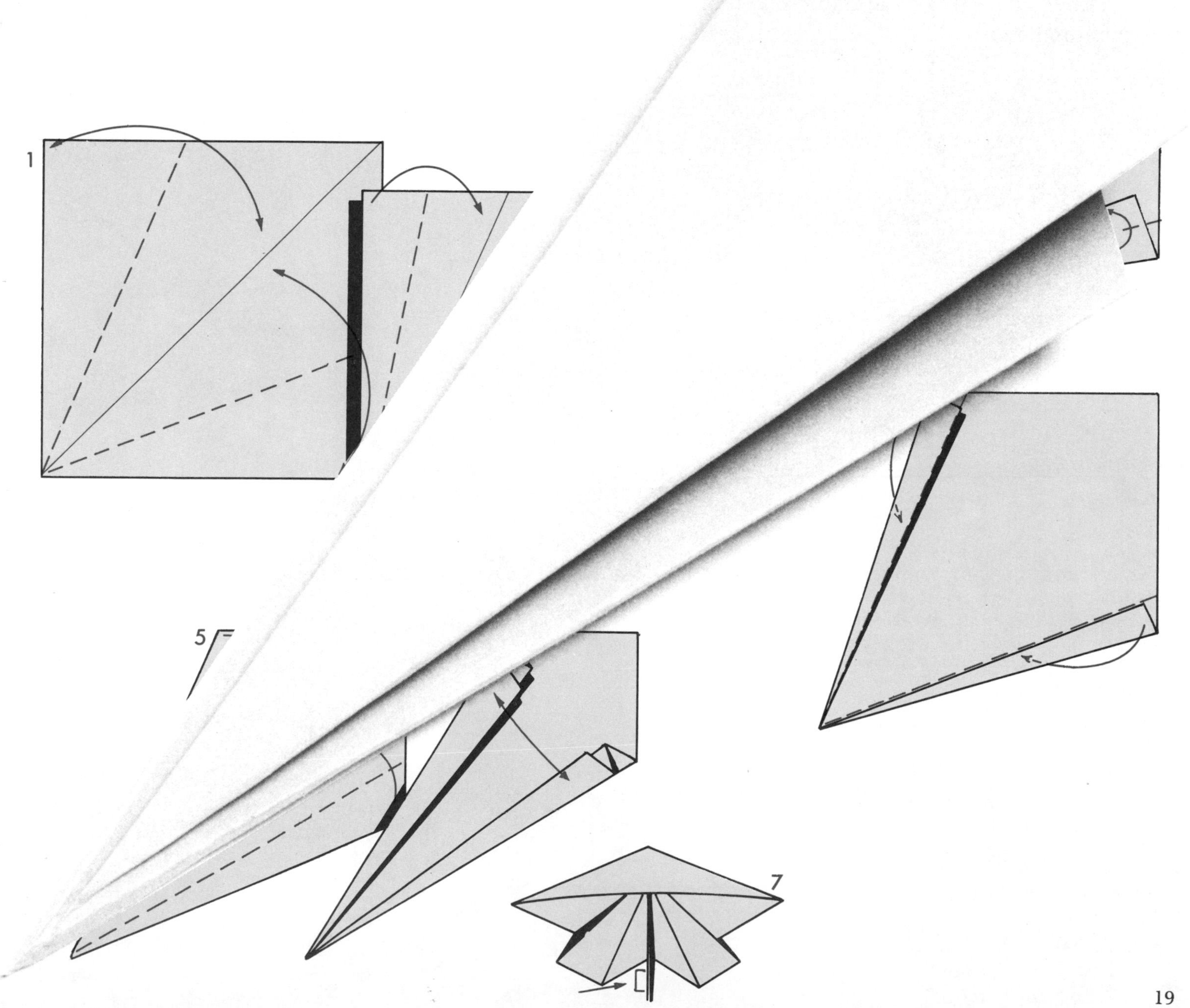

WINGS

A latterday Chinese sage said that airplanes without wings wouldn't fly, but what about wings without an airplane? Wings are designed to compensate for the weight of the fuselage and it is quite possible to leave the fuselage out altogether. At least that is the principle behind Wings. One of the first models in *Scientific American* International Paper Airplane Competition, it opened up a whole new area of interest. It is probably the easiest of the models to make. The wing tips may be curved up and down so the plane makes graceful swoops and spirals rather like a seagull in a storm. It is important to master the art of launching it too.

5

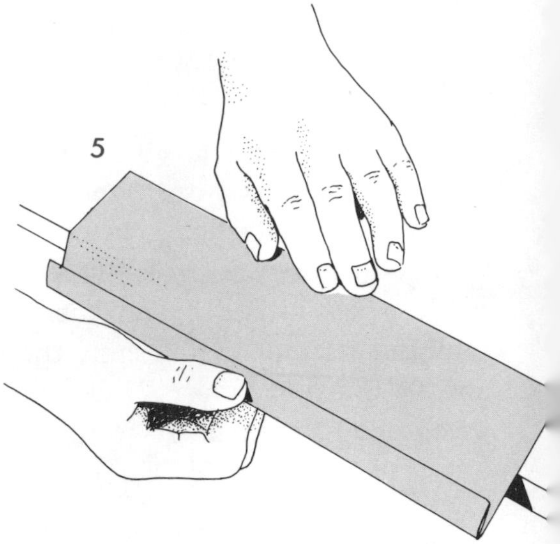

5 Stretch the single layer of paper across the edge of a table to give a gentle curve.

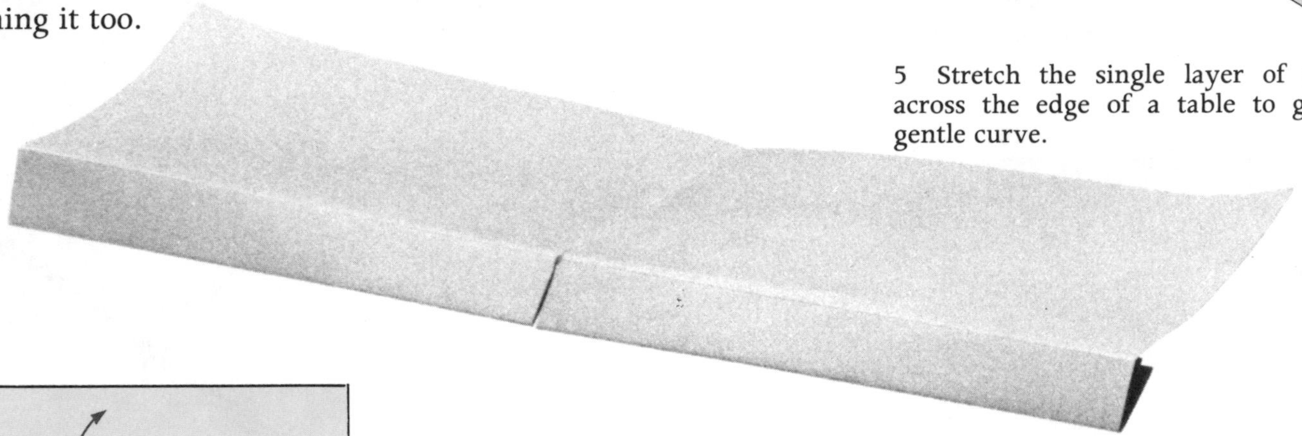

Wings are usually designed to compensate for the weight of the fuselage; it is possible to simply leave out the fuselage . . .

1

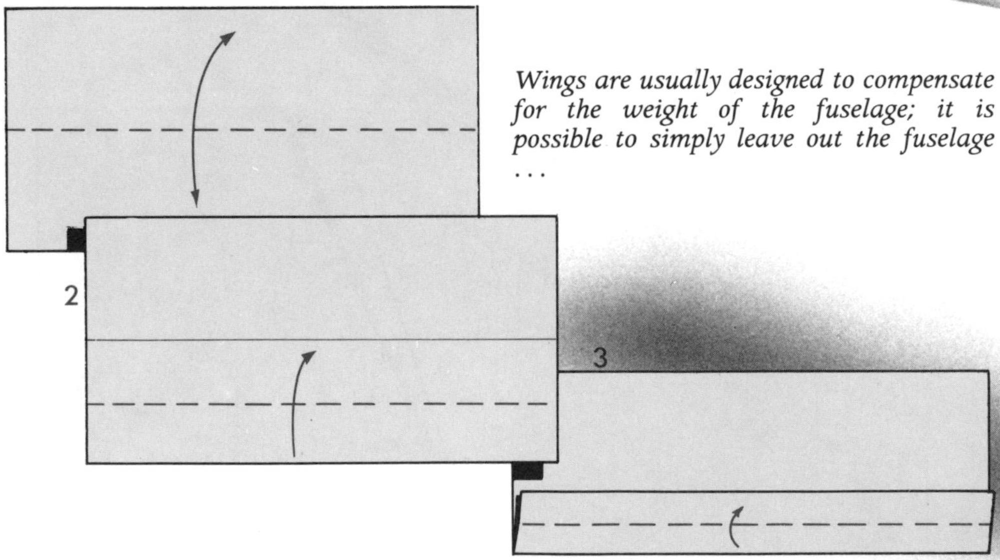

1 Fold a piece of paper 16 × 30cm (6 × 12in) in half lengthways and then open it out again.

2 Fold the lower half up to the middle.

3 Fold this in half again.

4 Stick the edge down with Scotch tape then make a slit in the center.

4

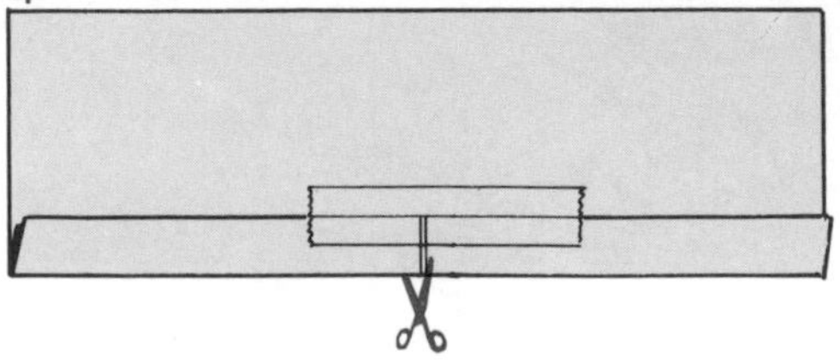

6

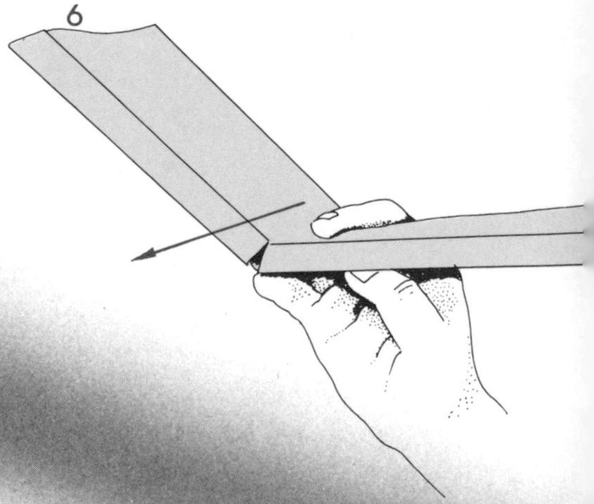

6 Wings is now ready for take-off and is launched horizontally from between the forefinger and the thumb. Do not throw a paper airplane forward too vigorously; speed is not important and most models perform most effectively if you allow them to glide away from your hand. Others require a light shove.

ROCKET

This section clearly illustrates how to make the high-performance Rocket from a piece of paper 30 × 30cm (12 × 12in). The Rocket is a fast-flying aircraft which, when accurately trimmed, also performs stunts. In addition, this is an excellent basic design to use for some original creations.

1 Make two diagonal folds in a piece of paper 30 × 30cm (12 × 12in) along the dotted lines so that the two edges meet along the center diagonal line. Open flat.

2 Fold each of the two triangles in half along the dotted line.

3 Fold each of the outside triangles in half again along the dotted line.

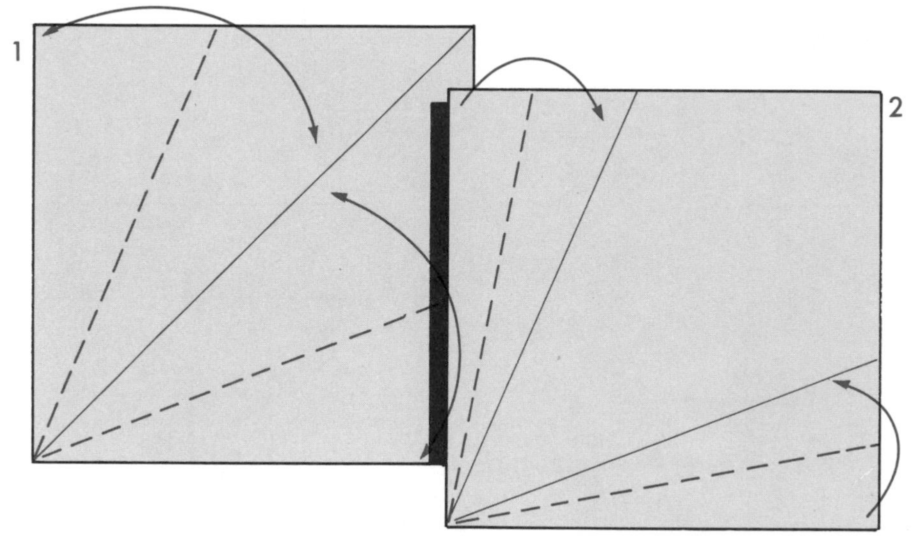

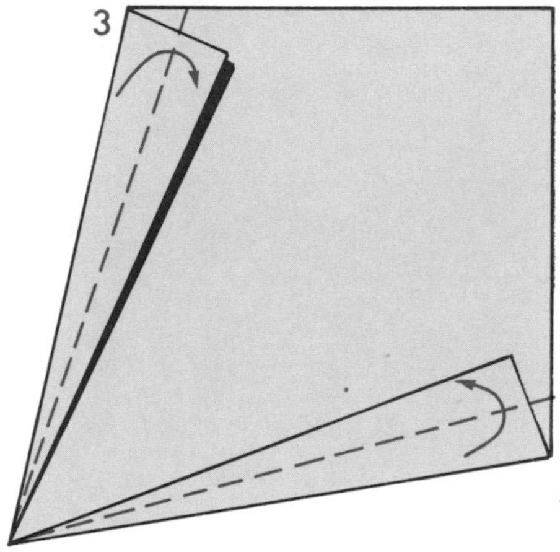

4 Fold each side backwards along the dotted line.

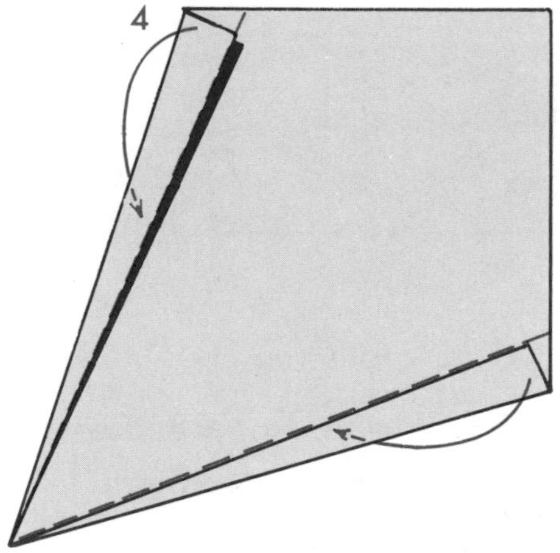

5 Now fold the two sides forwards again.

6 You now have a series of concertina folds. Unfold them gently to produce the Rocket shape.

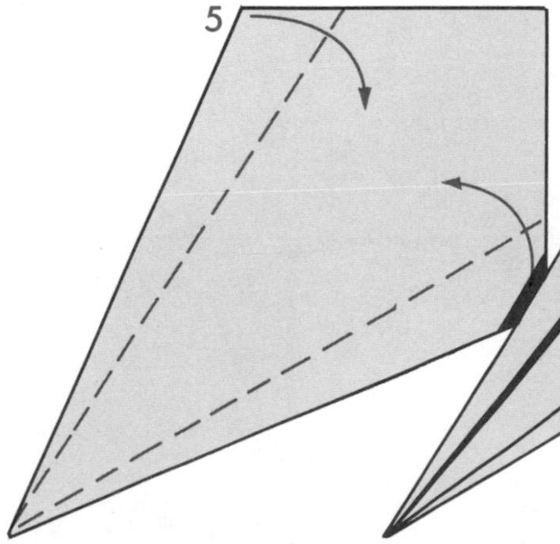

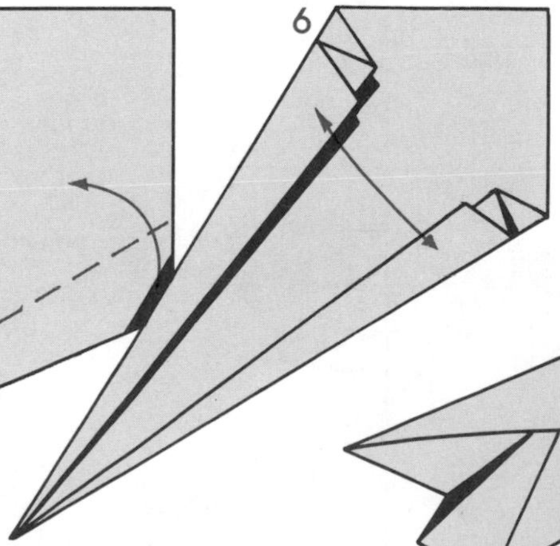

7 Fasten the two innermost folds together with a staple as illustrated in the rear view picture. The Rocket is ready to fly. With the point of the tail you can determine the flight path – the 'trim' as they say in flying jargon.

PAPER PLANE

This is the celebrated and infamous Paper Plane which your school friend could always make more successfully than you could. Not even if you offered your best comics would he disclose his secret. Now – better late than never – you can have your revenge. This Paper Plane is the archetypal model. If you become fully conversant with this model the rest of them will seem easy. The wings and the tail are made separately and then, having been folded, are joined together.

1 Take a piece of paper 20 × 30cm (8 × 12in) and cut off one end, putting this to one side to be used for the tail later on. Fold along the two diagonal lines illustrated, then make another widthways fold through the intersection of the diagonal fold. Make sharp clean creases by folding the paper backwards and forwards.

2 Fold the lower edge upwards while at the same time pressing in the sides in an inverted fold, resulting in the shape illustrated.

3 Fold the upper corners of the top layer down to the bottom point along the dotted lines.

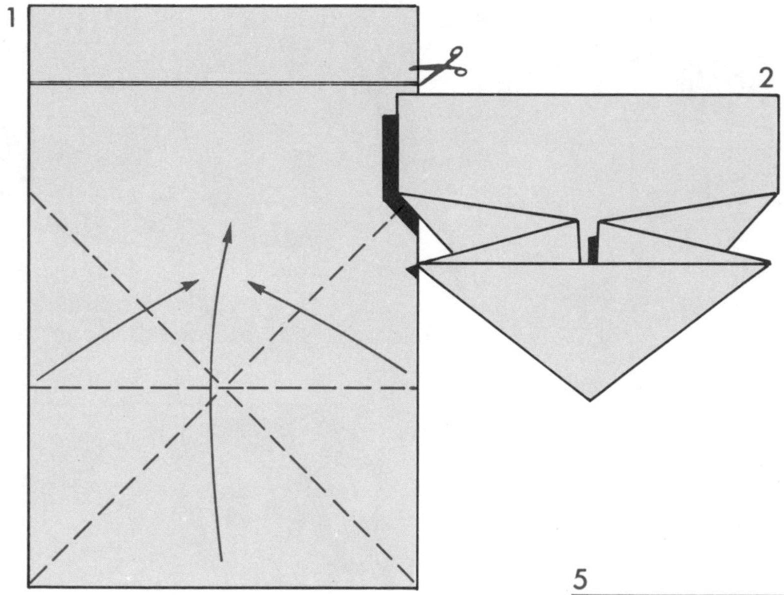

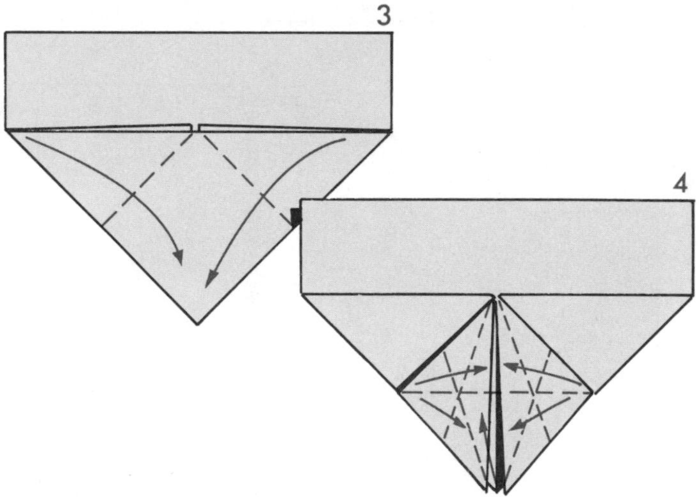

4 Now make folds along all the dotted lines shown in this diagram.

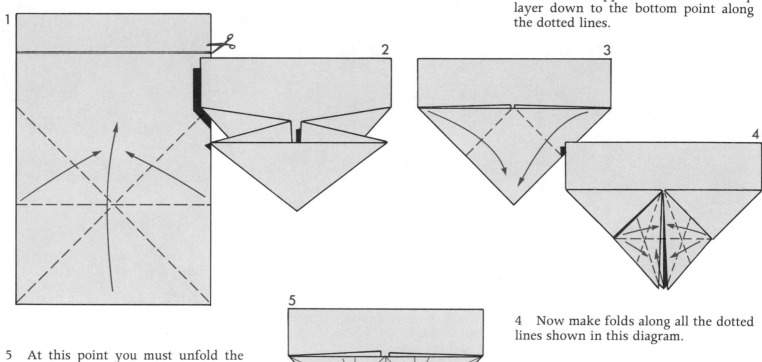

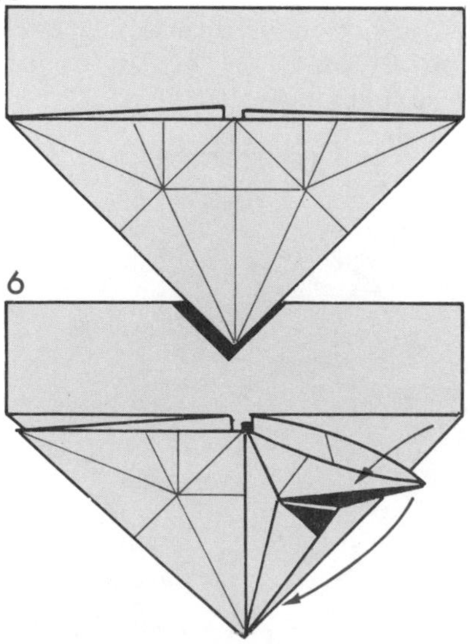

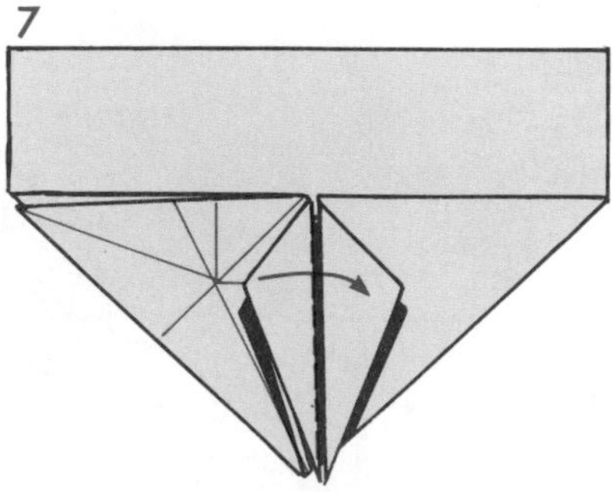

5 At this point you must unfold the model as far as the diagram for Step 2 so you can see all the creases shown here.

6 This is where it gets difficult. Study the diagram before making any moves and don't give up if it doesn't work the first time. If that confounded school friend could manage it, so can you with these instructions. Take hold of the righthand point, pull it towards you, fold it down to the bottom point and press it down flat.

7 Fold the left side of the figure just made over the right side.

Not even a pile of good comics could buy the secret of the Paper Plane . . .

8 Now repeat the process in reverse with the left point.

9 From the resulting figure fold the right side over the left.

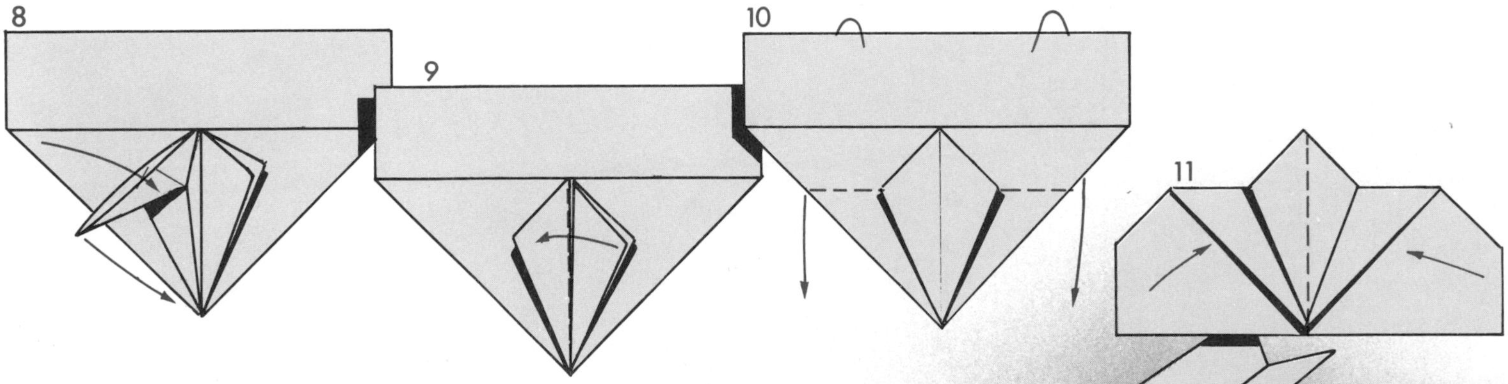

10 Bend the back section away from you along the dotted line.

11 Make a center fold bringing the sides towards you.

12 Arrange the wings in a V shape. Fold the tail piece in half lengthways and slide it into the wings. The Paper Plane is now ready for its test flight. Steps 6–9 are the really difficult ones which you have to tackle and master; then it is plain sailing.

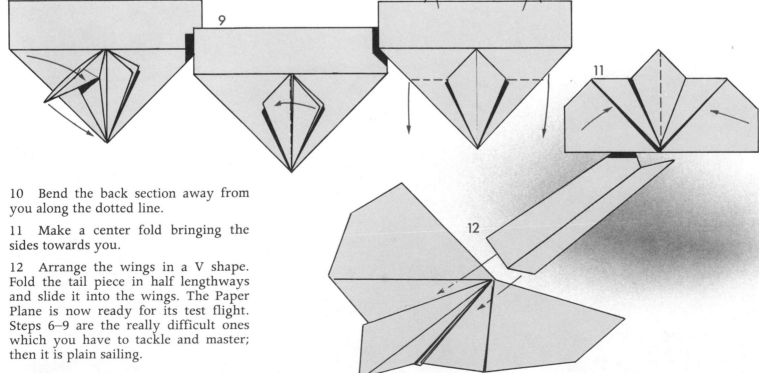

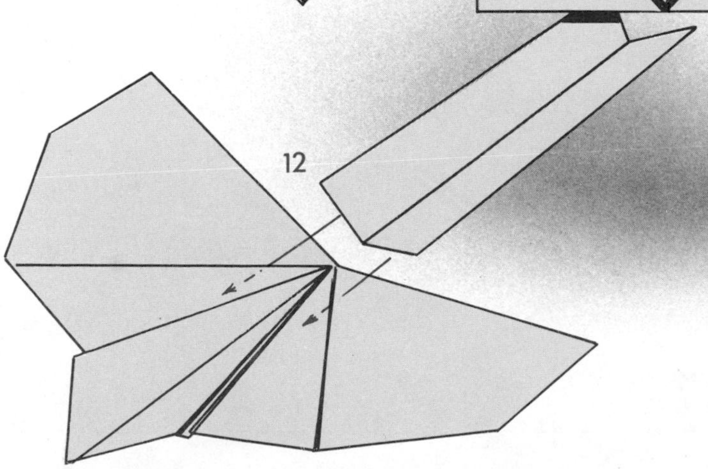

BAT

The level of difficulty involved in this model is not high but it does require perseverance. Having completed the relatively simple steps, the result is beautiful. The Bat can be made from somewhat thicker paper. Some people have said (but no longer say) that it doesn't really belong in the section for Fantasy Flyers. Our Bat is based on a very fast aircraft design.

1 Take a sheet of paper 20 × 30cm (8 × 12in) and fold it in half lengthways, then open it out flat. Take the top left corner across to the center fold so that the fold also passes through the top right corner.

2 Fold side 'a' along side 'b' and then open the paper out flat.

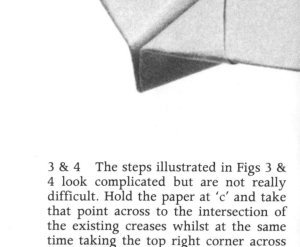

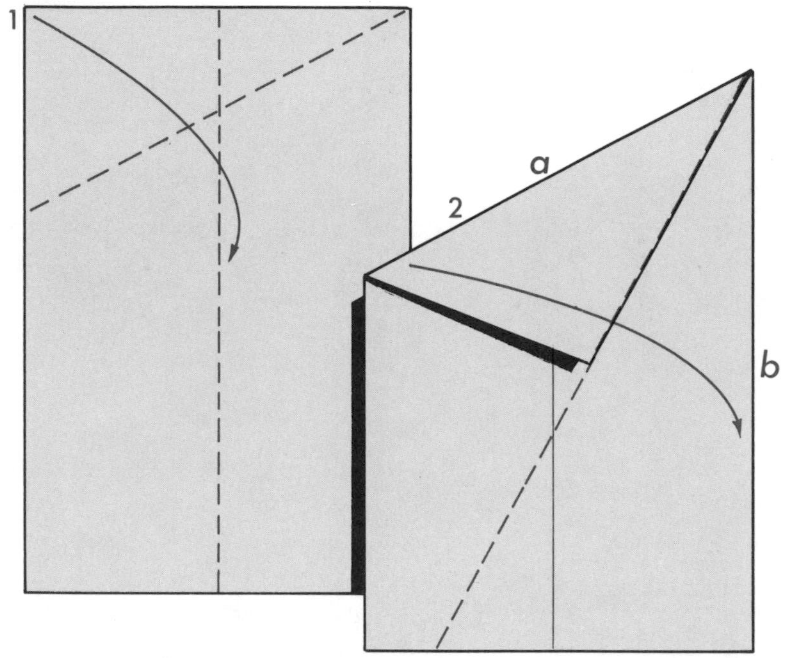

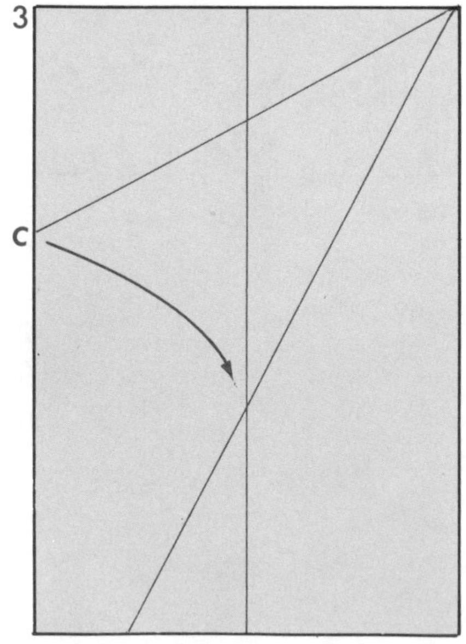

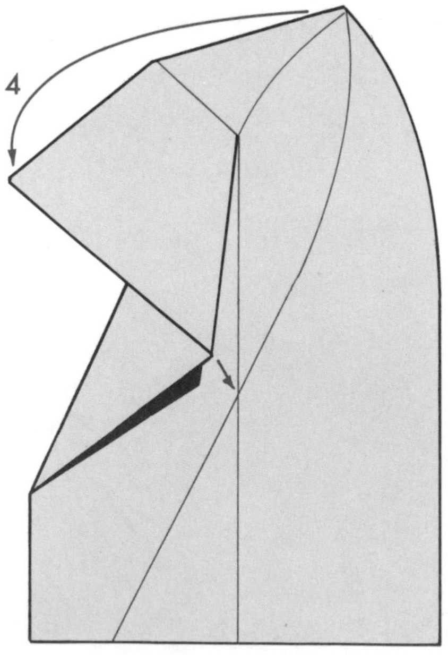

3 & 4 The steps illustrated in Figs 3 & 4 look complicated but are not really difficult. Hold the paper at 'c' and take that point across to the intersection of the existing creases whilst at the same time taking the top right corner across to the top left corner so that they lie flat.

Unfortunately this Bat cannot catch insects . . .

5 This is how your figure should look. Fold the top layer back to the right along the dotted line. Now bring point 'd' down towards you. Press flat.

6 Fold the top section in half as indicated by the arrow and then fold the whole figure in half lengthways along the dotted line.

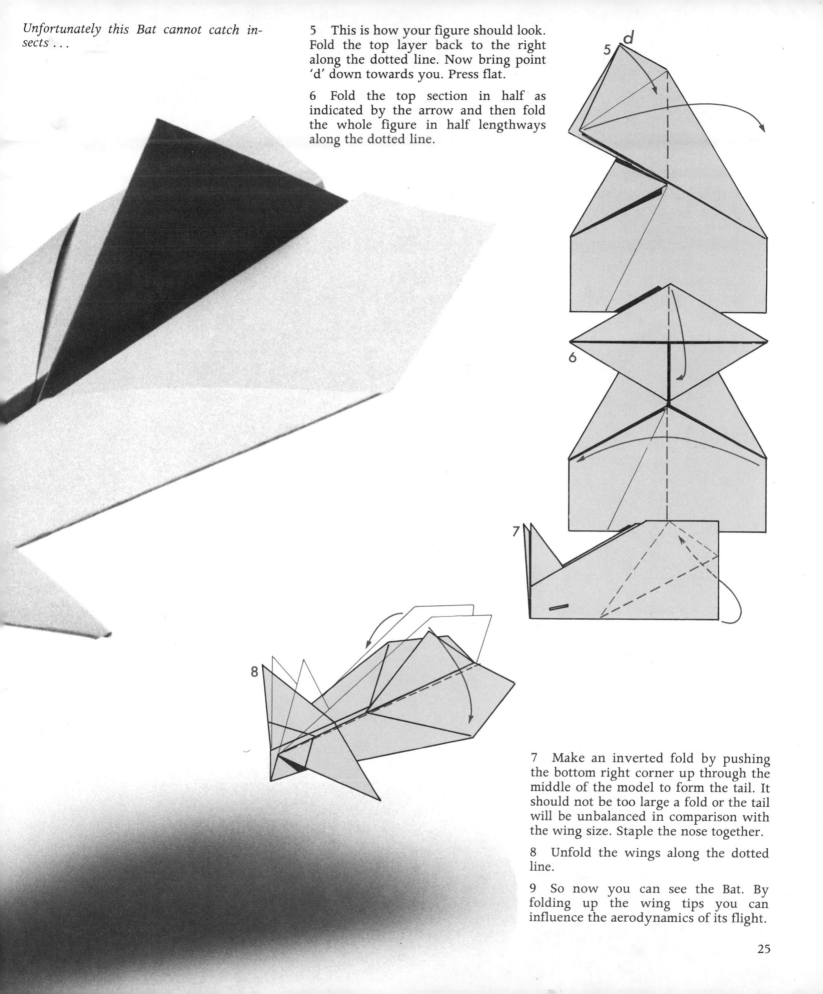

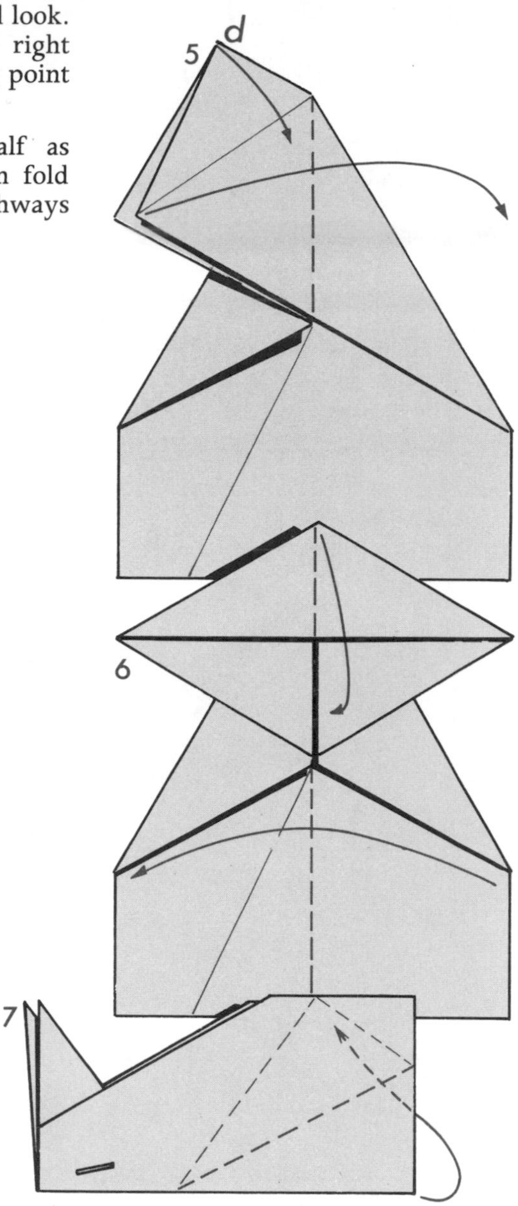

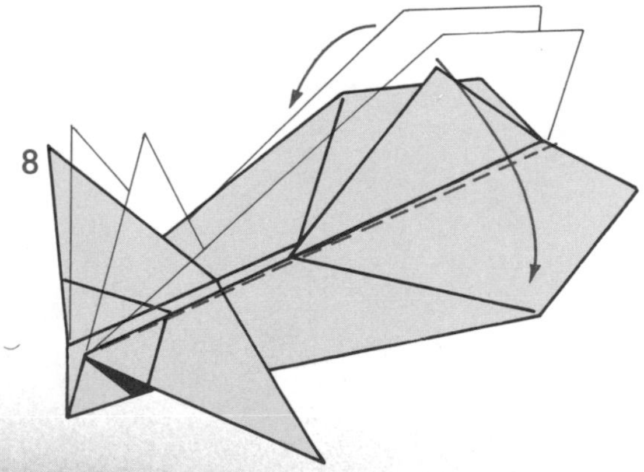

7 Make an inverted fold by pushing the bottom right corner up through the middle of the model to form the tail. It should not be too large a fold or the tail will be unbalanced in comparison with the wing size. Staple the nose together.

8 Unfold the wings along the dotted line.

9 So now you can see the Bat. By folding up the wing tips you can influence the aerodynamics of its flight.

The McDonnell, designed by R. Otte and produced by the McDonnell Aircraft Corporation . . .

McDONNELL

The McDonnell was the creation of aircraft designer R. Otte, who worked for the American McDonnell Aircraft Corporation. The first contribution to the *Scientific American* International Airplane Competition was produced using McDonnell company stationery. This airplane was obviously produced by someone with a particular talent for aeronautical engineering and it was frequently tested in a wind tunnel. It is best to use light paper for this model and to make its test flights on a still day.

1 & 2 Take a sheet of paper 20 × 30cm (8 × 12in) and make creases along all the dotted lines. Fold up the bottom edge, tucking in the two sides at the same time, to result in Fig 2.

3 Fold the two upper points of the triangle down to meet the lower point.

4 Fold along all the dotted lines shown here.

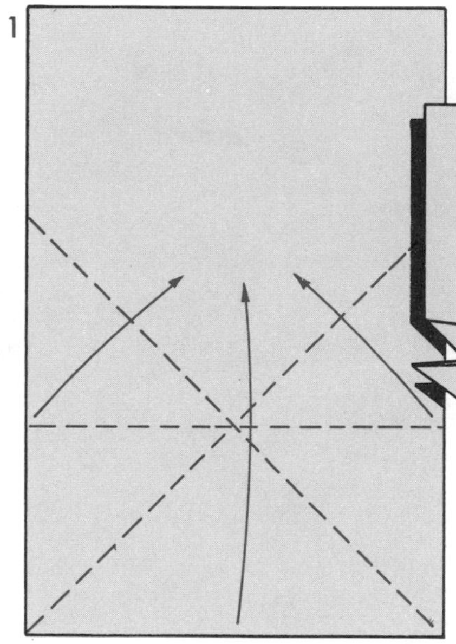

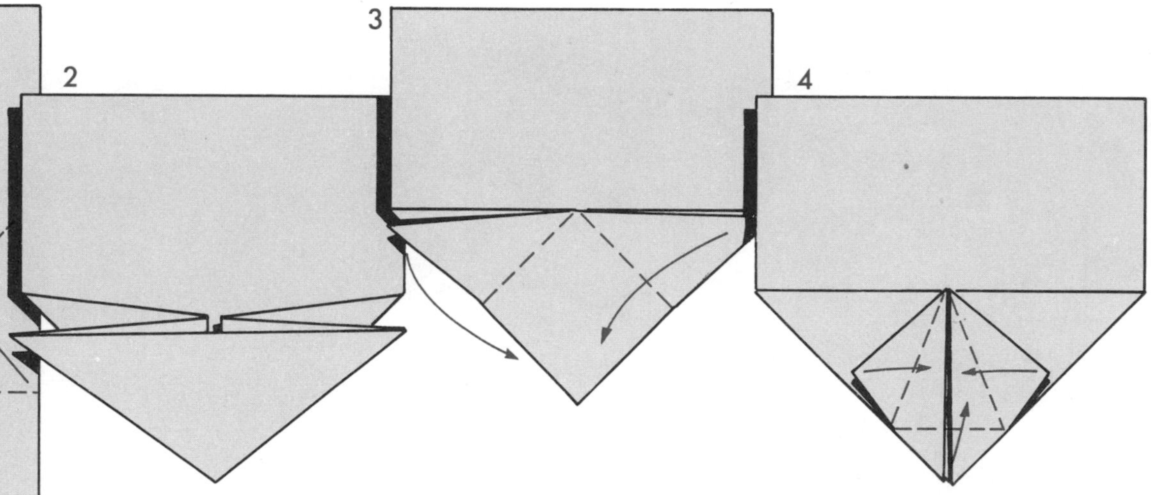

5 Tuck the two points 'a' into the 'pockets' formed in the lower triangle.

6 Turn the model over. Fold both sides in towards the center following the dotted lines.

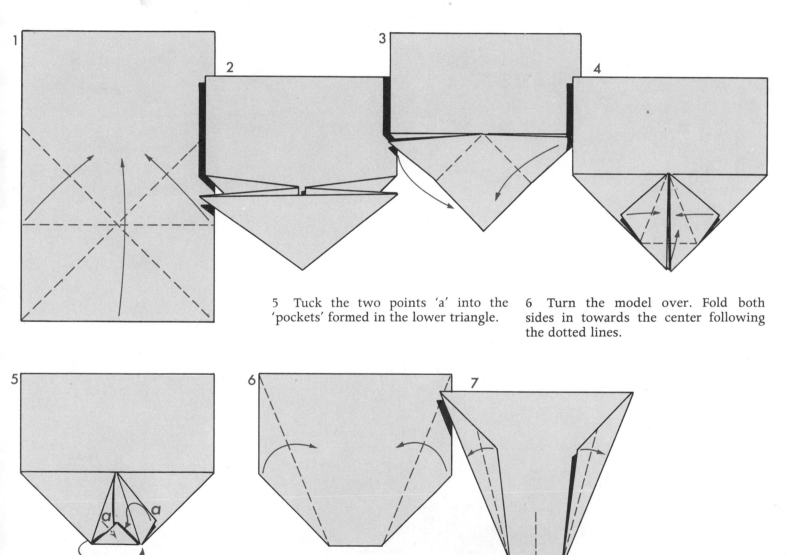

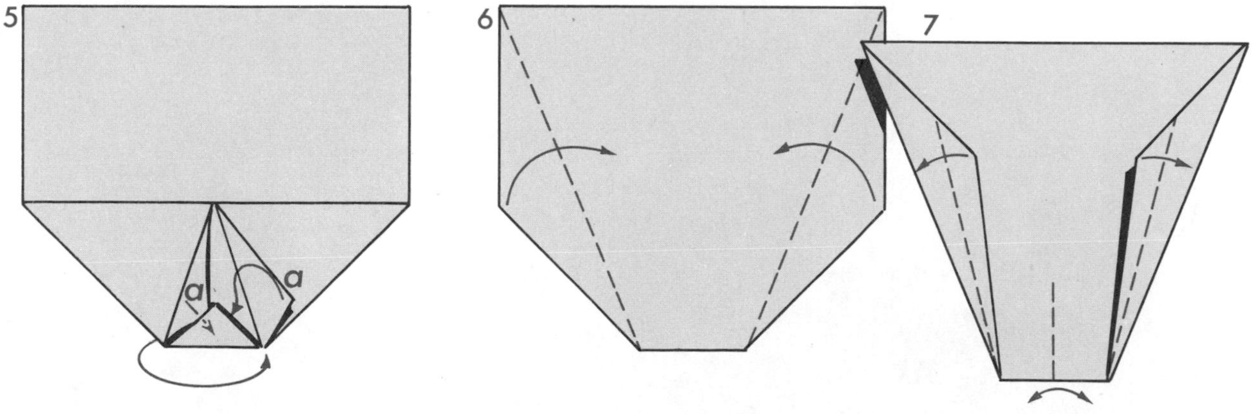

7 Fold the points of these flaps out again, as shown in the diagram. In fact the McDonnell flies very well without this additional detail. Finally make a light crease in the middle of the nose and now it's ready . . .

NB The flight characteristics may be varied by the amount that the points 'a' are tucked into the pockets in Step 5.

The SX 101 (PF) in its element . . .

SX 101 (PF)

SX 101 (PF) – it sounds mysterious, but many aircraft are identified in a similar way. In space travel work is proceeding on more projects – X-12, LVV-1034 etc, and these letter and number combinations are used for anything without an ordinary name. The SX 101 (PF) sounds like a rocket; it is the first model in the SX 100 range and the letters PF simply mean *Paper Flight*. Variations on this model may be called SX 102, SX 103 etc. You have to use your imagination with this series.

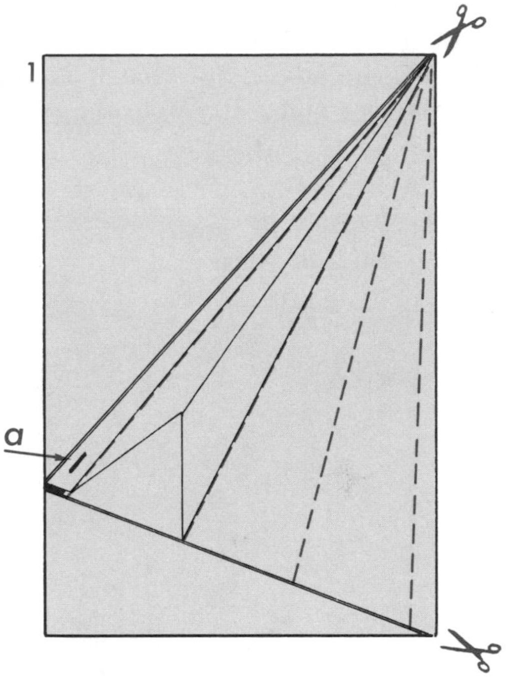

1 Take a piece of paper 20 × 30cm (8 × 12in) and cut out the triangle as directed. Make score marks along the dotted lines to ease folding. Fold the two narrow flaps on either side towards you along the dotted lines and then make the two middle folds away from you. Join the underneath at 'a' and the fuselage is ready.

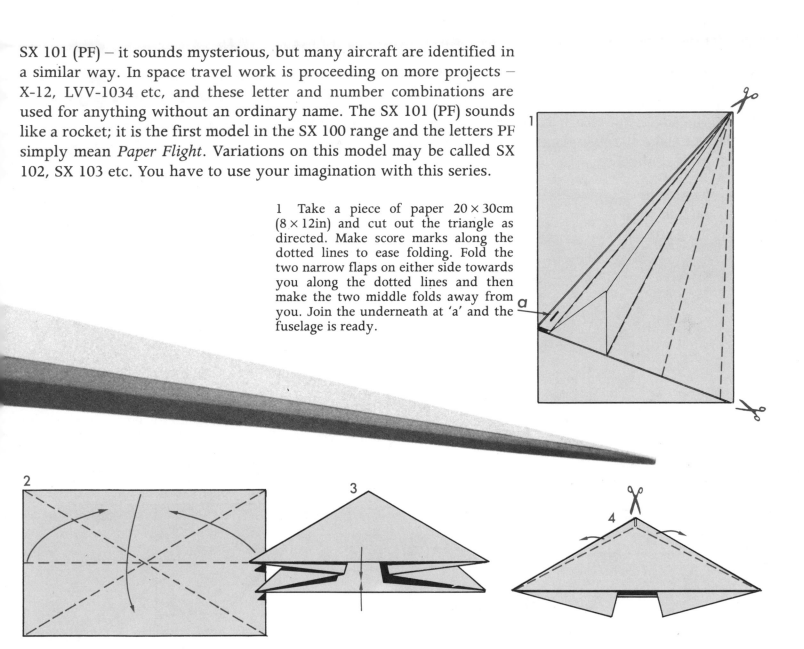

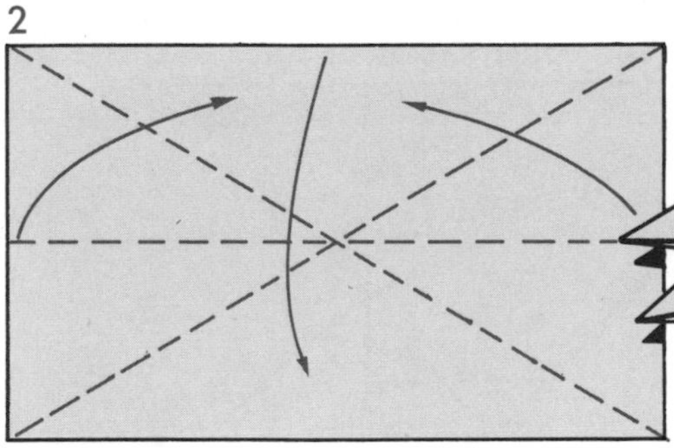

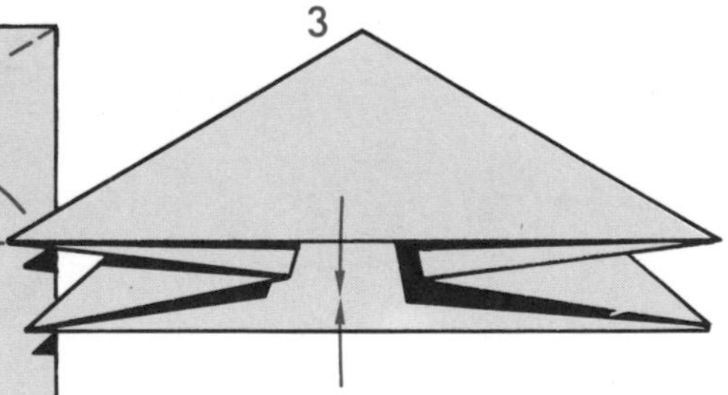

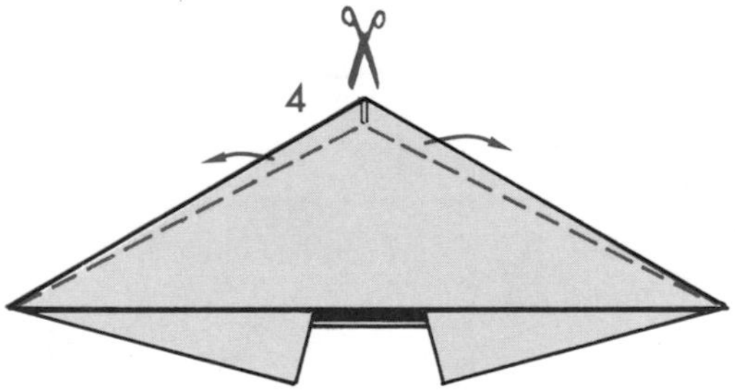

2 To make the wings, take a piece of paper 15 × 25cm (6 × 10in) and fold it across both diagonals and then in half lengthways at the intersection of the diagonals.

3 Fold the paper in half, tucking in the sides.

4 Make a short cut in the tip and bend both the top edges over following the dotted lines. Attach the front of the wings to the flat back of the fuselage as seen in the photograph. SX 101 (PF) is now ready. It is one of the simplest models to launch but, being a rocket, it will need plenty of propulsion.

PTERODACTYL (PTERANODON)

The final model in this chapter on Fantasy Flyers is descended from primeval times. It is called the Pterodactyl due to its similarity to the prehistoric flying reptiles. These beasts were not to be trifled with: they seized anything that moved. The paper reconstruction is however more amiable. It is an even faster projectile than an airplane and has the advantage that it is not too complicated to make. For the best results make the Pterodactyl out of very light paper because all the weight is in the nose.

1
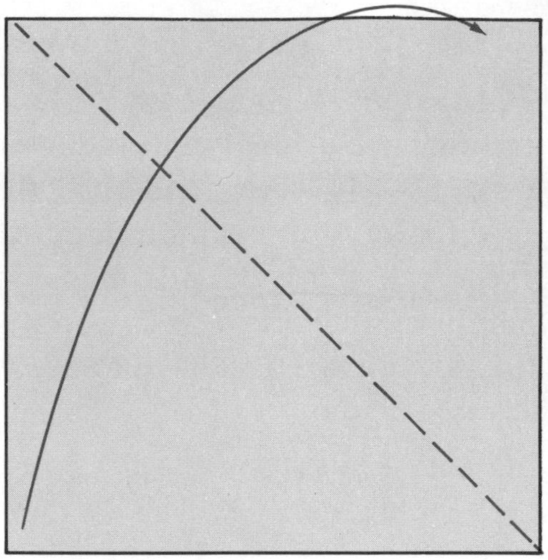

1 Fold a piece of paper 20 × 20cm (8 × 8in) in half diagonally.

2 Fold back the top corner so that it exactly lines up with the left edge.

3 Turn over and fold the whole figure in half.

2
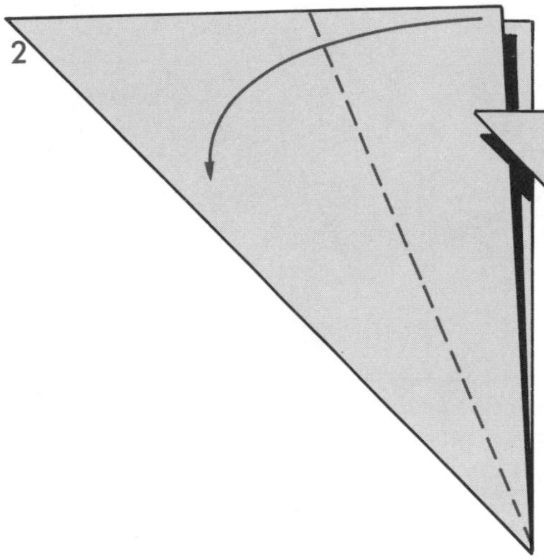

3
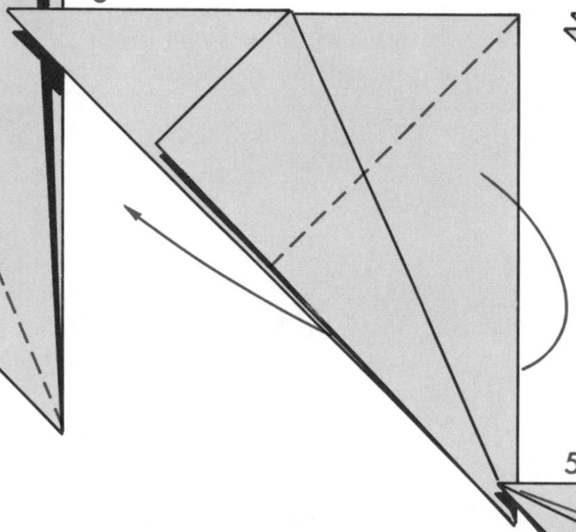

4
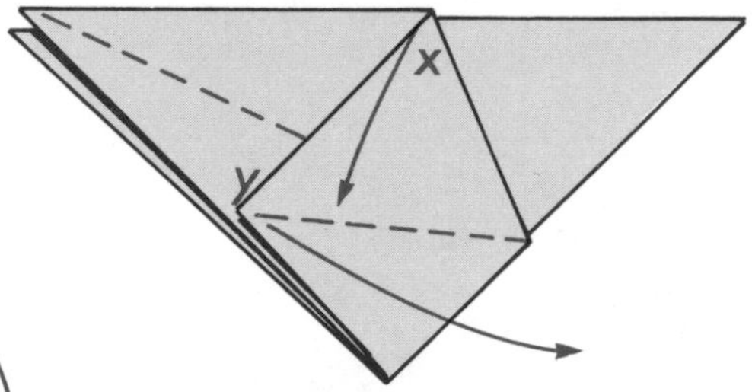

4 Simultaneously press point 'x' down and pull point 'y' down and over to the right so that there are folds along the dotted lines.

5 Open out the model by folding back the upper half along the dotted line.

5
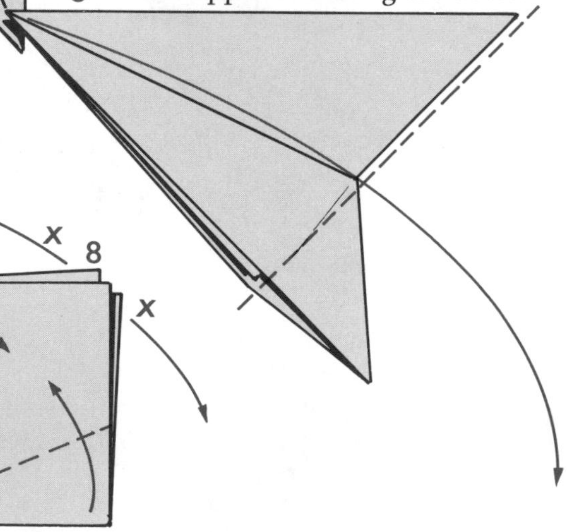

6
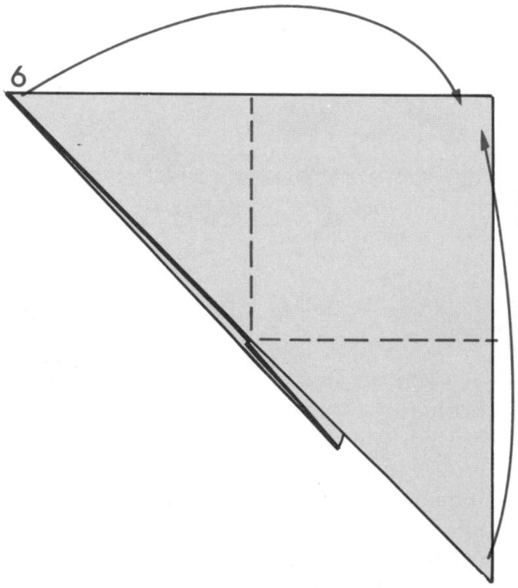

7
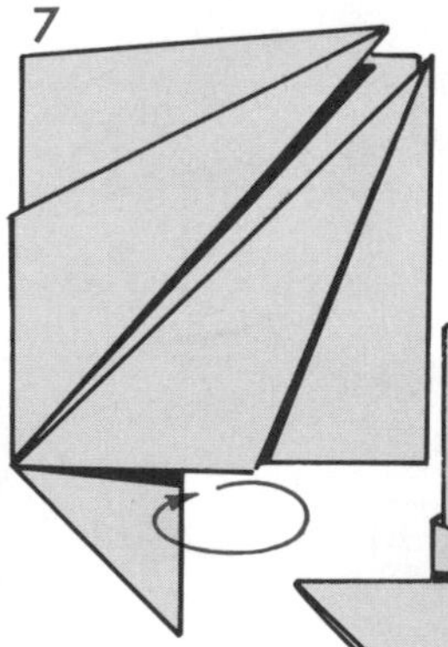

8
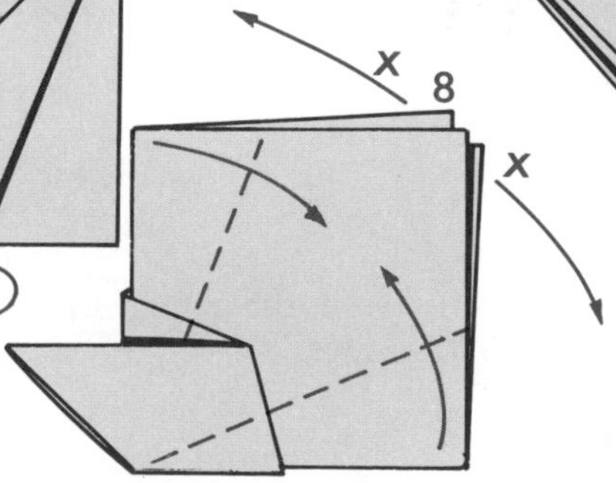

6 Fold in both points along the dotted lines, as illustrated, to result in Fig 7.

7 If everything has been done correctly, this is what it should look like. Now turn it over.

8 Fold the edges in to the center fold as the dotted lines indicate and at the same time, the two points 'x' lying underneath, out to either side.

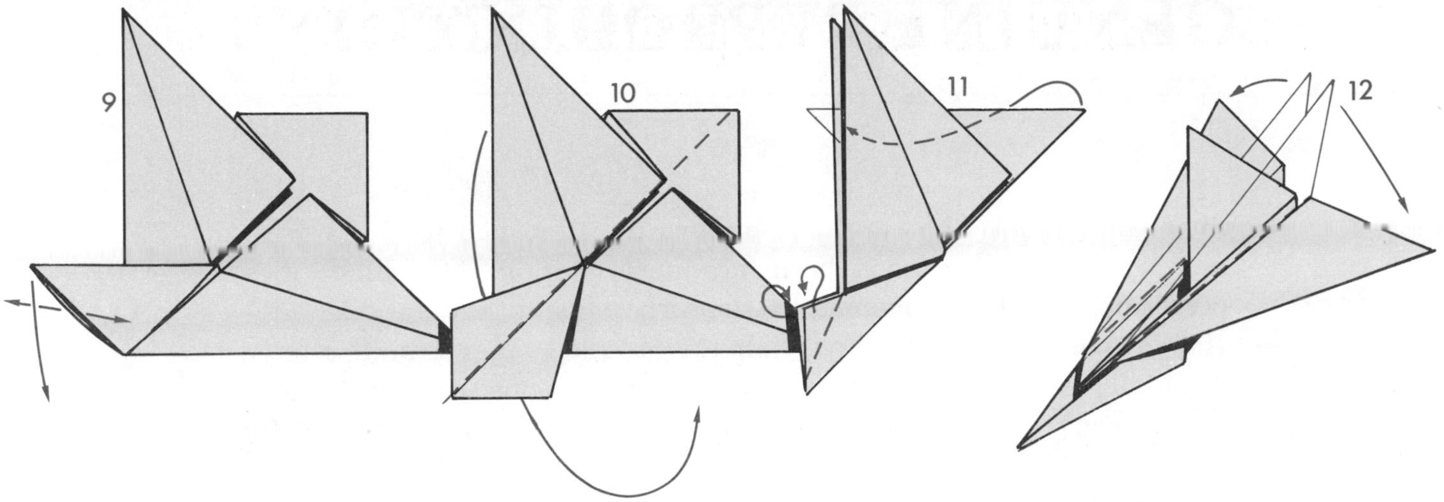

9 Open out the upright triangle and fold it down flat as the arrows direct.

10 Now, fold the whole thing in half away from you.

11 Tuck in the two points on the nose as directed by the arrows and then, using an inverted fold, push the tail up and in.

12 The only thing left to do is to unfurl the wings along the dotted lines and the Pterodactyl will be reborn after millions of years.

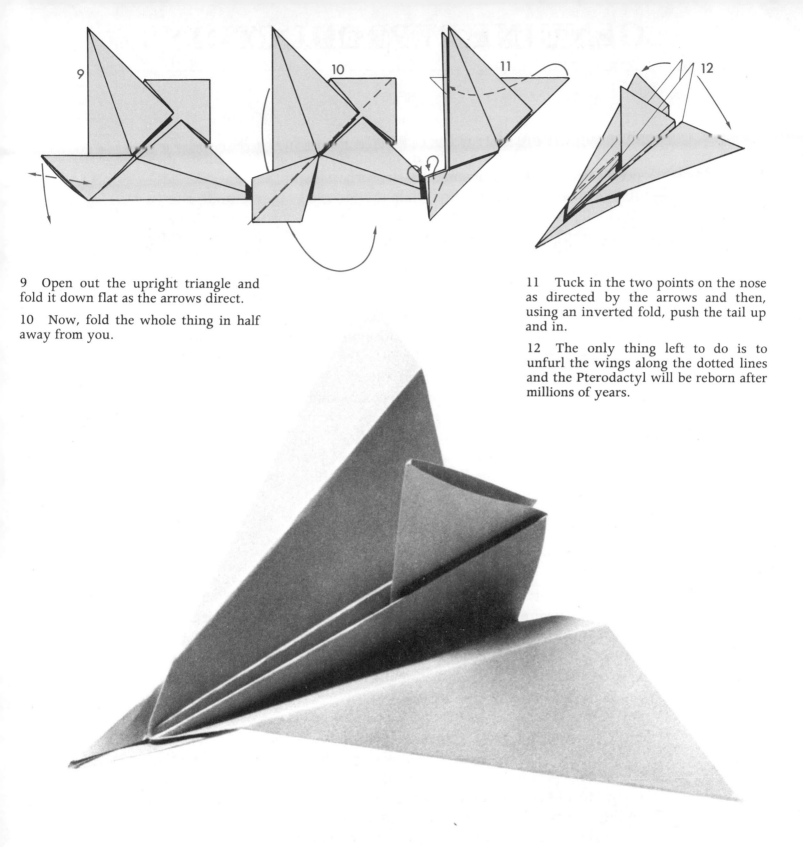

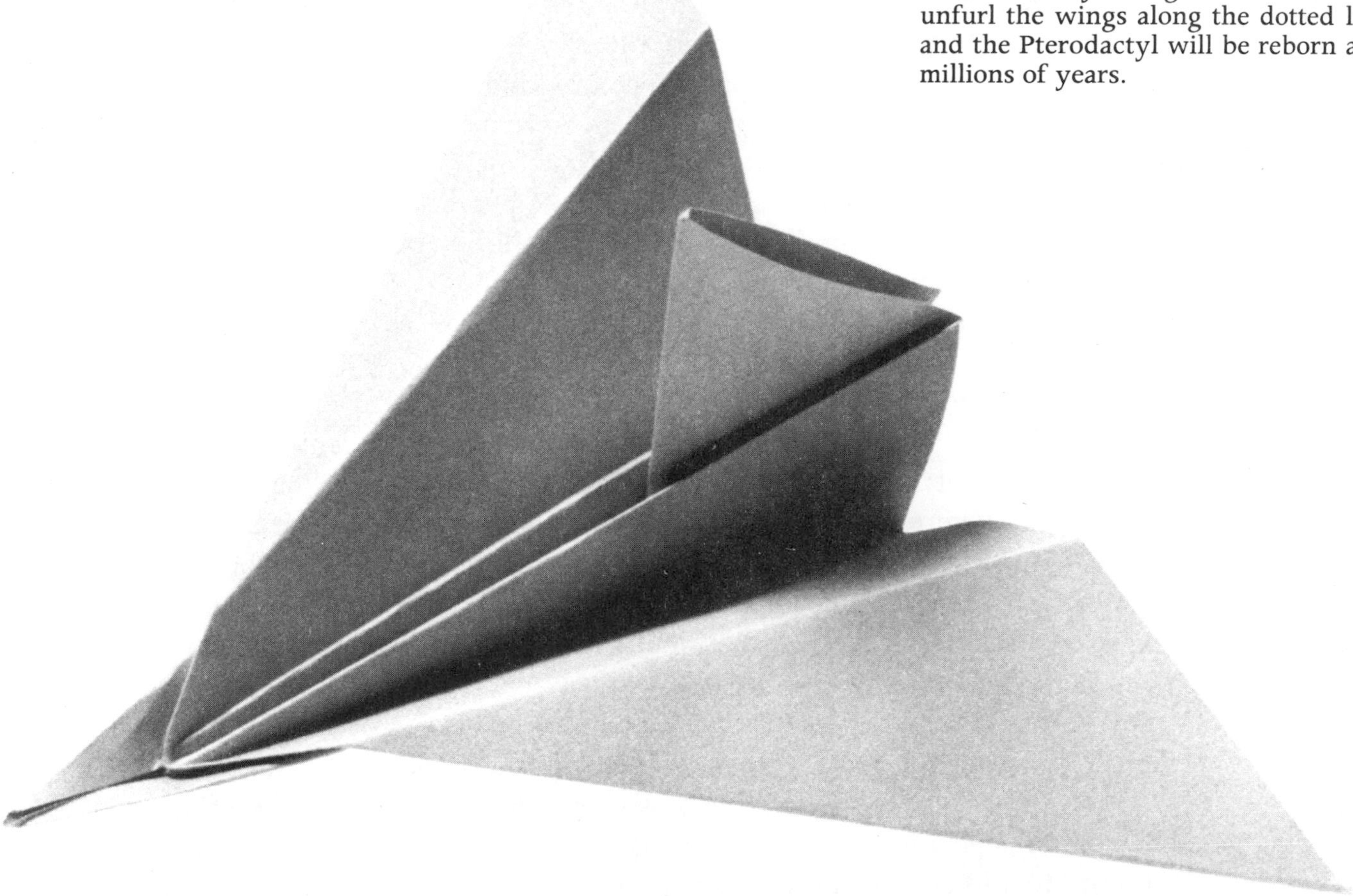

The final model in this section on Fantasy Flyers is descended from prehistoric times . . .

GENUINE REPRODUCTIONS

Ever since the Wright brothers became the first men to fly, a great number of airplanes has been produced, not all of which have performed exactly as planned. In the early days, if they did take off – and in many cases they never left the ground – they would plunge suicidally back down to earth. Many great creations were smashed to smithereens all too soon, leaving the bewildered pilot totally disillusioned.

These were the teething problems of a new technological era, the memory of which was captured in the silent movies and newer reproductions. During the First World War the unquestionable value of the airplane was established and ever since then most airplanes have been able to fly efficiently although one does ask oneself just how a Jumbo Jet can remain in the sky and remark on how the Starfighter always had the appearance of a tumbling autumn leaf.

But enough of teething troubles; man is well in control of the sky. When Charles Lindbergh became the first to fly across the Atlantic Ocean in the *Spirit of St Louis*, thousands of people came to greet him and the Parisians became victims of mass hysteria. Today we board the Concorde without a second thought, to cover the same distance at supersonic speed. Flying has become nearly as commonplace as travelling by train.

Nevertheless most people have at some time dreamed of piloting a jet, or flying a fighter plane. In this chapter your dreams can come true to some extent: these paper models imitate the real thing. There are five designs here with individual diverse characteristics, both famous and notorious. The French Mirage, the British Tiger Moth, the Swedish Saab 37 Viggen, the Russian Tupolev Bear and the American F-16 is a distinguished international gathering. Just a small comment on the F-16 which airplane enthusiasts will be quick to notice; the stabilizers of paper F-16 deviate somewhat from the original design but this need not detract from the general impression. After all, you do not expect to find details such as proper landing gear or a rotating propeller. The folded paper method is often quite difficult enough, and trying to add such complicated details will only result in your models flying a very short distance from the table to the wastepaper basket. Paper, however, is in plentiful supply and perseverance nearly always brings success.

The paper model tries to imitate the real thing. The French Mirage in full flight . . .

MIRAGE

The Mirage, made by the French aviation company Dassault, has proved itself to be one of the best jet aircraft ever produced. The delta-wing design which many aircraft engineers had long forgotten, was used again and gives the Mirage its characteristic shape. Like the Swedish Saab 37 Viggen, it is easily recognizable in the air, even to the uninitiated, so long as it isn't flying too high of course.

The paper model of the Mirage bears many of the same characteristics as the original: it regularly takes part in speed and aerobatic contests and is easily recognizable by its delta wings. Of course, there is a certain difference in the price . . .

1 Take a sheet of paper 20 × 30cm (8 × 12in), fold over a strip on the left-hand side then fold the sheet in half widthways.

2 Make a double crease along the top edge by folding it backwards and forwards along the dotted line.

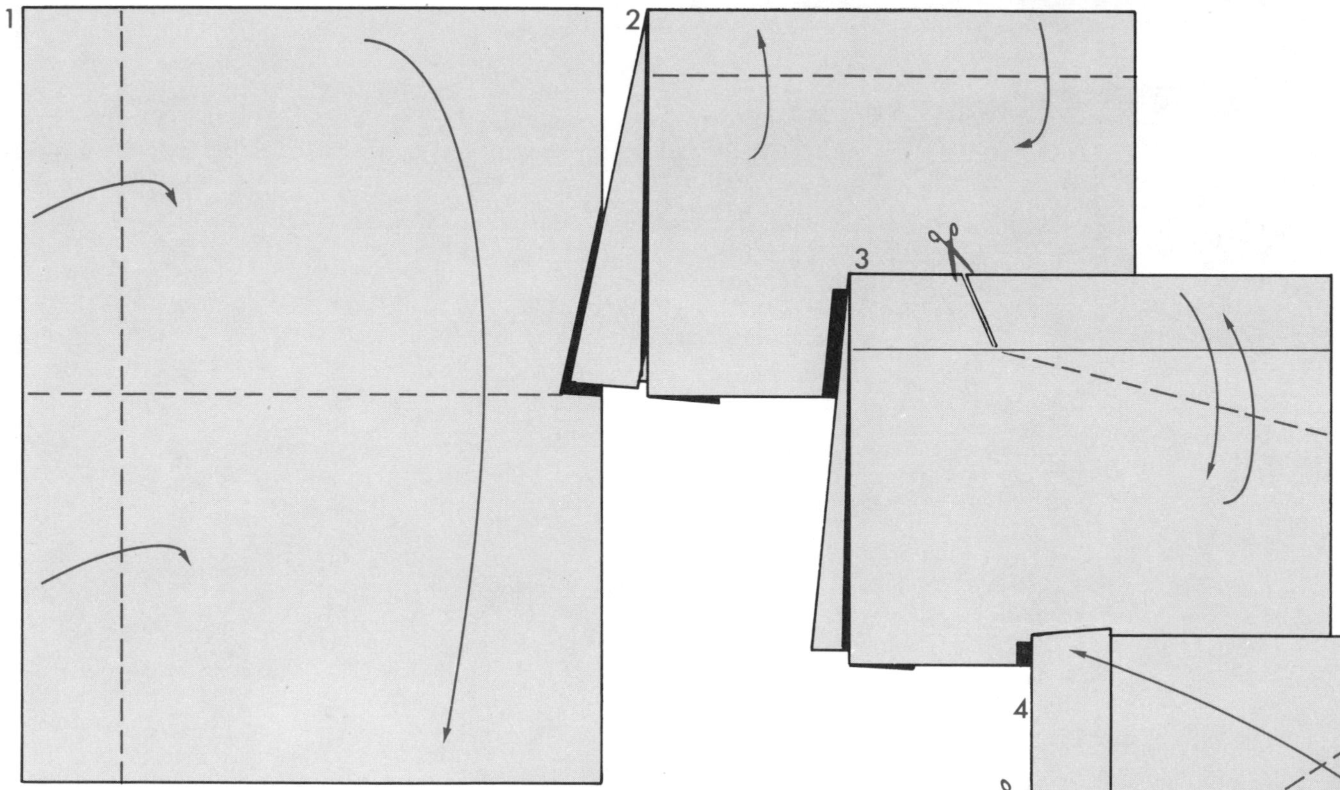

3 Cut down to the crease as indicated and then make another double crease along the dotted line illustrated.

4 Open out the figure except for the center section which remains double. Make a crease along the diagonal dotted lines and make two cuts from the left-hand edge just beyond the double layer, as indicated in the diagram.

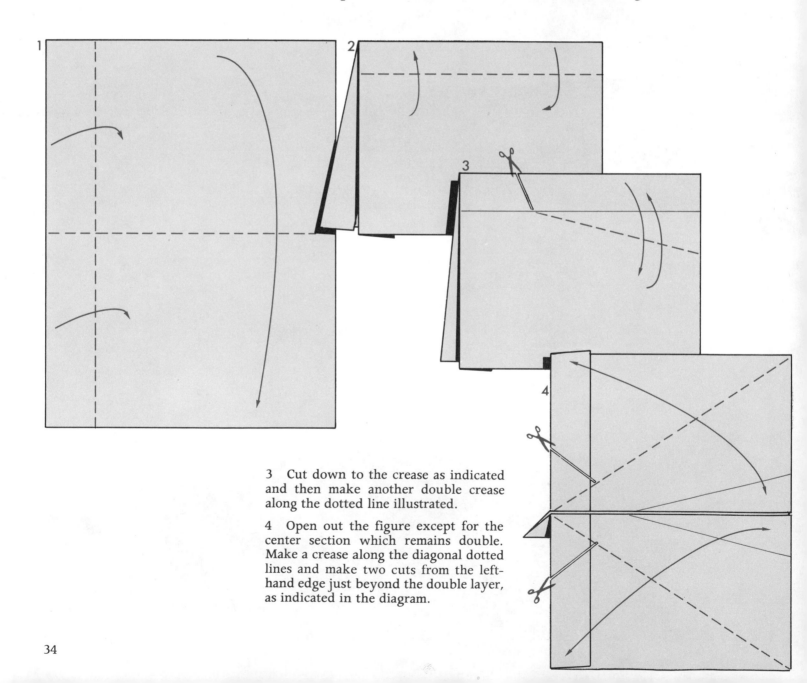

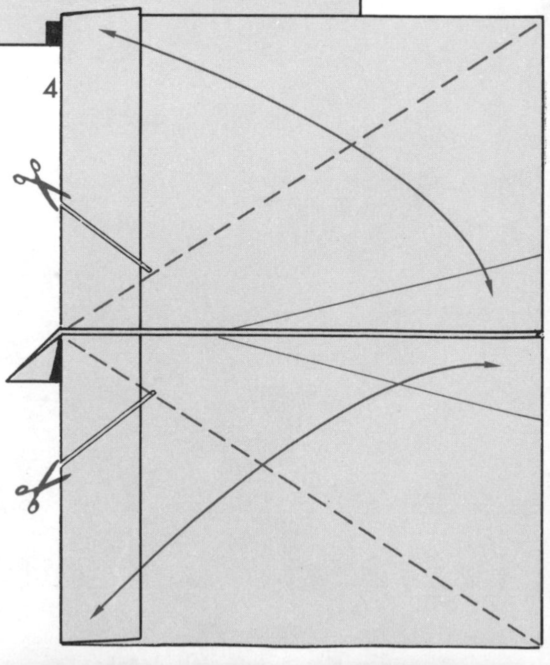

5 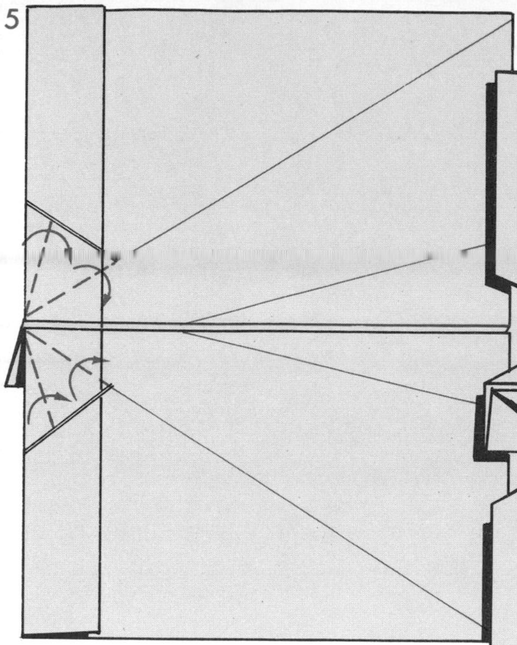

6 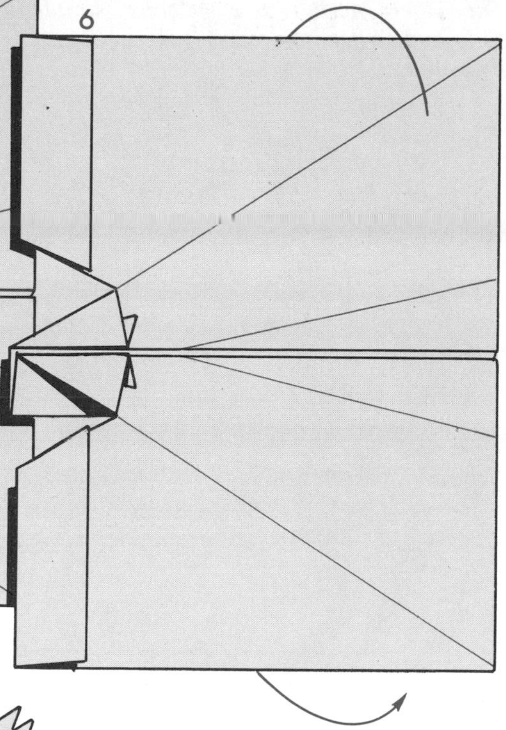

5 Fold over the section between the cuts and the center twice inwards, towards the middle, so that the folded edges meet at the center line.

6 Now fold the whole figure in half away from you.

7 Fold the two top left corners down along the dotted diagonal lines – one to either side of course.

8 Turn up the flaps which are to become the air intakes by making folds following the line of the fuselage.

7 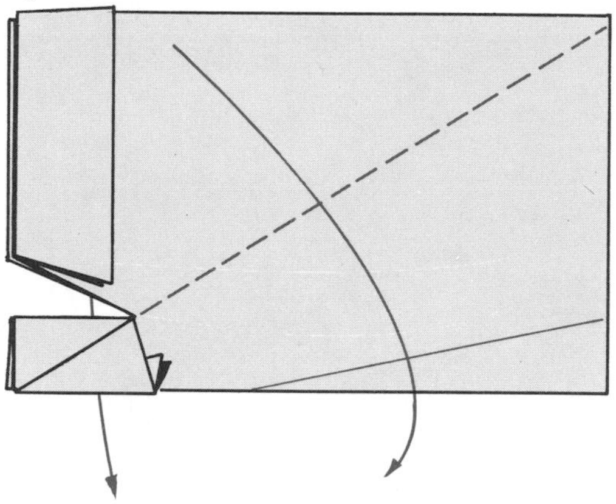

8 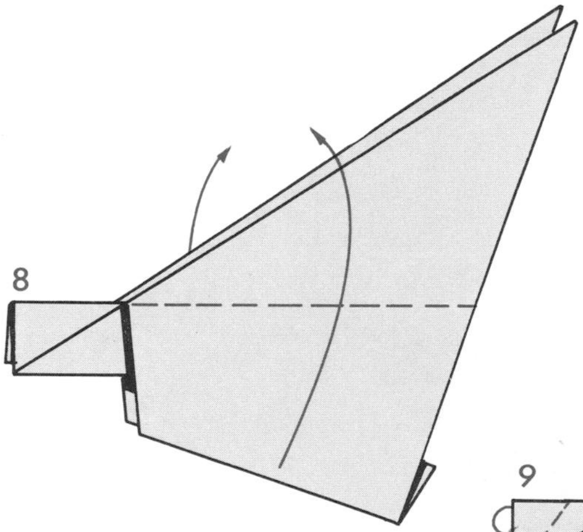

9 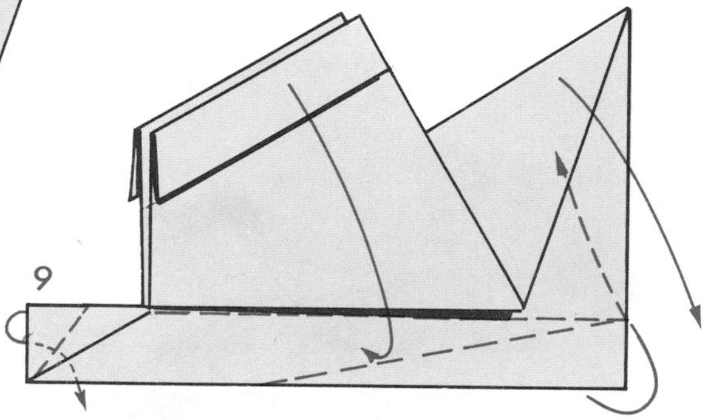

9 Make an inverted fold to tuck the nose in and then staple it down. Make an inverted fold in the tail. You can now see how important the cut was in Fig 3. If you have done it right, you can simply slip the front corner of the tail section into the slit in the fuselage and the whole thing takes shape (see Fig 10).

10 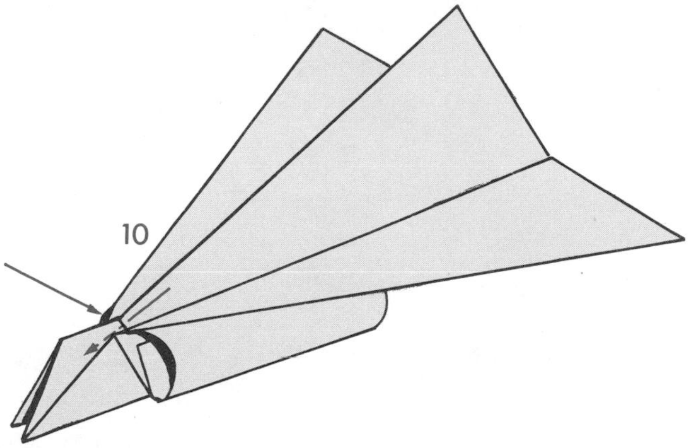

10 Form the air intakes for the jet engines by attaching both folded edges to the side of the fuselage with the inside edge lying flat against the fuselage. You will find it helpful to curl the paper round your finger to make the right shape. This modification is necessary for good aerodynamics. Finally, if you fold down the wings carefully over the fuselage and air intakes, you will see a genuine replica of the Mirage. Later on you can put flaps in the wings and the next step after that is the rudder on the tail. Your Mirage should then be able to fly in various directions and in time you and your friends could organize formation flights.

The Tiger Moth: graceful loops, simple rolls and, when something goes wrong, a nose-dive . . .

TIGER MOTH

Although this plane is still in existence and may often be seen in flying displays, it was designed long before the Second World War. Sir Francis Chichester, the celebrated round-the-world yachtsman, made this airplane famous when he flew one to Australia in the "twenties". For many years after that it was a popular airplane for training pilots. We are, of course, talking about the most famous biplane of all time, the Gipsy Moth, on which our paper airplane was modelled. Contemporaries from the First World War were the legendary Sopwith Camel and the Spad and many will have read the thrilling tales of the Red Baron and Biggles. Today the biplane is, compared with other designs, one of the slowest aircraft and yet it has an unbeatable record of aerobatic feats. It is used for stunt flying and its slow air speed of 60kph (36mph) means it is useful for crop-spraying.

Fuselage

1 The initial steps seem easy but be warned: this model is classed as *extremely difficult*. Take a sheet of paper 30 × 40cm (12 × 16in) and make a crease down the center. Fold both sides in half to meet along this center crease.

2 Make two short cuts through both the top and bottom layers, as the diagram illustrates. A quick look at Fig 3 would be helpful before making the cuts.

3 Make two more cuts as indicated in the top layer only. Fold the two flaps back.

4 Make a diagonal crease in each flap. Fold the top corners down to meet this diagonal line.

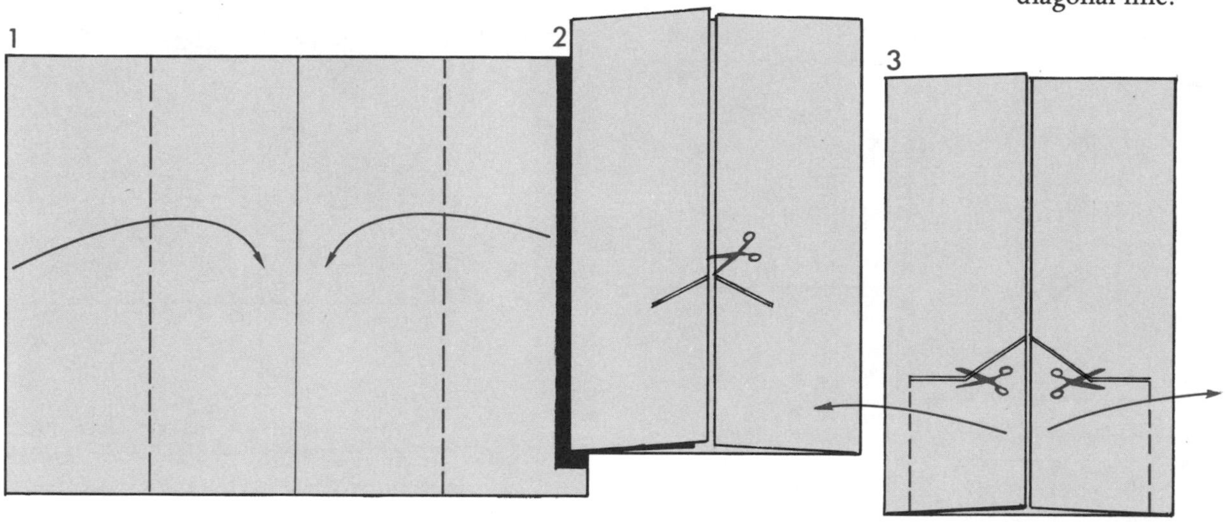

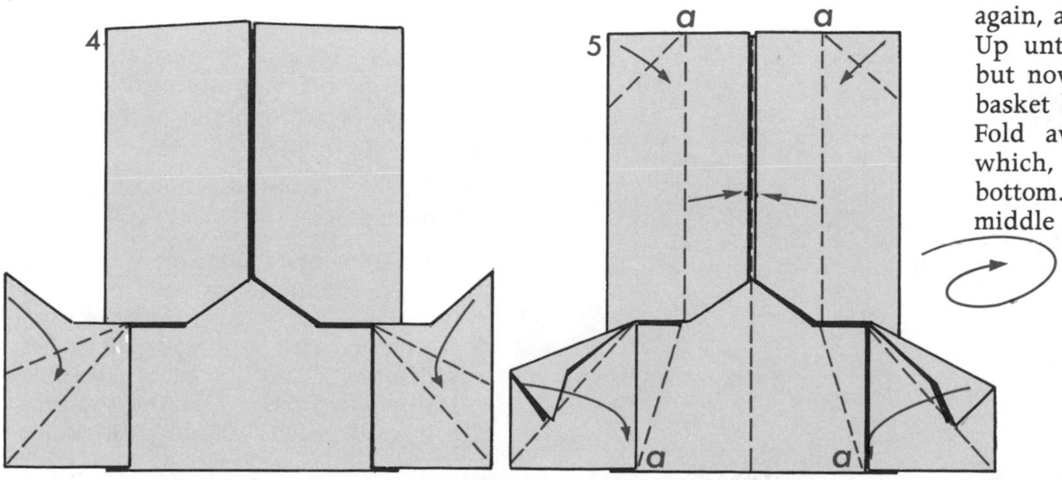

5 Fold these two edges inwards, once again, along the dotted diagonal crease. Up until now it has been fairly easy but now keep close to the wastepaper basket because it is going to get tough. Fold away from you along line 'a' which, you will see, is slanted at the bottom. (NB The lines 'a' are not in the middle of each side, but nearer to the center.) Make a fold along the center line towards you so that lines 'a' of the fuselage all meet along the center fold. The tip which will become the nose must be folded inwards. Turn the model over.

6

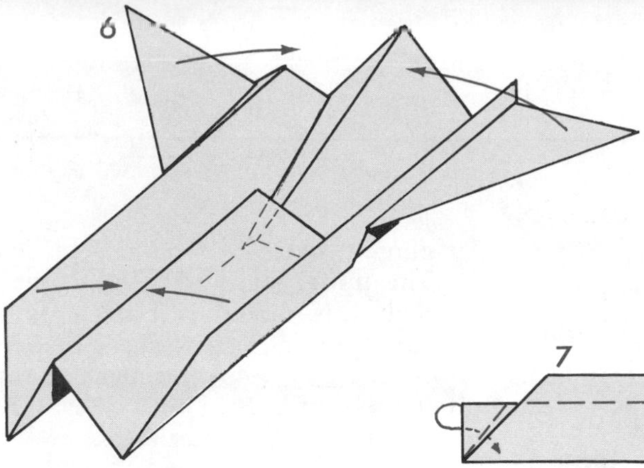

7

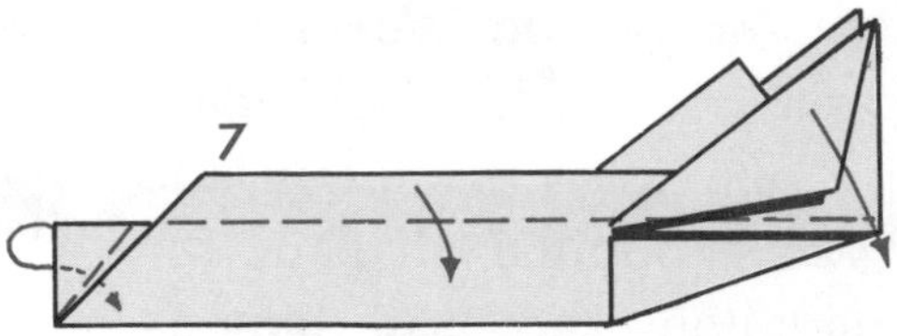

8

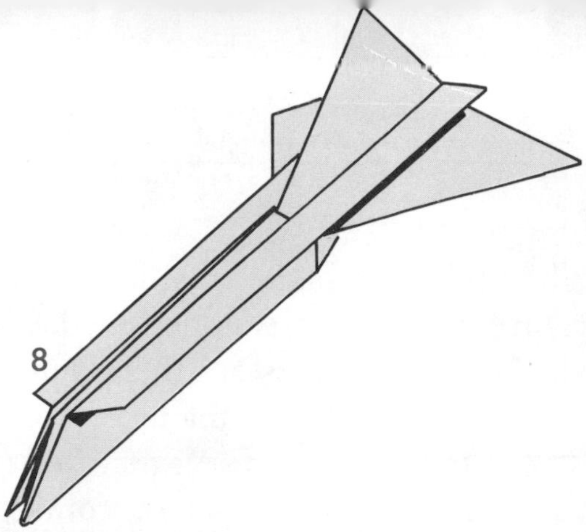

6 This is how the model should look if the whole thing has been folded according to the instructions. The base of the tail slots into the slit in the fuselage.

7 Tuck in the nose with an inverted fold. Fold the two top sections outwards, along the dotted line, following the line of the fuselage.

8 This is how the fuselage should look.

1

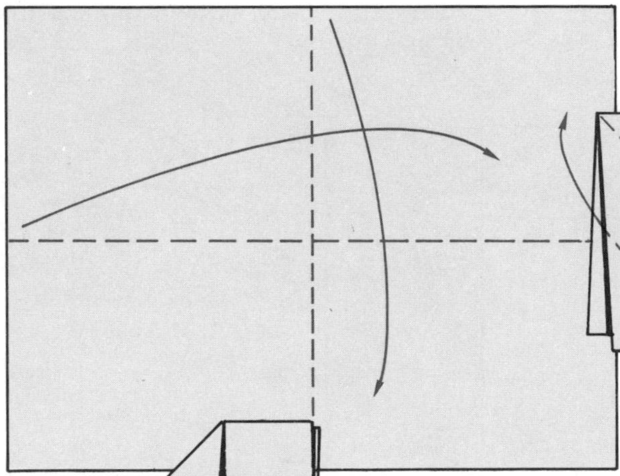

2

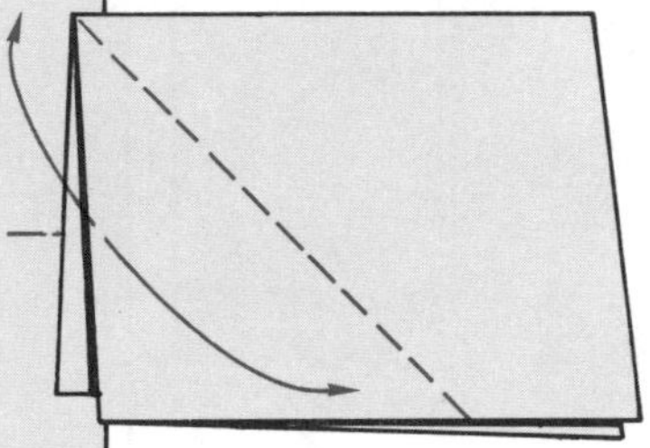

3

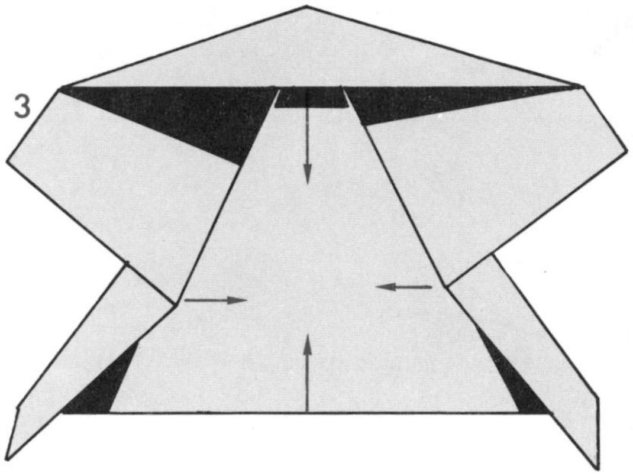

4

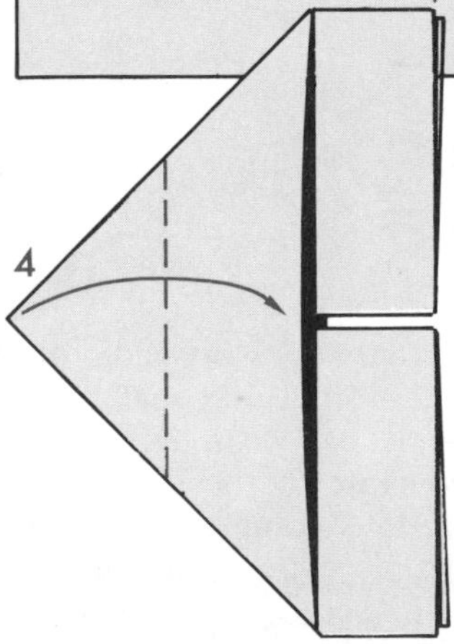

5

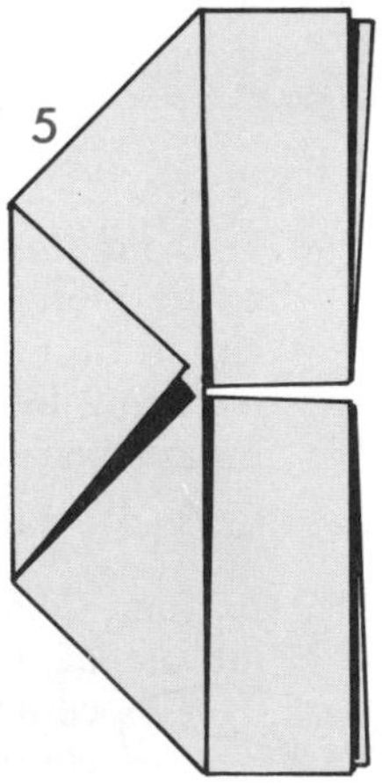

6

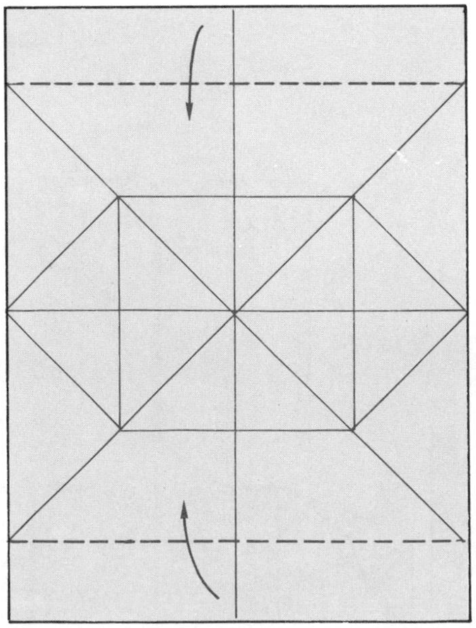

Wings

1 Take a sheet of paper 30 × 40cm (12 × 16in) and fold in half, first widthways and then lengthways.

2 Fold up the top layer of the bottom lefthand corner along the dotted line, doing the same with the bottom layer. Unfold the paper.

3 Lift two outside ends of the center line on the long side until they meet, then press the figure down flat as shown in Fig 4.

4 & 5 Fold the point over along the dotted line.

6 Now open out the sheet of paper. Make the four additional creases shown in Fig 6 so that all the creases on the paper match up with those on the diagram. If you are satisfied that everything is correct, fold the shorter edges inwards, as indicated by the dotted line.

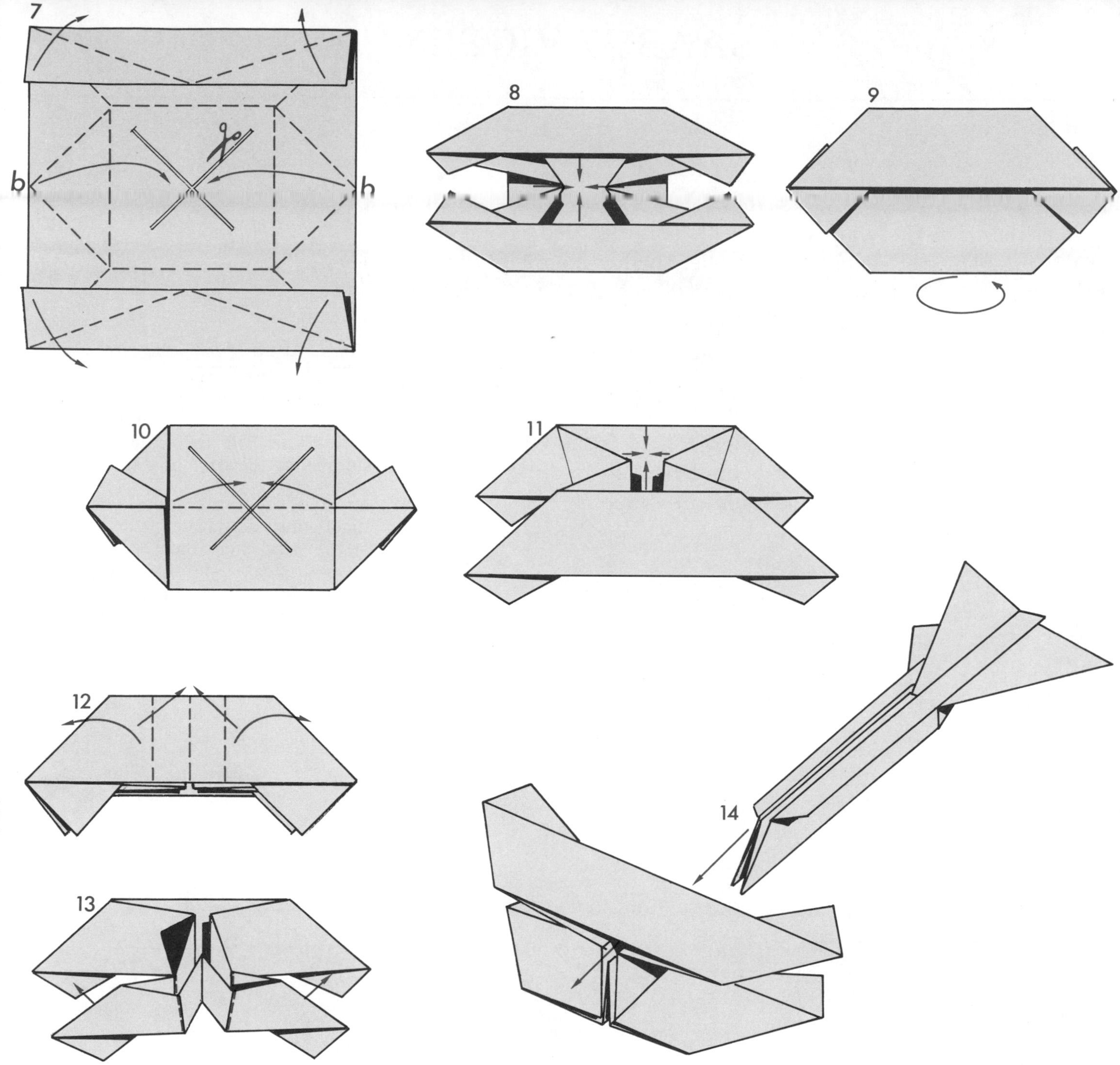

7 Now fold out the four corners of these flaps and make cuts in the places indicated. It is important that a balance exists between the length and size of the model. Push the points 'b' together and press the whole figure down flat so that the four corners of the model lie on top of one another.

8 It looks harder than it really is. This diagram should make it clearer.

9 Your model should look like this when pressed flat. Now turn it over.

10 Lift the two points indicated by the arrows towards the center following the fold along the dotted line and press flat.

11 This diagram clarifies the preceding steps.

12 Make a fold towards you along the center dotted line and a fold away from you either side along the dotted lines.

13 It should look like this.

14 Finally, push the fuselage through the hole in the wings and attach them together. The Tiger Moth is ready to make a flight. Soon your model will do acrobatics and stunt flying, after you have made the first ten . . .

SAAB 37 VIGGEN

The pride of the Swedes is the Saab Viggen, a delta-wing jet which, despite criticism of the wing structure, is still regarded as one of the most advanced fighter planes. The smaller, higher-mounted wings in front of the main wings aid stability at low speeds. The Viggen plays an important role in Sweden's defense plans.

The paper Viggen is a good example of the models of existing designs. It closely resembles the Viggen but, on closer inspection, plane enthusiasts will notice some variations. For example, the air inlets on the real Viggen run through to the front wings and the fuselage is proportionately higher behind the tail. In our model there is no undercarriage, no jet engine, and no weapons, but nonetheless our Viggen flies beautifully.

1 Take a sheet of paper 30 × 40cm (12 × 16in) and fold the two lefthand corners over to the dotted lines as shown. Fold over again along the dotted lines.

2 Fold the complete model in half widthways with the flaps innermost.

3 Make cuts in the paper as indicated and crease the tail by folding it backwards and forwards over the diagonal dotted line. Fold the wings up on both sides along the straight dotted line.

4 Fold the front edges of the large delta wings down along the dotted lines at the cuts, then fold the wings down on both sides along the straight dotted line as shown in the illustration.

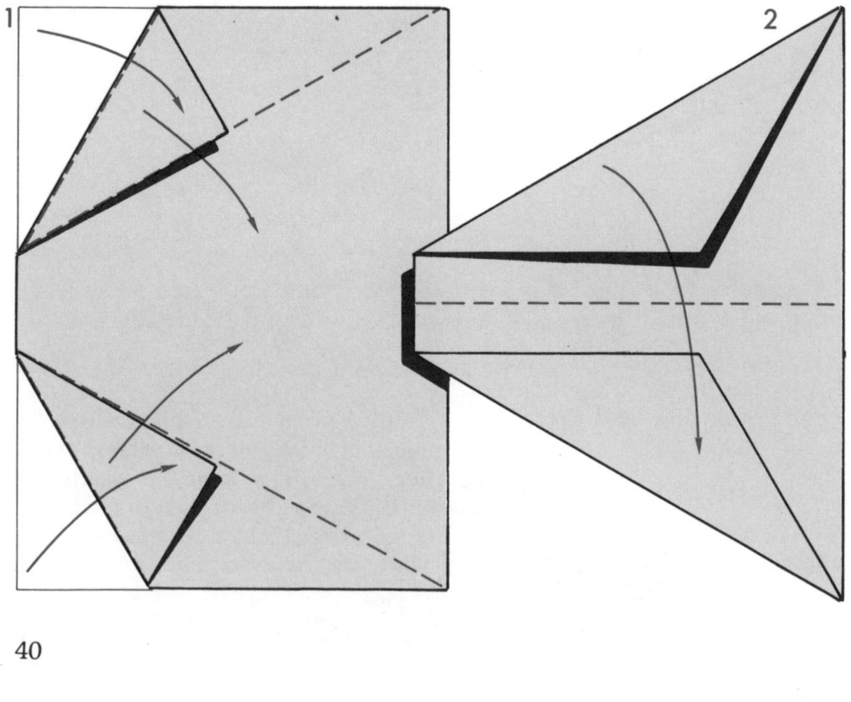

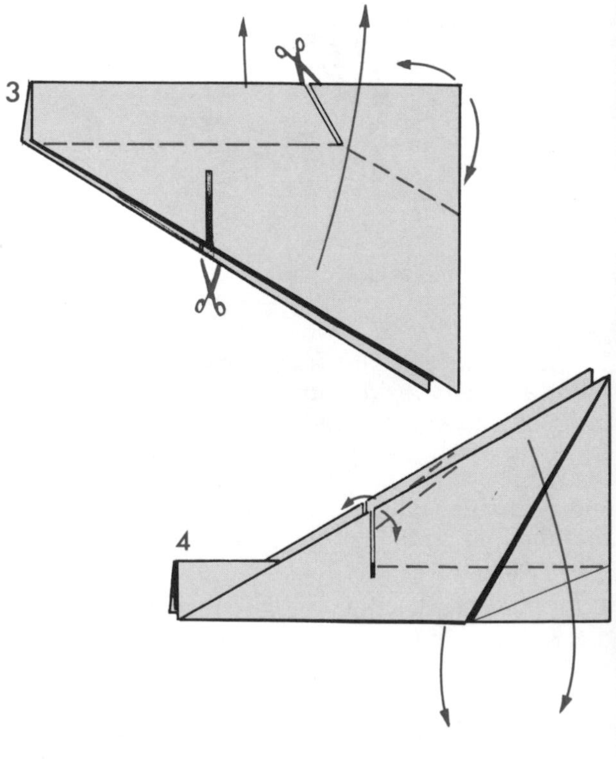

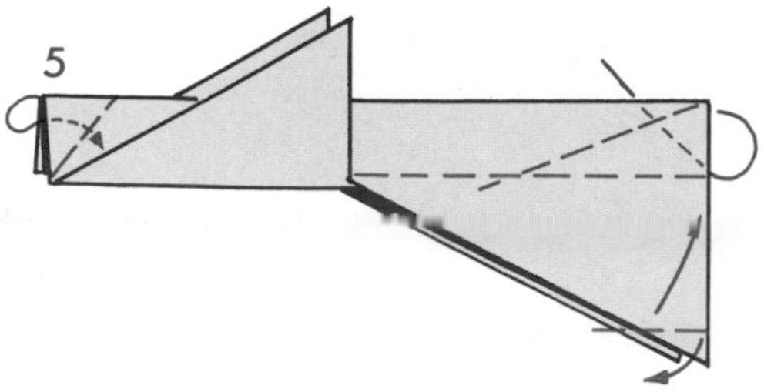

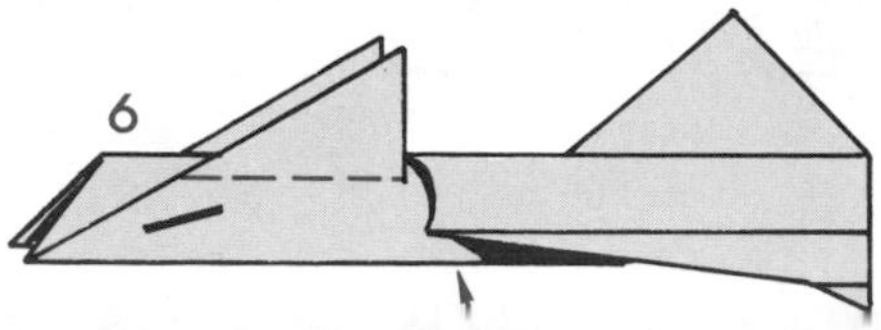

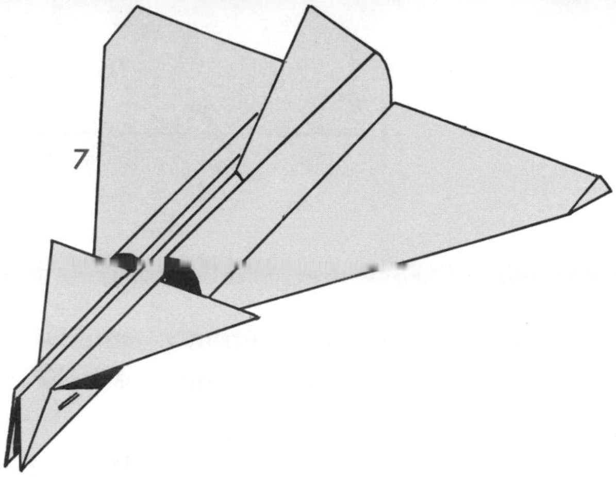

5 Make an inverted fold in the tip of the nose and push the base of the tail through the slit. Fold the wings up along the dotted line and the tips of the delta wings under as shown.

6 Secure the nose with a paper-clip or staple. Push the base of the delta wings up slightly to form air inlets for the jet engine and then staple or glue in place (see arrow). Fold the small front wings along the dotted line.

7 If your Saab 37 Viggen looks exactly like the illustration, it's ready for take-off.

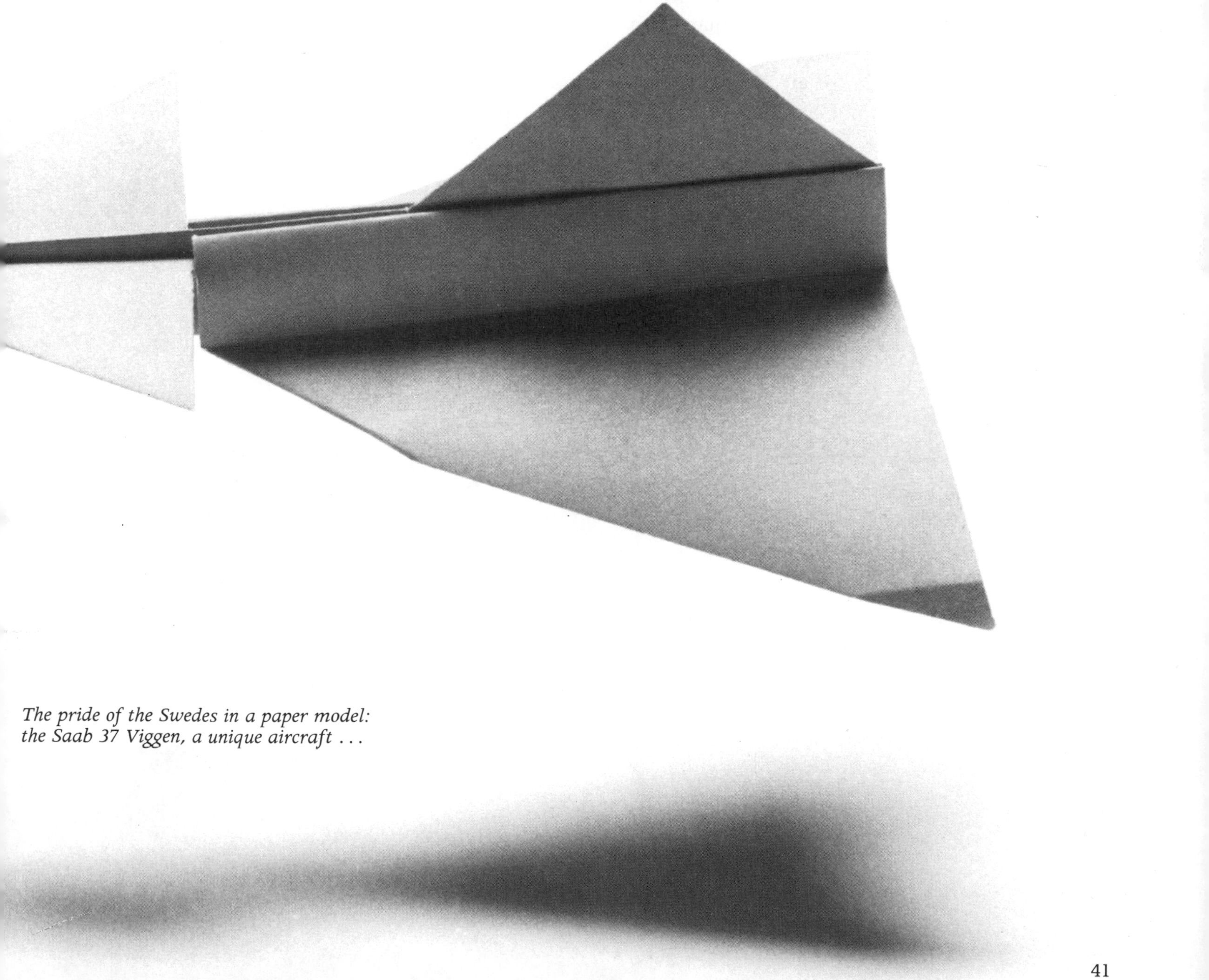

The pride of the Swedes in a paper model: the Saab 37 Viggen, a unique aircraft . . .

TUPOLEV (BEAR)

The Russian Tupolev is a unique airplane in aircraft history. The 'Bear', as it is commonly called in the West, is one of the largest aircraft in the world and was believed – wrongly – to be a jet. It has huge V-form wings and the four turbo-jets power immense propellers to move the craft through the sky. Experts in the field of aviation have said that its design should inhibit it from flying but the Tupolev proves the opposite. There are reports which say that the gigantic propellers explode against one another due to the vibrations of the aircraft. If necessary this enormous plane can remain in the sky for twenty-four hours. The same goes for its little brother although it is all relative and the length in the air must be seen as proportional. A flight lasting twenty-four seconds is, however, not impossible. This Bear is also a wonderful glider. The turbines and propellers have obviously been omitted.

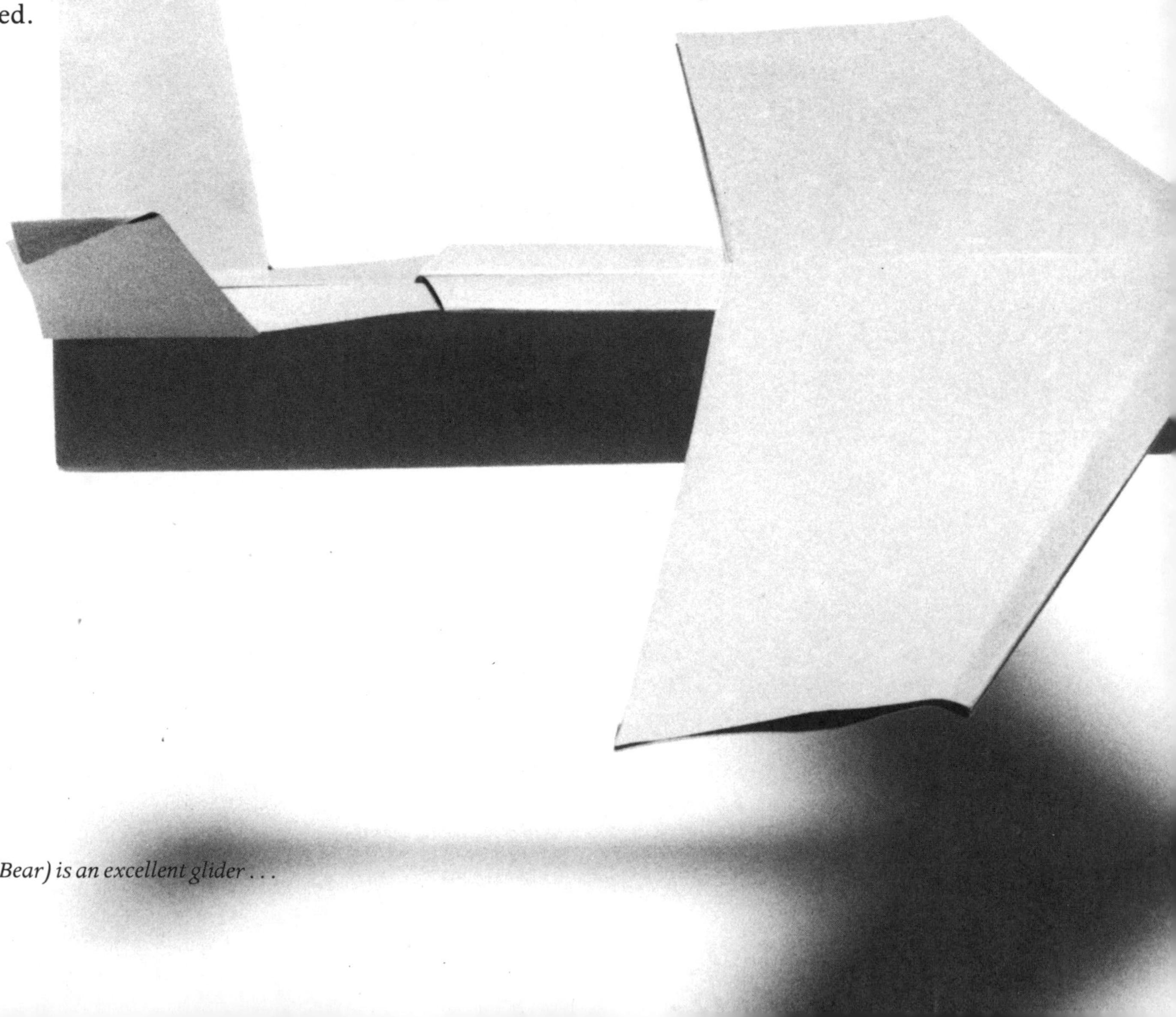

The Tupolev (Bear) is an excellent glider . . .

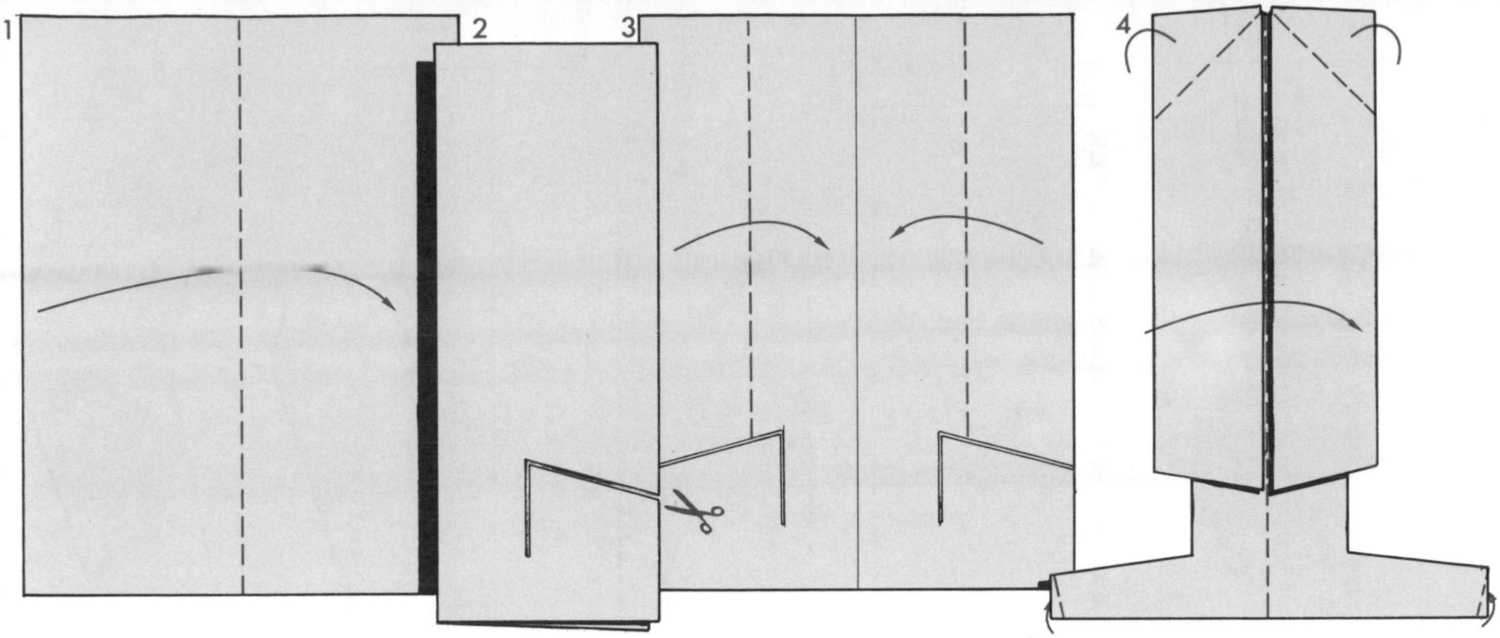

Fuselage

1 Take a sheet of paper 30 × 40cm (12 × 16in) and fold in half.

2 Make a cut through both layers of paper as indicated.

3 Open the paper out flat and fold both sides inwards to the center along the dotted lines.

4 Fold back the top corners to make the nose. Fold under the loose flaps of the tail section and fold under the tips of the tail as indicated. Now fold the whole model in half.

5 Fold over the top edge of the whole fuselage to either side, as indicated.

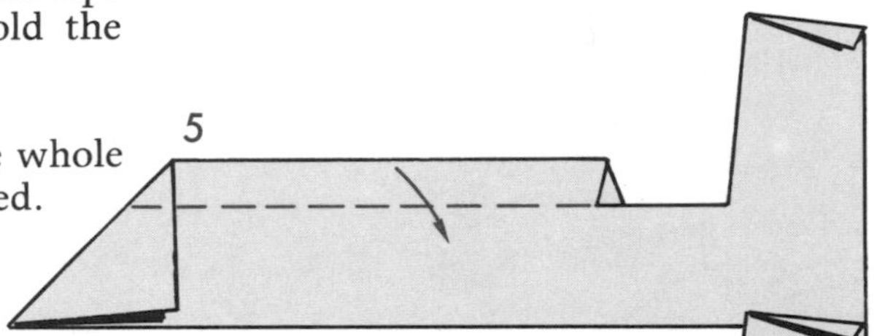

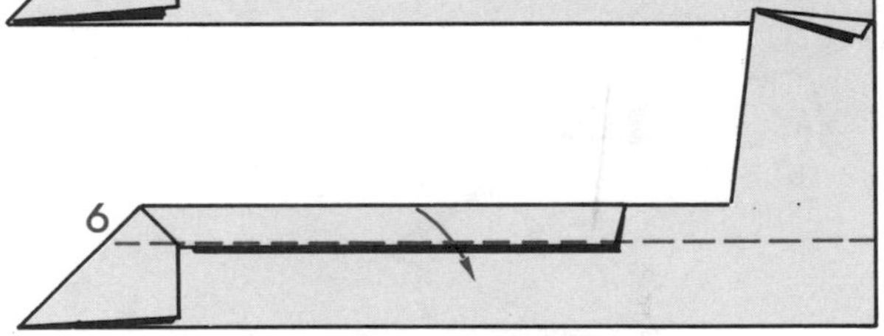

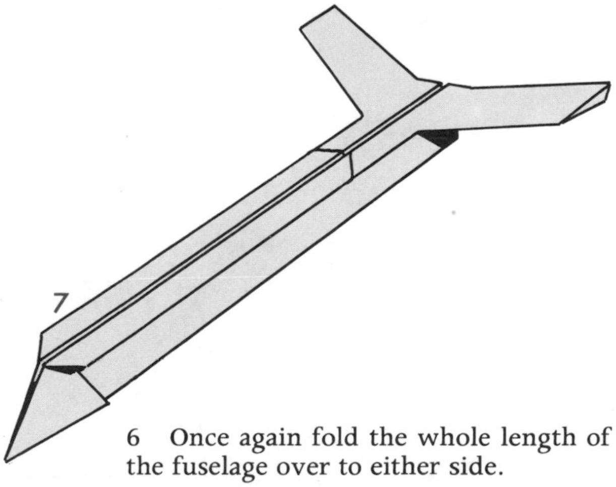

6 Once again fold the whole length of the fuselage over to either side.

7 This is the result when the fuselage is completed.

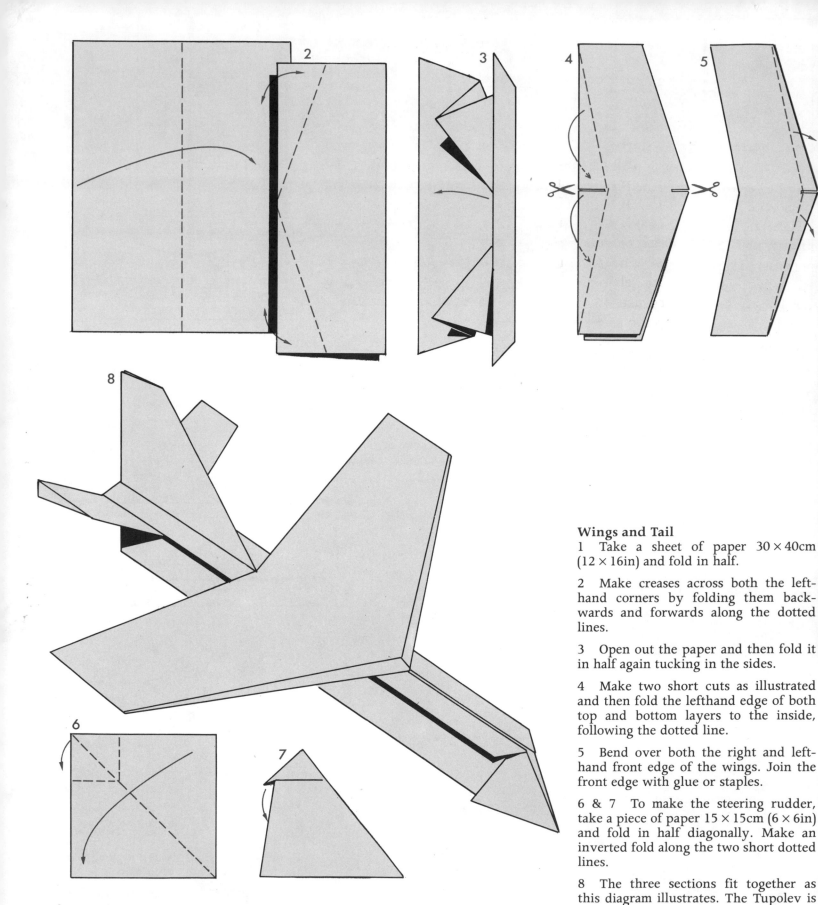

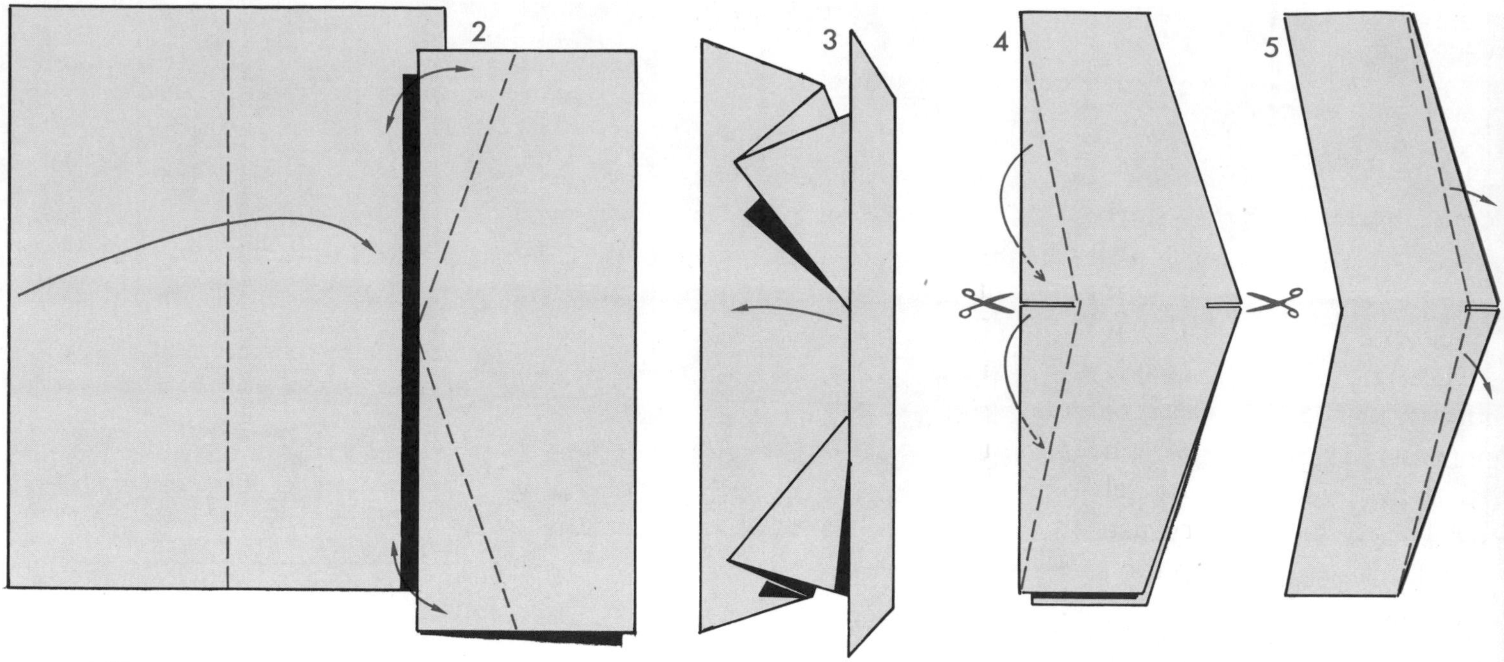

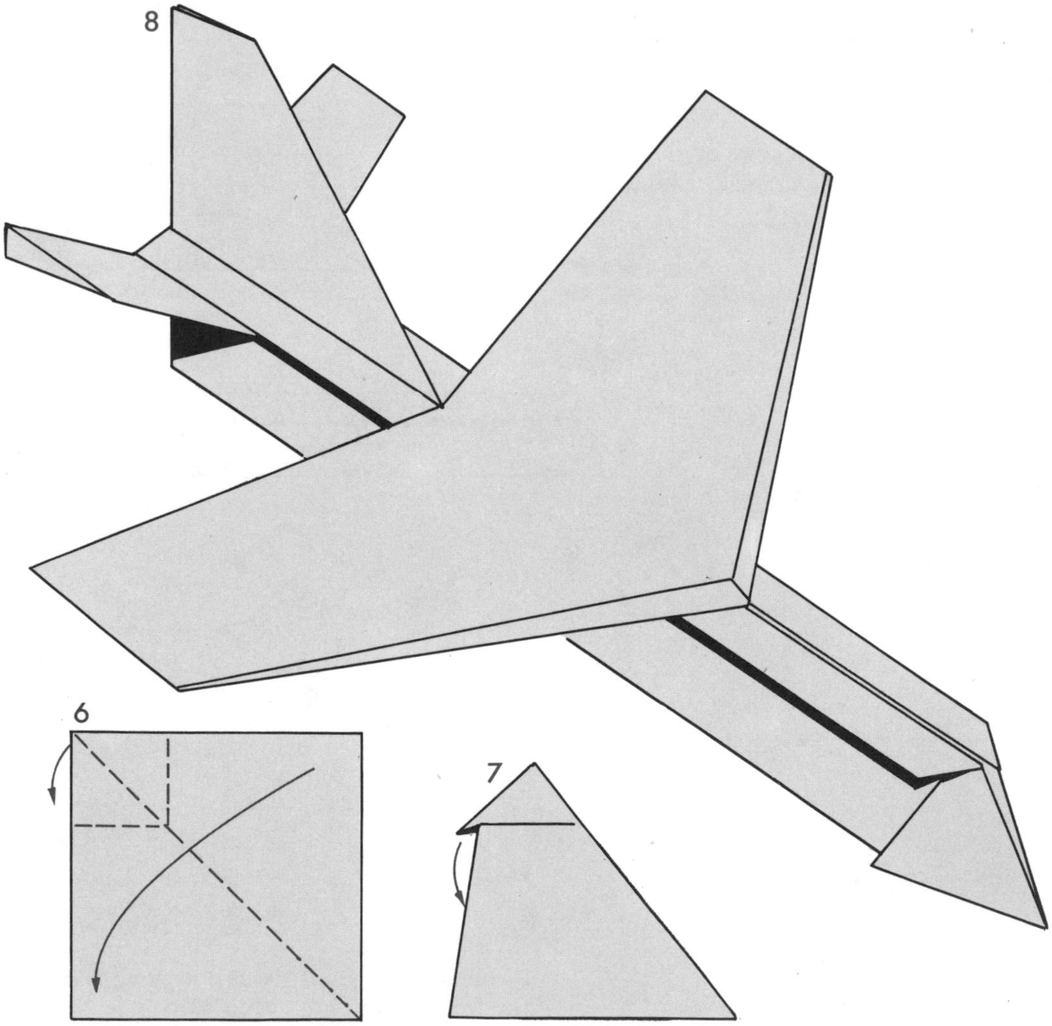

Wings and Tail

1 Take a sheet of paper 30 × 40cm (12 × 16in) and fold in half.

2 Make creases across both the left-hand corners by folding them backwards and forwards along the dotted lines.

3 Open out the paper and then fold it in half again tucking in the sides.

4 Make two short cuts as illustrated and then fold the lefthand edge of both top and bottom layers to the inside, following the dotted line.

5 Bend over both the right and left-hand front edge of the wings. Join the front edge with glue or staples.

6 & 7 To make the steering rudder, take a piece of paper 15 × 15cm (6 × 6in) and fold in half diagonally. Make an inverted fold along the two short dotted lines.

8 The three sections fit together as this diagram illustrates. The Tupolev is now ready.

F-16

The F-16, manufactured by General Dynamics, has become a controversial aircraft during its brief history. It is a jet with extraordinary potential and the most up-to-date equipment. Computers perform an important role; it might be said that it is not the pilot who flies the F-16, but the F-16 which flies the pilot.

The paper F-16 was modelled on a design by Eiji Nakamura, a well-known Japanese expert on folded paper planes and the shape is perhaps the most pleasing in the whole series. Apart from that, the F-16 is a very good model which flies quickly and can perform aerobatics. You can try using different types of paper for making it but don't use anything too light.

Fuselage

1 Take a sheet of paper 30 × 40cm (12 × 16in) and fold the top corners inwards along the dotted lines.

2 Fold inwards again along the dotted lines making sure that all the folds meet at the top center point.

3 Fold the outside edges inwards along the dotted lines for the third time and then cut off the corners as directed. Fold the whole model in half away from you along the center line.

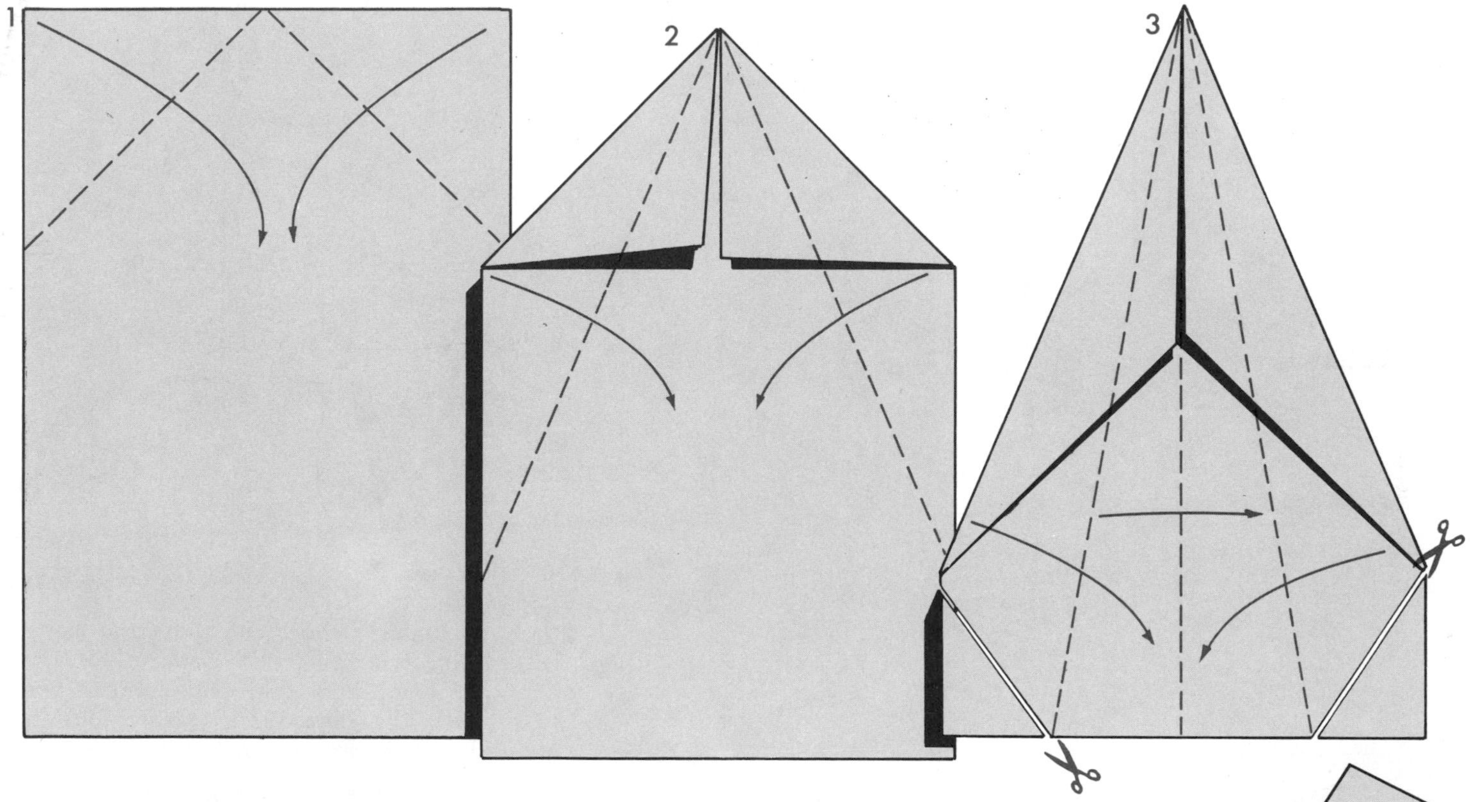

4 Fold the tail section backwards and forwards along the dotted line, and push up the center using an inverted fold.

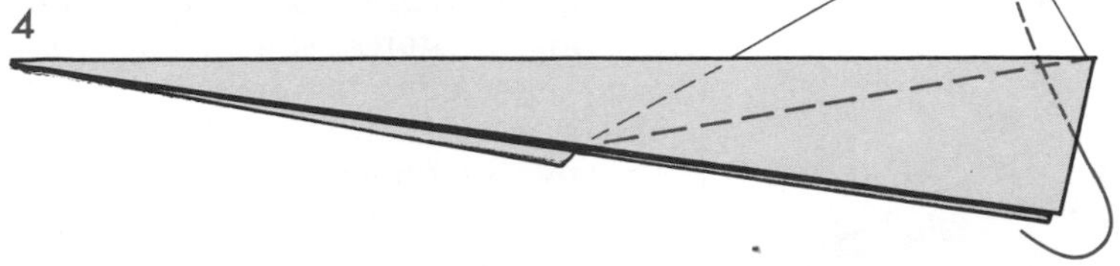

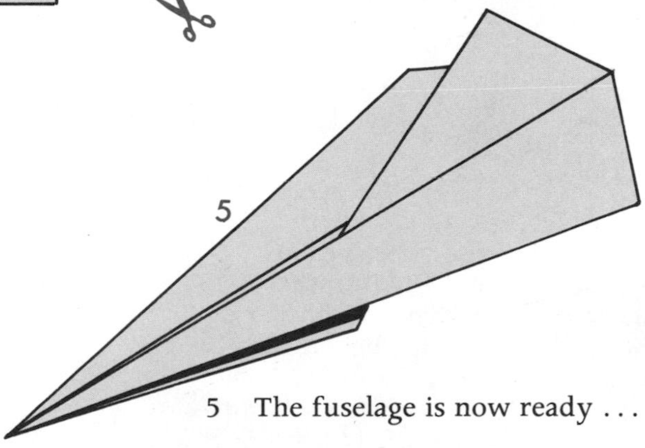

5 The fuselage is now ready . . .

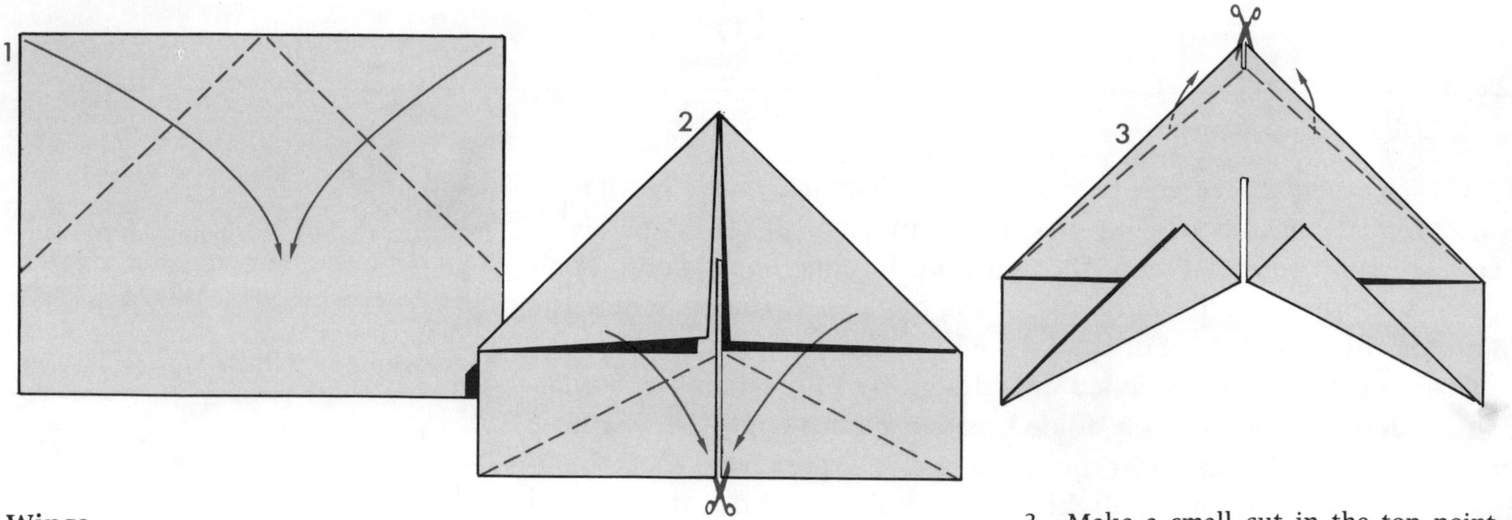

Wings

1 Take a sheet of paper 20 × 30cm and fold in the two top corners of the long side so that they meet in the middle.

2 Make a cut as shown and fold the resulting flaps upwards along the dotted lines.

3 Make a small cut in the top point, and bend the edges towards you along the dotted lines. This view is of the underside of the wings.

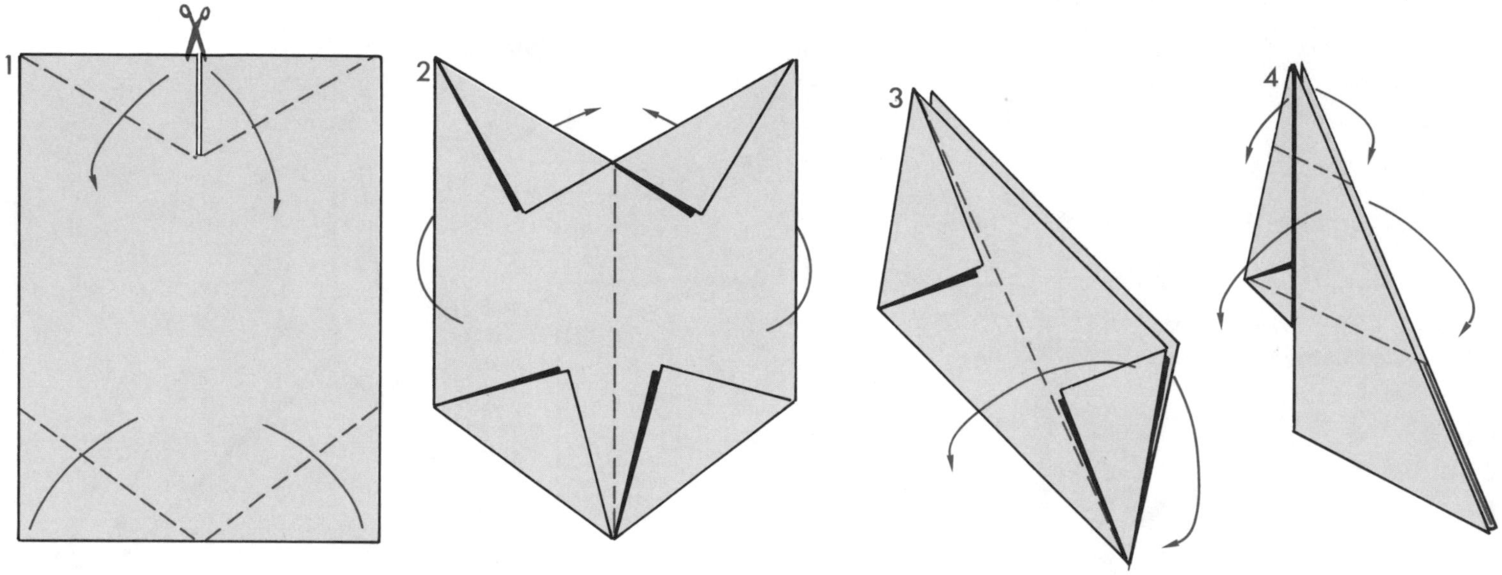

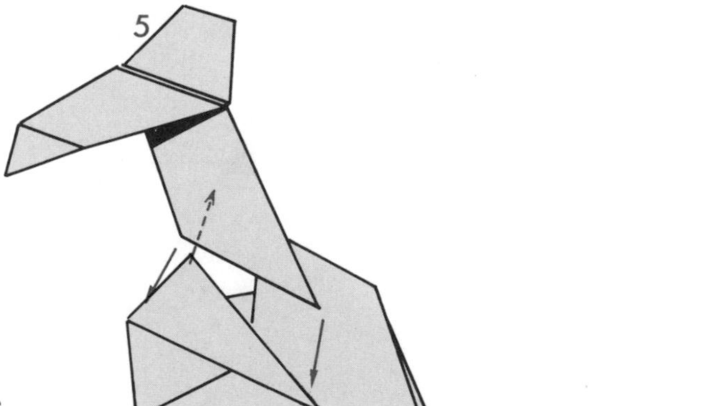

Tail

1 Make a short cut along the center line of a piece of paper 20 × 30cm (8 × 12in) and fold the corners over along the dotted lines. Now fold the lower corners upwards as indicated.

2 Fold the whole model in half away from you along the dotted line.

3 Fold down each flap to either side along the diagonal dotted line.

4 Fold the tip of the tail open to either side along the dotted line and then fold the tail open along the lower dotted line again to either side. Glue the edges of the bottom half together.

5 Attach the wings to the top side of the fuselage so that the tail end fits into the ready-made groove, and glue the whole thing together. Attach the tail by slotting it over the fuselage. Now the F-16 is ready for its maiden flight.

The paper F-16 was modelled on a design by Eiji Nakamura, a well-known Japanese expert on folded paper planes.

EXPERIMENTAL MODELS

Man had been experimenting with paper aircraft long before he conquered the skies. It is therefore logical to use paper for designs of the future. A number of different models are tested in this section; it would be interesting to see the performance of full-size versions. Futuristic models based on energy-saving principles are included; the Catapult Plane (pp 54/5) could prove useful in reality and also, perhaps, the revolutionary new helicopter design (pp 62/3). The Star Ship (pp 52/3), based on a cross between a traditional airplane and a flying saucer, creates a new concept in the flying world. And the future? Well, don't forget that it took years to develop the Concorde but after all that, it closely resembles the schoolboy's traditional paper plane. Why should history not repeat itself? The eight models on the following pages are just preliminary designs, so carry out further experiments or make your own modifications if you think they will improve the model. In years to come your ideas may well be quite realistic . . .

A saucer that really flies and will amaze your friends . . .

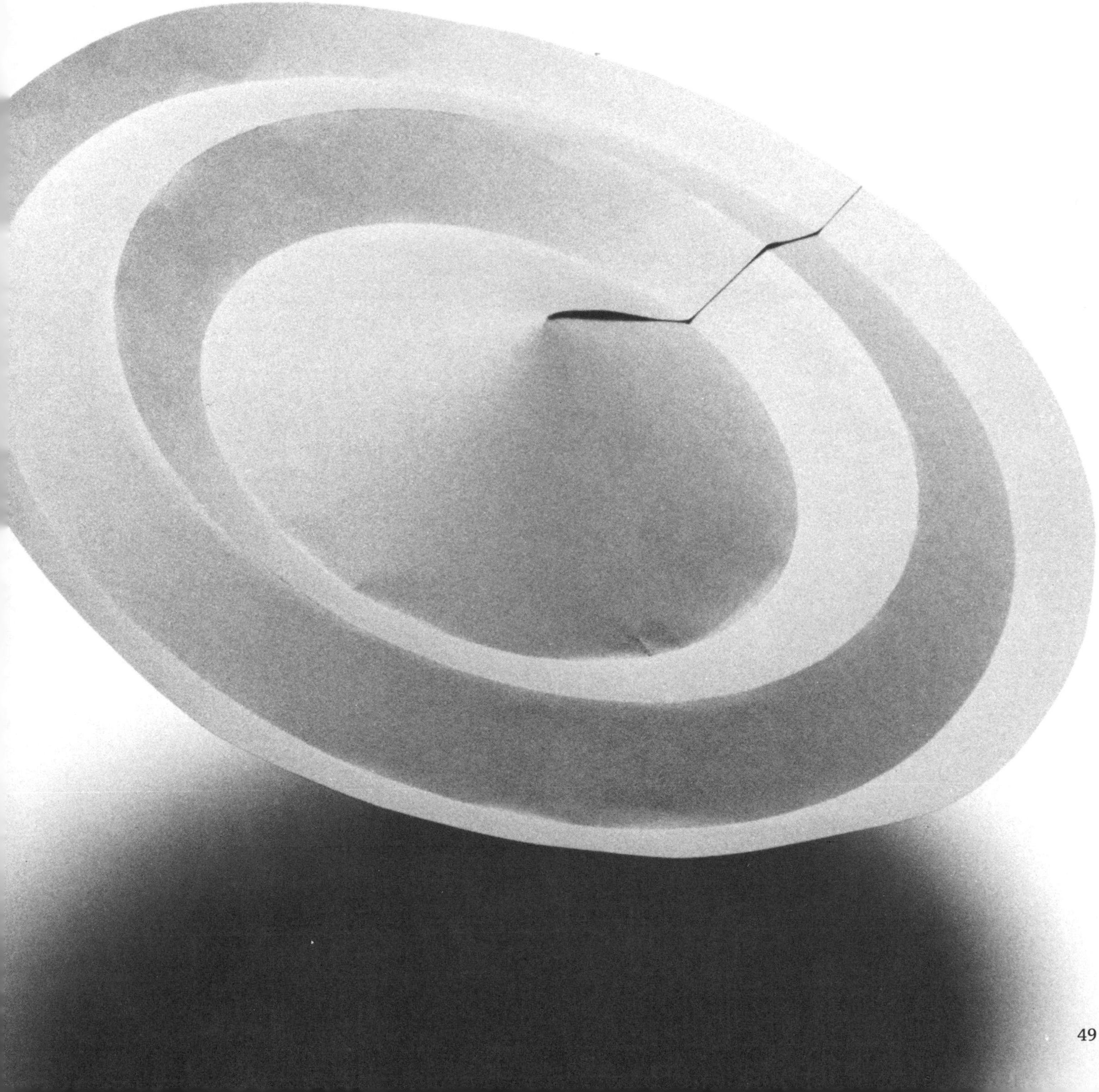

FLYING SAUCER

In a section covering designs for the future, the Flying Saucer just cannot be left out. A Flying Saucer that flies really well is cause for some excitement, just like the UFOs. The Flying Saucer is not too easy to make; using a pair of compasses or dividers will make it a little easier and with some improvisation you should succeed.

1 Cut out a 30cm (12in) diameter circle from a piece of stiff paper or thin card. A plate or a bowl could be used for the outline.

2 Mark the three circles 'a', 'b', and 'c' with a compass, spaced equidistantly.

3 Turn the model over and draw the circles 'a' and 'b' on the other side. Score these lines using the pointed end of the compass or a pair of dividers.

4 Turn the model over again and score circle 'c'.

5 Cut out the section indicated, fold the circles as illustrated in the cross-section diagram and glue lines 'e' and 'd' together.

The Flying Saucer flies in much the same way as a frisbee, hovering if you spin it. This model is an ideal one to paint – the effects will be very eye-catching as it spins through the air.

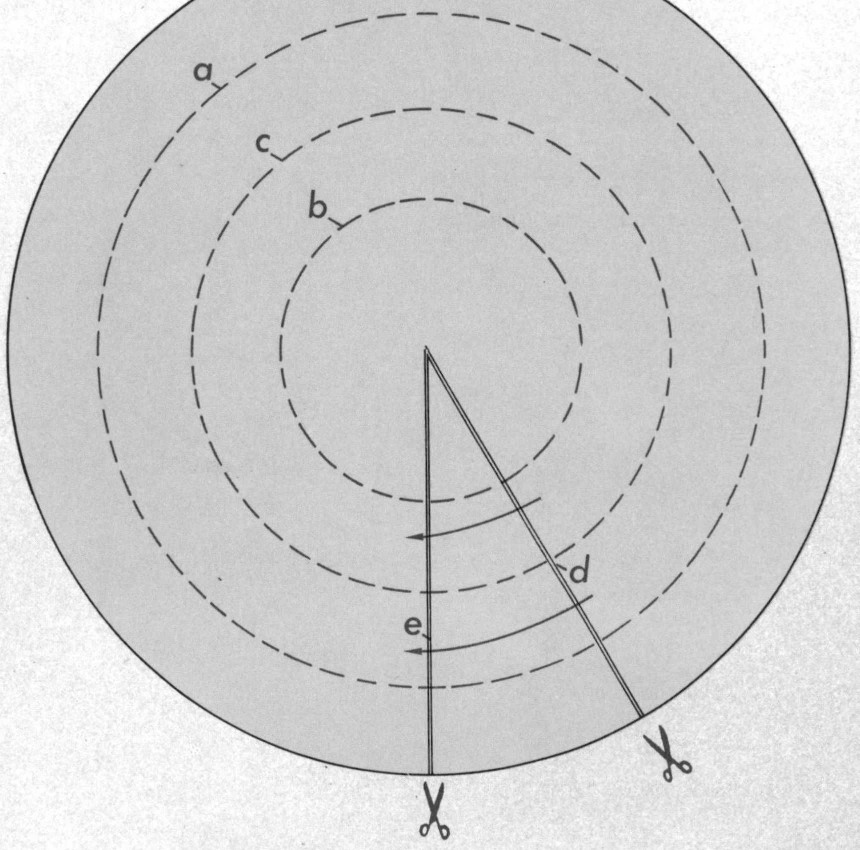

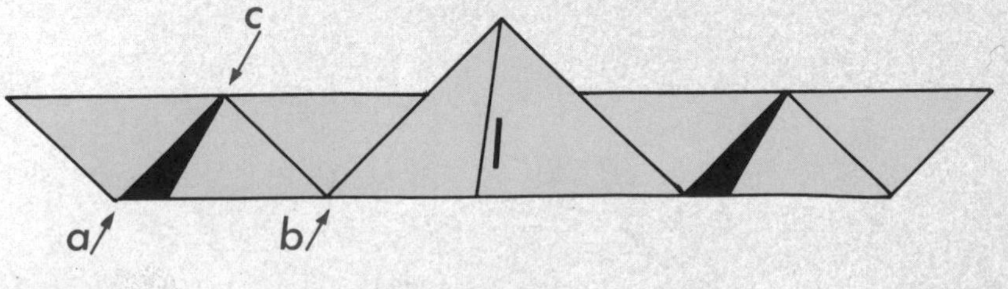

MATCHSTICK ROCKET

This is the only model in the book which has nothing to do with paper and very little to do with flying. So what exactly does it do does a rocket fly or is it propelled? There are no wings so it cannot glide and without power it would fall like a stone. To a certain extent, this applies to a great number of the models in this book. This Matchstick Rocket is a genuine rocket; it requires a paper clip, a box of matches, a piece of aluminum foil and a pin. Place the matchstick and the pin side by side with the pin point by the matchhead, roll up the top half in aluminum foil and then carefully withdraw the pin. The rocket is now ready to launch; pavements make excellent launching pads. Bend open a paper clip and lay the rocket on the top part of it. Hold a burning match underneath and the rocket will take off. Forget the "countdown" procedure because the take-off of this rocket cannot be planned around a tight schedule. If everything goes well, it should fly two or three meters. What could also happen is shown in these two photographs: in the top photograph the model has been carelessly ignited and the launching is a disaster; in the lower photograph the rocket veers suddenly to one side and makes a magnificent somersault. *DO NOT* launch your Matchstick Rocket indoors. The Matchstick Rocket may land on clothing so take great care to see that nothing is scorched or set on fire.

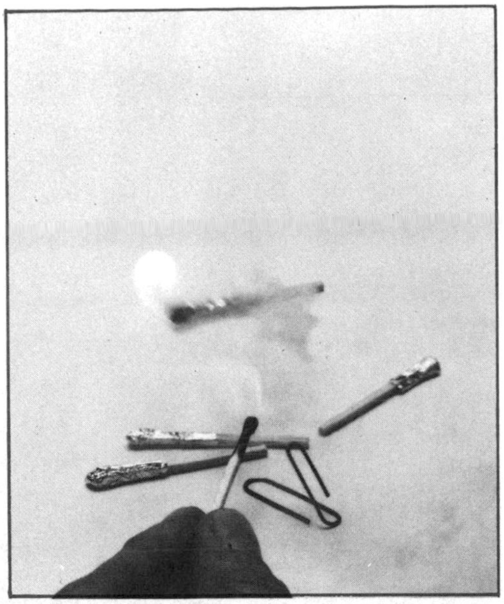

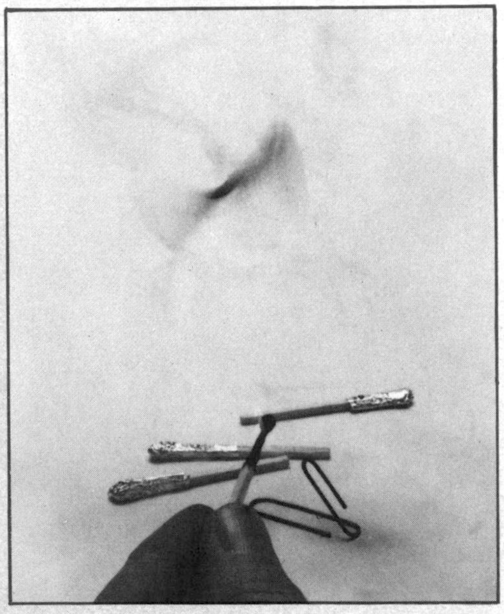

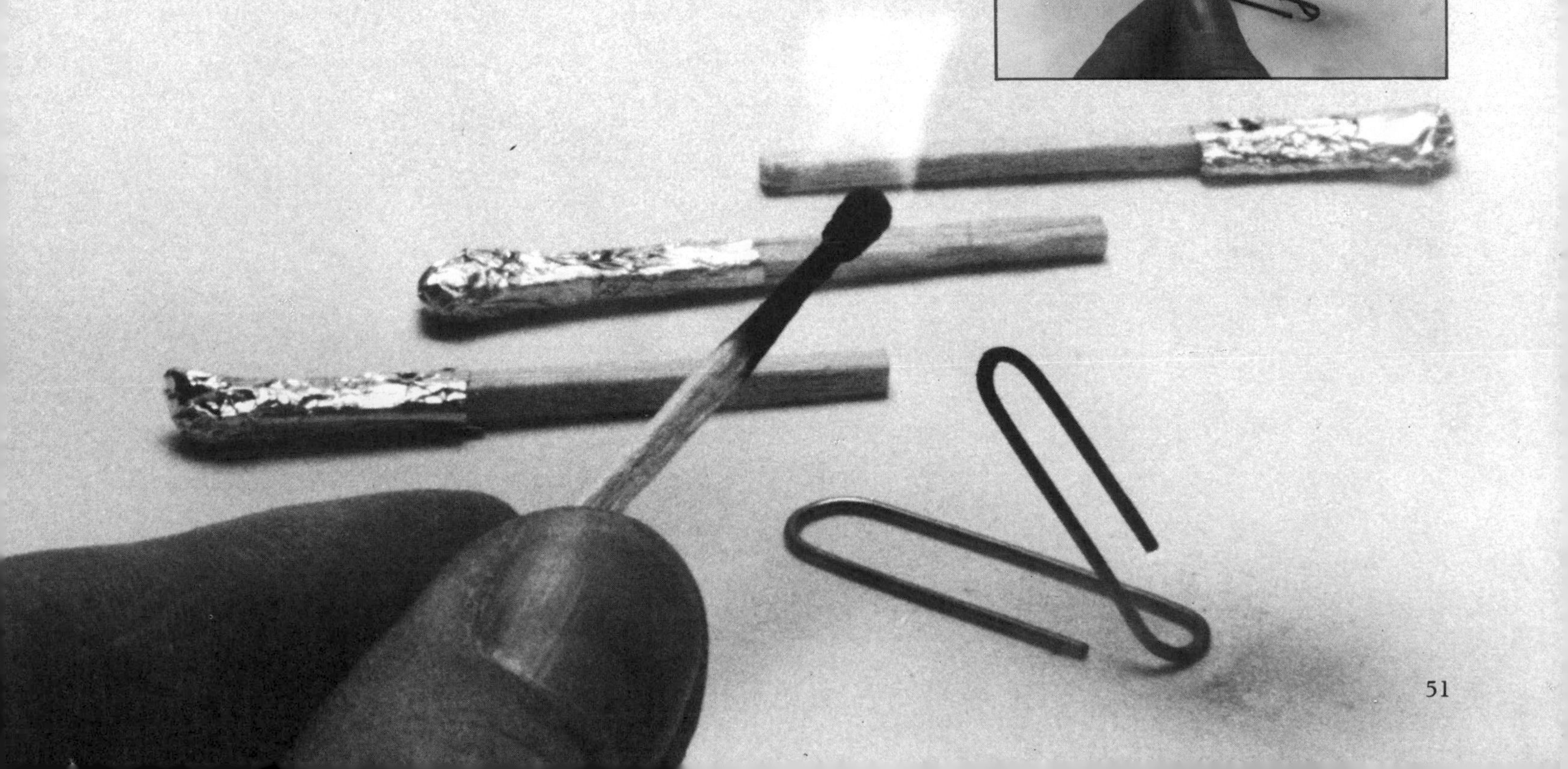

STARSHIP

This futuristic combination of a flying saucer and a traditional aircraft is made out of cardboard. There is not very much folding as most of the work is cutting out and slotting the sections together. It flies excellently but is particularly suited to long-distance flights. It does not perform aerobatics.

1 Take a round piece of cardboard of approximately 20cm (8in) diameter and make 3 cuts as illustrated to form the large wing section.

2 Cut out the rudders as the diagram illustrates, making the two cuts as indicated.

3 Cut out the fuselage, fold it in half lengthways and make a slit as shown in the diagram.

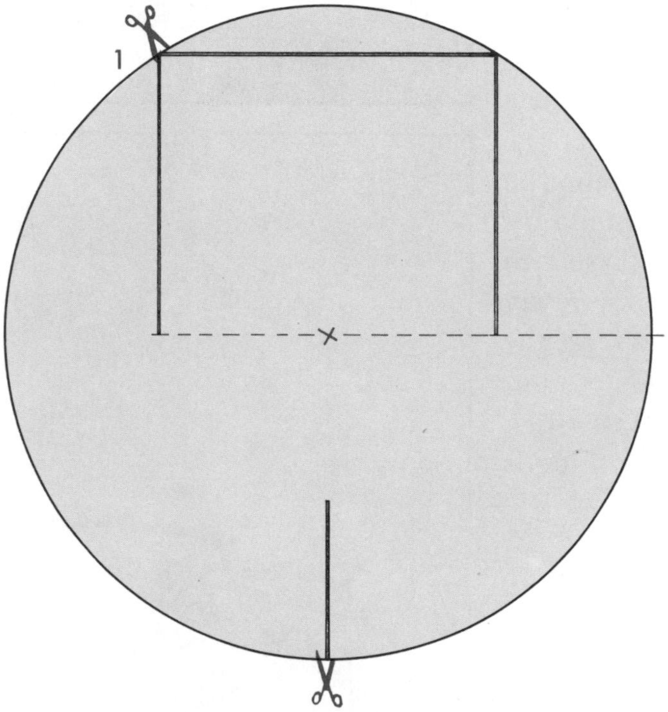

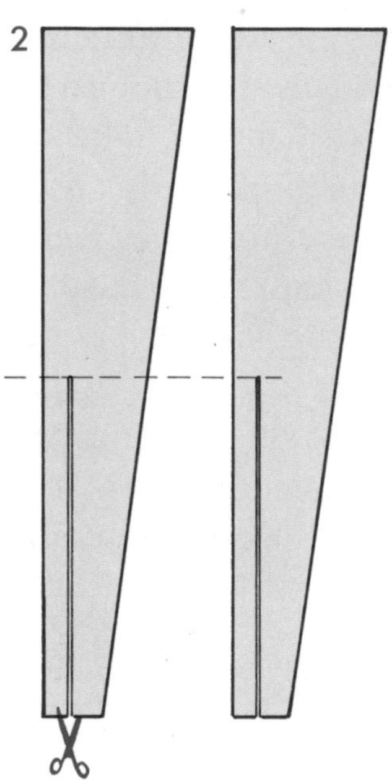

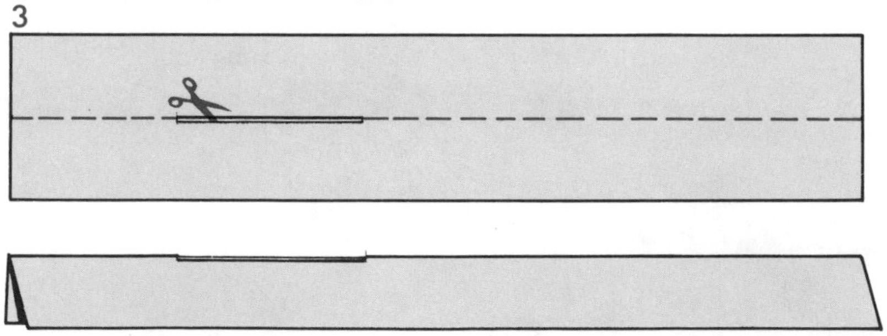

4 Cut out the nose section and make a slit as illustrated.

5 Cut out the stabilizer and fold down the two ends.

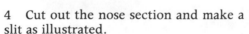

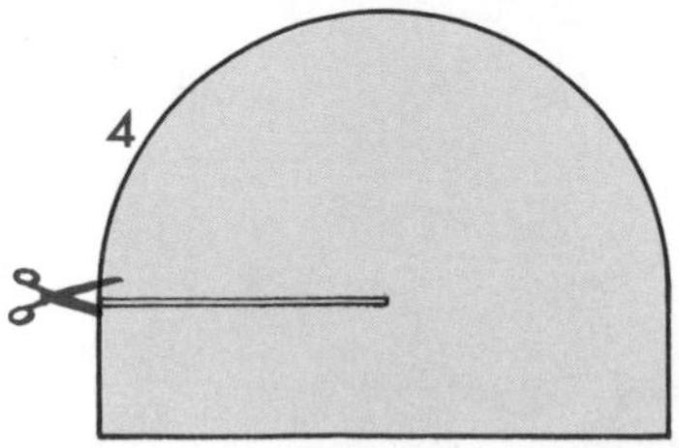

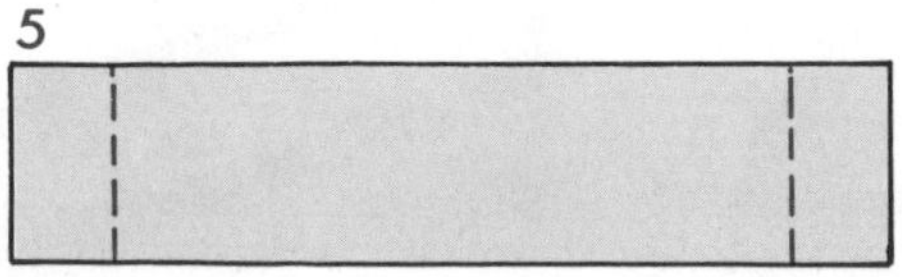

A futuristic design combining a flying saucer and a traditional aircraft . . .

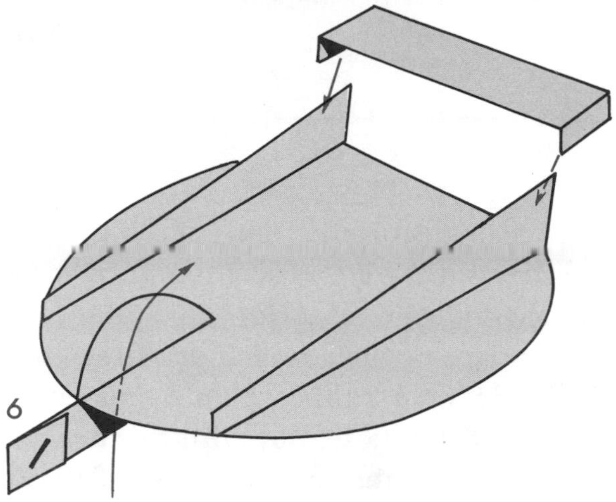

6 Fit the lower edge of the nose section through the slit in the fuselage and then slot the nose and the wing sections together. Attach the folded-down ends of the stabilizer to the rudders in the position indicated, fold back the front of the nose and staple it, and now your Starship is ready for launching.

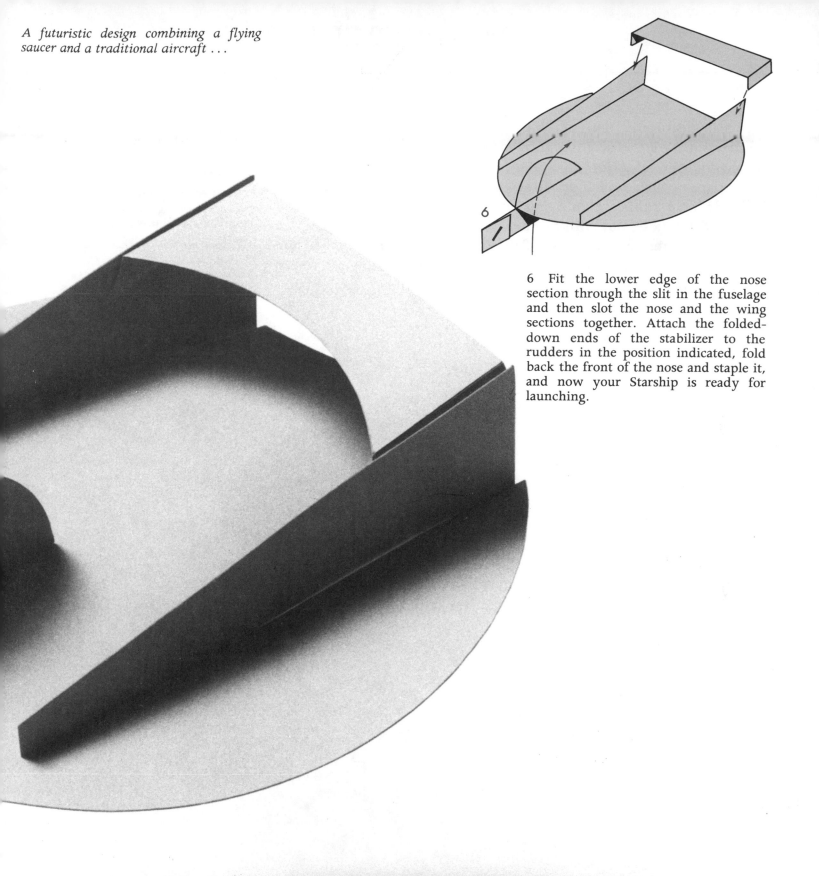

CATAPULT PLANE

The main feature of the Catapult Plane is its great speed. Its firing mechanism is very efficient and it has been used as a weapon of war throughout the centuries. This catapult is fired in just the same way as those paper pellets which are fired in the classroom (or office!) with the help of a rubber band. You could easily get blisters on your thumbs from those, but with this design there is no danger of that and plenty of fun too. It is a design of the future because no one believes that this firing technique will really work without using enormous rubber bands! It is best to use very thin paper for the Catapult Plane.

Fuselage

1 Take a sheet of paper 20 × 20cm (8 × 8in) and fold in the two sides along the dotted lines.

2 Fold each of the outside triangles in half again to give double thickness, then turn the figure over.

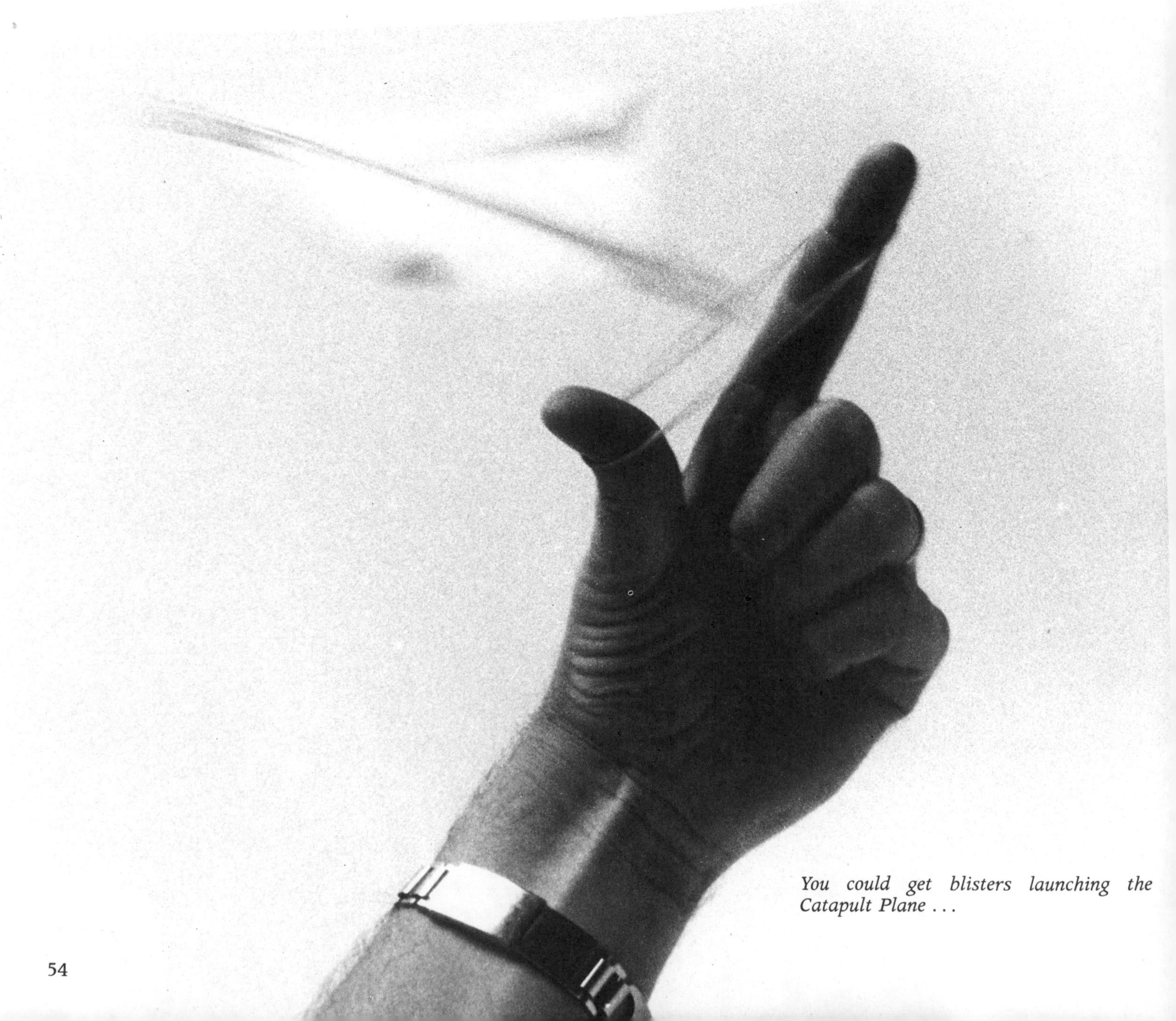

You could get blisters launching the Catapult Plane . . .

1

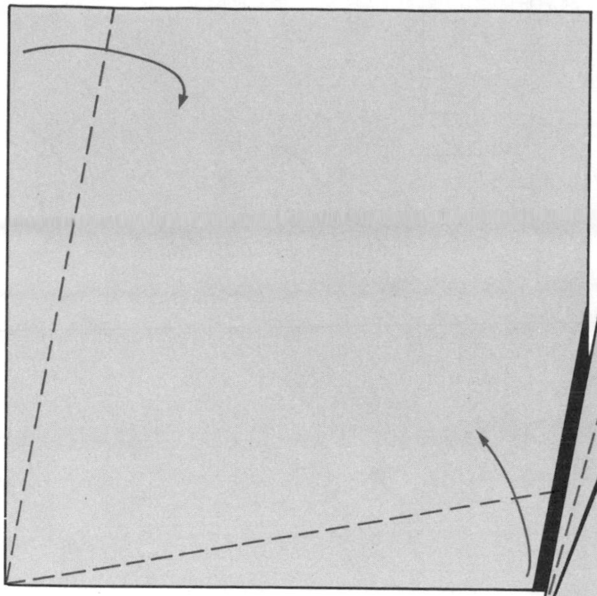

2

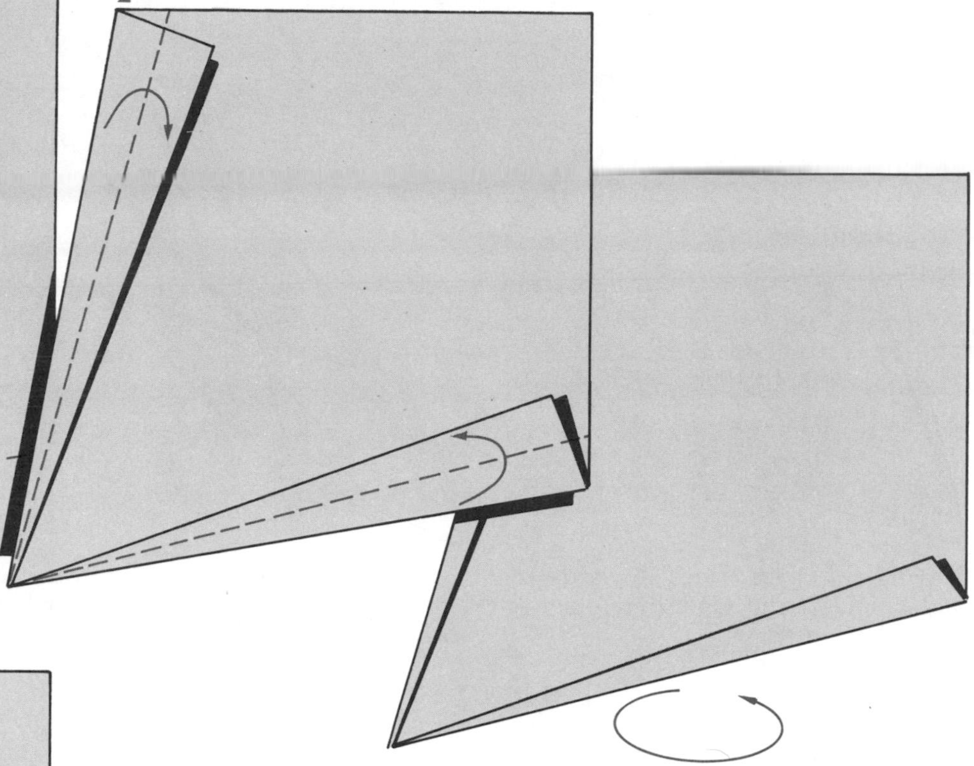

3

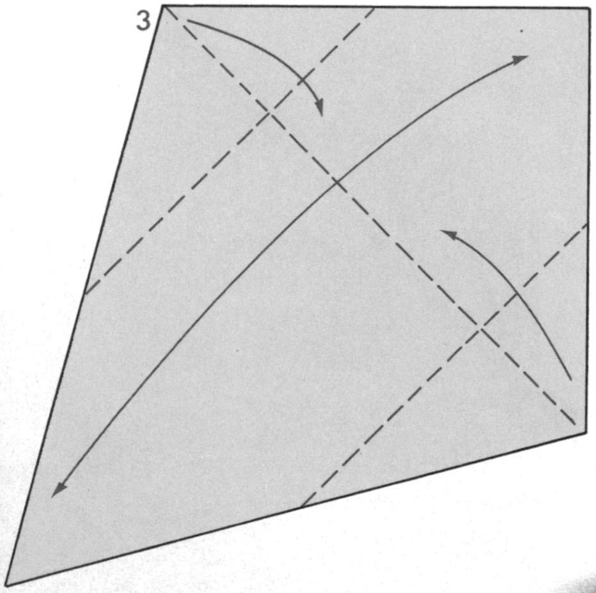

4

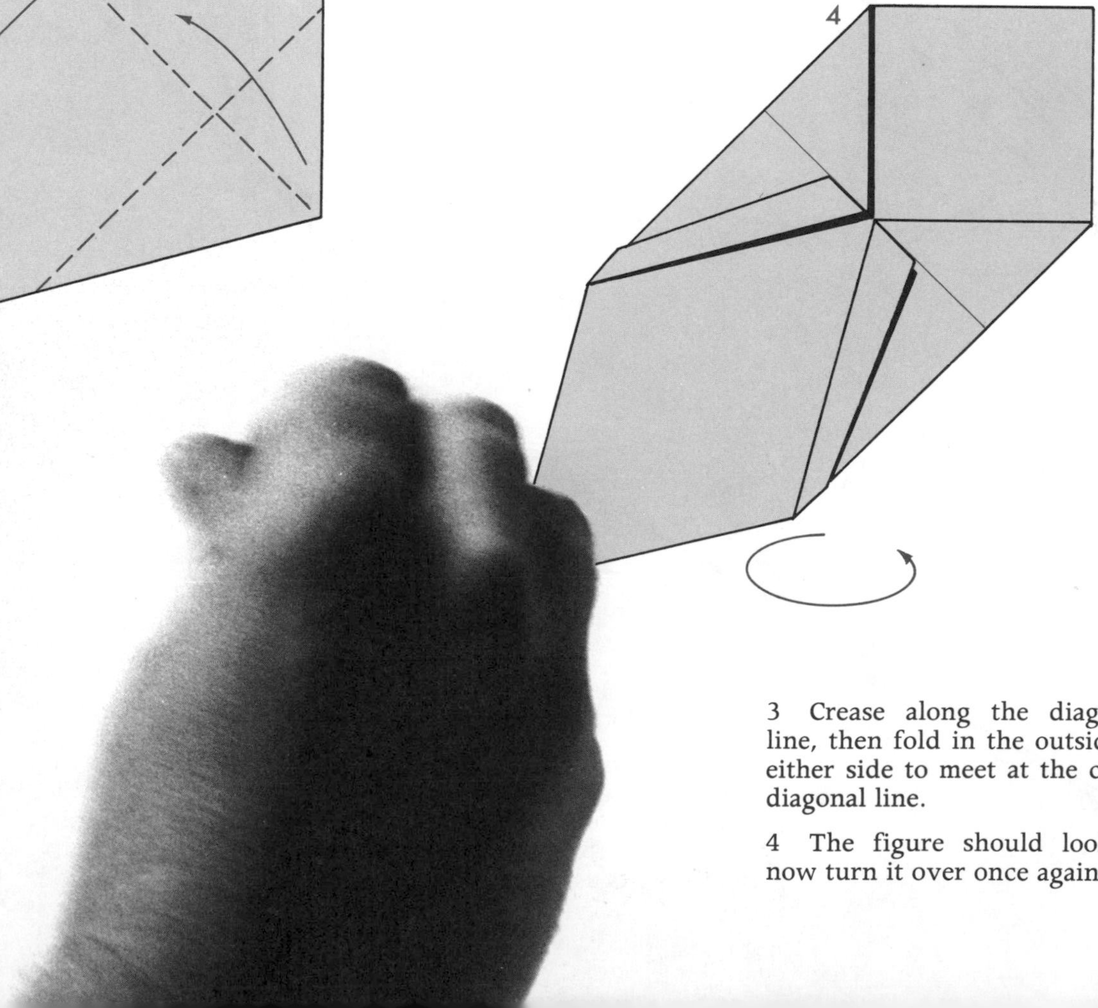

3 Crease along the diagonal dotted line, then fold in the outside points on either side to meet at the center of the diagonal line.

4 The figure should look like this; now turn it over once again.

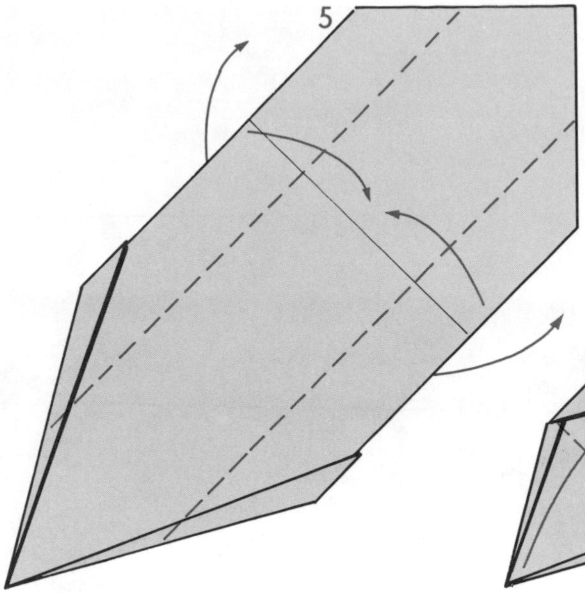

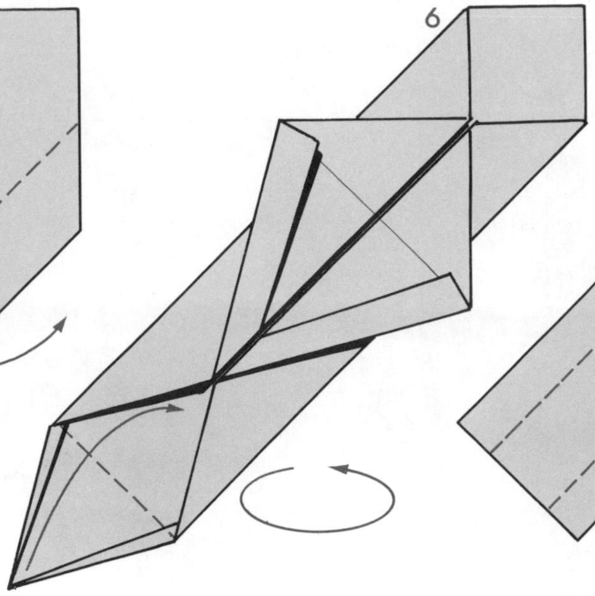

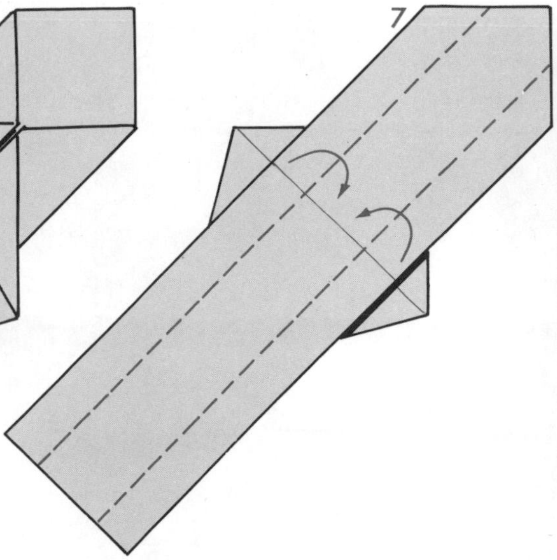

5 Fold in both sides towards the center, and at the same time open out the underlying flaps.

6 Fold up the nose tip and tuck it in as the diagram indicates, turn the whole thing over again.

7 Fold along the dotted lines, as the arrows indicate.

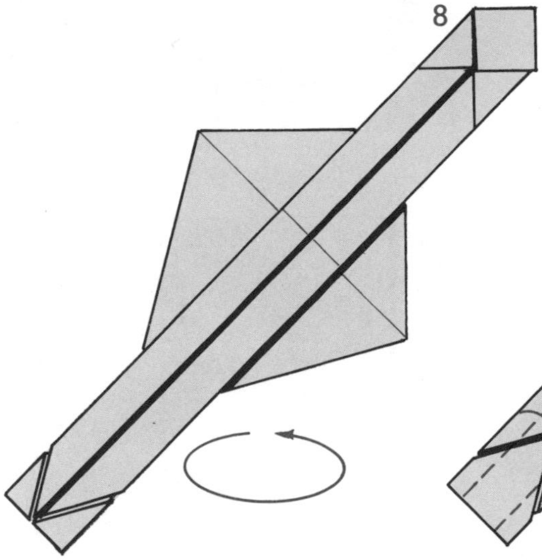

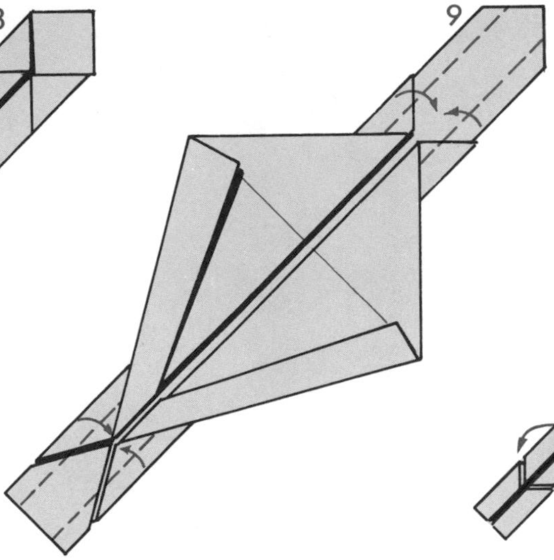

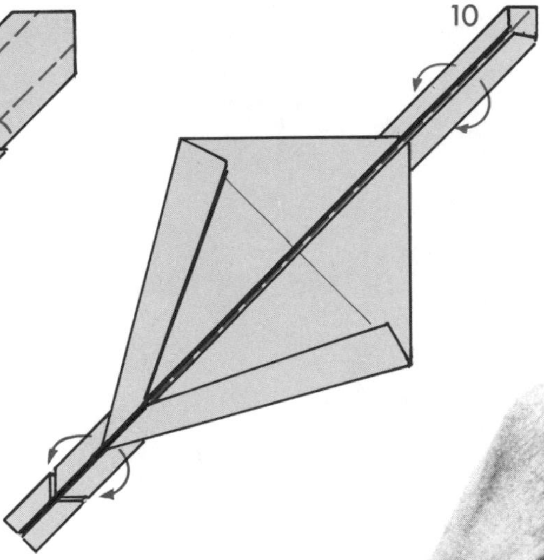

8 Turn the model over.

9 If you have produced a model which looks like this you may give yourself a pat on the back and then fold both edges underneath the wings in half.

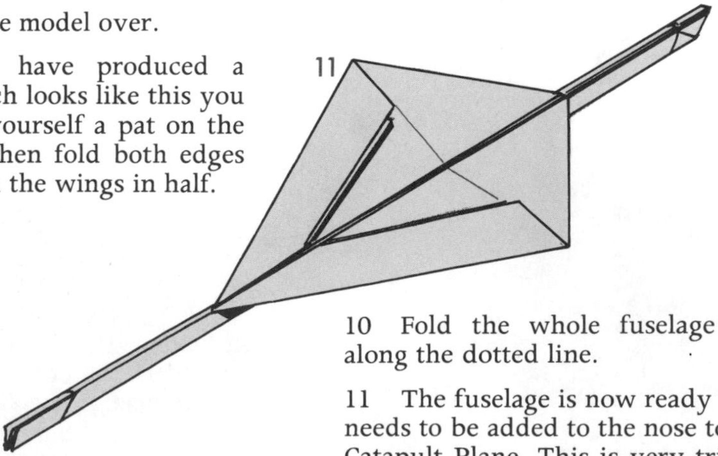

10 Fold the whole fuselage in half along the dotted line.

11 The fuselage is now ready but a tip needs to be added to the nose to fire the Catapult Plane. This is very tricky and can only be folded successfully if very thin paper is used.

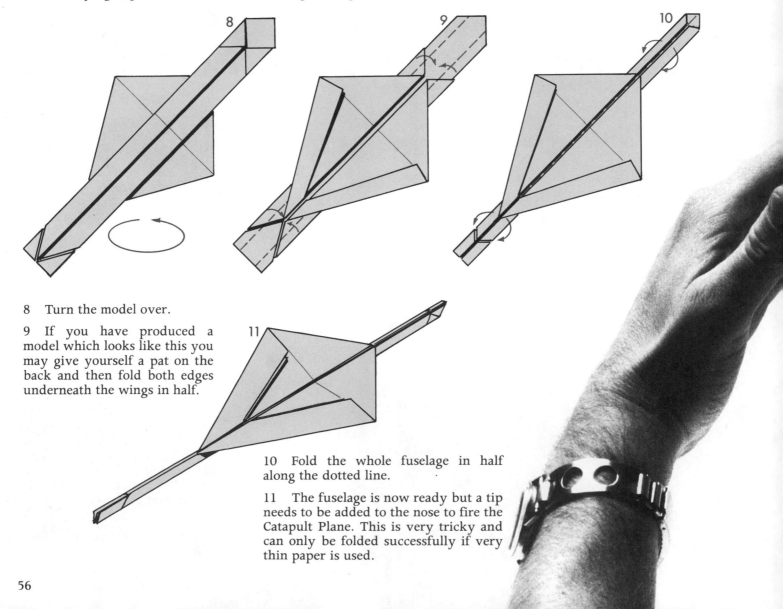

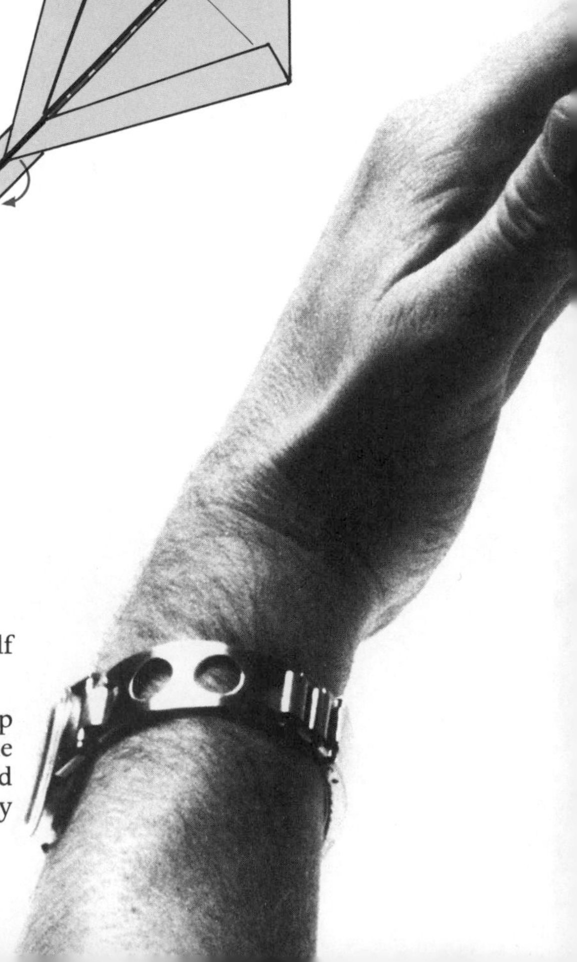

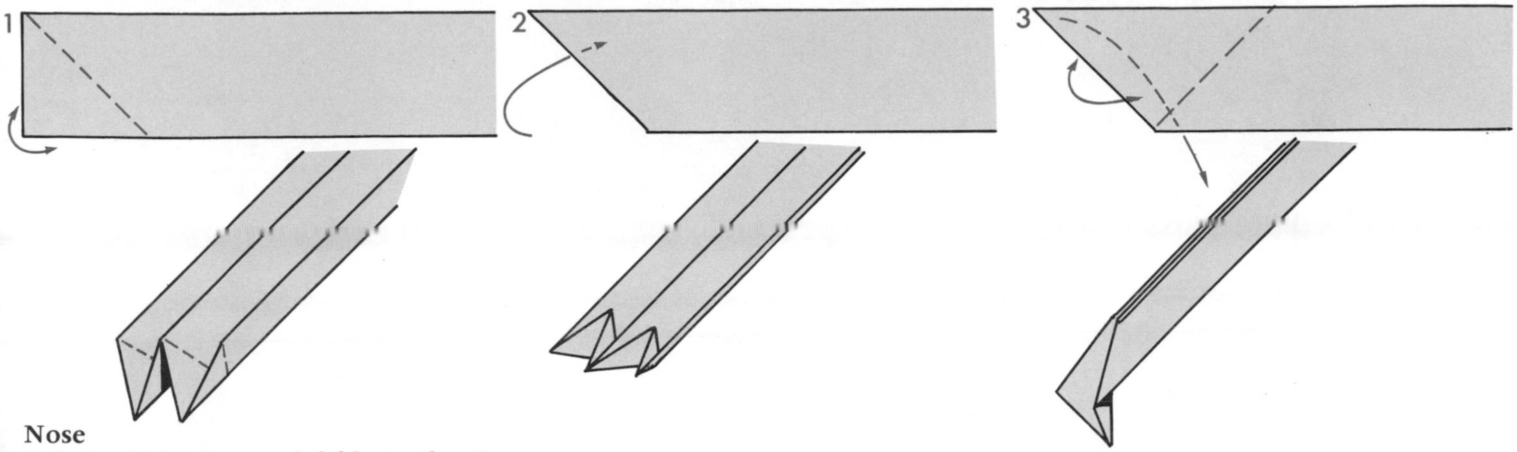

Nose

1 & 2 Make inverted folds in the tip by folding backwards and forwards along the dotted line, then tuck in both tips.

3 Fold the resulting point backwards and forwards along the dotted line and push it downwards through the middle.

4 Secure the upper side of the nose with Scotch tape.

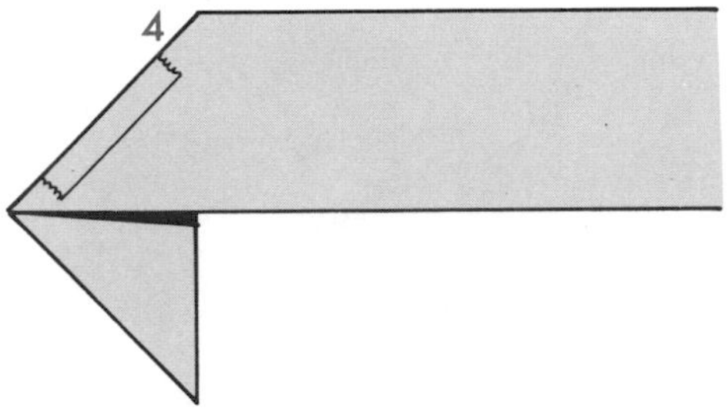

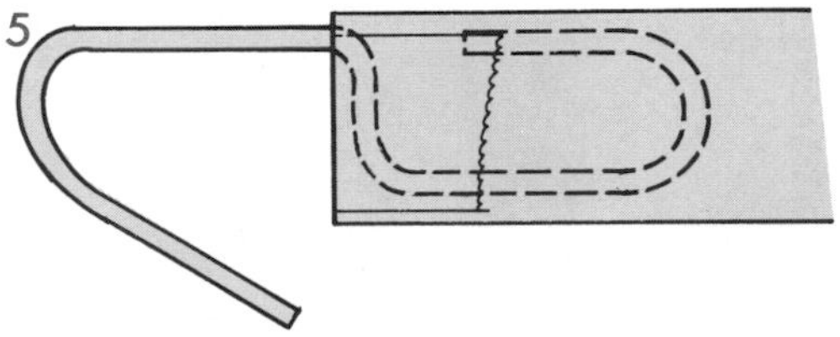

5 As was said earlier, this is a tricky job but the final result is fantastic. However, if the paper becomes too creased it is difficult to make any kind of shape with it, so the best thing to do is to go back to step 11, where the fuselage is complete. Now, simply twist open a paper clip, insert it into the nose and secure it with Scotch tape or glue. This isn't perfect, but it can save blood, sweat and tears. The Catapult Plane is fired with a rubber band. This can be done by stretching a rubber band between the thumb and the forefinger and shooting the plane by the familiar 'paper pellet' method. It is even more effective to attach the rubber band to a small stick with Scotch tape.

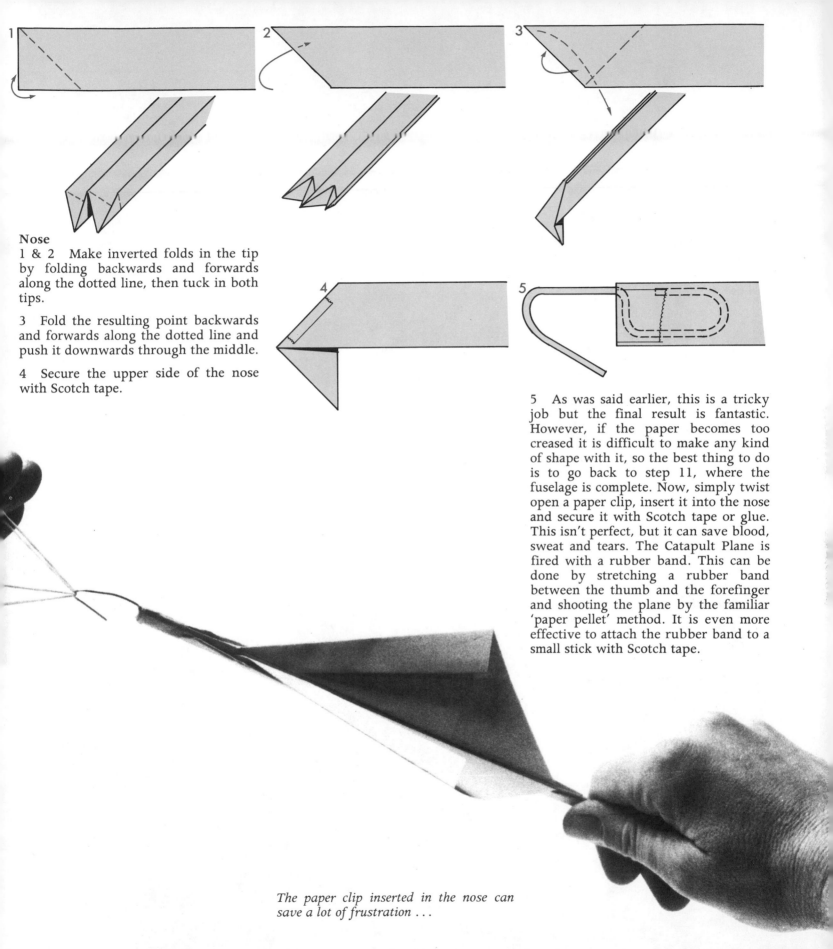

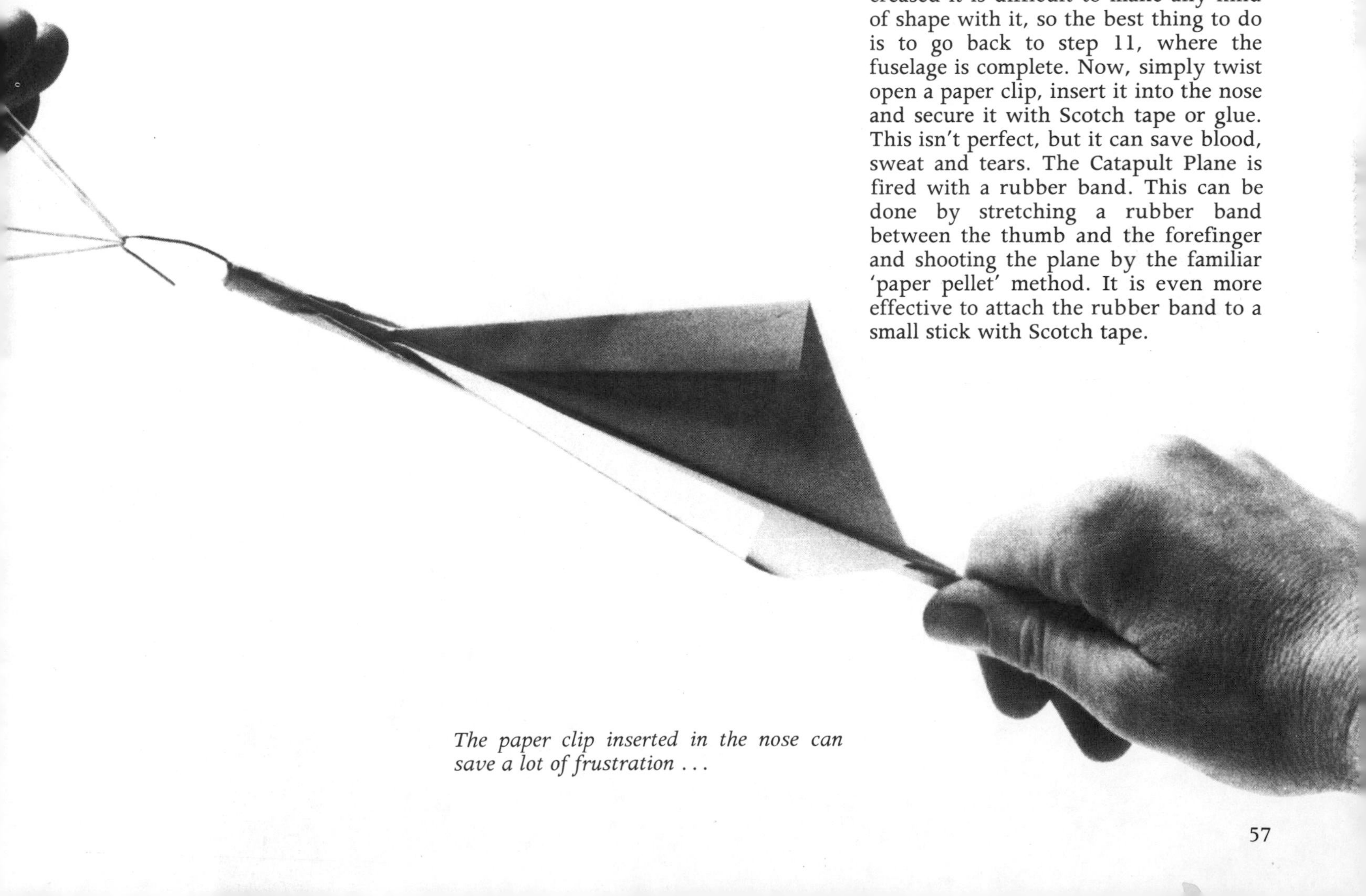

The paper clip inserted in the nose can save a lot of frustration ...

The Flying Fish is quite unique and combines the features of an airplane and a fish . . .

FLYING FISH

The striking looks of the Flying Fish make it very special. The shape combines the features of an airplane and a fish – hence the name. The flight performance is extraordinarily good and you could well imagine it leaping out of the water and feeling equally at home in the air. The method is rather unusual: all the folds are made first and then the Flying Fish is shaped in a single action. If you paint a face on it, the effect can be startling. The flight of the Flying Fish is quite unique and can be achieved by having the elevator in the right position. That in itself needs practice . . .

1 Take a sheet of paper 20 × 30cm (8 × 12in), fold over a 2cm (¾in) strip and fasten it down.

2 Make folds backwards and forwards along all the dotted lines. Do this very thoroughly because it facilitates the final folding. Make cuts in the places indicated on the left side, then fold over the resulting flaps and glue them down.

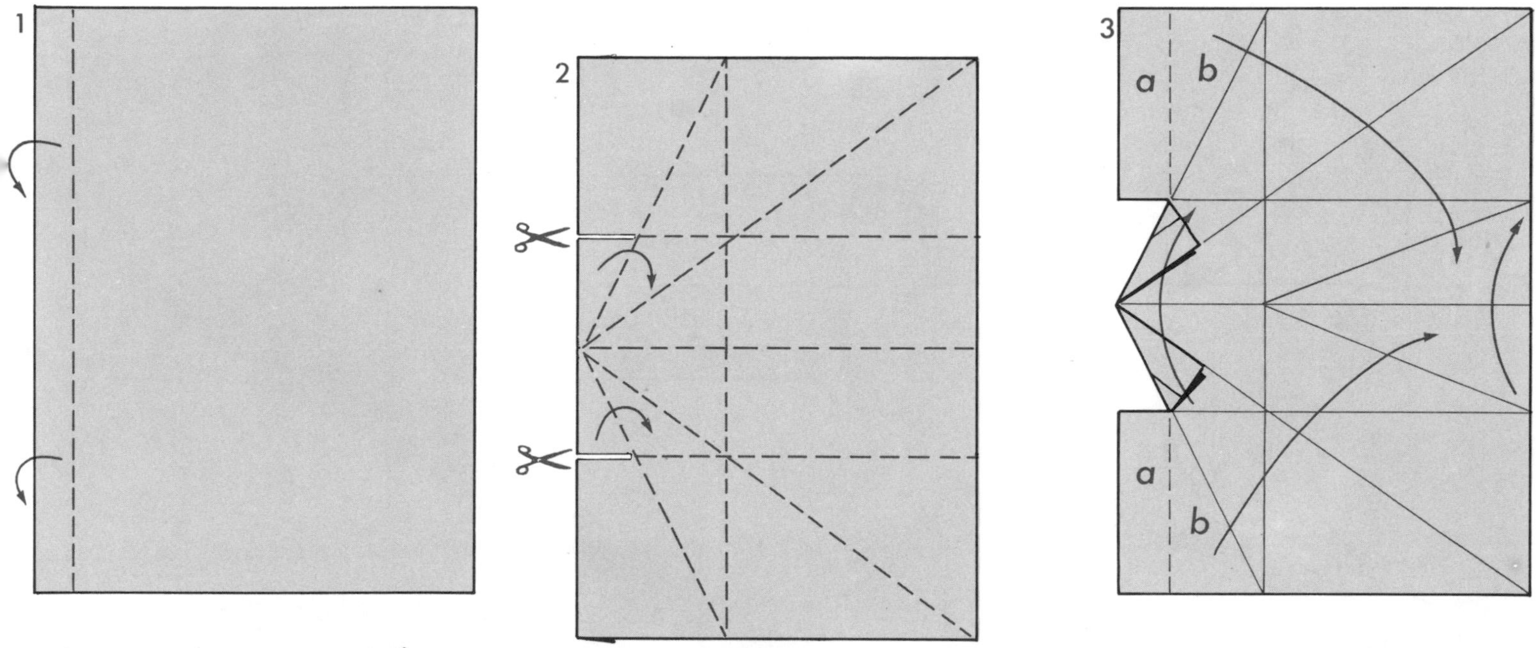

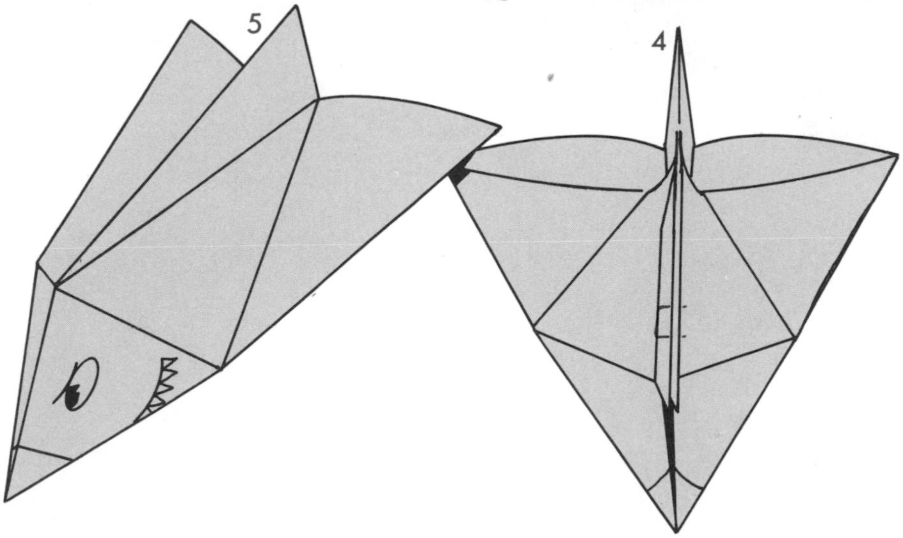

3 Now fold the whole thing together. Push the triangles 'b' together, fold the tail as illustrated and staple or glue flaps 'a' together.

4 This clearly shows what the model should look like underneath.

5 Like fighter planes in the Second World War the Flying Fish would look more striking with a face painted on it. Here is an example.

FLYING ARROW

Many people have played with pea-shooters during their childhood. The arrow is made in much the same way as a traditional pea-shooter. It is best to try and make it from the pages of glossy magazines or even comics, although the latter are less successful. The real professional tears out a rectangular sheet of paper and rolls it up while licking the torn edge. The merging of the paper fibers glues the coils together very effectively. Having made this, you add the tail section and the result is an excellent paper plane, although it is hard to believe it just from the picture.

Fuselage

1 Roll up a long piece of paper . . .

2 . . . then, keeping the paper rolled, stretch out the roll until you get a long point and secure it with Scotch tape.

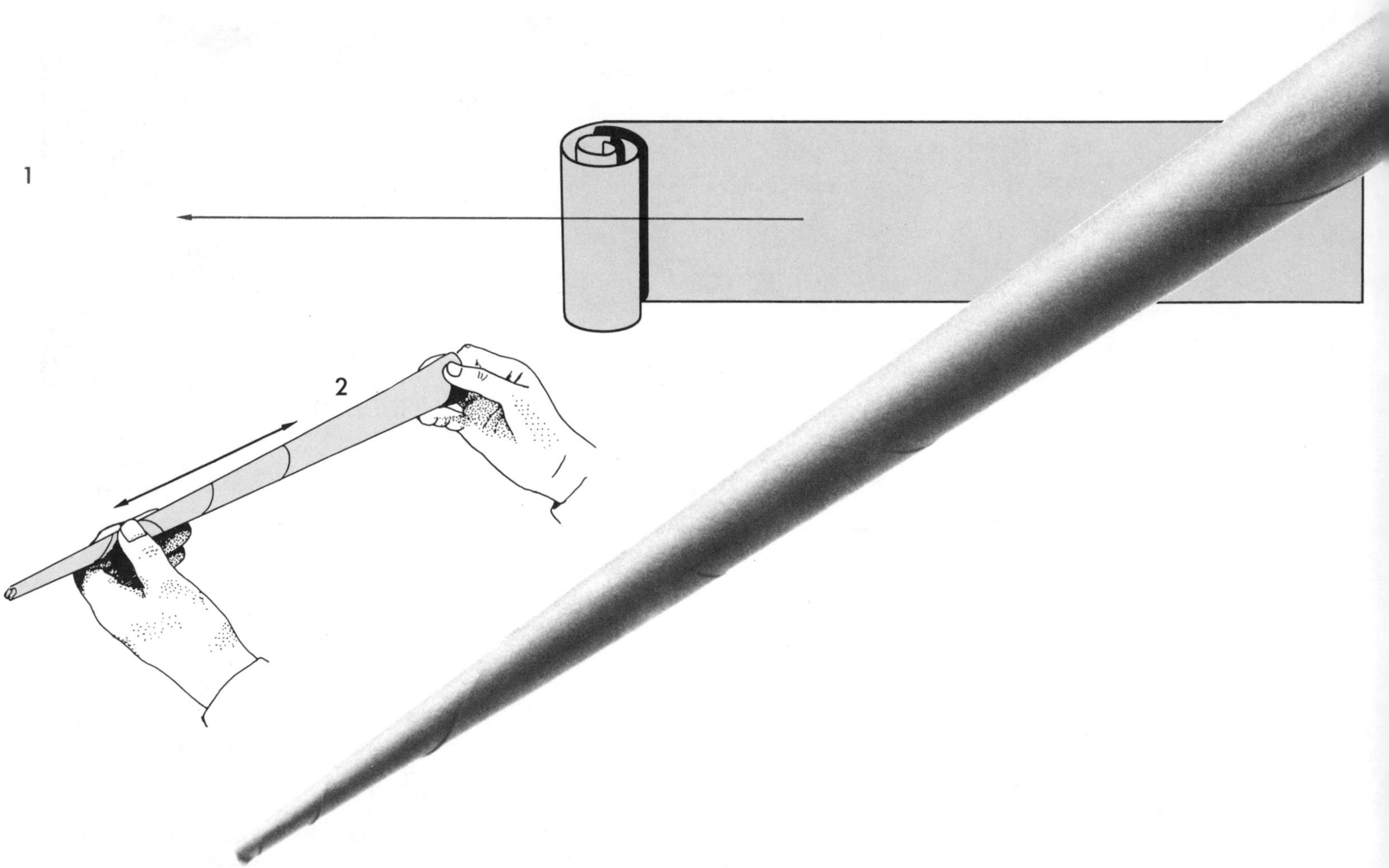

The Flying Arrow is reminiscent of the old familiar paper arrow and it flies beautifully . . .

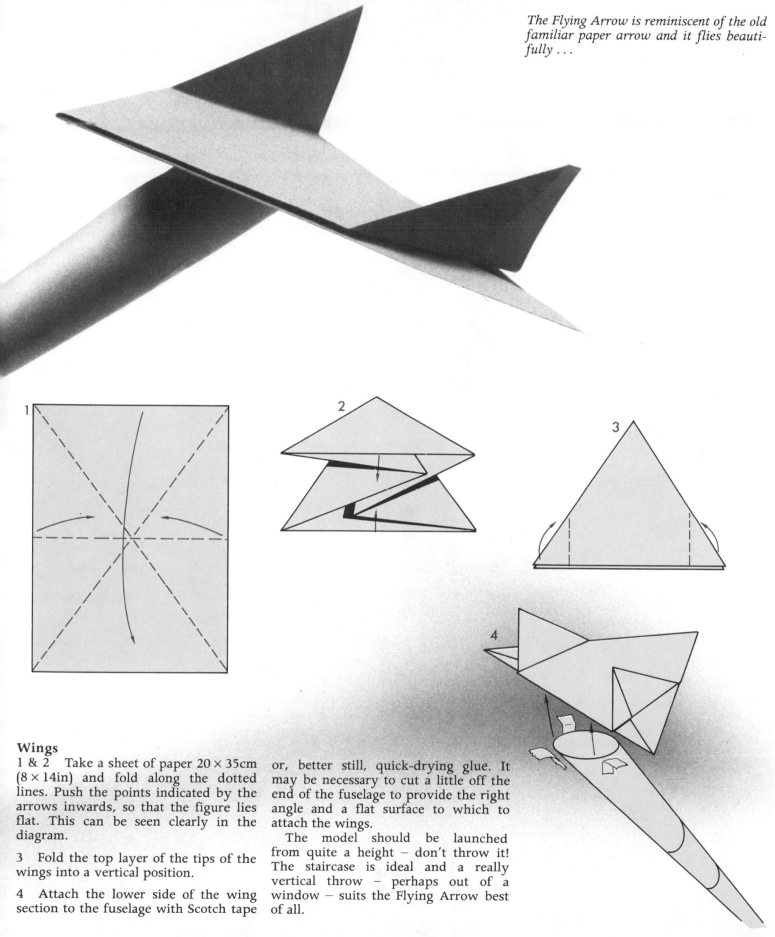

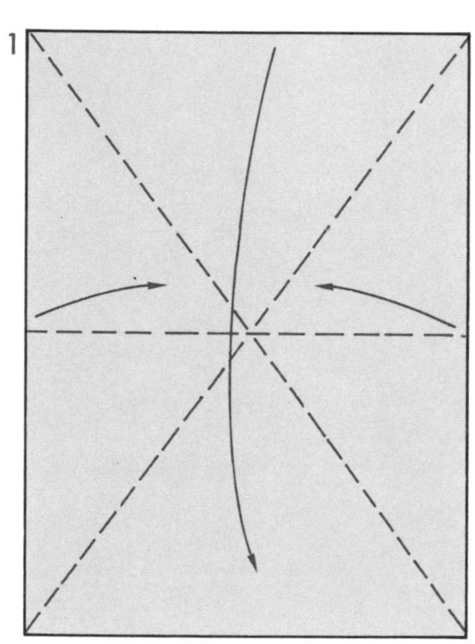

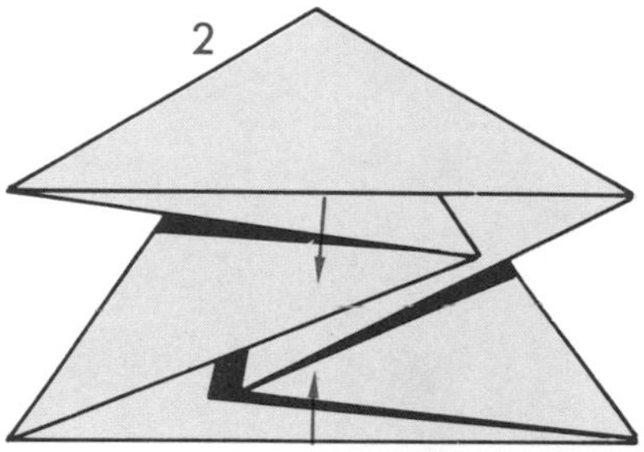

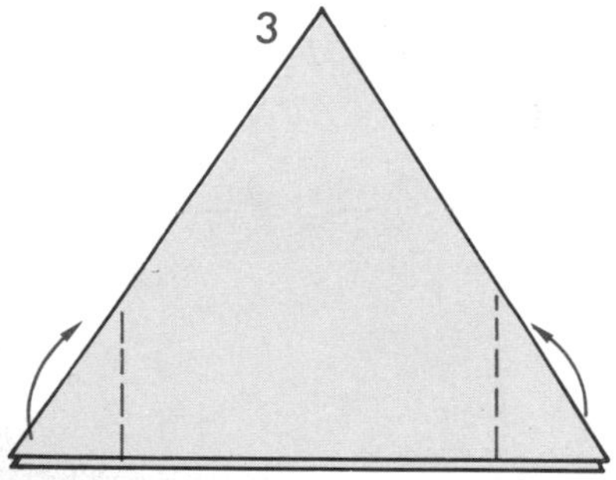

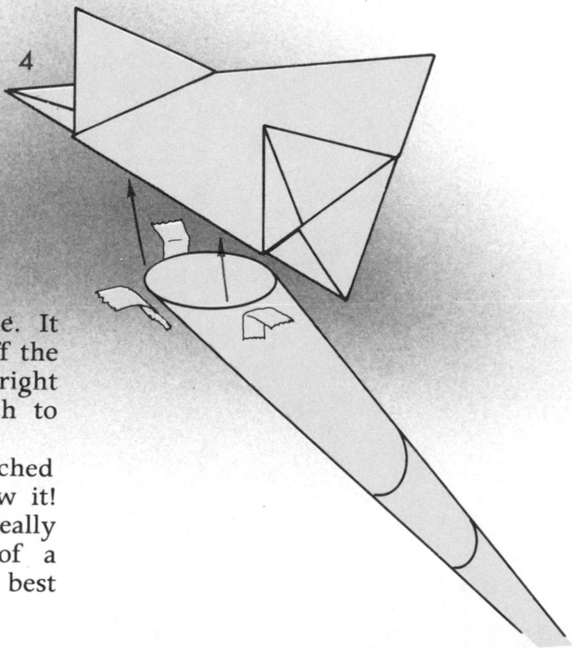

Wings

1 & 2 Take a sheet of paper 20 × 35cm (8 × 14in) and fold along the dotted lines. Push the points indicated by the arrows inwards, so that the figure lies flat. This can be seen clearly in the diagram.

3 Fold the top layer of the tips of the wings into a vertical position.

4 Attach the lower side of the wing section to the fuselage with Scotch tape or, better still, quick-drying glue. It may be necessary to cut a little off the end of the fuselage to provide the right angle and a flat surface to which to attach the wings.

The model should be launched from quite a height – don't throw it! The staircase is ideal and a really vertical throw – perhaps out of a window – suits the Flying Arrow best of all.

The Paper Helicopter is in fact a gyroplane – the forerunner of the helicopter. It is very easy to make and flies beautifully, spiralling to the ground like the wings of a sycamore seed.

PAPER HELICOPTER

This is probably the easiest model to fold and yet its performance is quite original and very effective. The Paper Helicopter is another model from the *Scientific American* International Airplane Competition and it functions in the same way as a real helicopter. Strictly speaking, it is a gyroplane, which was the forerunner of the helicopter we know today. This was an airplane with freely rotating overhead blades and used only as a freight carrier. The concept was put aside when the helicopter was invented. If launched from a high place, our Paper Helicopter can cover a distance of one hundred meters or so using no power and with the rotary blades operating just like those of a real helicopter. Who knows what may happen in the future. This reliable parachute design may even become a viable commercial proposition. Although the gyroplane has been obsolete for more than thirty years, the popularity of the paper model may well inject new life into it.

1

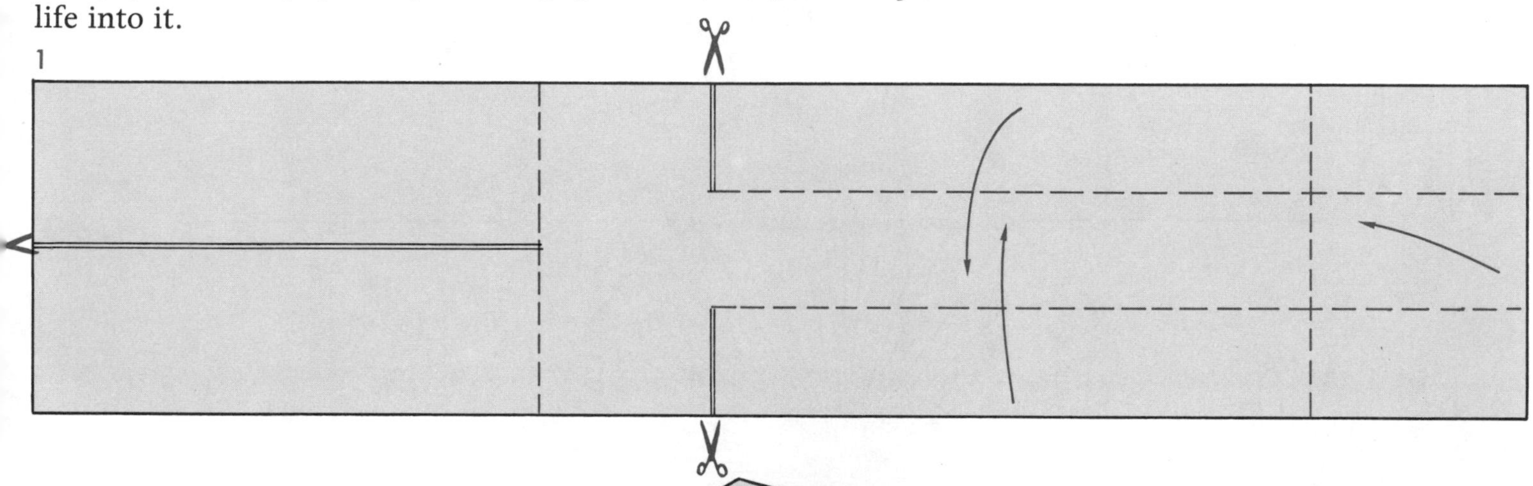

1 Take a sheet of paper 30 × 7cm (12 × 3in) and make cuts in the three places indicated. Fold the two resulting flaps on the lefthand side along the dotted line – one forwards and one backwards. On the righthand side fold the edges in along the dotted lines and then turn up the end.

2

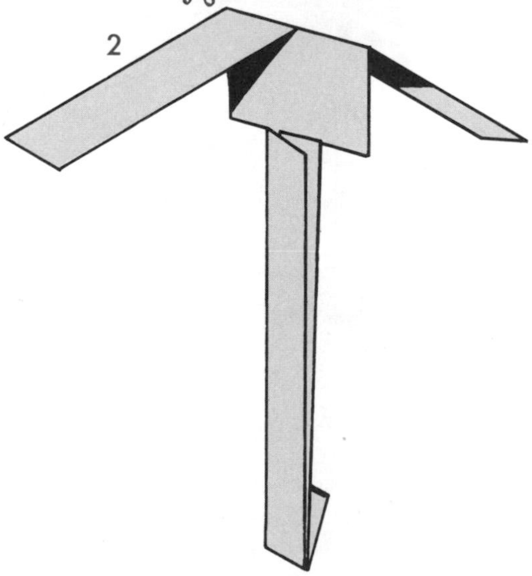

2 Once the Paper Helicopter has been glued or stapled together, it is ready for its maiden flight but remember that you should launch it from as high a point as possible.

CAROUSEL

This paper Carousel will remind you of the fairground and it whirls around, exactly as the name suggests. It is an interesting variation on the Flying Saucer, and is based on the theory of the turbine engine. It is a contemporary application of the ancient fly-wheel. The paper Carousel has the advantage of being self-propelling and thereby maintains a horizontal flight path if you throw it from a great height. It could even be used to propel the Flying Saucer. The Carousel hardly ever crashes which is a bonus, but it may disappear out of sight. It is therefore advisable to put your name and address on this aircraft because it would take you a long time to make a new one!

1 Fold a strip of paper 100 × 20cm (40 × 8in) like a concertina in 2cm ($\frac{3}{4}$in) sections.

2 When all that work is completed pierce a small hole through one side using a needle and thread. Thread the whole length and tie both ends of the thread together.

3 Open it out into a circle and staple the ends together.

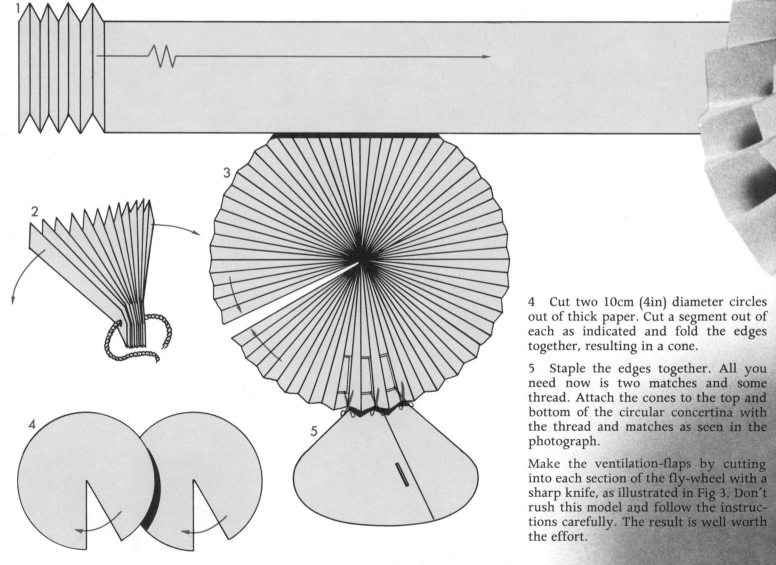

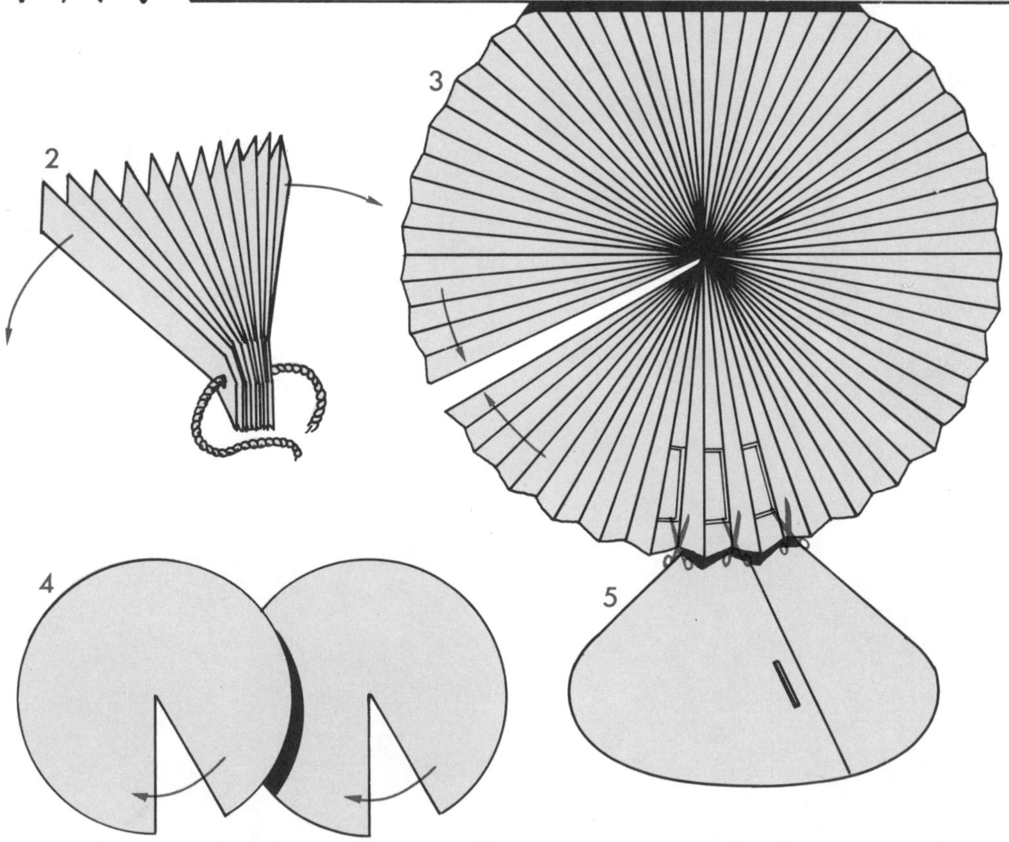

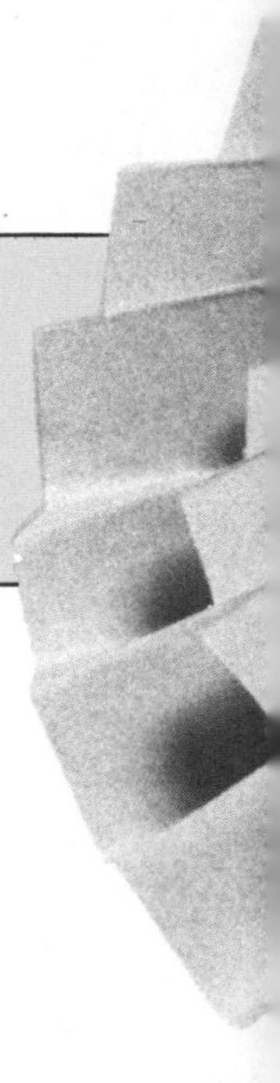

4 Cut two 10cm (4in) diameter circles out of thick paper. Cut a segment out of each as indicated and fold the edges together, resulting in a cone.

5 Staple the edges together. All you need now is two matches and some thread. Attach the cones to the top and bottom of the circular concertina with the thread and matches as seen in the photograph.

Make the ventilation-flaps by cutting into each section of the fly-wheel with a sharp knife, as illustrated in Fig 3. Don't rush this model and follow the instructions carefully. The result is well worth the effort.

The Carousel doesn't crash but rather enjoys vanishing out of sight . . .

COMPETITION CRAFT

There is no sport without competition and flying paper airplanes is now considered to be a sport. America has already got off to a flying start, and the rules for these contests originated there. The categories are as follows: the longest flight in meters (or, if you are lucky, kilometers), the longest time in the air, the aerobatics class, and the best loops or the most impressive nose dive. Obviously there could be further classes. Competition has always been an important element in flying; more than just a few half-crazy pilots made valiant efforts to cross the Atlantic in rickety little planes before Charles Lindbergh succeeded in the *Spirit of St Louis*. The round-the-world yachtsman, Sir Francis Chichester, attempted to fly around the world in a Tiger Moth. Amelia Earhart was the first woman to complete a non-stop flight from America to Japan. These are examples of the feats which the model flyers try to emulate on a smaller scale. You could, for instance, find a large pond in a nearby park and try to reach the other side with your best competition craft, or you could organize speed contests.

All competition craft should be very carefully folded; there are ten designs here. You can experiment with different types of paper and decide for yourself which is the best and, if necessary, make small modifications to improve performance. Care should always be taken to see that there are enough models entered in each class. Learn the abilities of each model and the best method of launching them. The aerobatics performed by competition craft are similar to those performed by other models. Numerous stunts can be attempted: a loop, in which the airplane turns a full circle, is obtained by turning the flap upwards. A roll, in which the plane revolves around its axis, is

The Sprinter, a very fast fighter plane.

achieved by folding one flap up and the other one down. A corkscrew is a special kind of roll. If the paper airplane also has tail flaps, many more aerobatic maneuvers are possible.

Stunts may be carried out in many different ways and sequences. Naturally there is always the risk of crashing when performing aerobatics, but you can always make a new airplane. For formation flying you should only use sturdily built models.

The Cirrus 75 is a long-range specialist.

CIRRUS 75

The name Cirrus 75 was not chosen at random. This model was named after the best and most up-to-date glider because it has the same qualities as its big brother. The Cirrus 75 can make long-range flights, being especially successful if it starts from a high point such as a balcony or upstairs window. Therefore this plane is particularly suitable for 'the longest flight and the longest lasting flight' competition classes. It is best to use lightweight paper.

1 & 2 Take a sheet of paper 20 × 30cm (8 × 12in), fold it along the illustrated diagonal lines and then make a horizontal fold through the intersection as illustrated. Tuck in each side while folding up the bottom edge; see Fig 2.

3 Fold down the two corners along the dotted lines.

4 Cut out the sections indicated in the top half; to make the sides symmetrical fold the model in half before cutting them out. Once this is completed, fold the airplane in half along the center line and then fold back the wings along the dotted lines either side of the center. Fold over the tail tips along the dotted lines. The procedure is explained more clearly in the diagrams.

5 Fasten or staple the sides of the tail together below the fold. The flaps on the wings can be folded upwards or downwards so that aerobatics and boomerang stunts are possible.

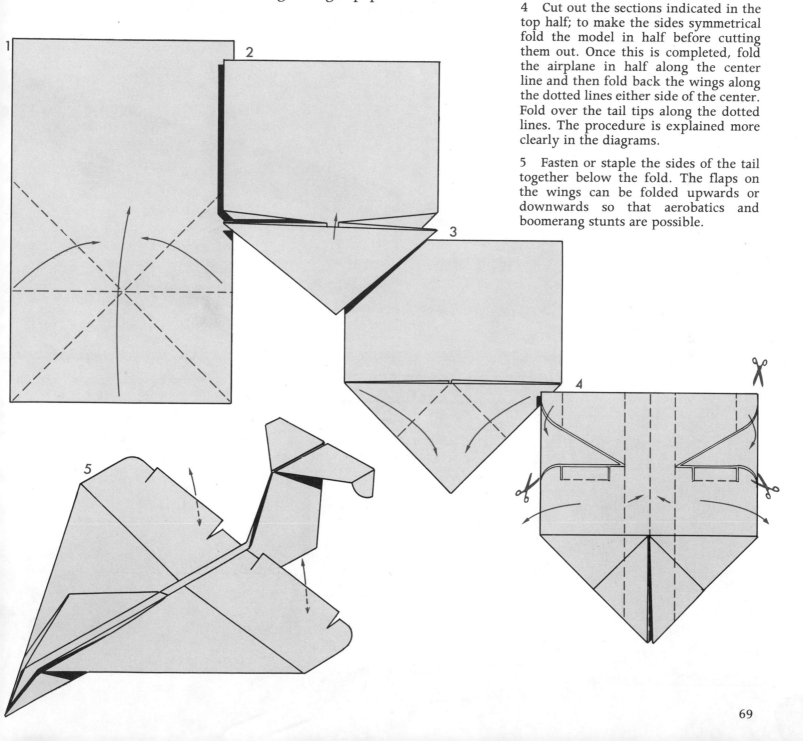

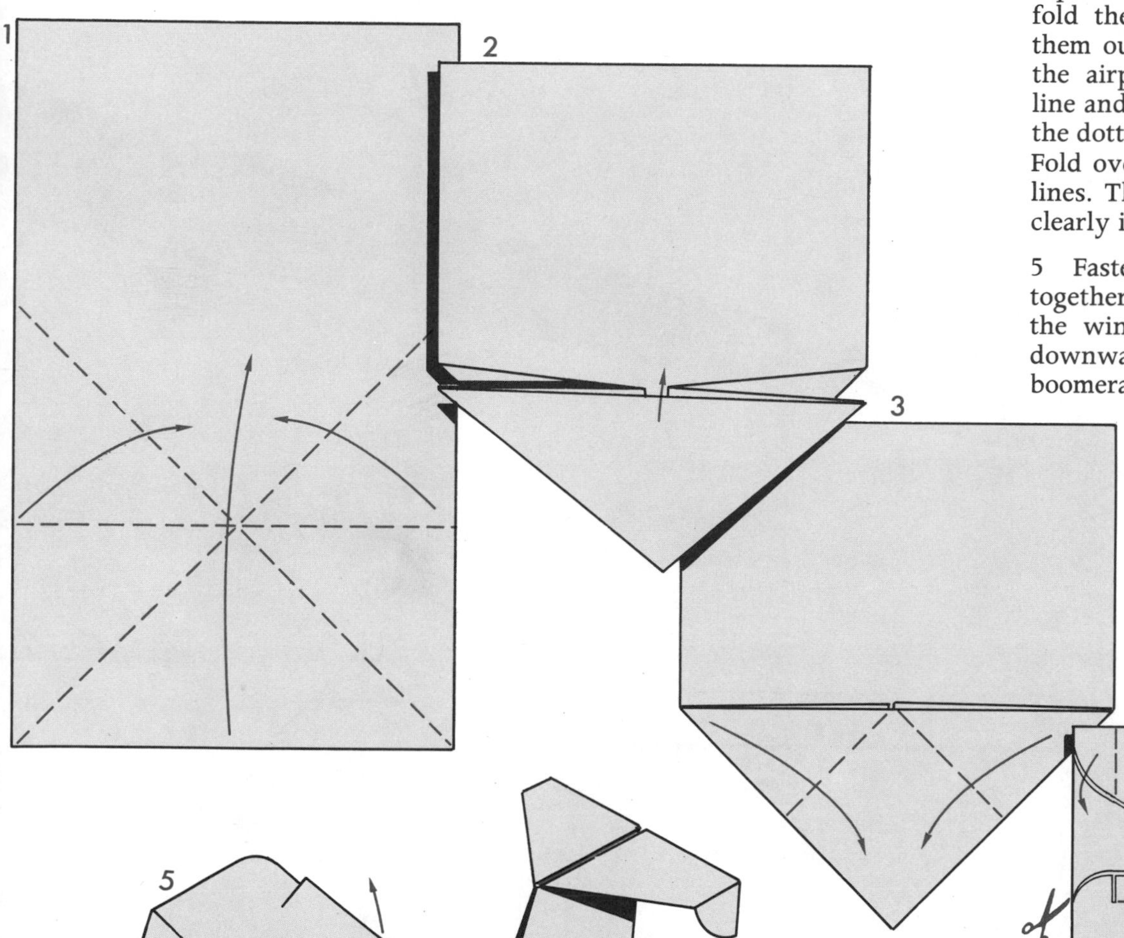

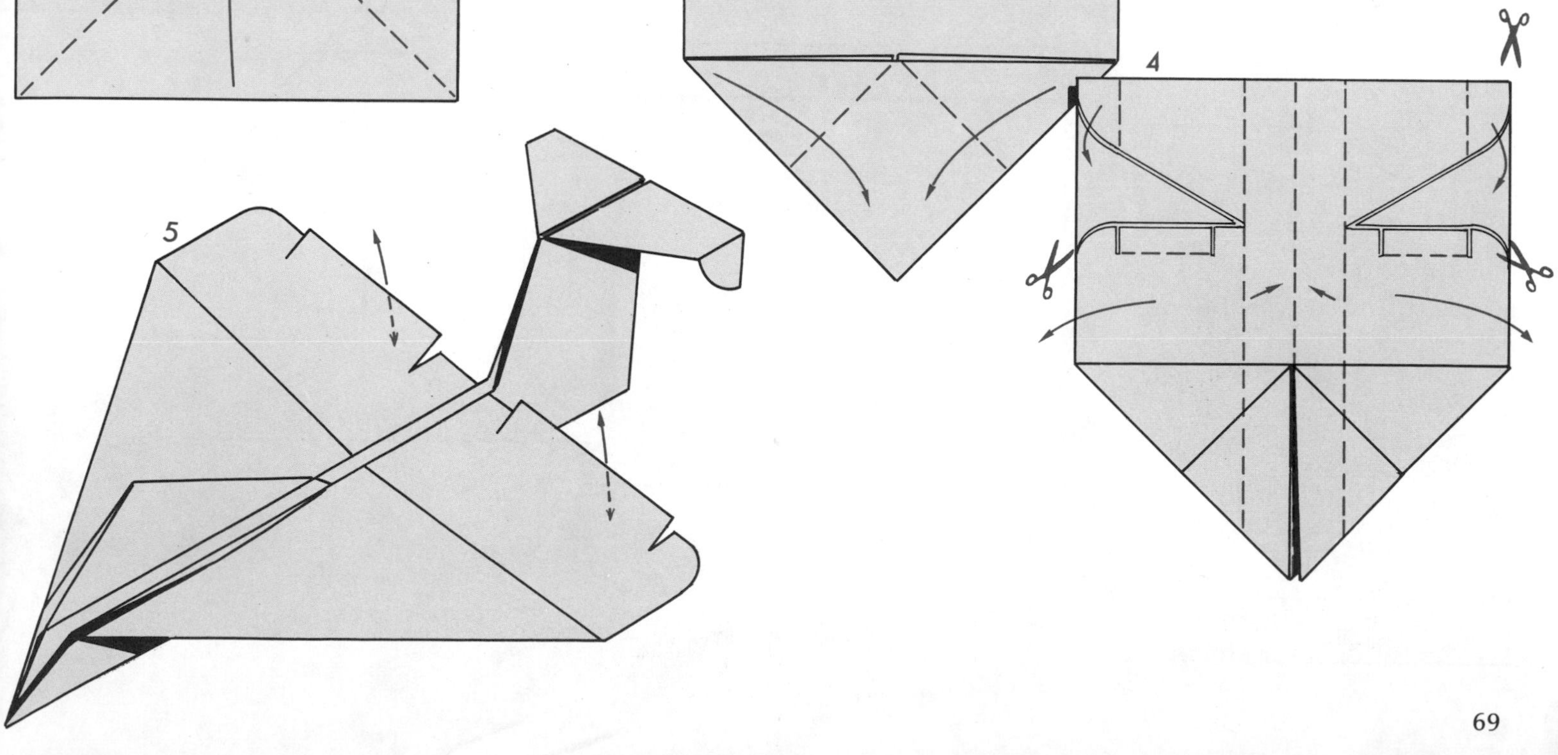

HUNTER

Although when you look at this airplane you will not immediately think of the familiar British Hunter, its flight performance will certainly remind you of the fantastic jet airplane. The delta-wings are the dominant feature of this plane. The large tail section guarantees it sufficient stability and the flaps on the wings, based on what is known in aeronautics as the "slotted flap" principle, improve its gliding efficiency. The Hunter is extremely fast and will produce some startling performances after a short training period.

1 Take a piece of paper 25 × 30cm (10 × 12in) and fold the top edge over three times to make a thick edge.

2 Make a center fold and then fold the top corners back along the dotted lines.

3 Fold the whole model in half.

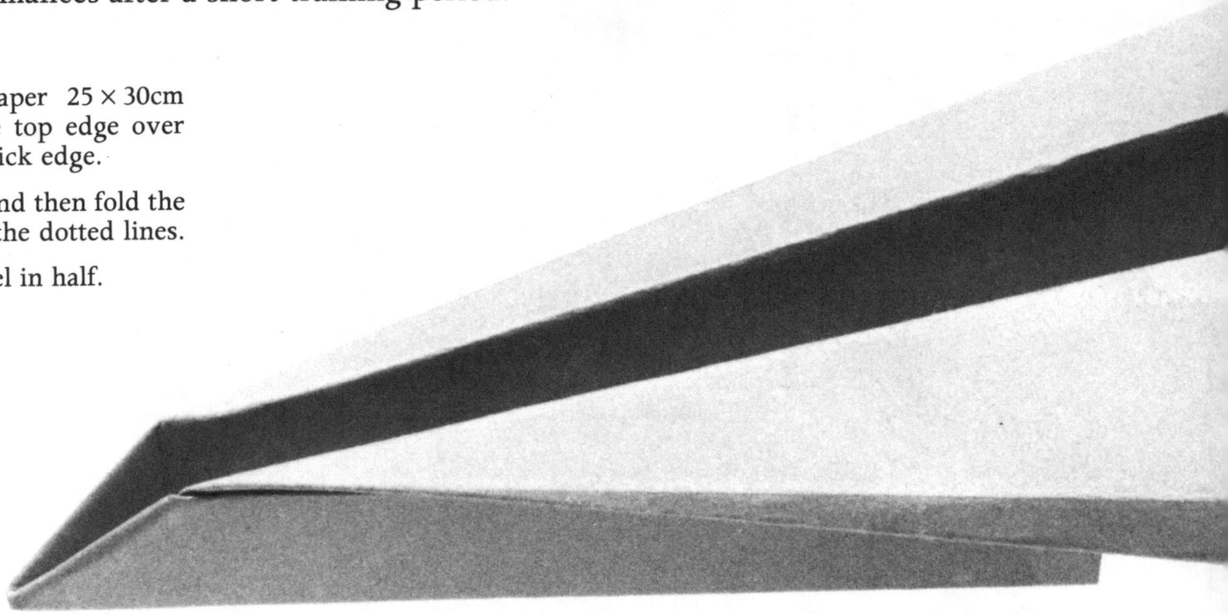

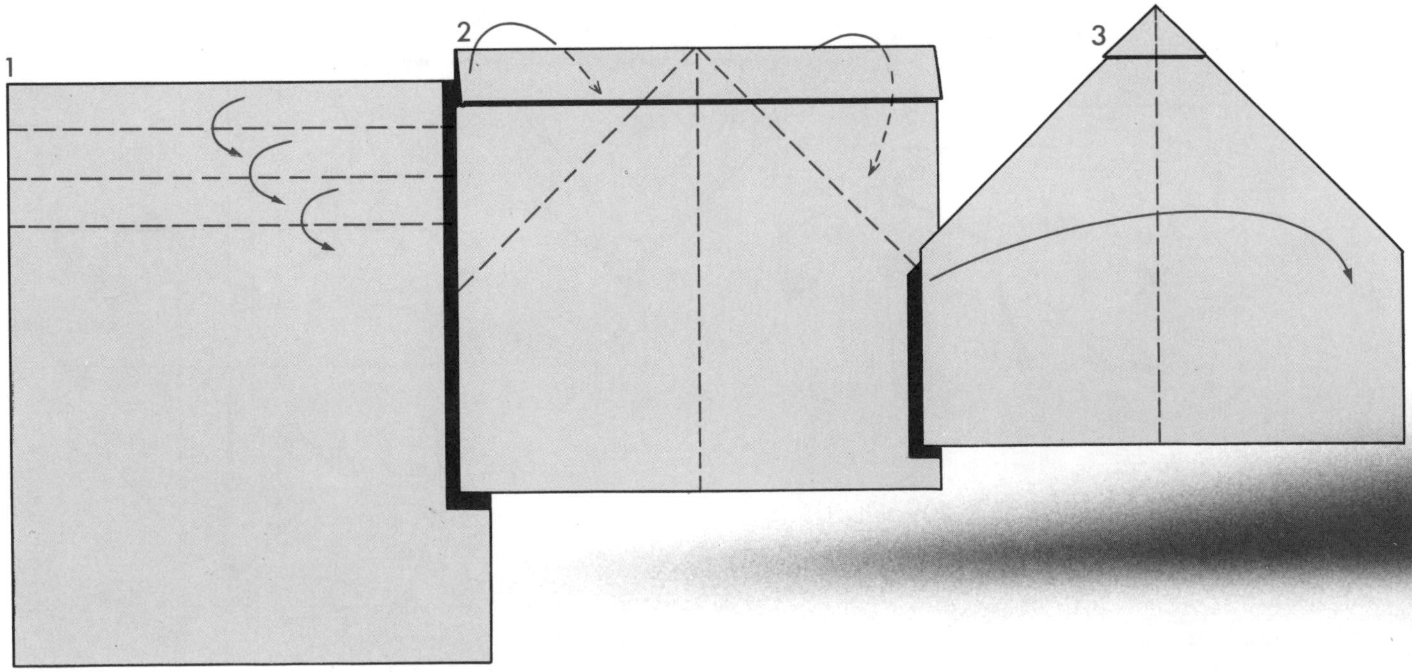

The Hunter is a very fast airplane which will produce some startling performances after a short practice.

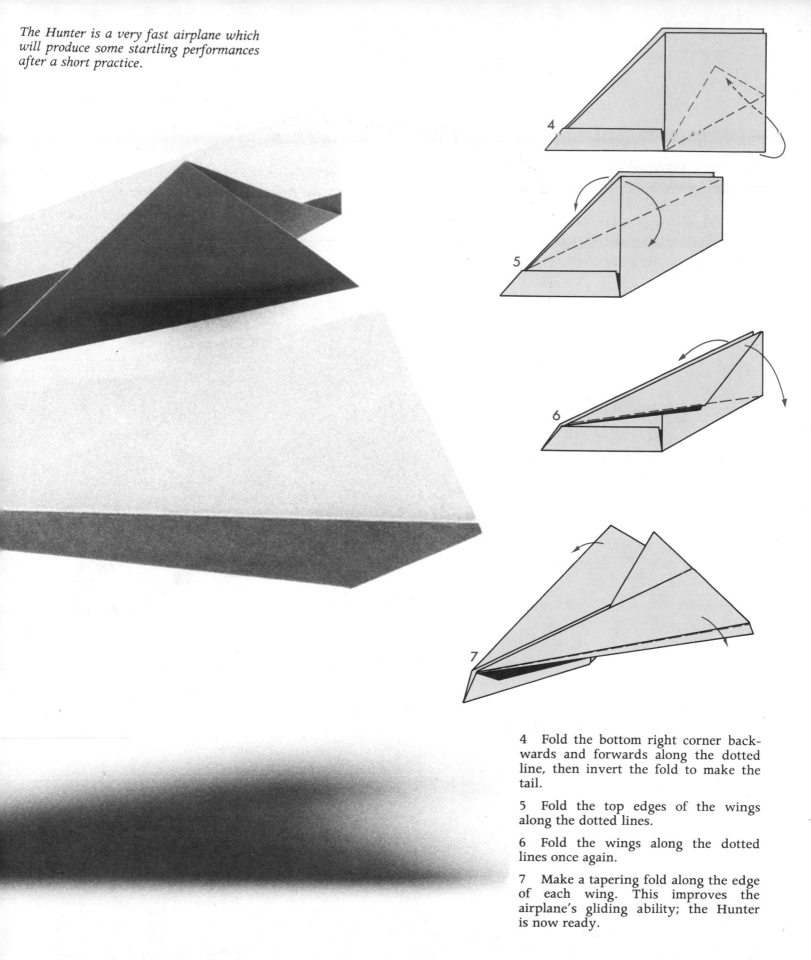

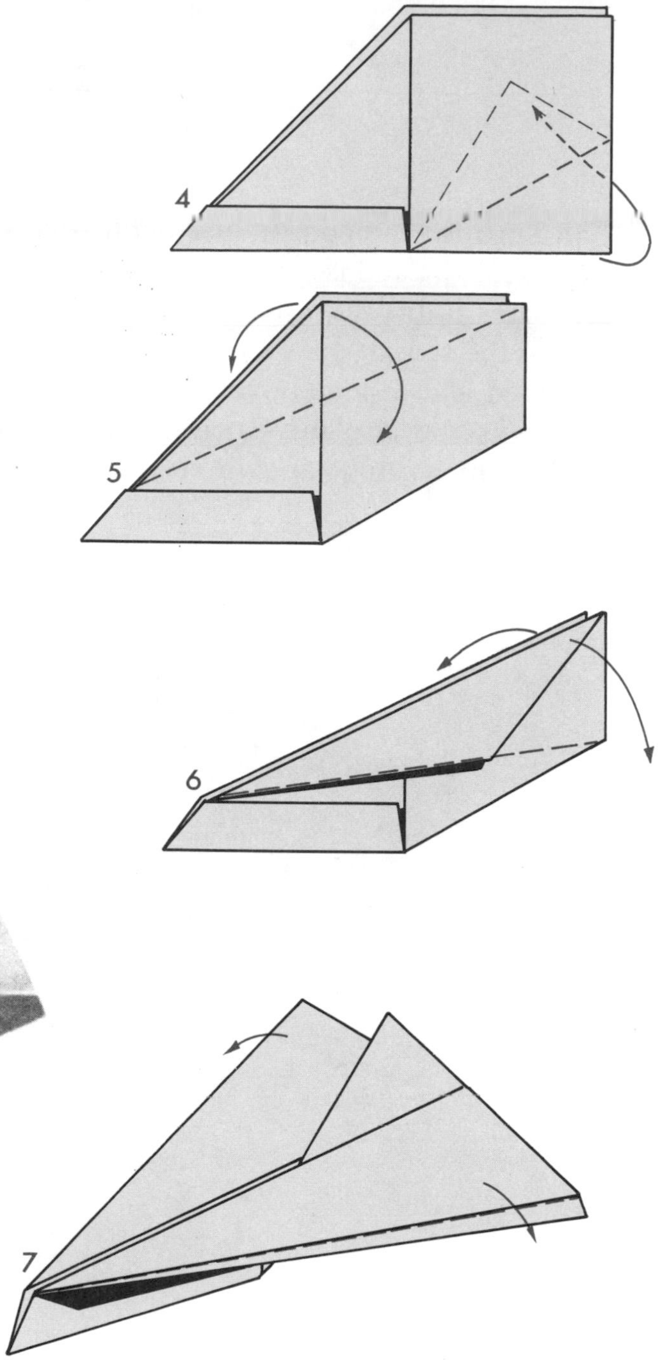

4 Fold the bottom right corner backwards and forwards along the dotted line, then invert the fold to make the tail.

5 Fold the top edges of the wings along the dotted lines.

6 Fold the wings along the dotted lines once again.

7 Make a tapering fold along the edge of each wing. This improves the airplane's gliding ability; the Hunter is now ready.

SPRINTER

The Sprinter is good at just about everything. It is shaped like a supersonic jet and is capable of winning top marks in competitions. Its aerobatic ability does not compare badly with other models either, due to the special design of the middle section whereby the nose flap is folded and fastened over the wings. This widens the fuselage and improves the airplane's performance. The Sprinter is an all-round model which can go anywhere and be used at any time.

1 Take a sheet of paper 30 × 35cm (12 × 14in) and make a lengthways center fold. Fold both sides in half so that they meet on the center fold.

2 Fold the corners backwards and forwards along the dotted lines.

3 Fold the corners over to meet the folds you have just made.

4 Once again fold the top edges over along the dotted lines.

5 Make creases along the long diagonal dotted lines by folding backwards and forwards. Fold in the top corners to meet these dotted lines.

6 Fold the whole model in half away from you.

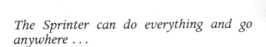

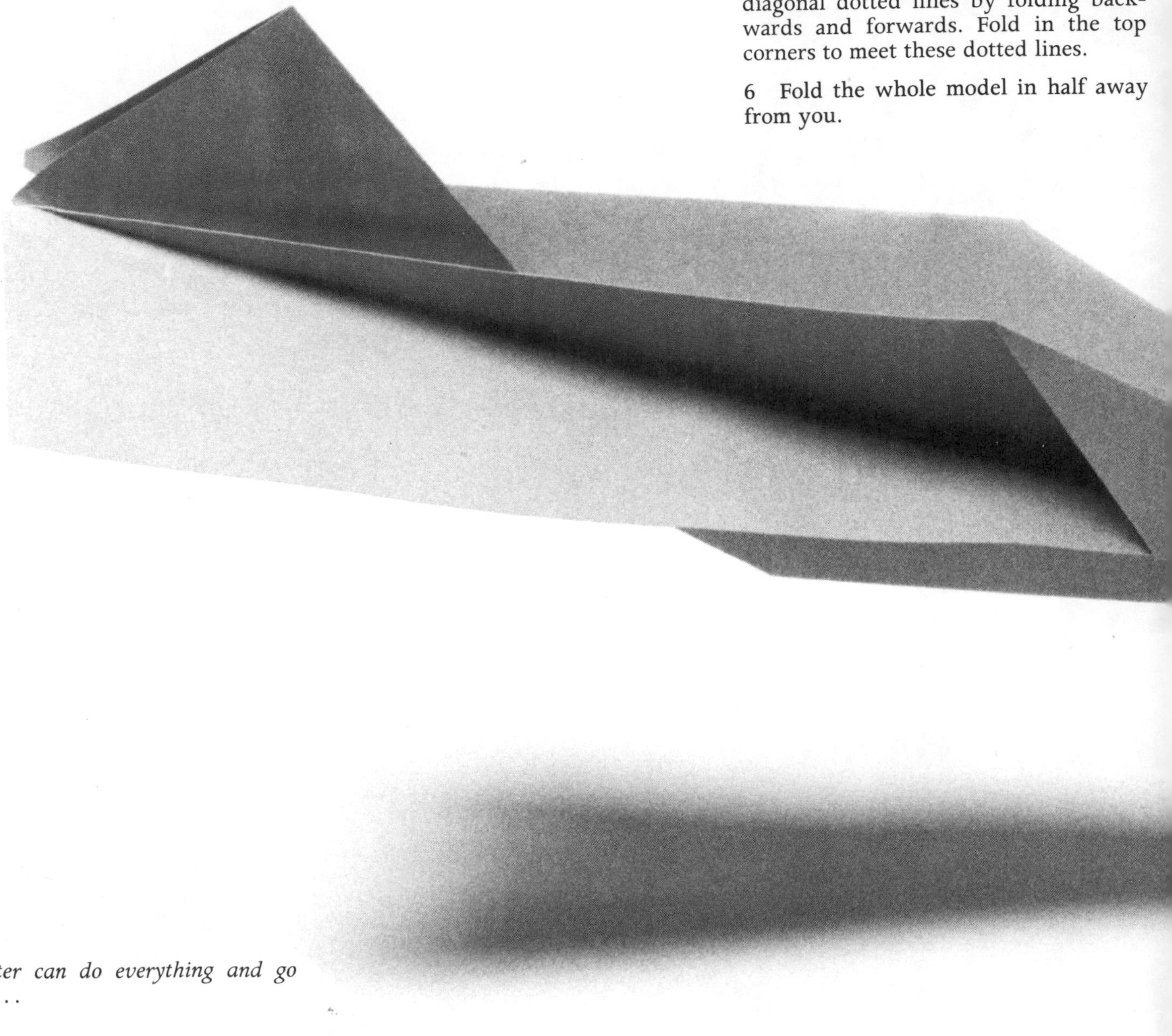

The Sprinter can do everything and go anywhere . . .

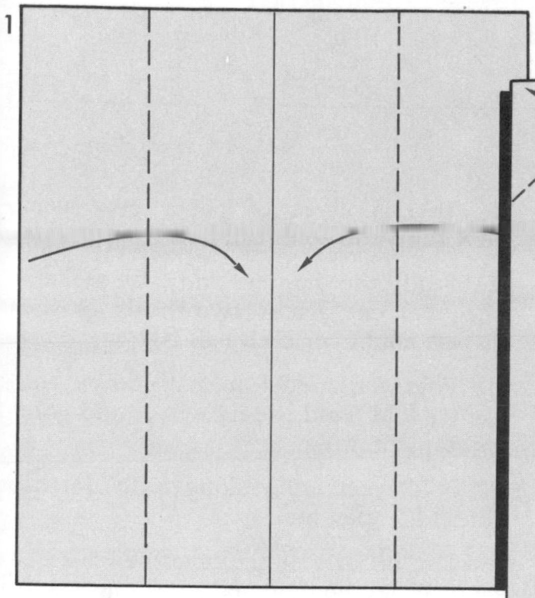

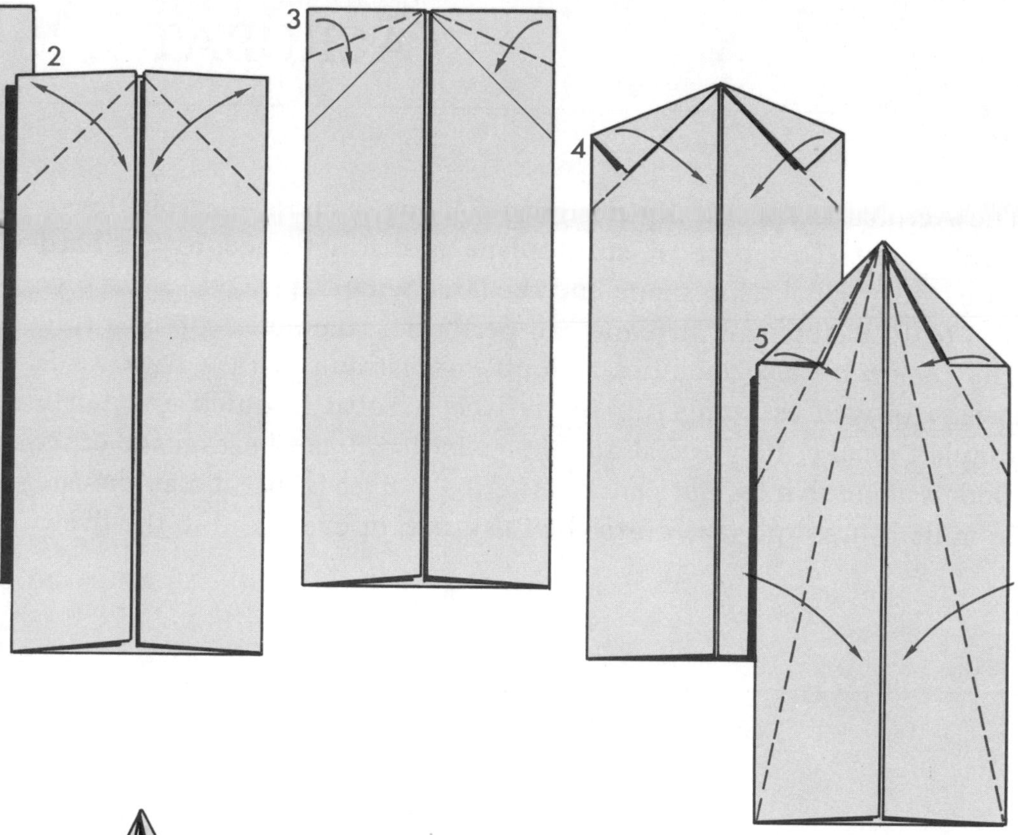

7 Fold up the wings along the existing crease. Make an inverted fold in the tail following the dotted lines. Now open out the wings.

8 Finally fold the nose section over the wings to either side and glue or staple to the underside of the fuselage. You will find that, by easing the outer folds open, the folds fit inside each other neatly. Flaps may be made at the back of the wings but the form these take really depends on the class you want your Sprinter to fly in.

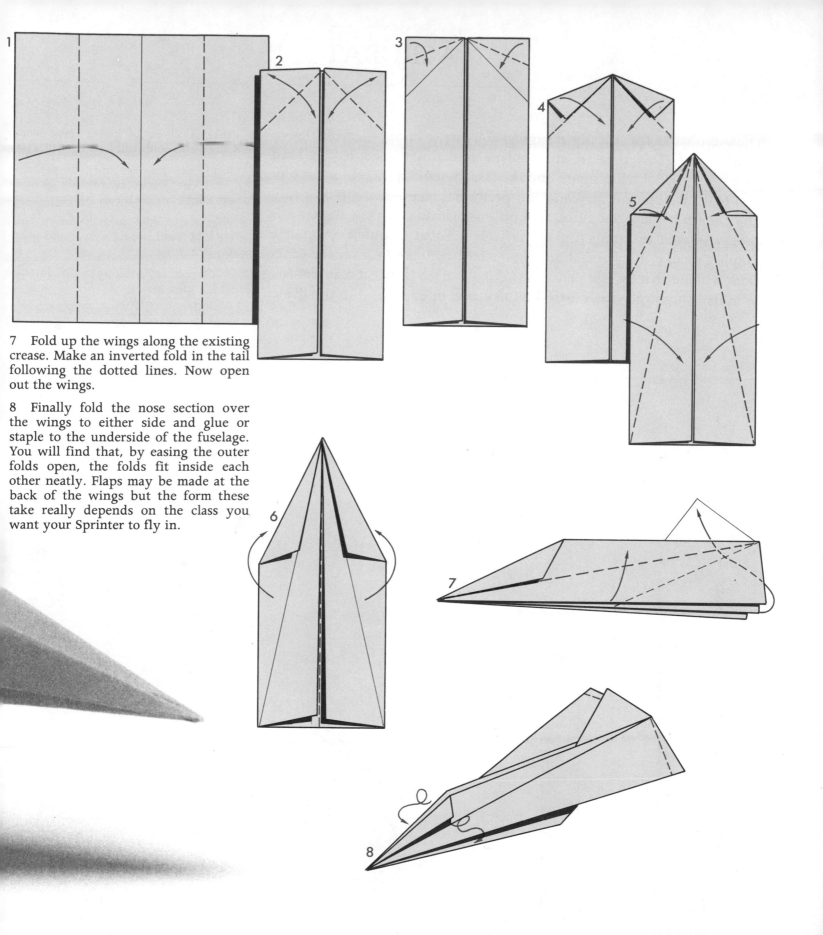

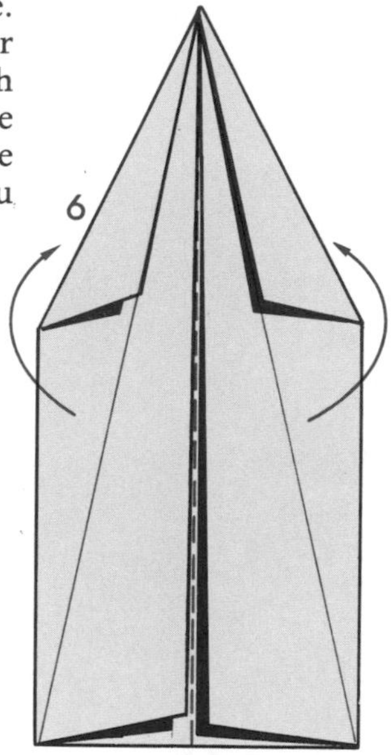

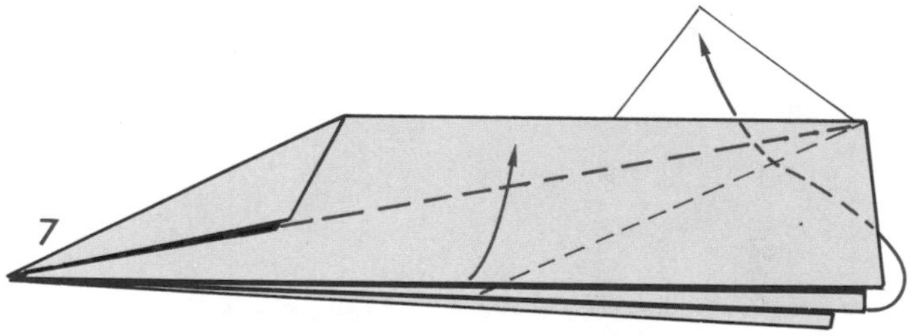

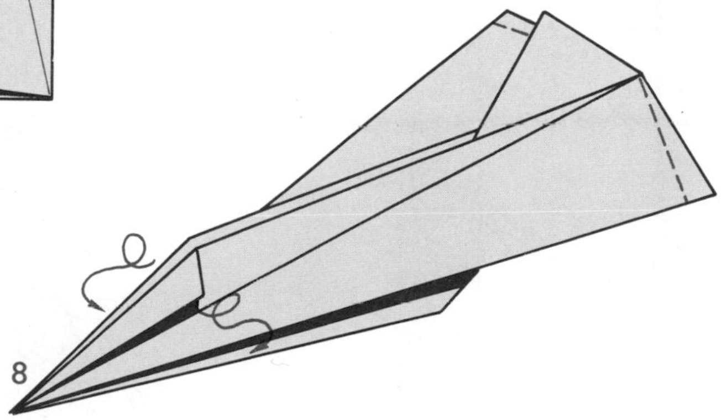

ACROBAT

The Acrobat is specifically designed for one purpose – aerobatics or stunt-flying. This type of stunt plane is distinguished by its hard nose, the original wing shape and the large wing flaps. Over a distance of 5 to 10 meters this airplane can perform a complete loop or a roll. The repertoire also includes a double somersault with a backwards twist. As well as being fun to fly, the Acrobat is quick and fairly simple to make. Its greatest advantage is that it can beat all the other models at aerobatics. But watch out – the danger is that it may deviate from its course and crash into the furniture, or even land in the fire!

1 Take a sheet of paper 20 × 30cm (8 × 12in) and fold it in half.

2 Study the diagram and then make a diagonal cut across two-thirds of the paper. Fold over each half twice.

3 Fold the model in half down the center fold. Fold the nose over and glue or staple it down.

4 Fold each wing along both dotted lines and open out.

5 Cut off the inner corners of each elevator as shown and fold the flaps either up or down, depending on how you would like your Acrobat to perform.

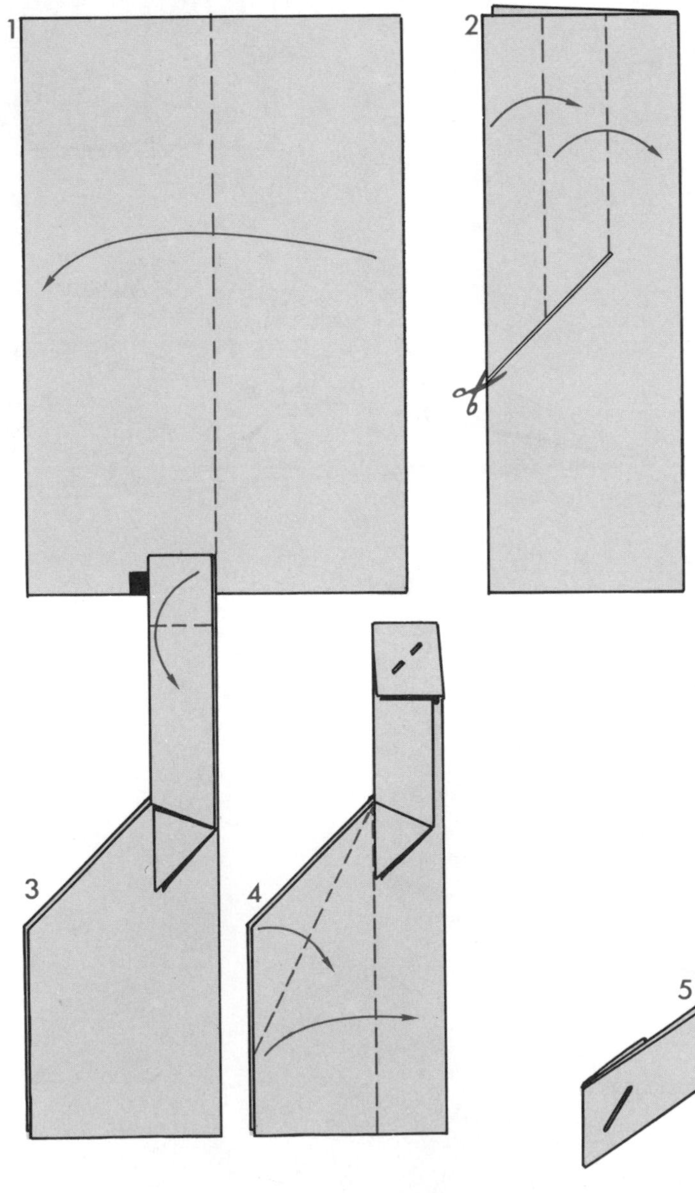

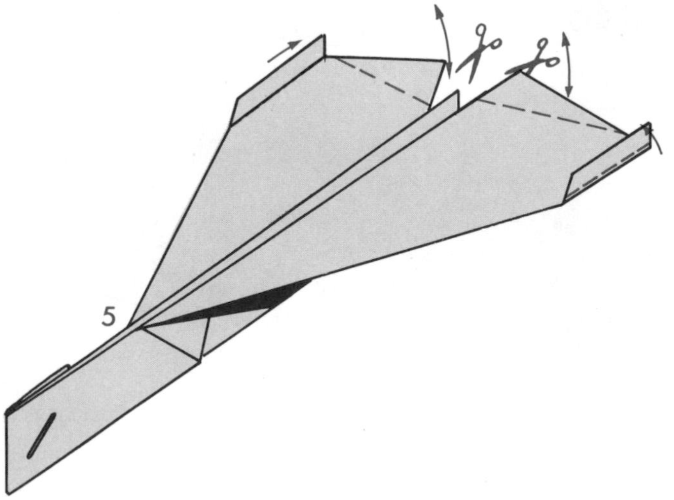

Over a distance of 5–10 meters, this model can complete a roll or a loop . . .

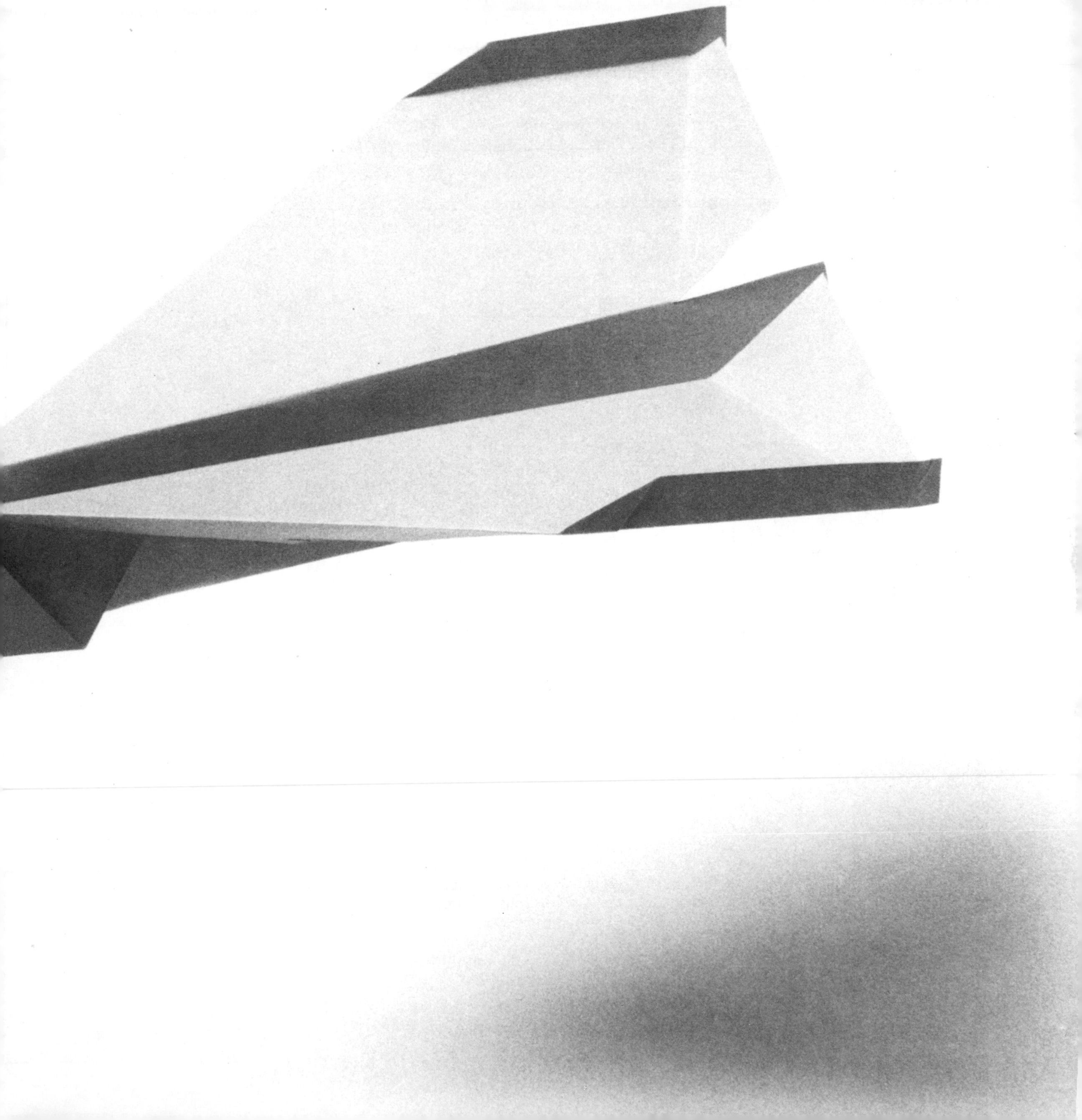

SAILPLANE

This model is extremely headstrong. Its flight begins like that of a jet but, once in the air, it unfurls its wings and demonstrates its fine gliding abilities, a feature which enables it to cover great distances. Because of this, the Sailplane is particularly suited to long-distance flying competitions. The design is based on sound aerodynamic principles which account for its fine performance. Put some weight behind your throw to get it going. You will see how the flight happens in two phases – first the rapid take-off and then a slower glide during which the wings expand considerably. The Sailplane is a first-class contender for a prize in the long-distance class. Experience has shown that light paper is best to maximize the duration of its flight.

1 & 2 Cut out a sheet of paper 40 × 40cm (16 × 16in) as the diagram illustrates. The bottom section is 20cm (8in) wide. Make folds along both diagonals of this section, and then fold in half through the intersection. Tuck in the sides and fold the bottom corners up to meet the top corners as shown in Fig 2.

3 Fold the two corners of the top layers and the bottom point backwards and forwards along the dotted lines.

1

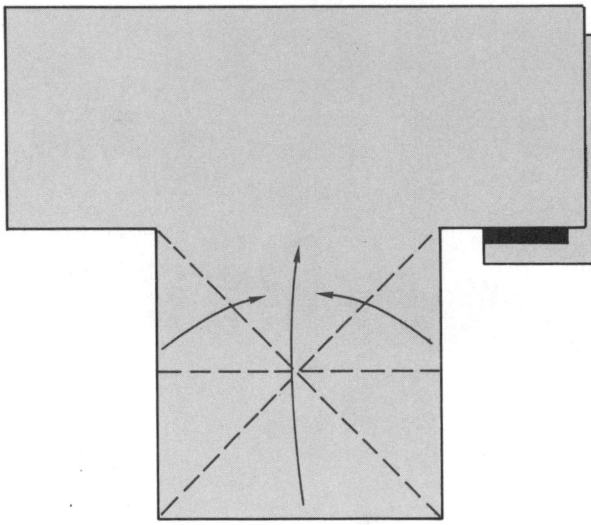

2

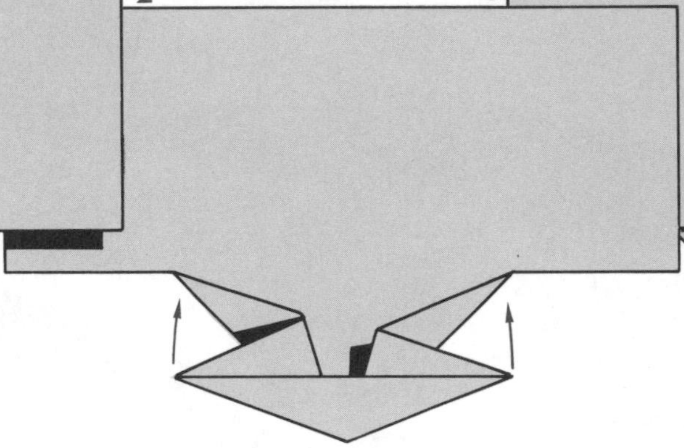

3

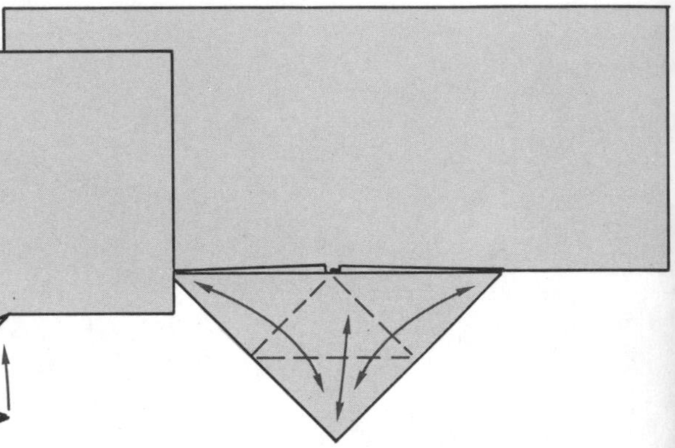

4 & 5 This part is complicated. Push the outside corners of the triangle inside the top layer and down so that the points lie inside the point at the bottom of the triangle. This is far easier if you have already made good folds in the previous step.

6 As soon as this is successfully completed, fold the whole figure in half along the dotted line.

7 Make a long diagonal fold from the nose as indicated by the dotted line and then fold the bottom corner backwards and forwards along the dotted line and push it up in an inverted fold to make the tail. Unfold the wings along the diagonal fold.

8 All that remains is to fold up the wing tips along the dotted lines.

4

5

6

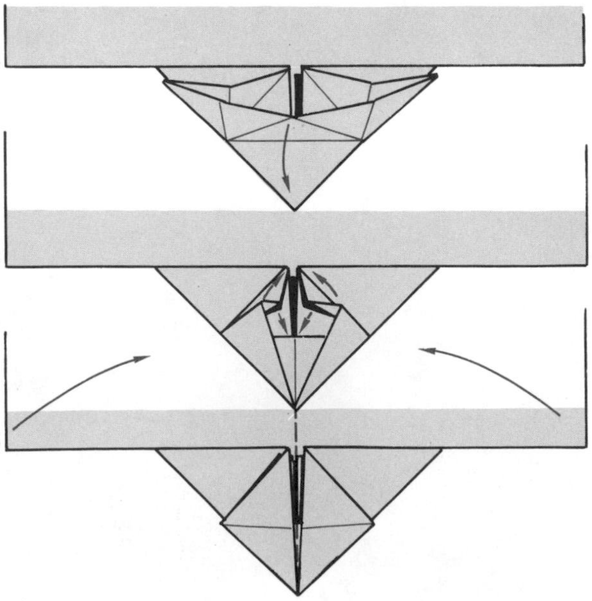

7

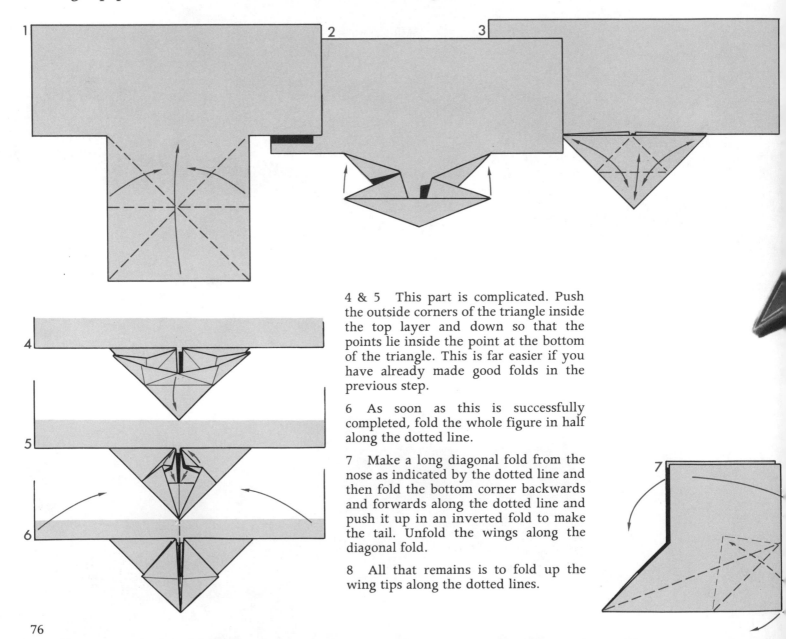

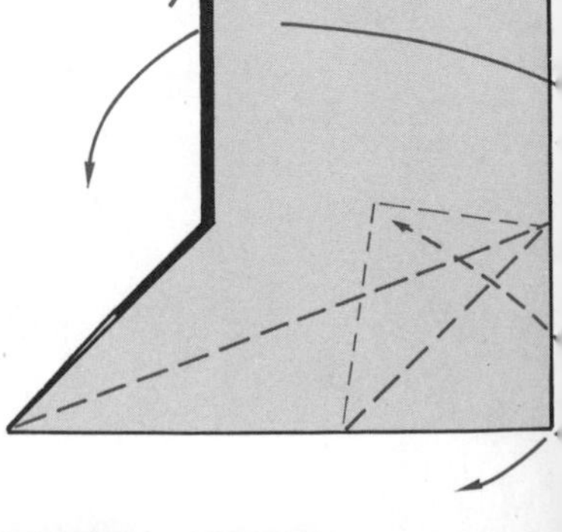

An extremely willful plane which takes off like a jet but then behaves like a real glider, these features enabling it to glide great distances . . .

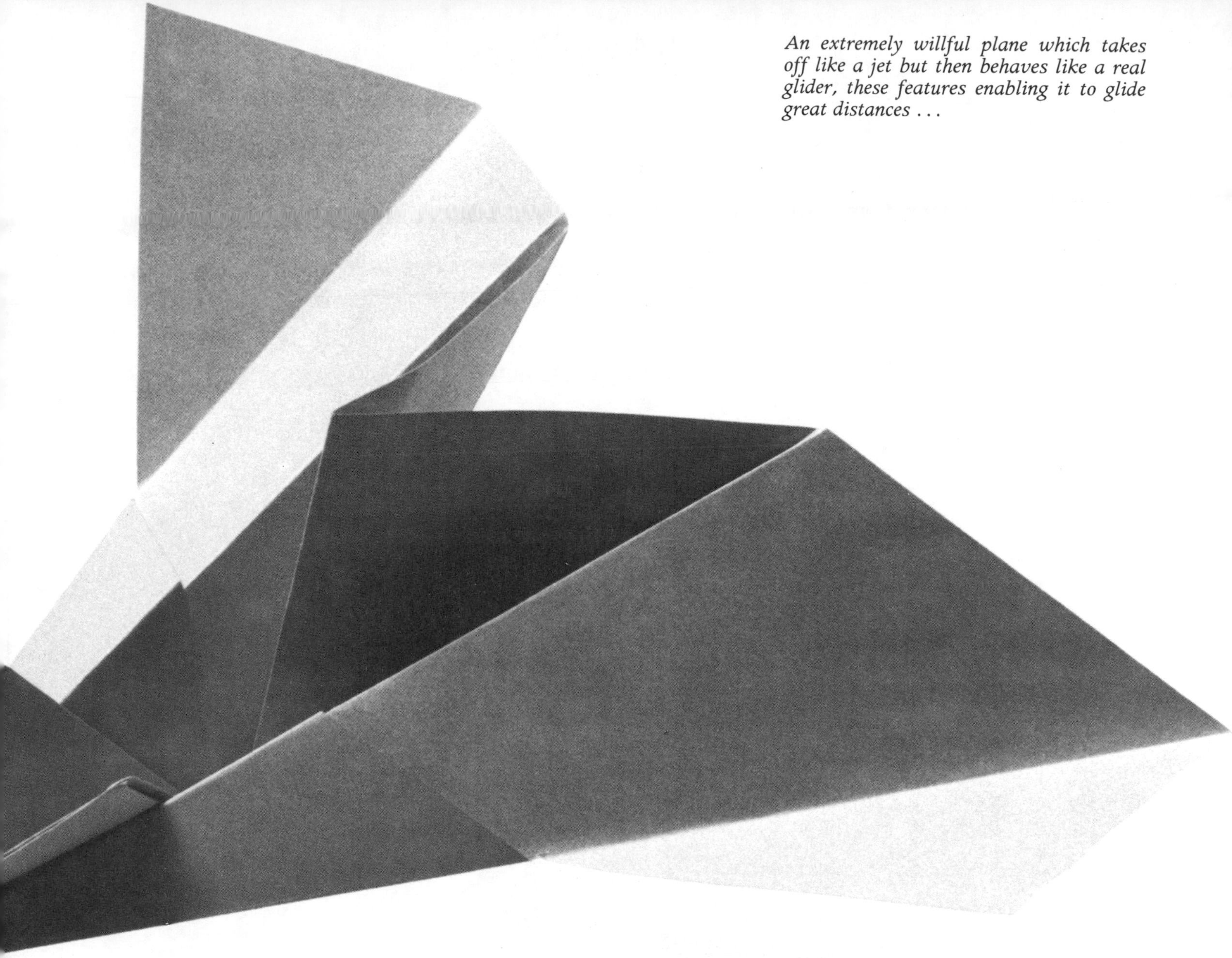

SAKODA

This superb airplane which won a prize at the *Scientific American* International Airplane Competition was designed by the Japanese professor and origami expert, James M. Sakoda. This model is a fine example of origami, the Japanese art of folding paper. It is a very fast airplane and excellent for aerobatic stunt-flying. The Sakoda is not hard to fold. At first glance it could be a prototype for a new supersonic airplane – a powerful space-cruiser.

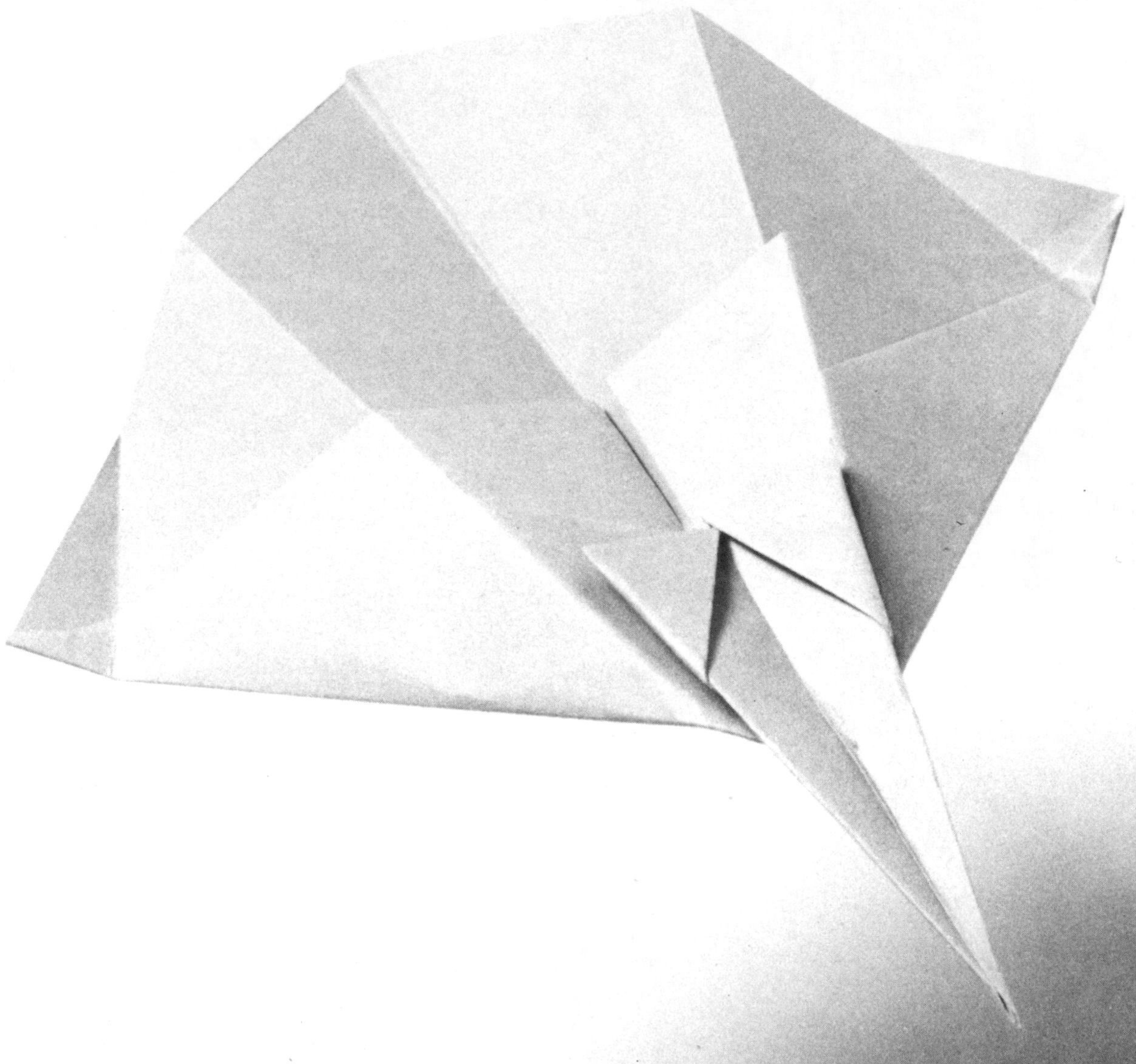

The Sakoda is not difficult to make . . .

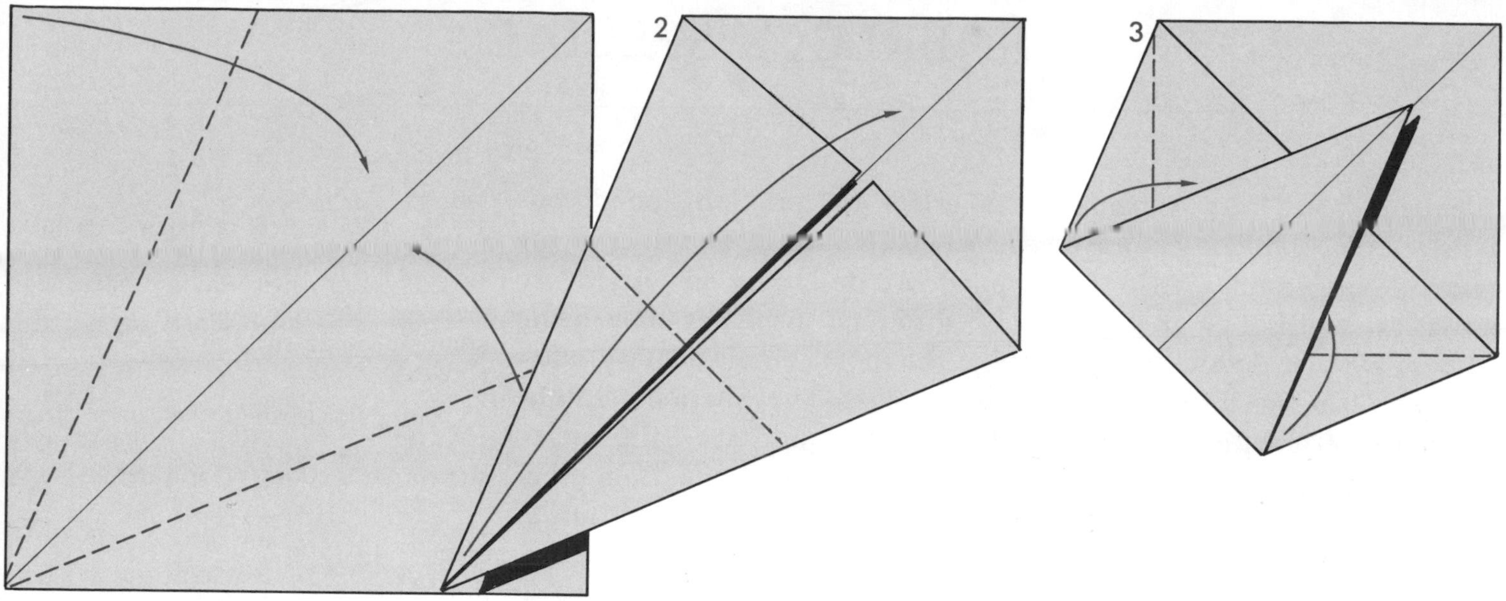

1 Fold in two corners of a sheet of paper 30 × 30cm (12 × 12in) to meet along a diagonal center line.

2 Fold up the resulting point along the dotted line.

3 Fold in the sides underneath the point you have just folded up.

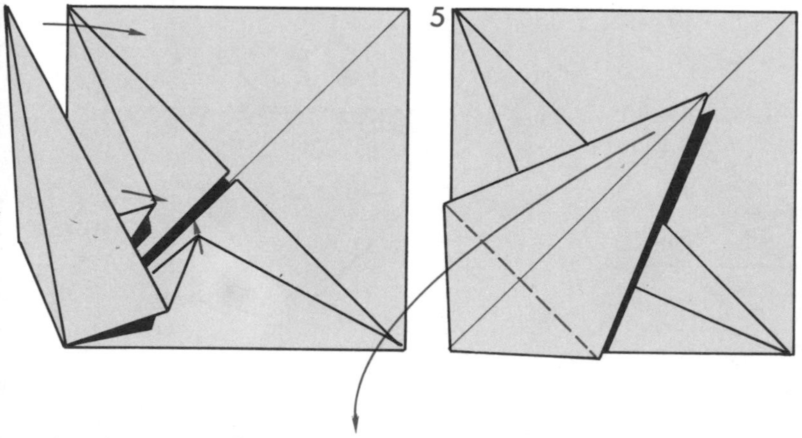

4 This diagram makes it clearer.

5 Fold the point back again along the dotted line and push the model flat.

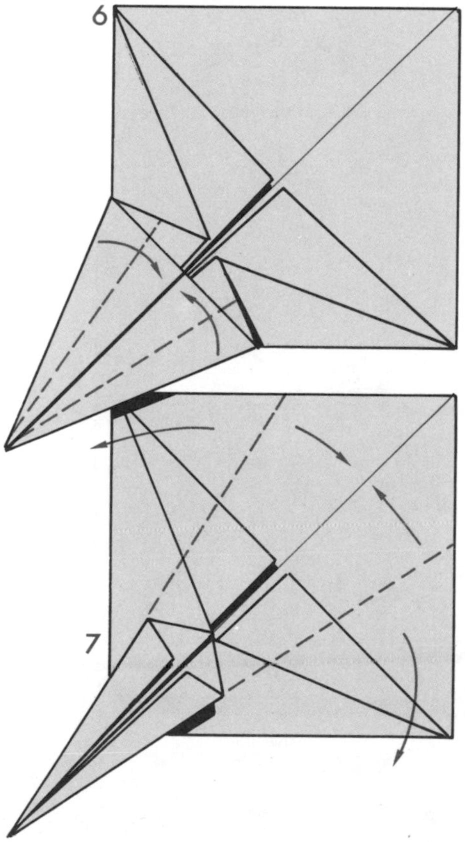

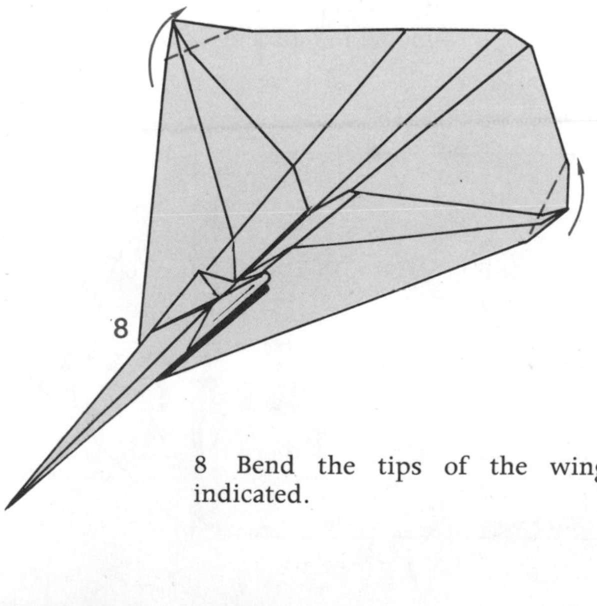

8 Bend the tips of the wings, as indicated.

6 Fold the two edges over to the center line as illustrated in the diagram and press down flat.

7 Fold the wings away from you along the dotted lines and then fold the whole model in half along the center line.

SHERLOCK SPECIAL

'Elementary my dear Watson', said Sherlock Holmes to his ponderous assistant on completing a fine piece of detective work. The skills of the great detective may also be applied to designing airplanes. By investigating particular features of different airplanes and using your powers of deduction to combine the most complementary ones, you may find a formula for a new design. The Sherlock Special combines certain features of the Flying Arrow and the Sailplane to produce the finest characteristics of both. Ideas have come from other designs in this book to solve one puzzle of aeronautical design but, as in many investigative affairs, there is more than one solution.

Wings

1 & 2 Fold a sheet of paper 20 × 30cm (8 × 12in) along both diagonals and then in half widthways. Having made good creases, fold the sheet in half while simultaneously tucking in the sides as shown in Fig 2.

3 Cut a slot through the center of the triangle. Fold up the top layer of both the corner sections as indicated.

1

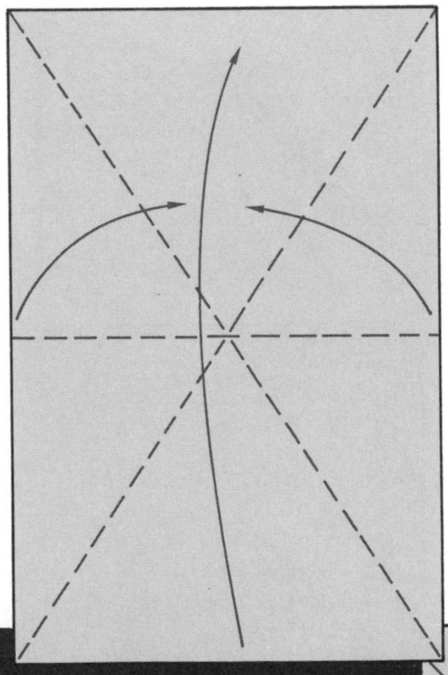

2

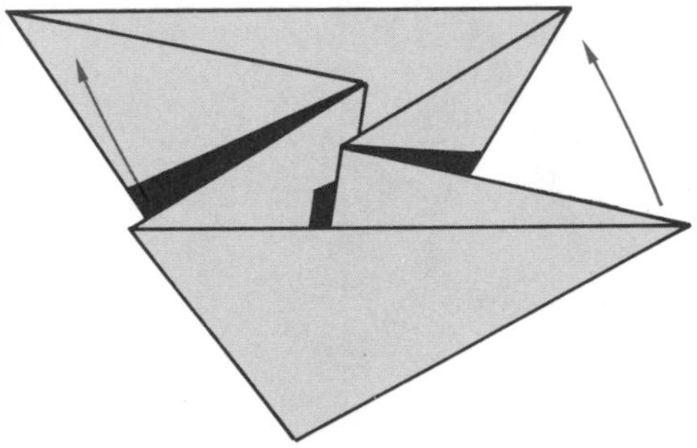

3

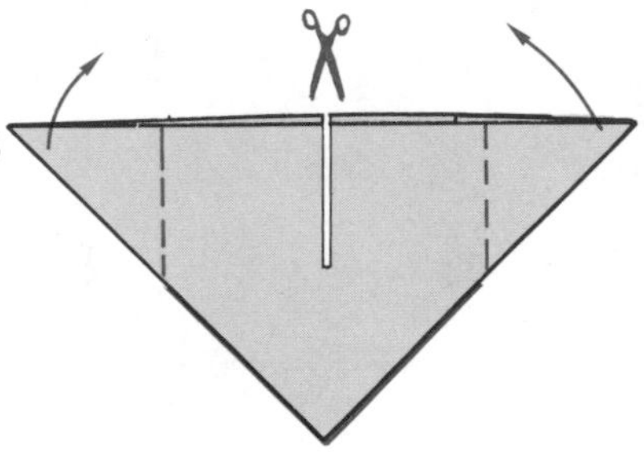

Fuselage

1 Fold a sheet of paper 20 × 40cm (8 × 16in) along the dotted lines, as you do with the wings and, in the same way, fold it in half tucking in the sides.

2 Fold in the outside points of the resulting triangles along the dotted lines to the center line. Lastly fold the whole model in half lengthways.

1

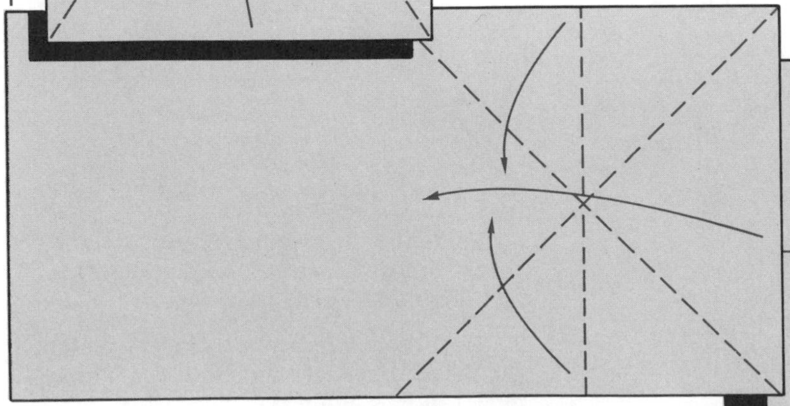

2

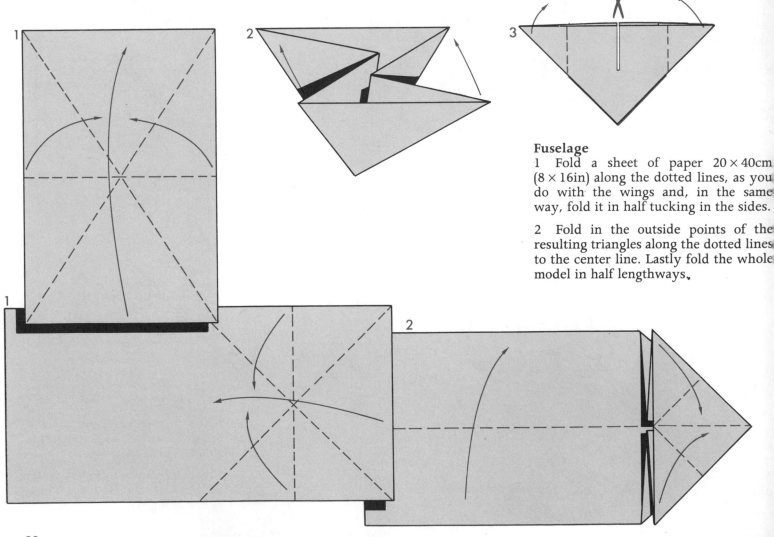

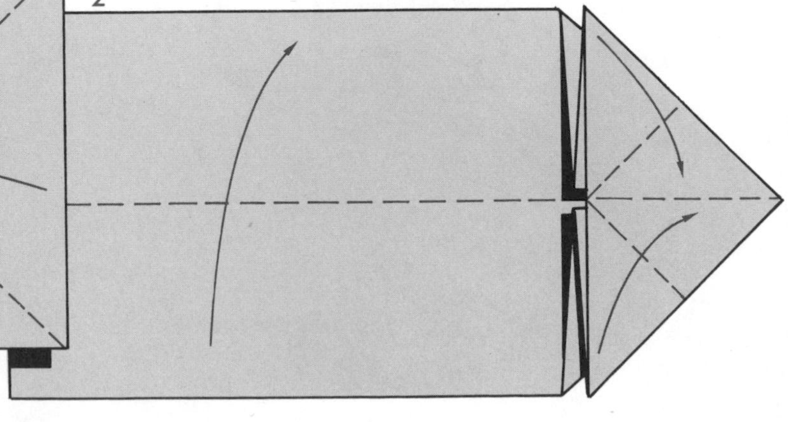

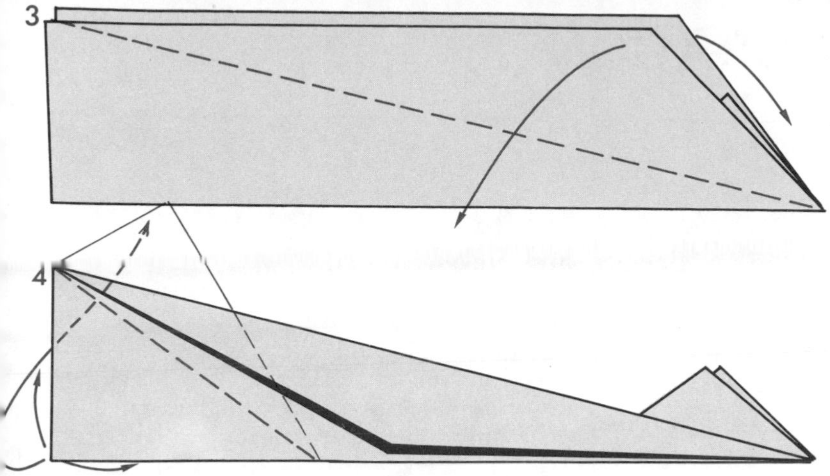

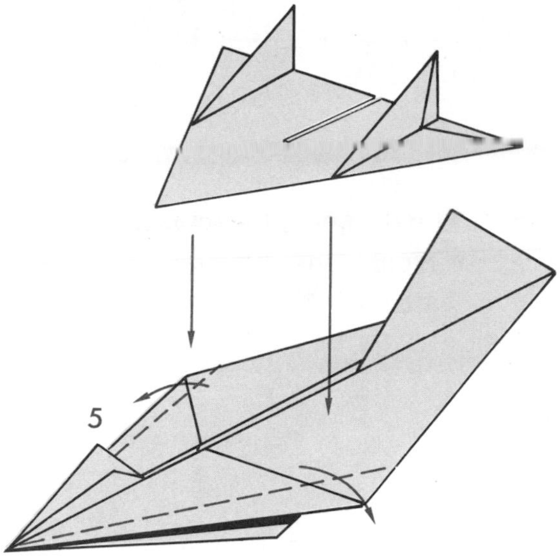

3 Fold each side outwards along the dotted lines.

4 Fold backwards and forwards along the dotted line to make an inverted fold for the tail. Fasten the nose with glue, Scotch tape or a staple.

5 Slot the wings over the tailpiece and glue the two sections together.

The Sherlock Special is now ready to explore high altitudes. A modification can be made by folding down the sides of the fuselage along the dotted lines; this makes the fuselage more compact and, with this refinement, it will perform loops and rolls with careful adjustment of the various moving parts.

The Sherlock Special – an airplane combining the finest characteristics of two other models.

FLYING DRAGON

By joining together several similar sections of a familiar design, an entirely original concept is created – one that has moved a few light years away from conventional paper airplanes. The resulting Flying Dragon is based on the Sherlock Special design but, as the picture clearly shows, it takes at least three airplanes to make one dragon.

Nose
1 & 2 Take a sheet of paper 20 × 20cm (8 × 8in). Make folds along both diagonals and then across the center intersection. Fold it in half, tucking in the sides as the arrows indicate. Turn down the corners of the top layer.

Nose

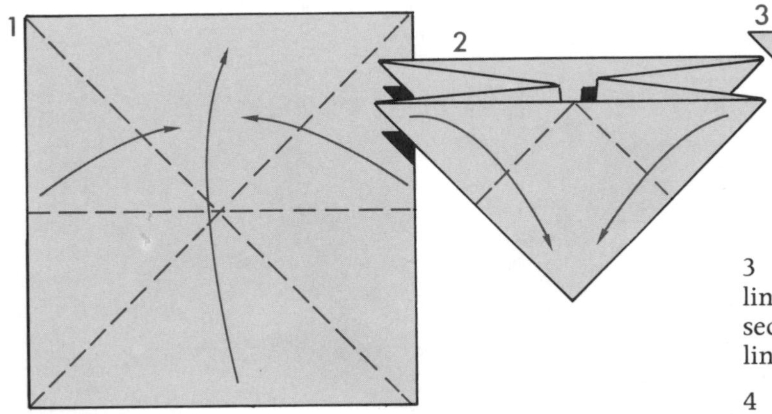

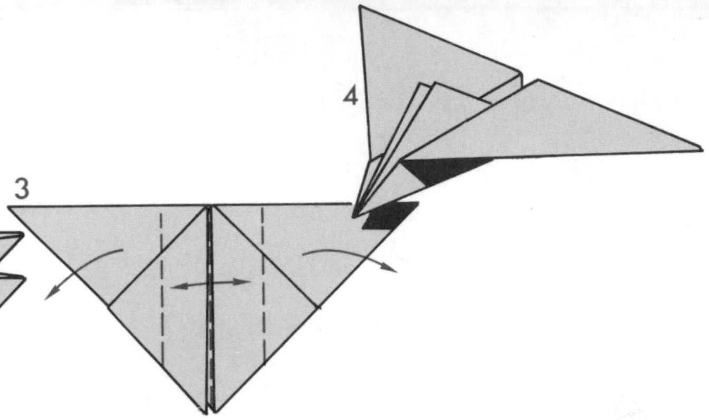

3 Fold in half along the center dotted line and then fold down the wing sections to either side along the dotted lines.

4 This is what the result should look like.

Wings

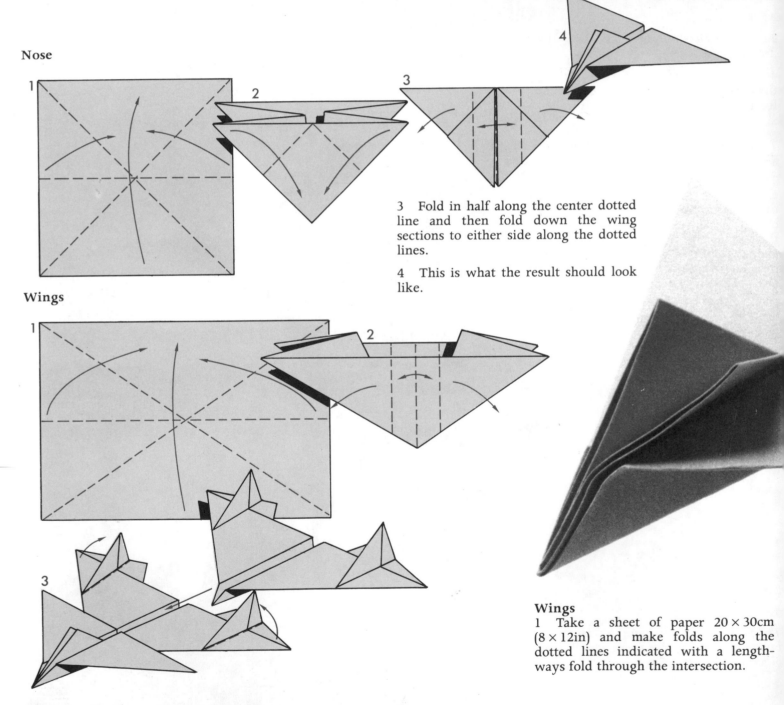

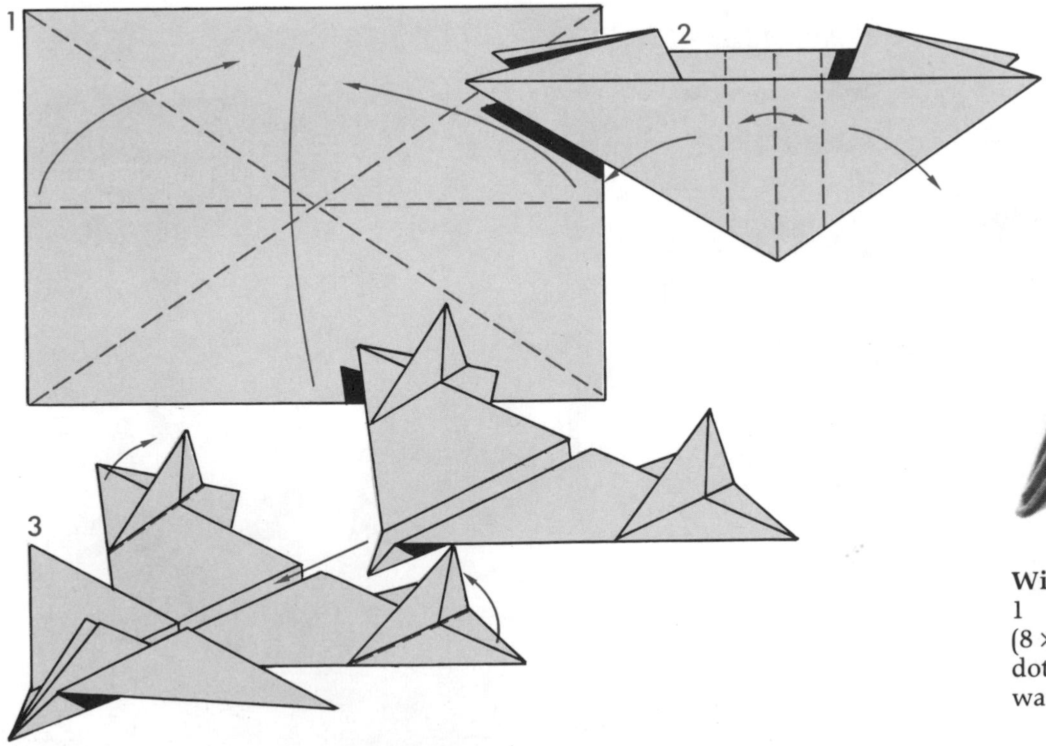

Wings
1 Take a sheet of paper 20 × 30cm (8 × 12in) and make folds along the dotted lines indicated with a lengthways fold through the intersection.

2 Fold in half as before, tucking in the edges. Following the diagram, fold the whole model into a V-shape along the dotted lines and turn up the top layer of the wing tips.

3 Insert the wing into the ready-made nose and fuselage section and glue it in tight, as the diagram shows. This is the first step of the assembly. You may then add on as many wing sections as required – two are shown here. It is best to test the flight performance in between adding each section. We added on five wings but had to stop there because the waiter in the Chinese restaurant didn't want us to use any more paper table napkins although he did have to agree that our creation looked like a real dragon. That was after it had made a crash landing in the chop suey five tables away. Heavy air traffic prevailed until closing time . . .

It takes at least three airplanes to make one Flying Dragon.

The same basic principle is used for both the Flying Arrow and the Flying Christmas Tree.

FLYING CHRISTMAS TREE

Creating new designs from standard models is fascinating – it remains to be seen how many different designs can emerge from one simple principle. In this case you simply follow the wing pattern for the Flying Arrow to make one section of a Flying Christmas Tree. It is up to you how many sections you add – it just depends on the size of tree required. So far there is no mention of it in the *Guinness Book of Records* . . .

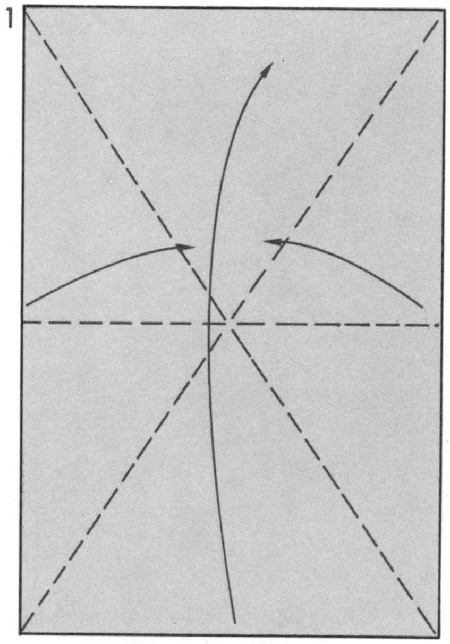

1 Make folds in a piece of paper 20 × 30cm (8 × 12in) along both diagonals and through the center.

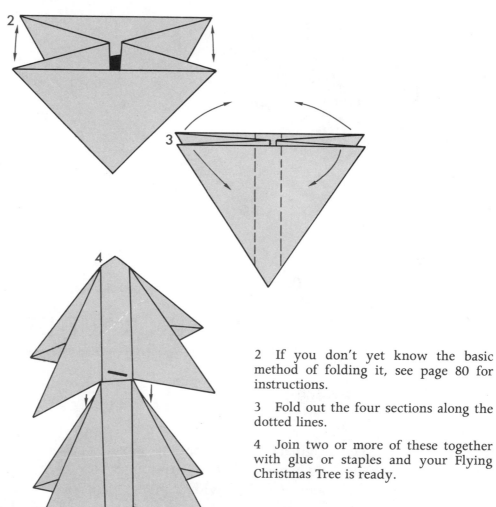

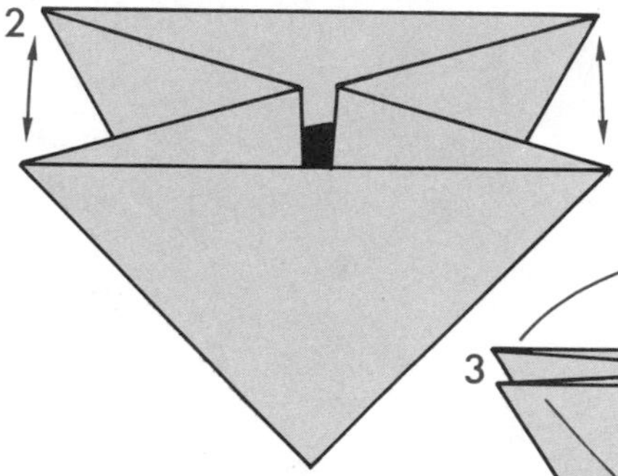

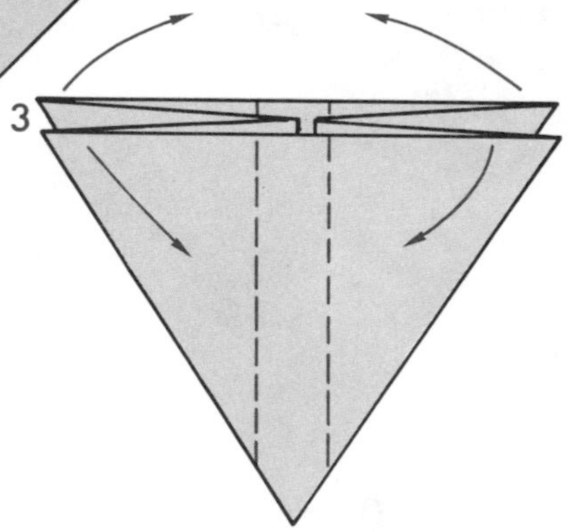

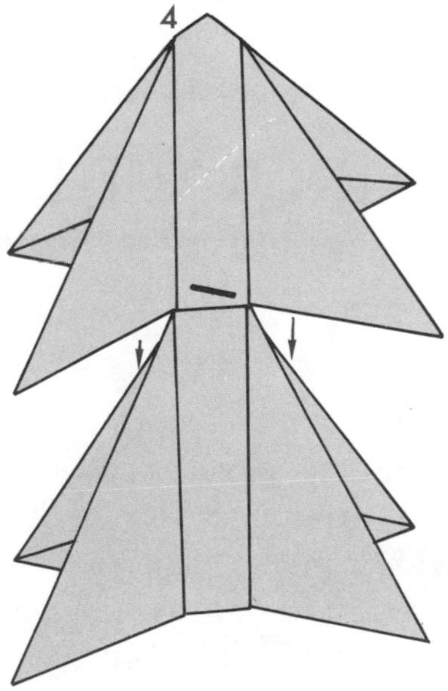

2 If you don't yet know the basic method of folding it, see page 80 for instructions.

3 Fold out the four sections along the dotted lines.

4 Join two or more of these together with glue or staples and your Flying Christmas Tree is ready.

A tiny paper pellet Anti-aircraft Device makes an attack on a powerful French Mirage . . .

ANTI-AIRCRAFT DEVICE

The original idea for making paper airplanes probably came from shooting paper pellets – a popular way of passing the time in the classroom. It also provided an excellent method of passing notes and other more shady information – a skill which has faded into the background with the advent of school computers and multiple-choice questions. Paper pellets can be made out of anything; the size and type of paper is not important although folded newspaper is hard to shoot with a rubber band. *Paper Flight* features a new use for the traditional paper pellet as a defense weapon. This game is best played in a group. One group tries to fly as many paper airplanes as possible from A to B and the other group tries to prevent them reaching their destination by shooting them down with pellets. Every airplane reaching B wins a point and every airplane shot down is a point to the anti-aircraft team. The larger the group, the more fun it is. You have to start thinking about tactics. Consider the best ways of defeating the enemy; should you fly in low over the ground or stay as high as possible? It is clear that a concealed battery of pellet launchers can decimate large numbers of flying airplanes at one go. There are endless possibilities . . .

1

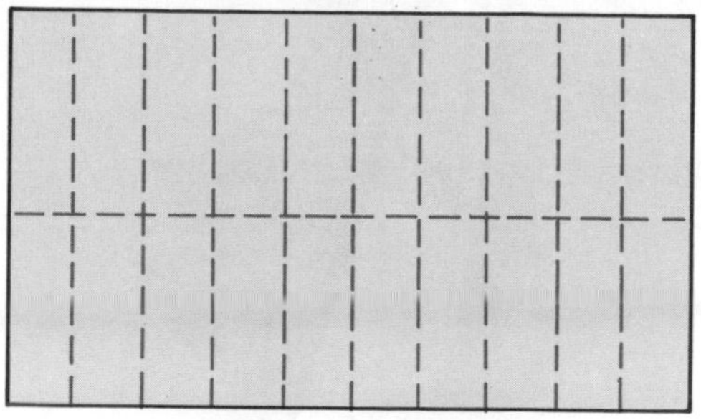

2

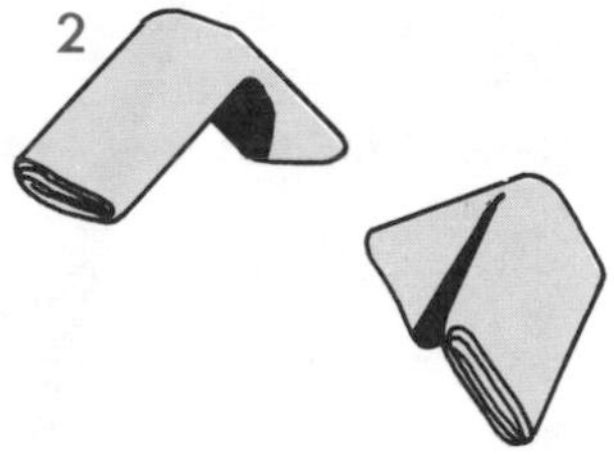

1 Fold a piece of paper in half widthways ten times and fold it lengthways.

2 The pellet should now look like this. Stretch a rubber band between the thumb and first finger, fit the paper pellet in the middle, stretch it backwards by holding the paper pellet in the thumb and forefinger of the other hand, pull and . . . fire!

The Catapult Plane is attacking the Sherlock Special; which will crash first?

CATAPULT DEFENSE CRAFT

The Catapult Plane (pp 54–7) also performs well in defense. You can either shoot it from the floor or use a sling but, whichever method you choose, it is very satisfying to shoot a friend's airplane out of the sky. The paper pellet is an anti-aircraft missile but the Catapult Plane, although launched in a similar way, is really closer to being a fighter plane. You can relive the Battle of Britain; if only the super powers had agreed to conduct the war in this way . . .

The symbolic significance of the Crane is well known.

Basic Crane
These diagrams illustrate the preliminary method for folding birds. In origami this is called the 'Basic Crane' because so many different cranes may be made from it; many of our models use this method for the preliminary stages.

1
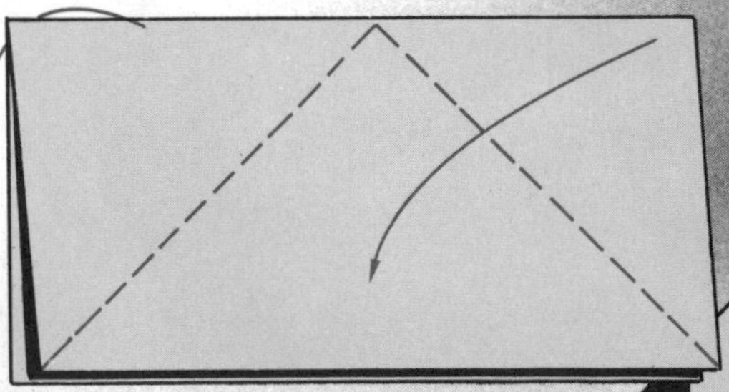

2
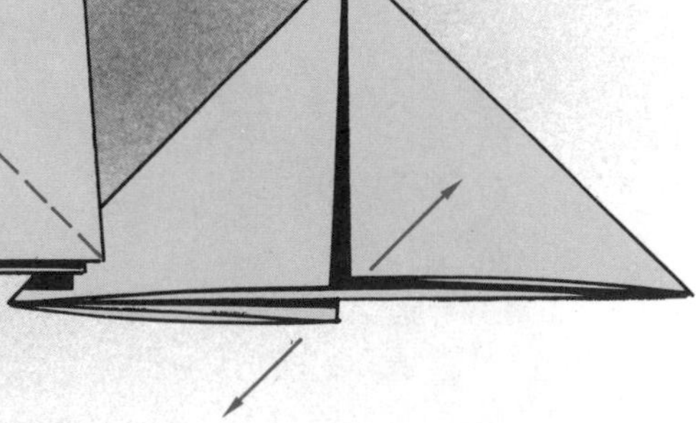

3
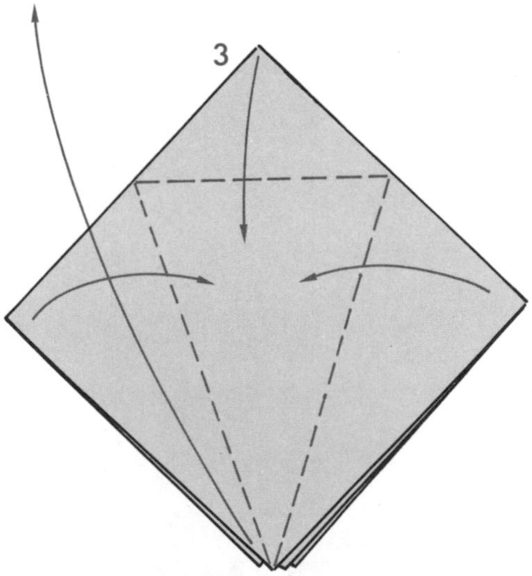

1 Take a sheet of paper 30 × 30cm (12 × 12in) and fold it in half. Fold in both corners along the dotted lines, one forwards and the other backwards.

2 Holding the triangle at the middle of the bottom edge, pull the sides open and press the figure down flat.

3 Fold three points in along the dotted lines and then open out again having made good creases. Take the bottom point of the top layer of paper and fold it back along the creases just made.

BIRDS

This chapter leads us further into the world of origami, the Japanese art of folding paper models and shapes. The techniques are age-old and several of the birds in this section are based on those origami principles. Whereas you can make up ideas for paper airplanes and give free rein to the imagination, making birds is slightly different. We need to look to nature in order to capture the inherent qualities of shape and form of the different birds which are necessary for producing realistic paper replicas. We are also talking about two completely different ways of flying. The flight of an airplane is straighter and smoother than that of a bird which has to move its wings in a way that man has never been able to imitate. This is the weakness of our paper birds – they fly like gliders, never moving their wings. However they look lifelike. The basic principles of origami are quite simple; the famous Crane design is used as the basis for a number of different birds. Only a few simple additions need to be made to this basic design to create other species.

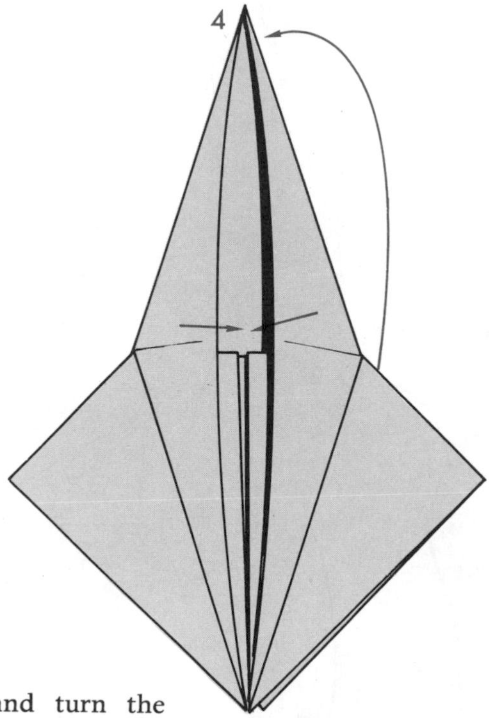

4 Press it down flat and turn the model over, repeating the procedure on the other side.

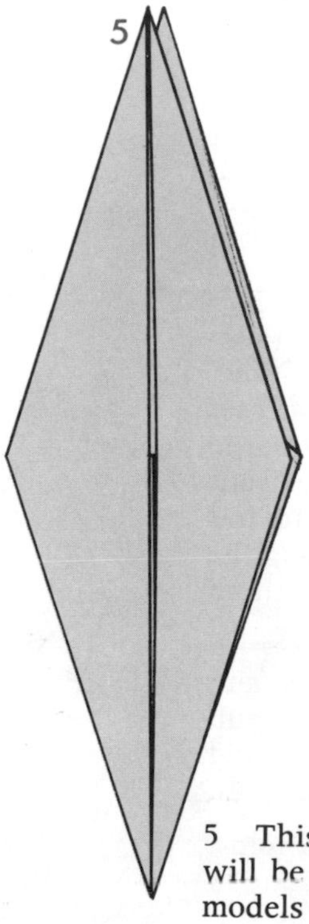

5 This is the Basic Crane which you will be referred to again as many other models are derived from it.

CRANE

The distinctive shape of the crane has made it a favorite model for origami enthusiasts. It is certainly a beautiful, majestic bird with grey or white plumage and an immensely long, powerful bill. A flock of cranes flying overhead must be a wonderful sight but unfortunately these birds are rarely seen in the western hemisphere. Here we have two alternative methods of folding cranes, both beginning with the Basic Crane explained on the previous page.

Method A

1 Having completed the Basic Crane (page 90) fold the edges along the dotted lines, the front edges forwards and the back edges backwards.

2 Fold the bottom points along the dotted lines backwards and then make inverted folds, one point to either side.

3 Fold the left point along the dotted line and make an inverted fold to form the head. Pull the wings open as indicated by the arrows.

4 The body which has now appeared can be pulled open further.

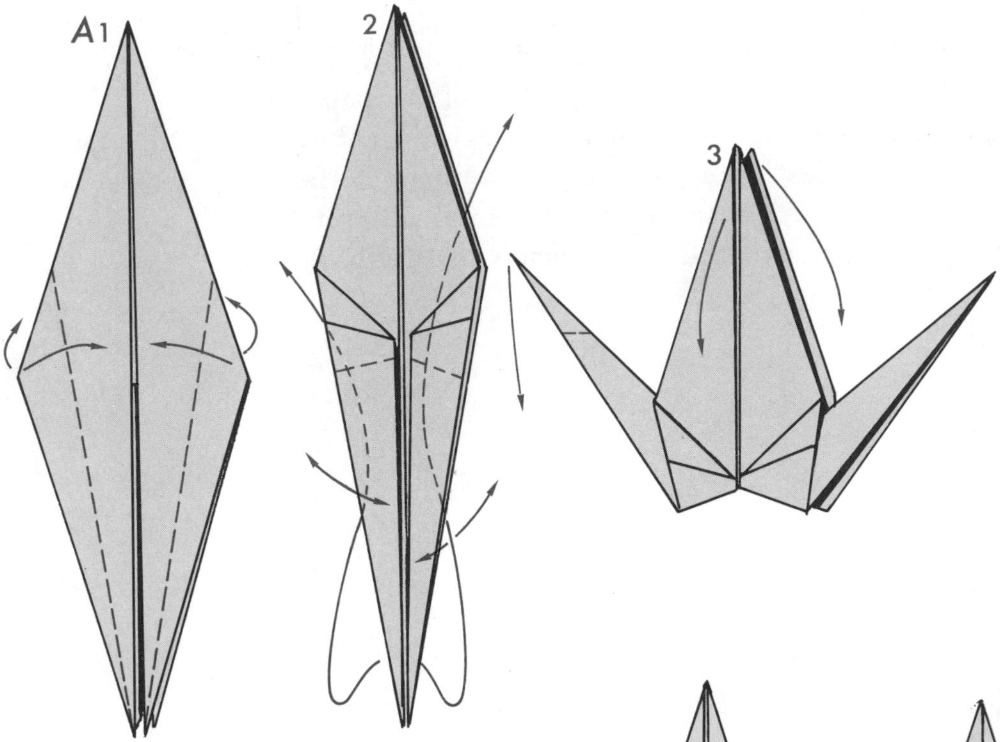

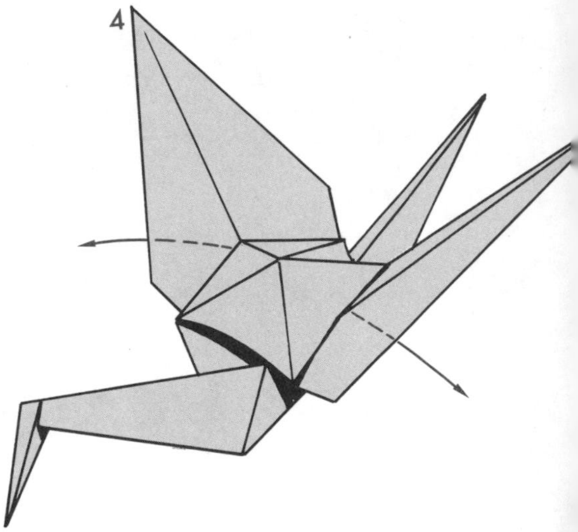

Method B

1 Follow steps 1–5 for the Basic Crane, fold the lefthand edge in to the center line as indicated by the dotted lines, the back folding backwards and the front folding forwards. Fold the righthand edge backwards and forwards along the dotted line and pull it through with an inverted fold.

2 Fold the left side backwards and forwards along the dotted line and pull it through with an inverted fold. Fold the sides inwards along the dotted lines.

3 Now make two more inverted folds, one in the bend of the head and one in the bend of the legs.

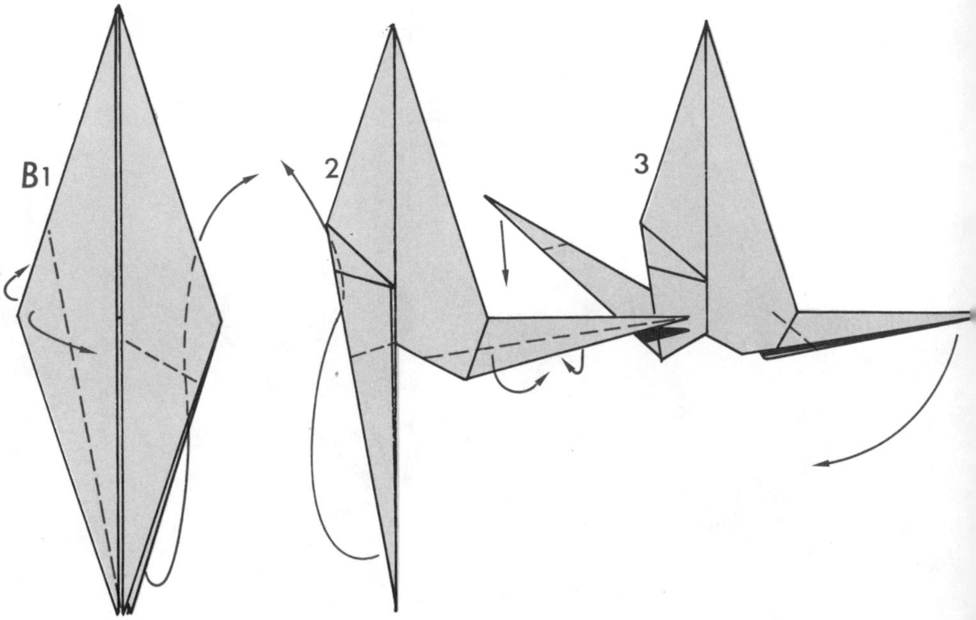

The Crane in flight: the result of following method B.

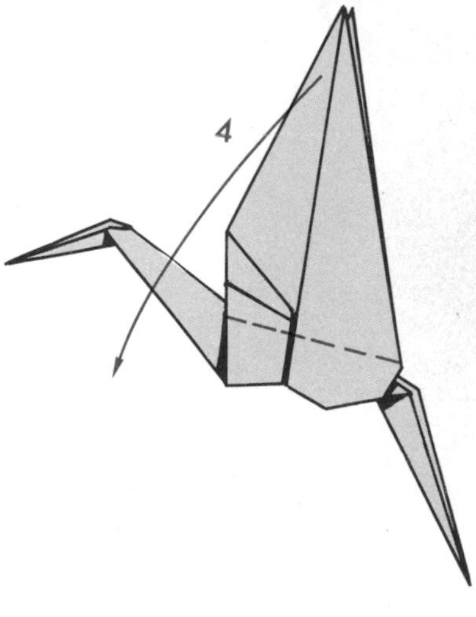

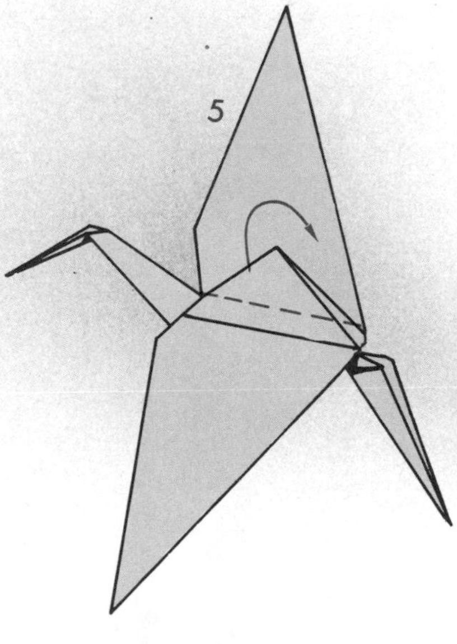

4 Open out the wings along the dotted lines.

5 Tuck in the point on the back as if it were an envelope.

HERON

Herons are found in or near the water, on rivers, lakes and sea shores. Although they have a reputation for being shy and retiring, they can sometimes be seen awaiting the spoils of a fisherman's catch, quite content to let someone else do the work for them. Herons have a very distinctive flight with the head back between the shoulders and legs extended, as illustrated in the paper model. The wing-beat is slow and powerful, even clumsy, yet in contrast they appear stately, elegant birds when standing motionless by the waters' edge waiting to spear a fish.

One can tell that this is a Heron and not a Stork from its beautifully arched neck.

Follow steps 1–5 for the Basic Crane; steps 1–3 are similar to method B of the Crane on page 92.

1 Fold over both lefthand flaps along the dotted line, one in front and one behind. Pull the right bottom tip up through the middle using an inverted fold.

2 Fold the edges inwards along the dotted line as shown.

1
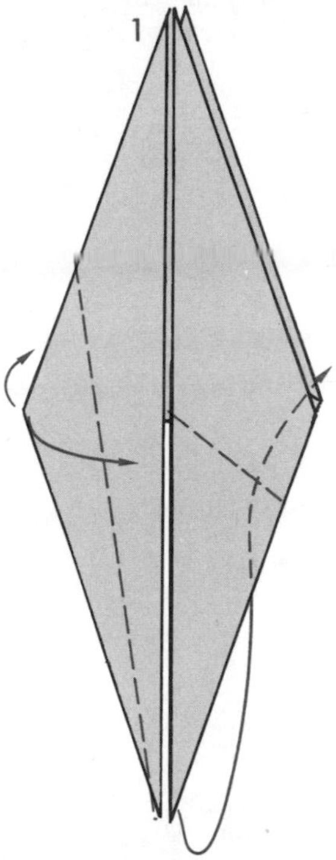

2
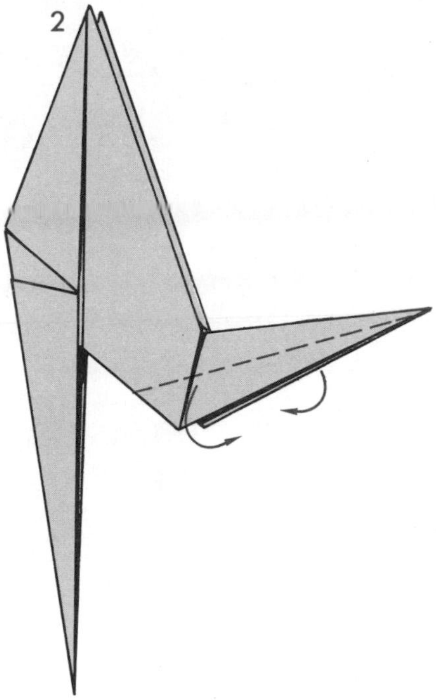

3

4
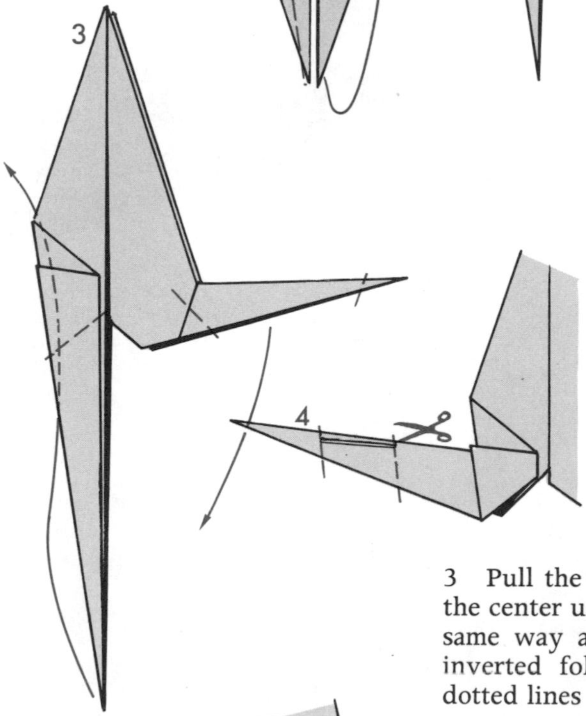

3 Pull the left bottom tip up through the center using an inverted fold, in the same way as the right tip. Make two inverted folds in this flap along the dotted lines to fashion the legs.

4 Cut the neck as indicated. Fold along the dotted lines and make two inverted folds to separate the neck from the head and the characteristic crown.

5
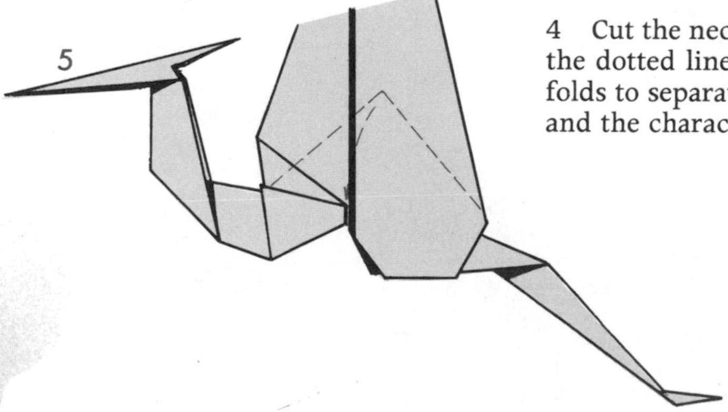

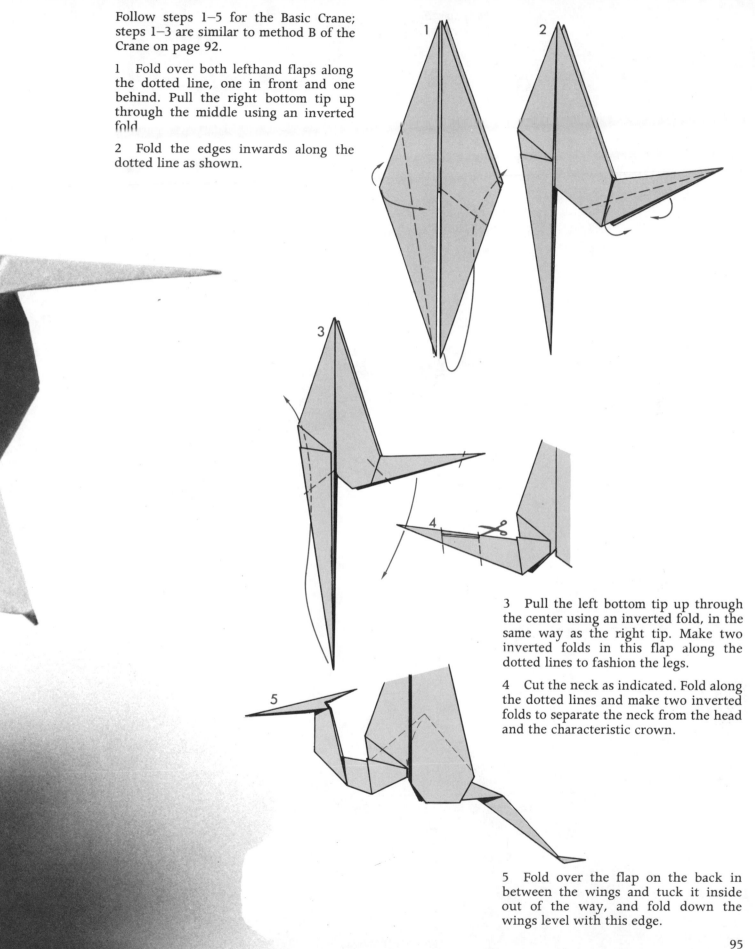

5 Fold over the flap on the back in between the wings and tuck it inside out of the way, and fold down the wings level with this edge.

*The paper Eagle is looking for a thermal –
a current of rising warm air . . .*

EAGLE

This king of the sky does not require the Basic Crane method – the majestic creature has its own folding method. The eagle glides well, expertly making use of currents of warm air to soar high in the sky. The wings hardly ever have to move. From a great height the eagle can spot a mouse amongst the grass with its extraordinarily sharp eyes. The eagle is a symbol of freedom and greatness and features in the coats of arms of many countries. Like his real life counterpart, this paper Eagle possesses the same ability to hover, so long as it finds some currents of warm air to provide the lift.

1 Take a sheet of paper 20 × 20cm (8 × 8in) and fold it in half diagonally.

2 Fold the triangle along the dotted line, as directed by the arrow.

3 Fold back the top layer following the dotted line.

4 Fold the whole model in half.

5 Fold the wings up along the dotted lines, one to either side and tuck in the tail with an inverted fold.

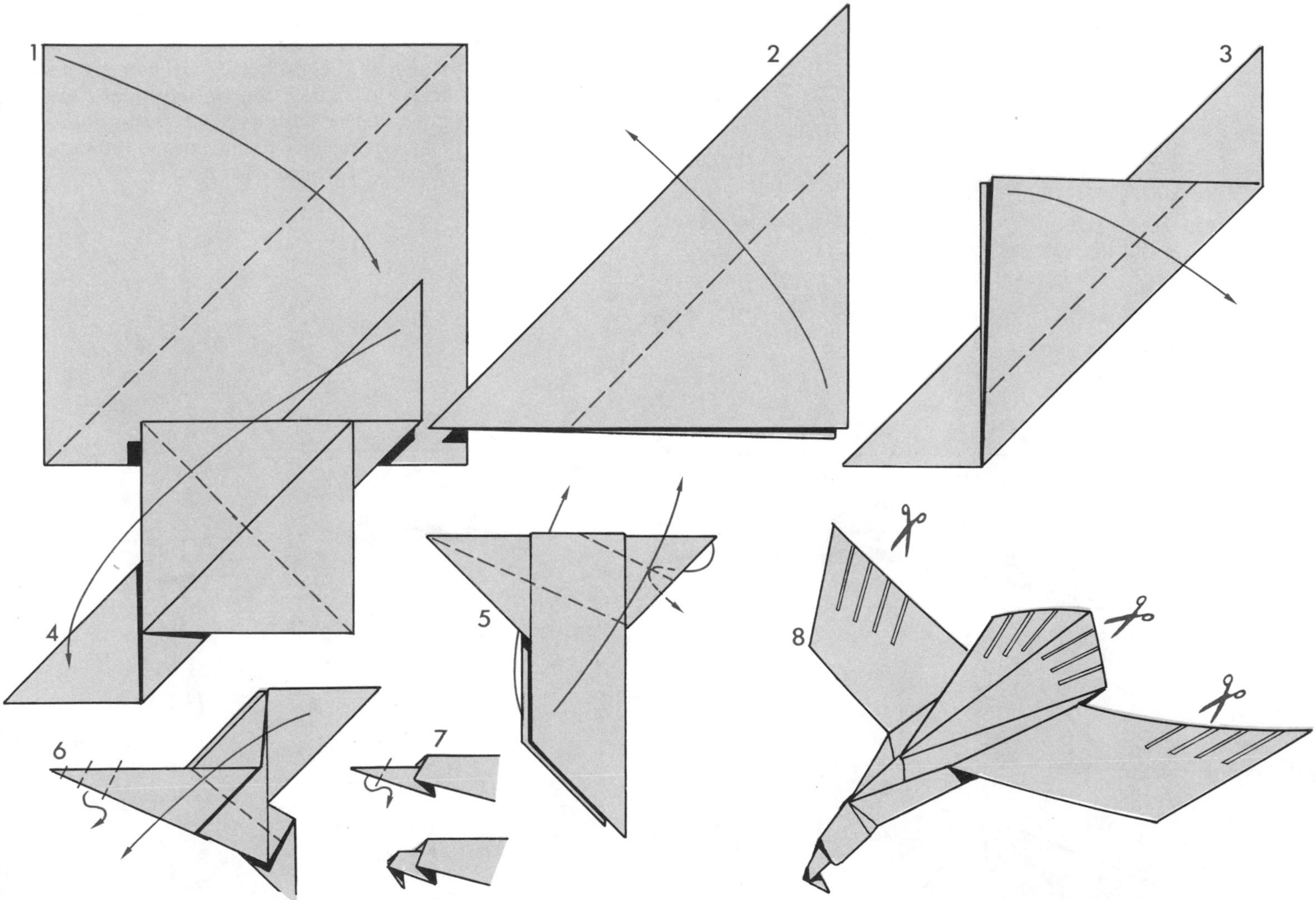

6 Make three good creases in the nose and then two inverted folds make the hooked beak. Bend the wings into the flying position by folding them down the dotted line.

7 These detailed diagrams show the nose and beak folds more clearly.

8 As a finishing touch, make slits in the wings and tail to represent feathers – this may even improve its flight. Now the eagle can go out and prey on the neighborhood.

SEAGULL

Be warned from the start; this Seagull is extremely hard to make even though it may look simple. The appearance is deceptive, a fact which also applies to the gull's temperament. This graceful white bird, immortalized in the film and book, *Jonathan Livingston Seagull*, is also a notorious thief, stealing the eggs of its own kind. Our Seagull flies very well and is an excellent glider. A variation on this design is to make a life-size model out of brown wrapping paper, the resulting bird being the Storm Petrel. This distant relation of the seagull mainly lives in the region of Cape Horn.

1 Cut out a triangle of the proportions shown in the diagram with a base twice as long as its height. The bottom of the triangle is 40cm (16in) wide. Make folds along all the dotted lines and bring the top point forward folding points 'a' down to points 'b'.

2 This diagram makes it clearer.

3 Fold the triangle over at point 'c' and push the right point down. Press the surface down flat.

4 This diagram shows the half-way point.

5 This is what the result of the last four steps should look like. Fold the sides of the top layer backwards and forwards along the dotted lines. Take hold of the bottom point pulling it up and back. This technique is similar to that for the Basic Crane.

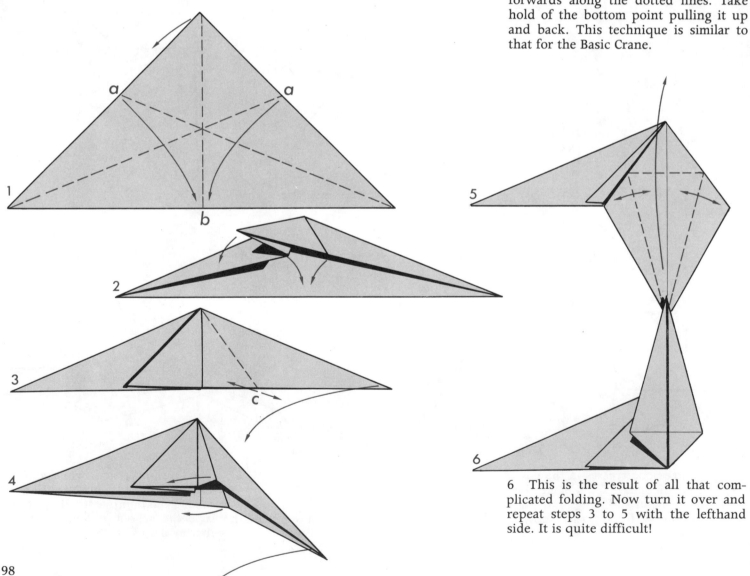

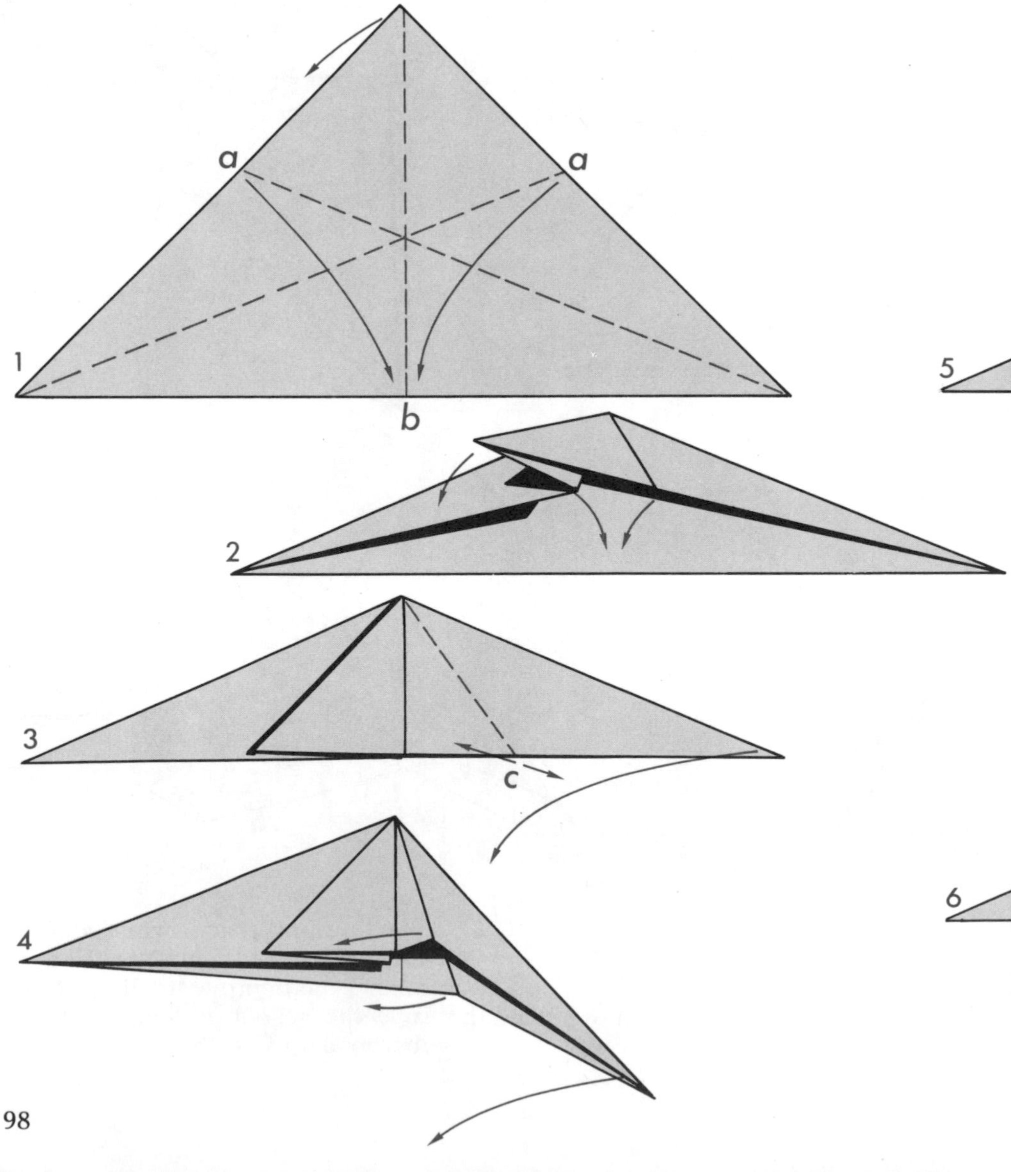

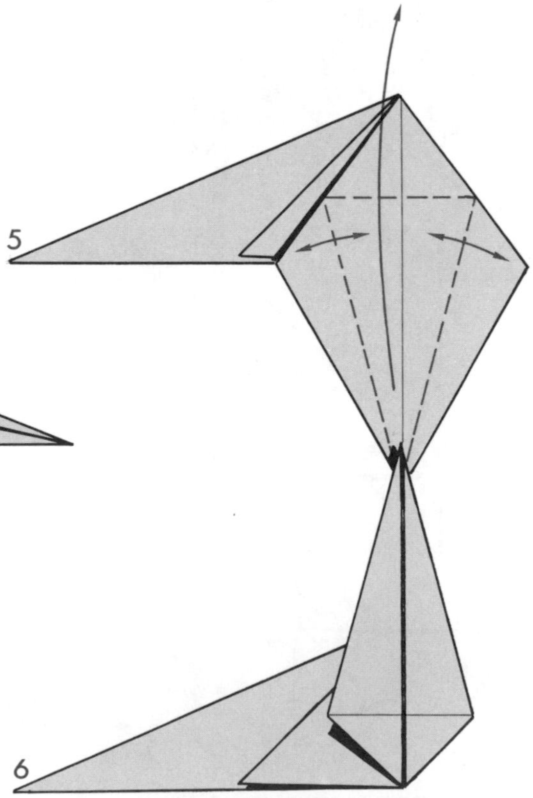

6 This is the result of all that complicated folding. Now turn it over and repeat steps 3 to 5 with the lefthand side. It is quite difficult!

Our Seagull is a fast flyer and an excellent glider...

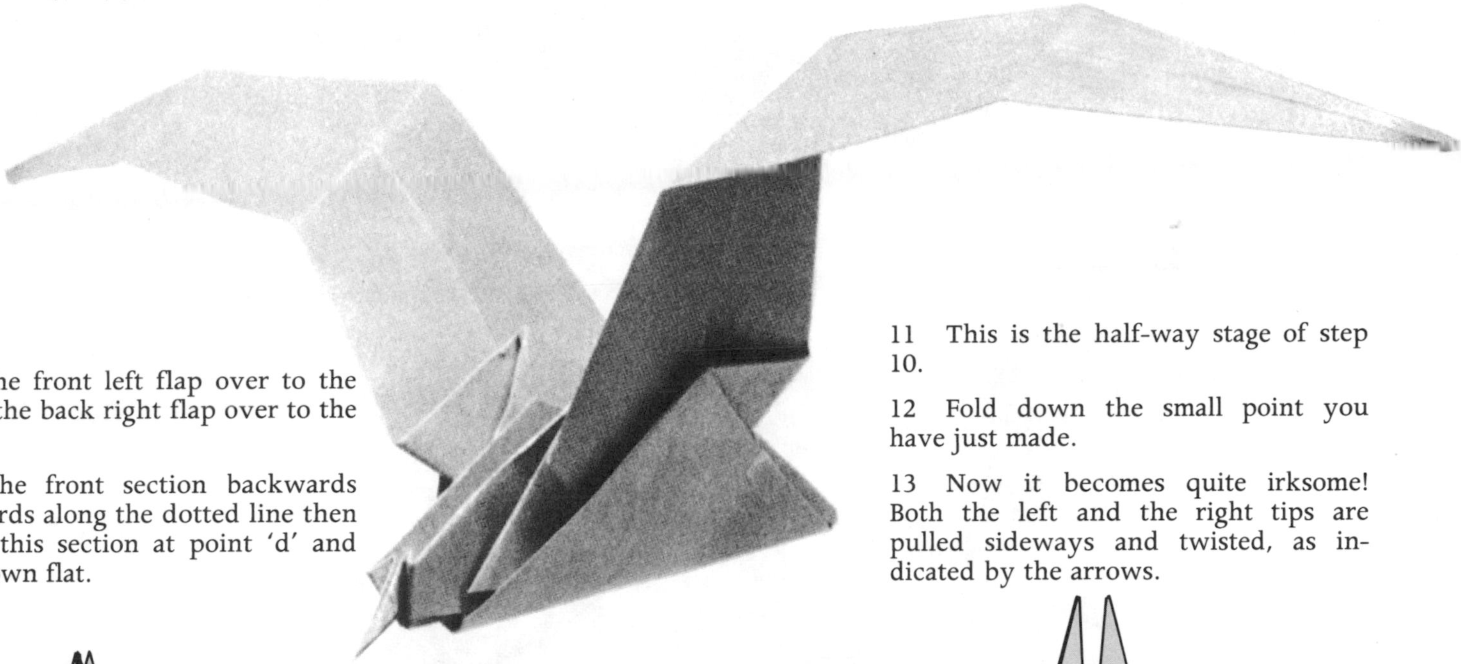

7 Fold the front left flap over to the right and the back right flap over to the left.

8 Fold the front section backwards and forwards along the dotted line then open out this section at point 'd' and press it down flat.

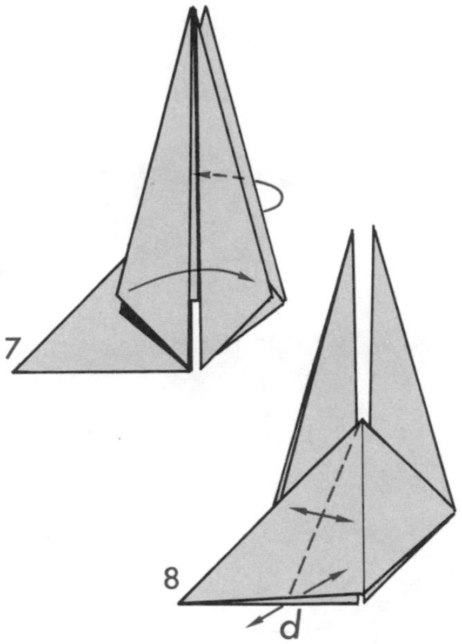

9 This diagram should make step 8 clearer.

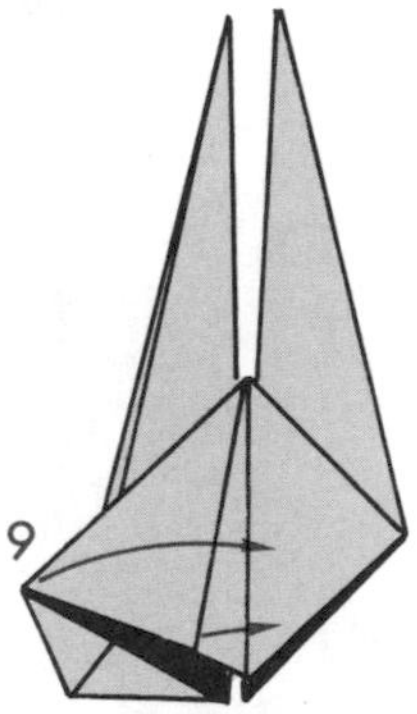

10 Make good creases along all the dotted lines and pull the bottom point up and press it down flat.

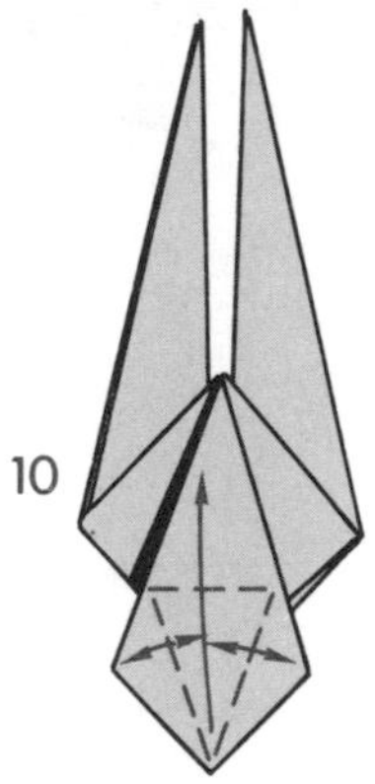

11 This is the half-way stage of step 10.

12 Fold down the small point you have just made.

13 Now it becomes quite irksome! Both the left and the right tips are pulled sideways and twisted, as indicated by the arrows.

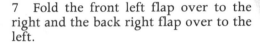

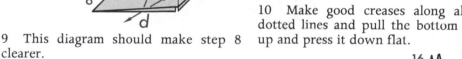

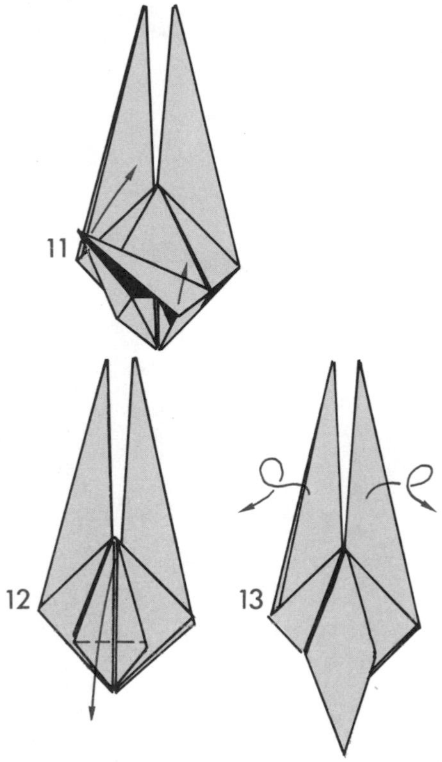

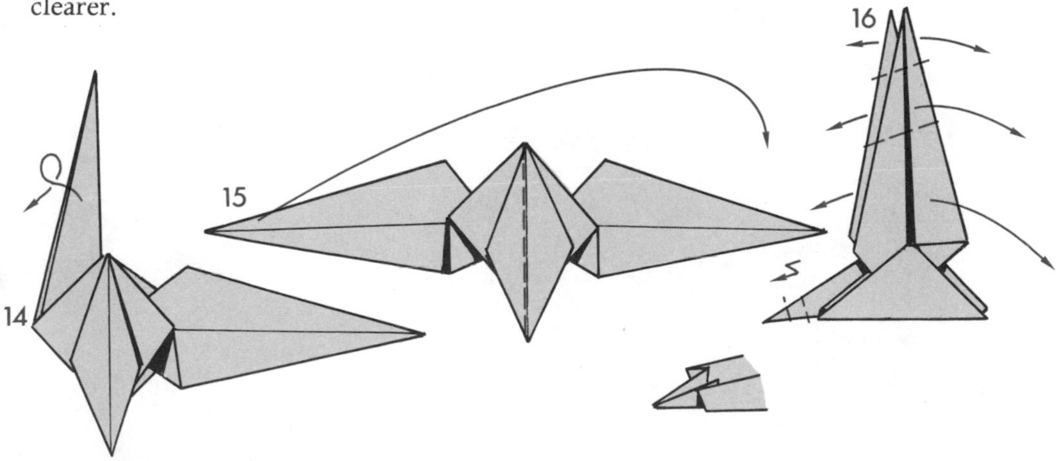

14 This drawing may make it clearer. Having completed this step, the model should look like the following diagrams.

15 Fold the model in half along the dotted line.

16 Open out both wings by folding along the dotted lines in the direction of the arrows. Fold the lefthand point once inwards and once outwards as the thunderbolt arrow describes to make the head. The detailed diagram makes it somewhat clearer.

The Wild Geese are very similar to Seagulls to make – although in reality the two are vastly different.

WILD GEESE

Wild geese flying overhead in V formation are a sure sign of the changing seasons. Our Wild Geese are made in a similar way to the Seagull, from a triangle of paper, though of course they look quite different. Geese have had many roles over the years – the Romans used them as watch-dogs, some farmers use them to mow the grass and the French make pâté out of them. They honk in a silly but amusing way on the ground, but in the sky their flight is breath-taking. Not only do they fly extremely well but they also make long-distance passages. These paper Wild Geese are versatile; for example you could make a beautiful mobile with four of these birds flying one behind the other and, if positioned over radiators, they will gently fly in the rising hot air.

1 Cut an equilateral triangle from a sheet of paper. To make the triangle draw a large circle with a pair of compasses and, keeping the radius constant, place the compass point anywhere on the circumference of the circle and mark the two points (a and b) where the compass bisects the circumference of the circle. Take a line from the pinprick on the circumference, through the center of the circle and mark point c. Join up points a, b and c and you have an equilateral triangle. Now cut out the triangle.

1

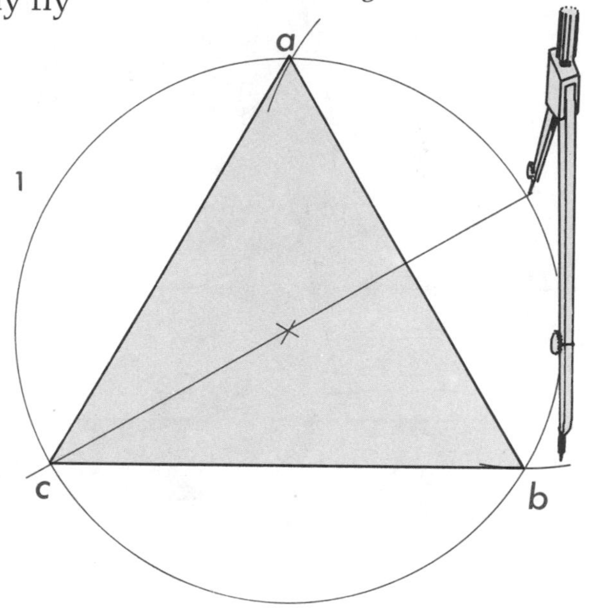

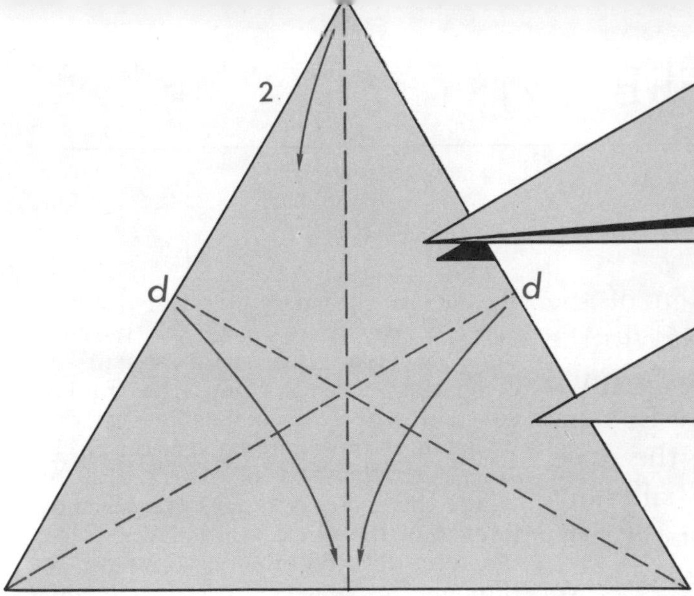

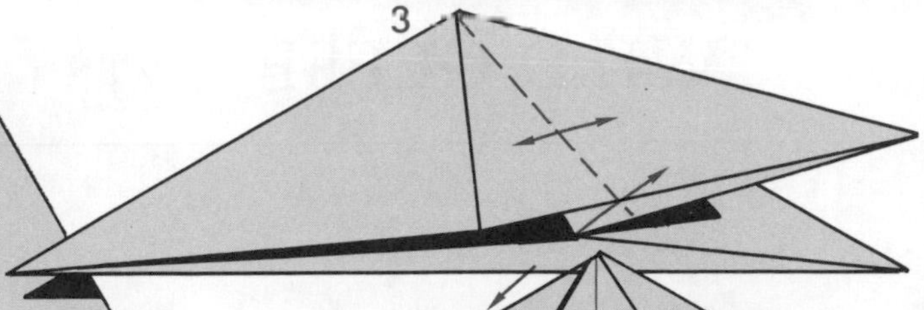

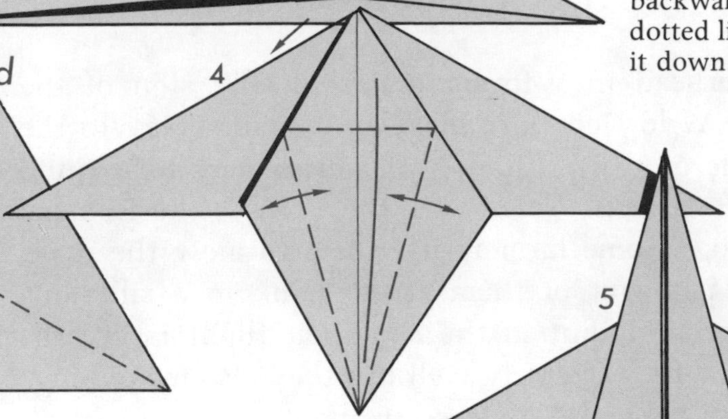

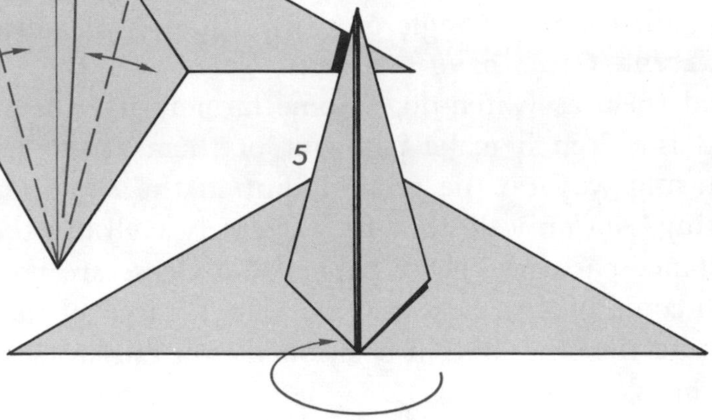

2 Fold along the dotted lines in-dicated. Fold the top point down, while at the same time pushing points d in to meet at e.

3 Fold the point which now stands up backwards and forwards along the dotted line. Open out this flap and press it down flat as indicated in Figs 3 and 4.

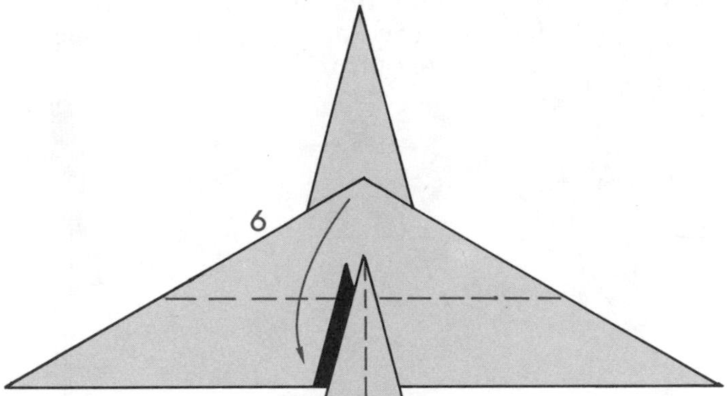

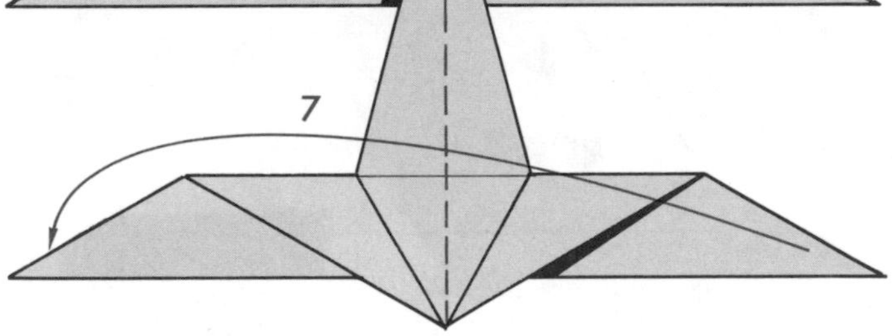

4 Make folds along the dotted lines and fold back the bottom point along the horizontal dotted line pushing the paper down flat along the folds just established.

5 Hopefully, your model now looks like this. Turn it over.

6 Fold the point nearest you down, along the dotted line.

7 Fold the whole model in half.

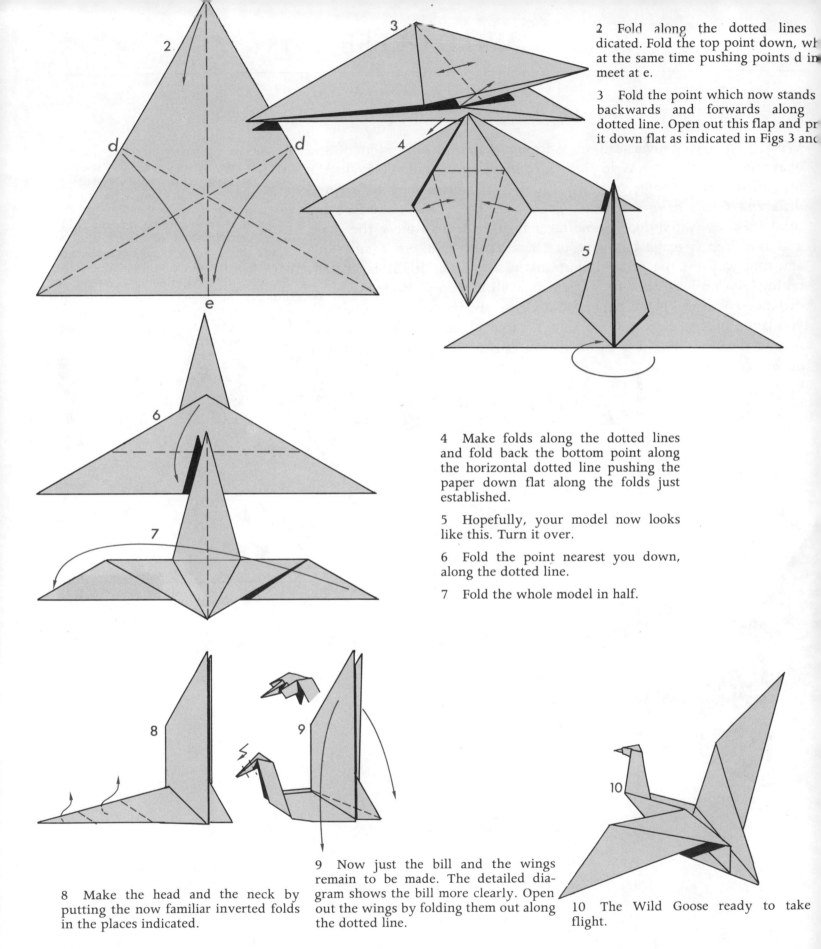

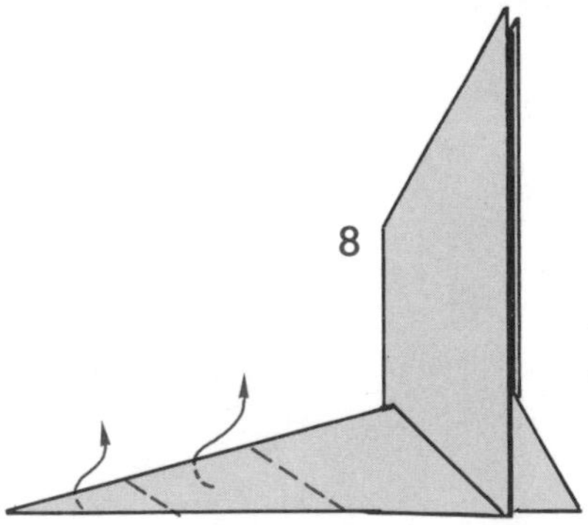

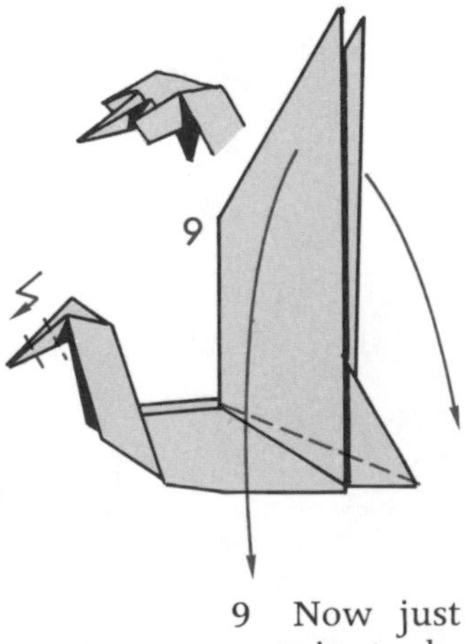

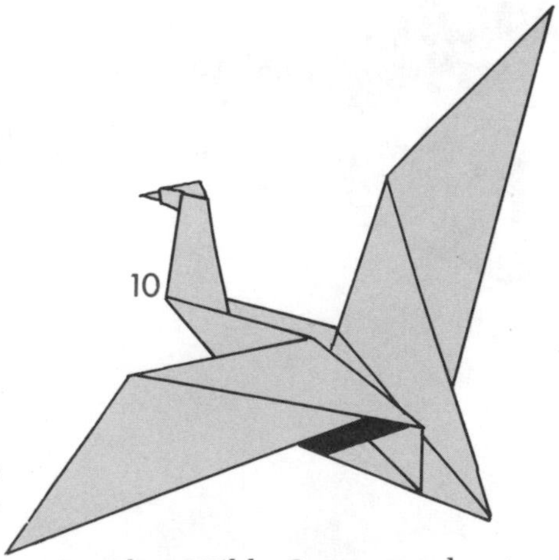

8 Make the head and the neck by putting the now familiar inverted folds in the places indicated.

9 Now just the bill and the wings remain to be made. The detailed diagram shows the bill more clearly. Open out the wings by folding them out along the dotted line.

10 The Wild Goose ready to take flight.

WILD DUCK

The Wild Goose and the Wild Duck have plenty in common. Both are wild, both fly and both are extremely good to eat. Only a minor alteration is necessary if you wish to transform a Wild Goose into a Wild Duck.

1 Follow the instructions for the Wild Goose as far as step 7. Now fold the wings down along the dotted line. Make the head and the neck with two inverted folds, following the arrows.

2 Fold the wings back up along the dotted line, as directed by the arrows.

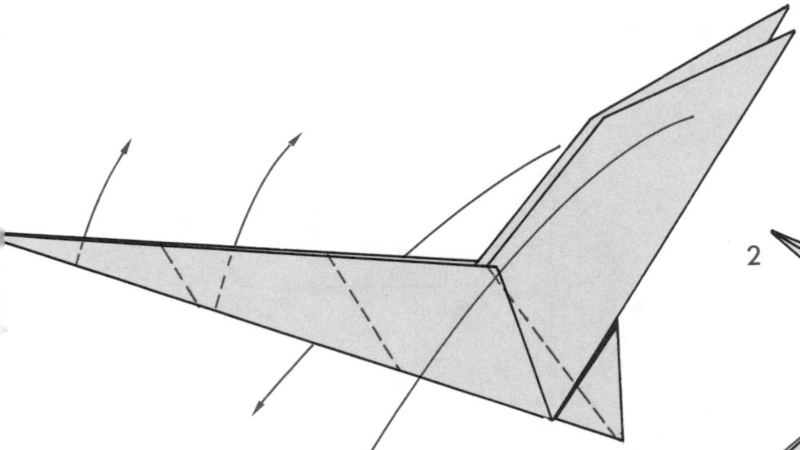

2

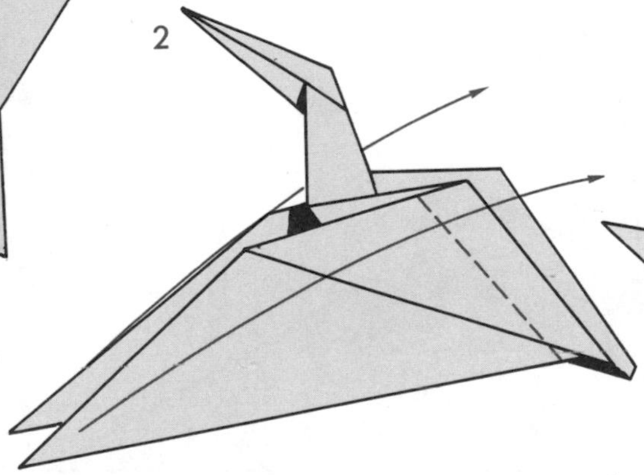

3 The duck wings are slightly different to those of the goose: fold the wings along the dotted line once more and tuck in the head with an inverted fold.

3

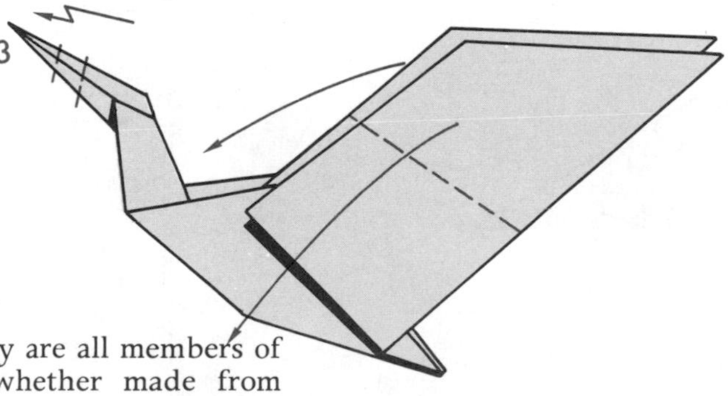

4 You can see they are all members of the same family whether made from feathers or paper.

4

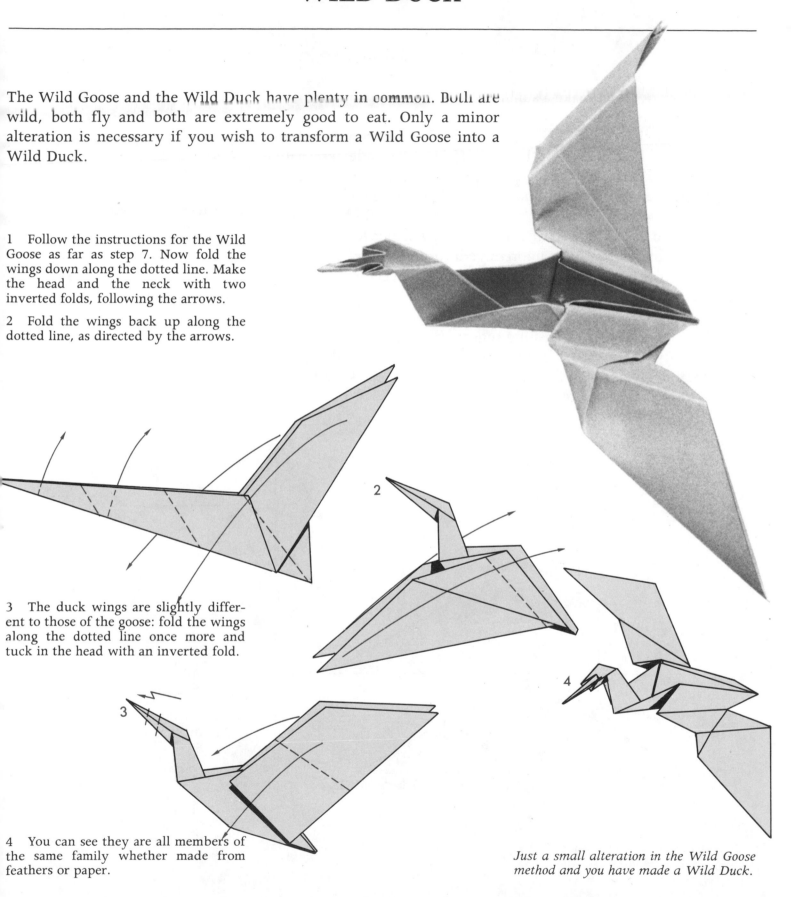

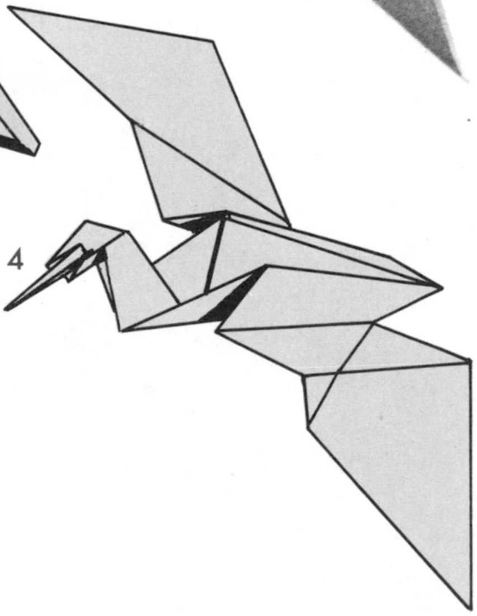

Just a small alteration in the Wild Goose method and you have made a Wild Duck.

SWALLOW

'One swallow does not make a summer' runs the well known proverb. There is another favorite saying about these quick-moving agile birds – that if they are flying high, the weather will stay fine, but if they are flying low, rain is on the way. There is a simple explanation for this: during fine weather the atmospheric pressure is high and the insects they feed on are found mostly at a high altitude whereas if the atmospheric pressure is low due to bad weather, they find food nearer the ground. In addition to their usefulness as weather forecasters, the swallows are among the most impressive birds in the sky. They spend most of their life on the wing, which means everything happens during flight, even sleeping. They settle briefly to lay eggs and hatch their young. The paper Swallow is not concerned with this but it imitates its namesake in its dashing flight.

You already know the initial assembly plan – steps 1 to 5 are folded in the same way as the Wild Geese. Then add the stocky body, the inset head and the characteristic forked tail.

1 Fold the center point at the back down away from you.

2 Fold the two sides in to meet down the center line.

3 Fold the top righthand flap over to the left.

4 Fold down the small tip of the front section, following the dotted line, and then fold the whole of this section back over to the right along the dotted line.

5 If you have succeeded in getting this far, repeat the last two steps and do the same to the lefthand flap.

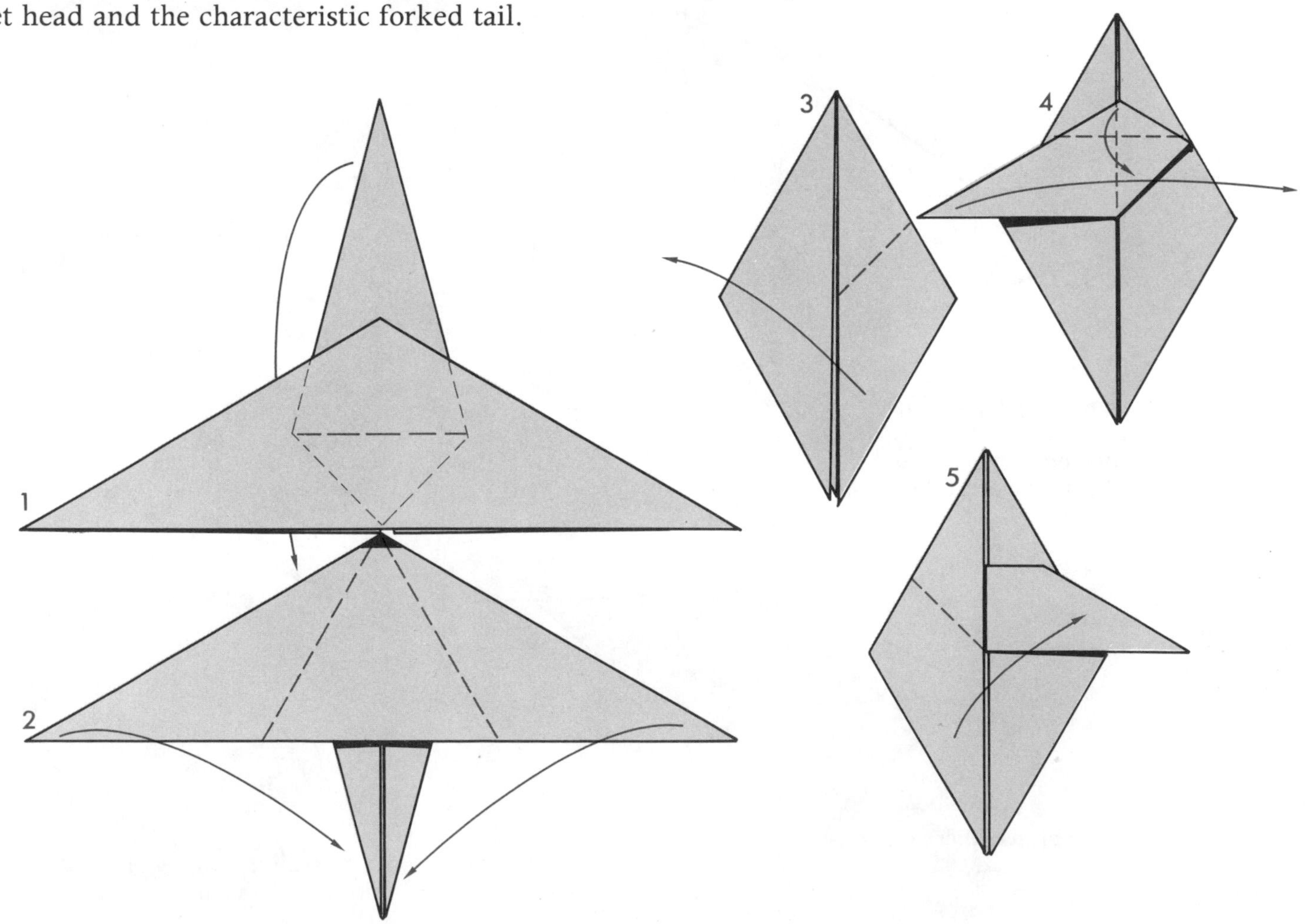

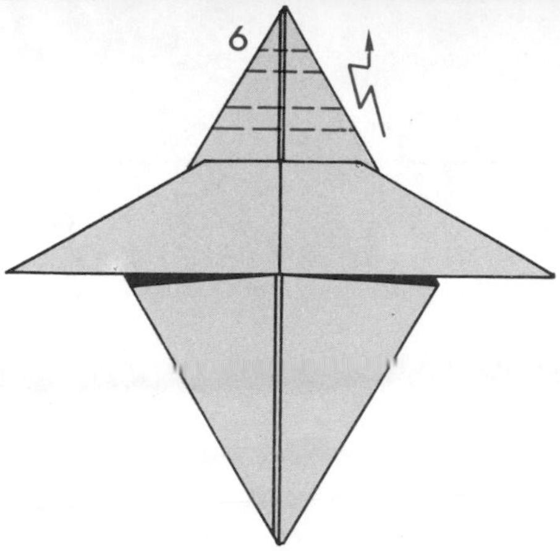

6 Now form the head and neck. Make fold along the four dotted lines in the direction indicated by the arrow and in the same proportions.

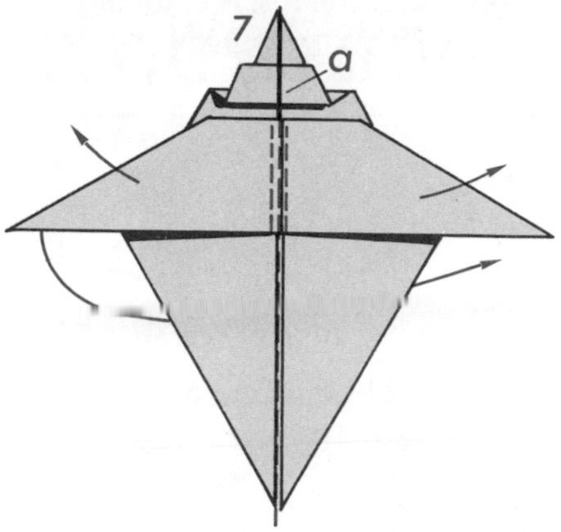

7 Fold the bird in half down the centre line away from you and fold the wings back up to lie flat. If your paper is too thick it may be torn but there is no need to be discouraged or to go right back to the beginning – the Swallow will not be spoilt.

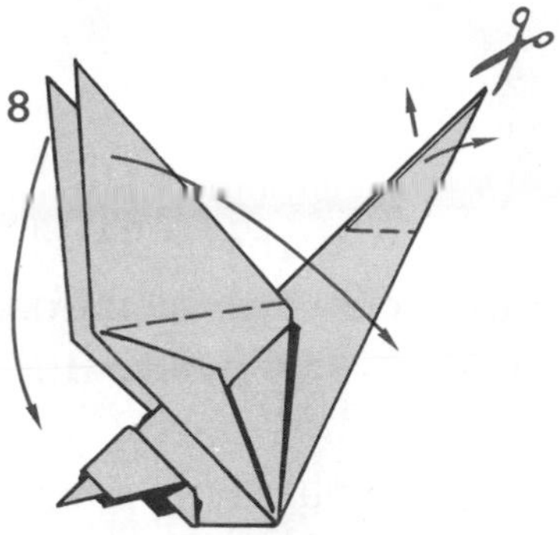

8 Fold the wings once more along the dotted line. Cut down the center of the tail section and fold each side out to make the fork as directed by the arrows.

Although one swallow does not make a summer, this paper bird will make you think of blue skies and fine weather . . .

WHITE DOVE

Simplicity is the main characteristic of these members of the dove family – only two main folds are made in a square piece of paper. Man uses doves for widely differing purposes – on the one hand the bird is a symbol of peace; on the other, man tries to make money with racing pigeons by organizing competitive flights. These birds are put in boxes or baskets and transported long distances before being set free to return home as quickly as possible. Their homing instinct is remarkable. Doves and pigeons have become something of a nuisance in the cities and have been nicknamed 'flying rats' because they spread disease. No such problem with this simple paper White Dove – it flies well too.

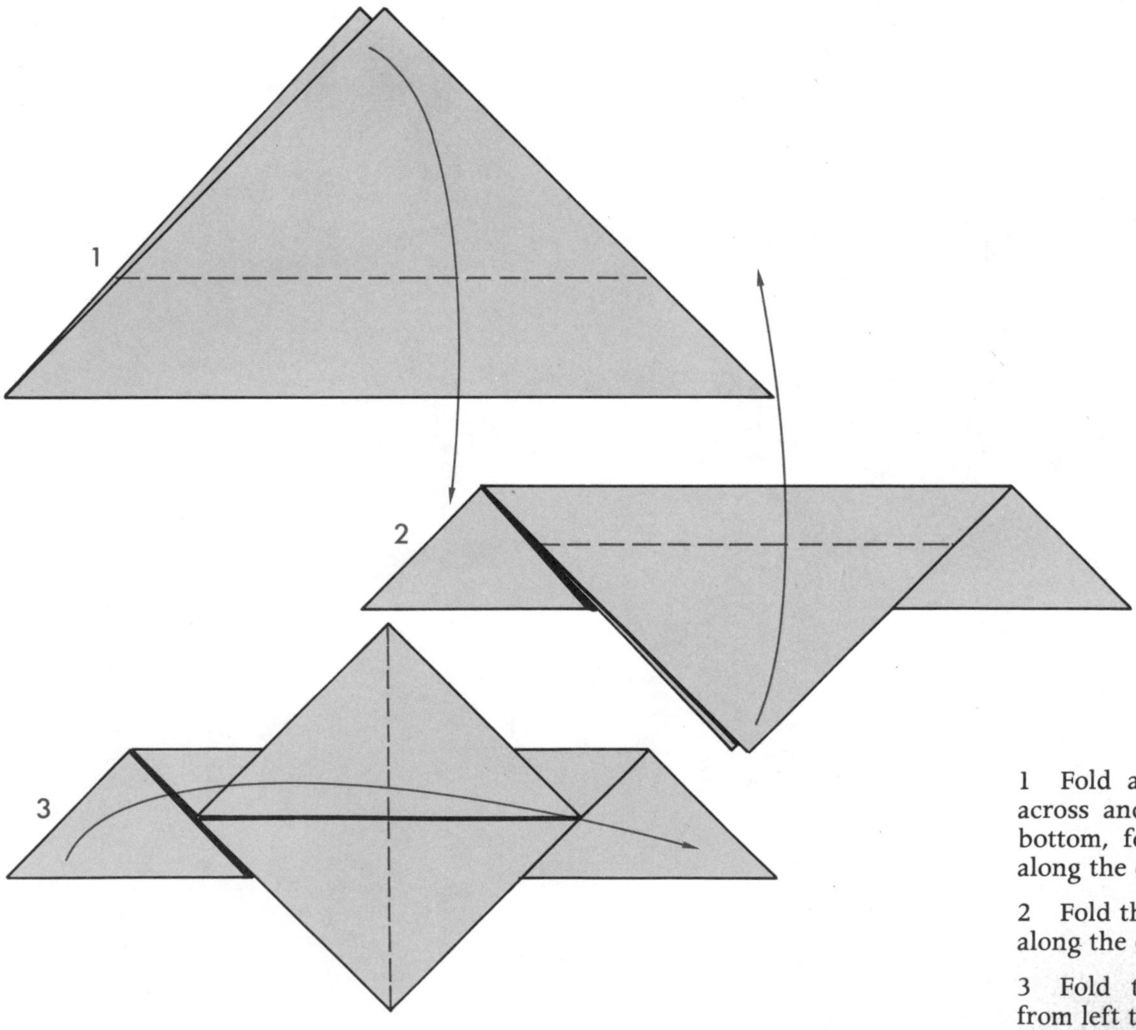

1 Fold a square of paper diagonally across and then, with the fold at the bottom, fold the two top edges down along the dotted line.

2 Fold the top flap only back up again along the dotted line.

3 Fold the complete model in half from left to right along the dotted line.

4 To shape the head, make an inverted fold and pull the point under as shown.

5 Now fold the wings up on both sides along the dotted line.

6 Bend the wing tips outwards along the dotted line.

7 The completed White Dove.

4
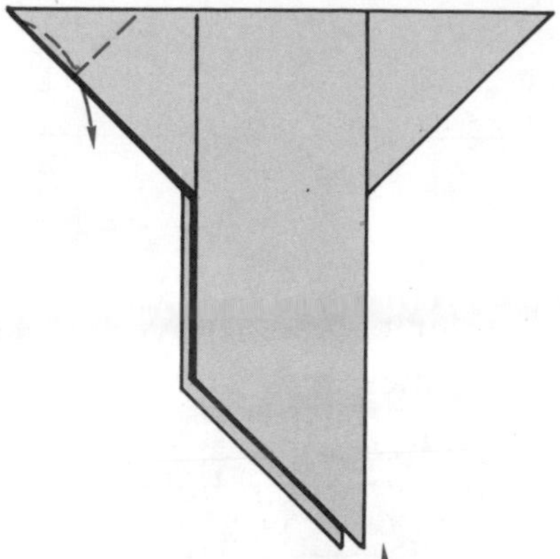

5
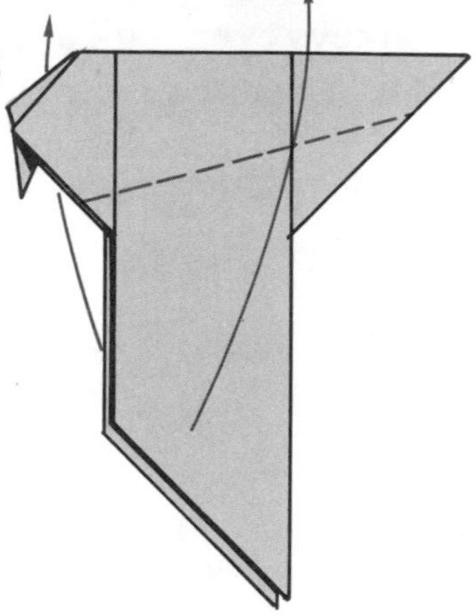

6
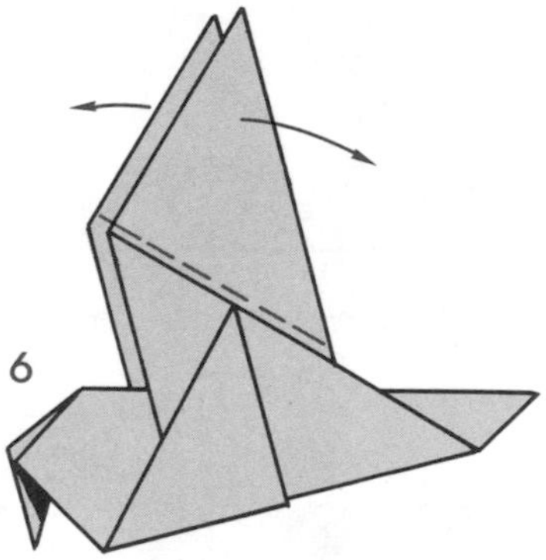

7
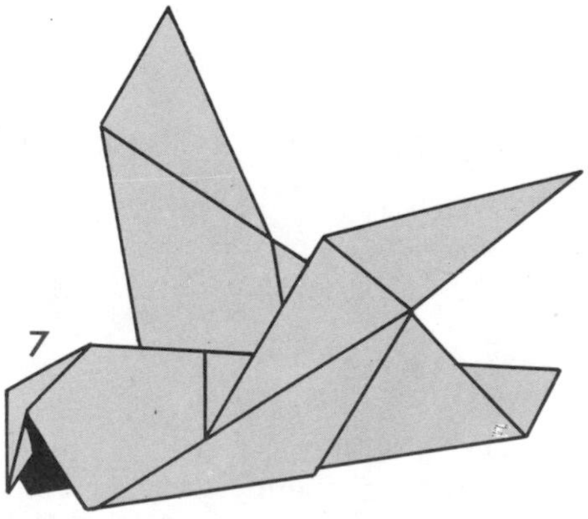

The White Dove is a symbol of peace

CARRIER PIGEON

Carrier pigeons played an important and heroic role in wartime. With vital messages and information placed in small capsules attached to their legs, they flew across the front lines in the teeth of the guns to return to their home bases. Many animals have characteristics that humans can relate to – dogs can offer a paw, parrots can talk, monkeys even look a little like people and carrier pigeons can play the rôles of express couriers. The carrier pigeon is a flying racing machine with built-in radar and a remarkable sense of direction – it always reaches its destination. Our paper Carrier Pigeon flies quickly; it will be difficult to time this bird because it's gone in a flash.

1 Start making the Carrier Pigeon in the same way as the White Dove, by folding a square sheet of paper in half diagonally and then folding the top corner down along the dotted line.

2 Fold this in half as shown by the arrow.

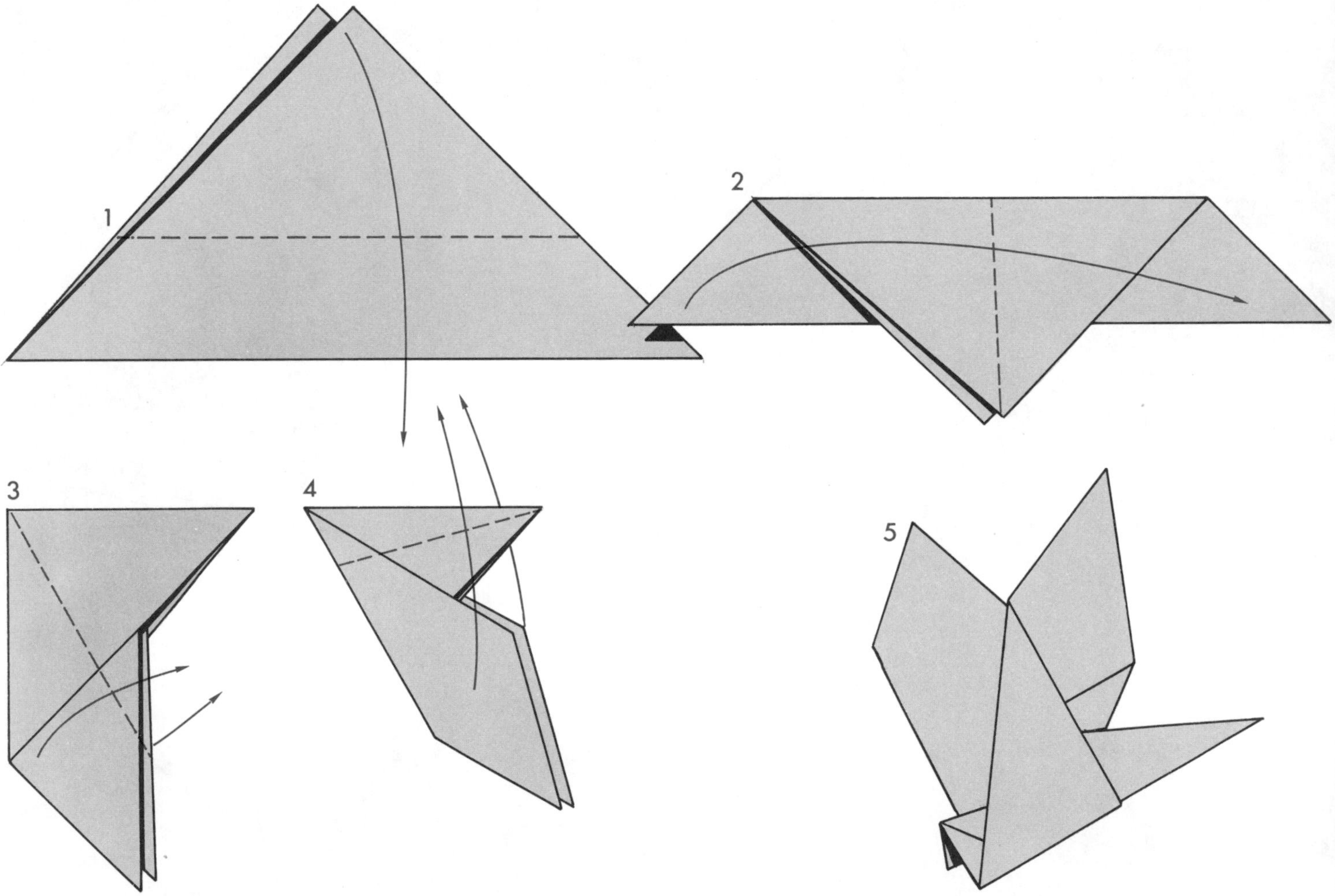

3 The sections which will form the wings are folded to the right along the dotted line, one to either side.

4 Fold both wings upwards, following the dotted line.

5 And now, fly away! A light throw is all that is necessary.

The paper Carrier Pigeon always gets there in the end . . .

In real life the Dragonfly's flight bears a resemblance to a helicopter but the paper replica cannot begin to match the flying ability of the original insect.

INSECTS

Insects are fascinating little creatures and yet many people dislike them. They fly in a completely different way to birds; they have wings of course but the flying motions are not like those of birds. For example, a dragonfly can fly up and down while keeping its body in a horizontal position, just like a helicopter, and still remain airborne. To make paper insects there are additional requirements: a steady hand, a magnifying glass and tweezers – especially if you intend to make them life-size. Their flight performance cannot be compared to that of the airplanes; insects are less powerful than airplanes and anyway the flying capability of an insect is not its most important characteristic. More important is their delicate shape and beauty. You will find that the Fly is a great success if you make it out of a cigarette paper. People envy birds their ability to fly, forgetting that in the insect world there are many creatures whose flying abilities are far superior to birds. When folding these insects be very patient and you will succeed eventually. Perhaps, as a result of carefully making these insects, you will think twice before thoughtlessly destroying live ones.

DRAGONFLY

The dragonfly is a beautiful insect. It is a timeless summer pleasure to lie on the bank of a river chewing a blade of grass and watching a dragonfly hovering over the water. The dragonfly, with its wonderful green, blue and indigo coloring, is on the lookout for its prey.

Our paper Dragonfly is one of the most attractive insects. It is difficult to fold but that shouldn't deter anyone who has got this far. It is very tempting to forge ahead because the result is so lifelike. It flies reasonably well but its performance will be improved if you don't cut the wings in the final stage. This however begs the question of whether or not it is still a Dragonfly. Start off with the Basic Crane (page 90).

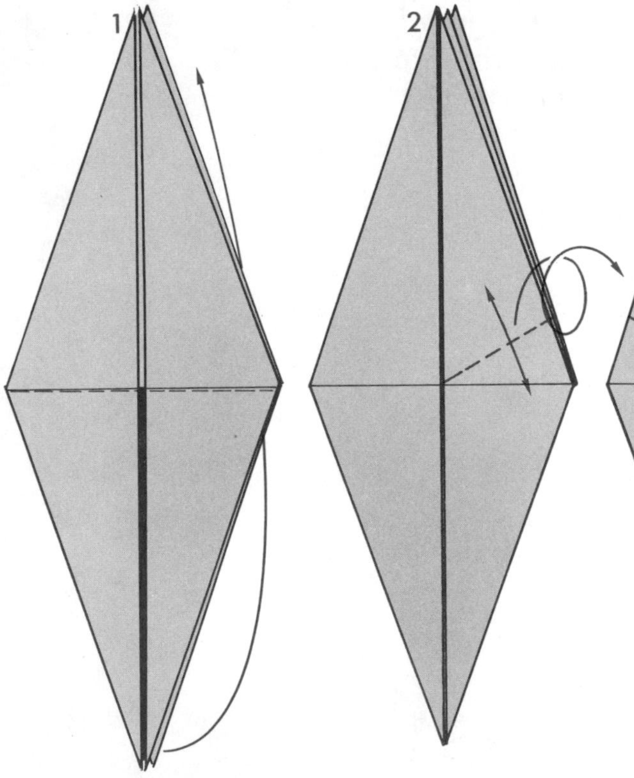

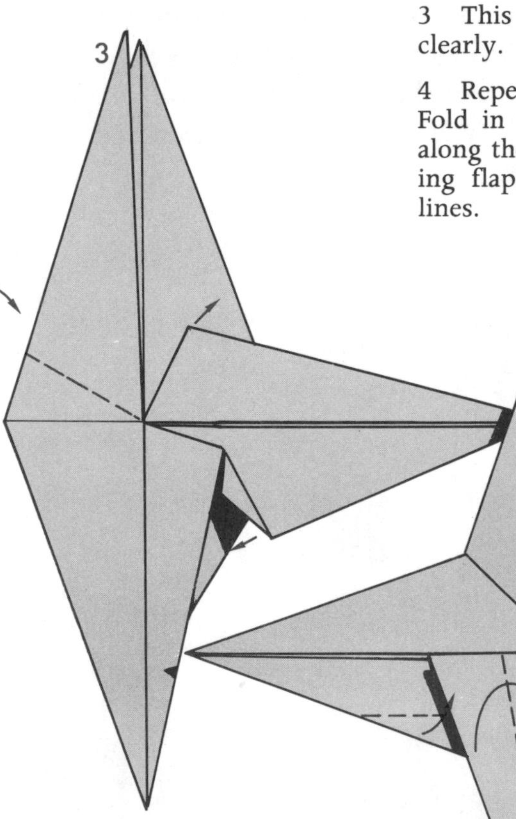

3 This diagram illustrates step 2 more clearly.

4 Repeat step 2 with the lefthand side. Fold in the sides of the bottom point, along the dotted lines. Press the resulting flaps down flat along the dotted lines.

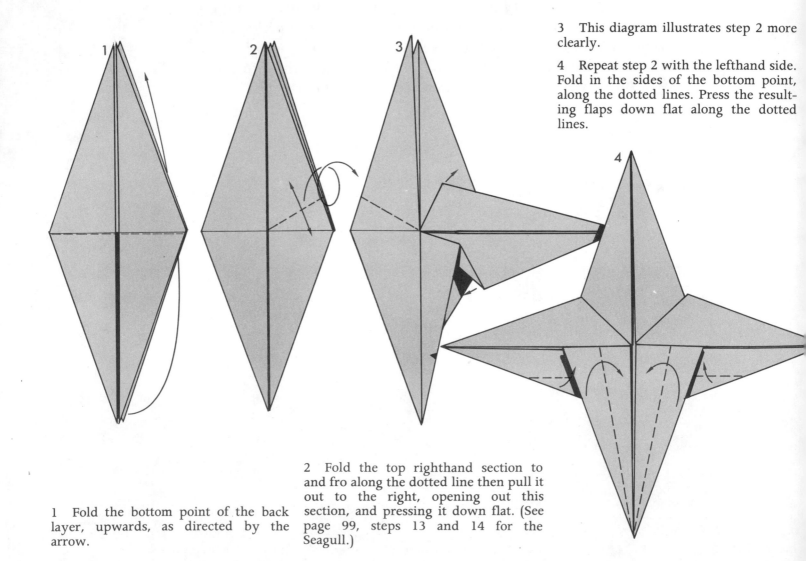

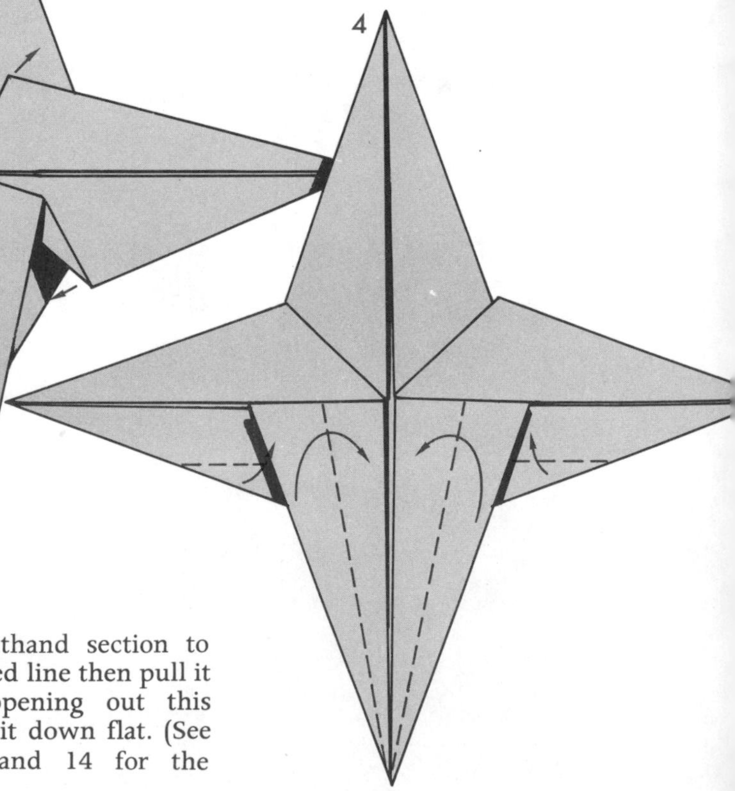

1 Fold the bottom point of the back layer, upwards, as directed by the arrow.

2 Fold the top righthand section to and fro along the dotted line then pull it out to the right, opening out this section, and pressing it down flat. (See page 99, steps 13 and 14 for the Seagull.)

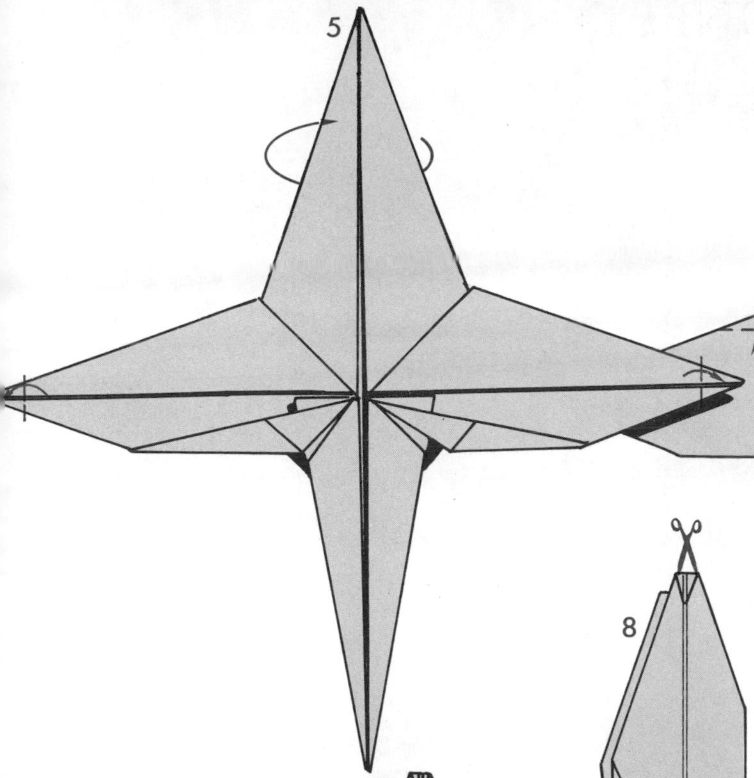

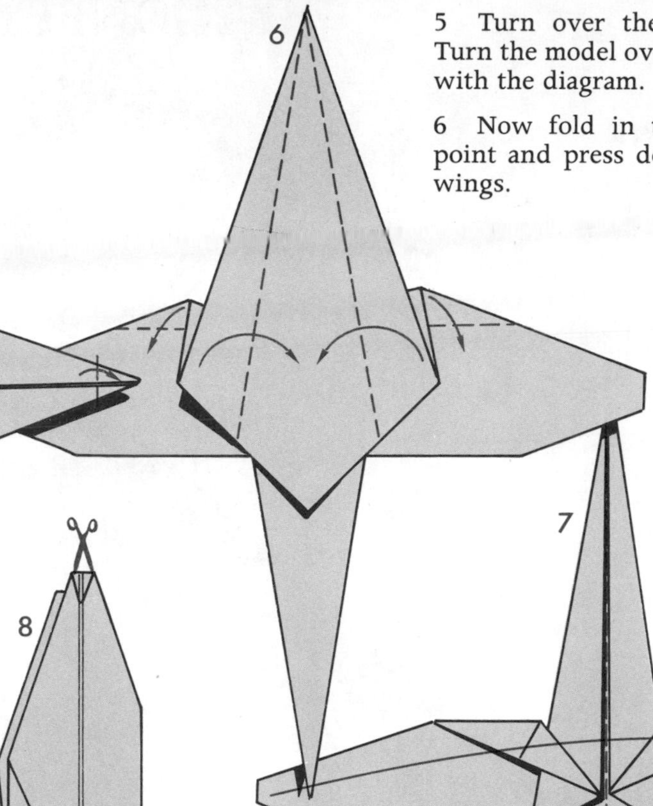

5 Turn over the tips of the wings. Turn the model over and compare yours with the diagram.

6 Now fold in the sides of the top point and press down the flaps on the wings.

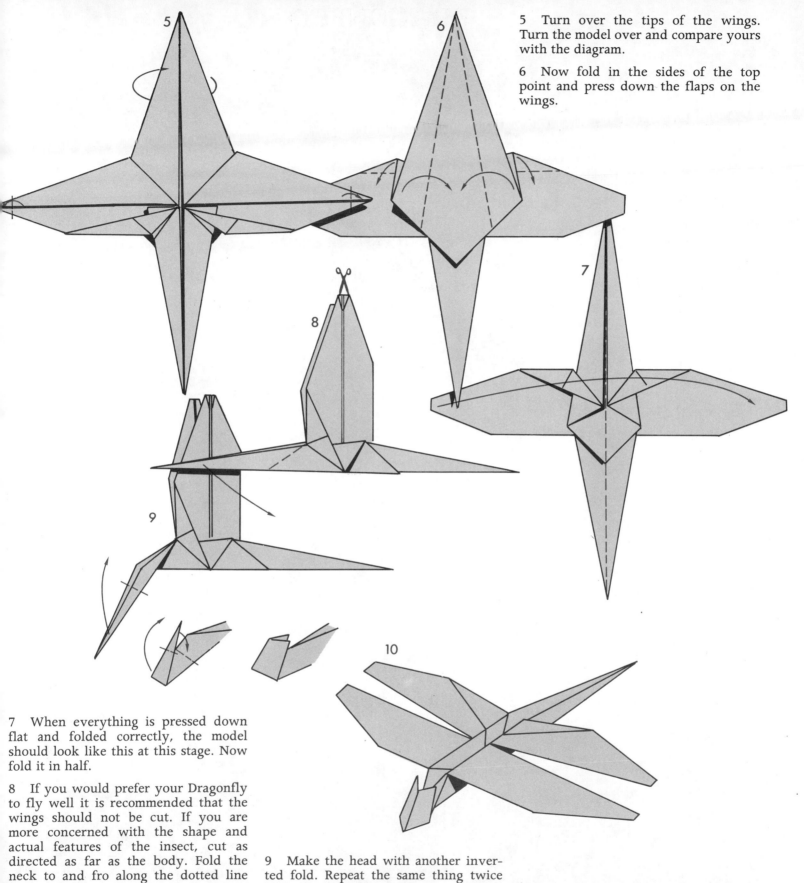

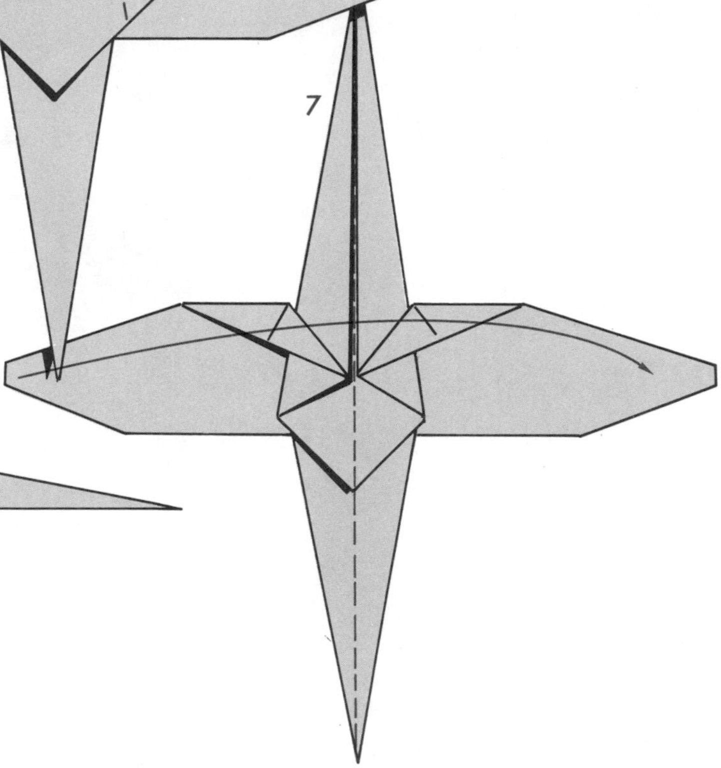

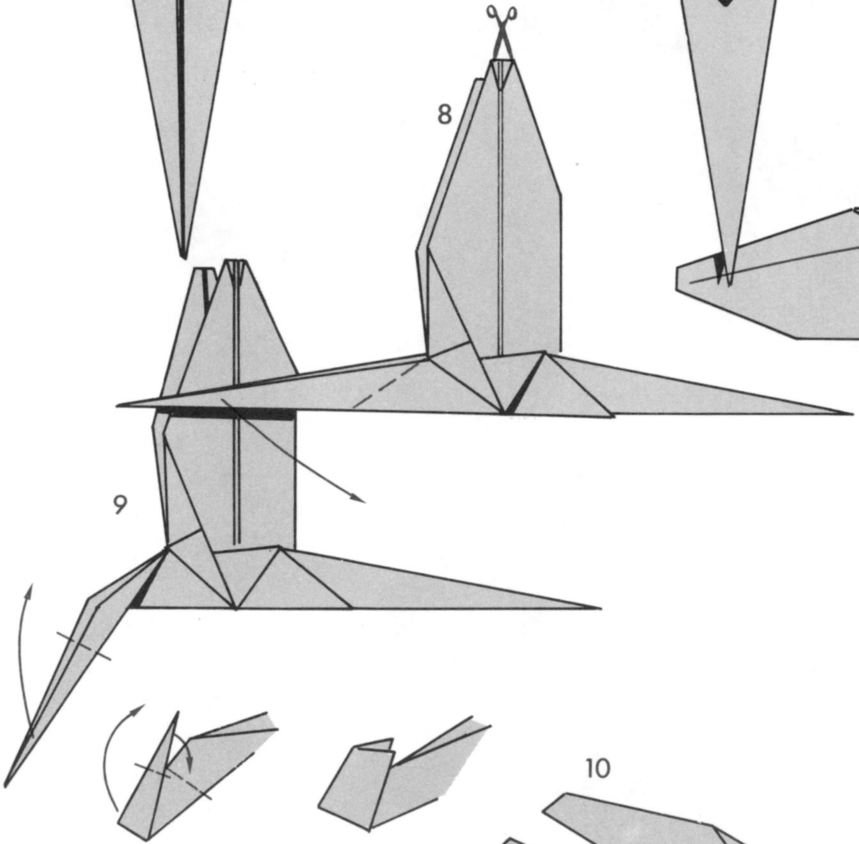

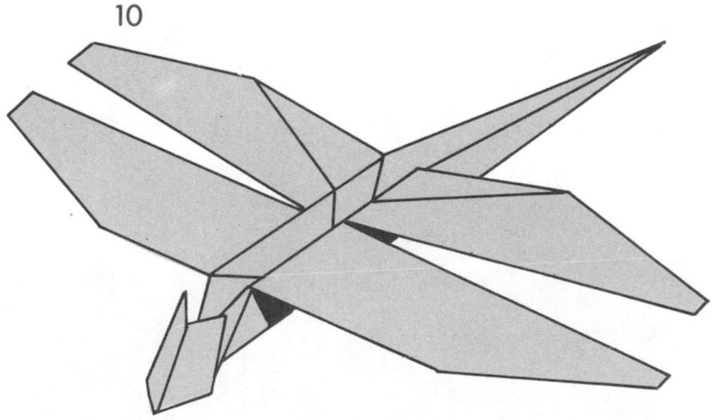

7 When everything is pressed down flat and folded correctly, the model should look like this at this stage. Now fold it in half.

8 If you would prefer your Dragonfly to fly well it is recommended that the wings should not be cut. If you are more concerned with the shape and actual features of the insect, cut as directed as far as the body. Fold the neck to and fro along the dotted line and push the whole thing down with an inverted fold.

9 Make the head with another inverted fold. Repeat the same thing twice along the dotted line and now you have the Dragonfly to add to your collection.

10 The finished Dragonfly ready to hover over the water . . .

Many people dislike moths as they can be a nuisance, but this paper one is charming . . .

MOTH

Some people are not particularly fond of moths, especially when they make uninvited visits to their wardrobes. Quite apart from that they seem to flutter rather than really fly. At night, moths are attracted to bright lights and the frenzied fluttering of a moth round the bedside lamp can be disturbing. However, moths are beautiful insects, often with attractive markings, and our paper Moth certainly won't eat holes in your best suit.

1 Take a sheet of paper 30 × 30cm (12 × 12in) and make folds along both diagonals and then another through the intersection as shown in the diagram. Fold the sheet in half while tucking in the sides at the same time.

2 Make folds along all the dotted lines and bring the two points together by pinching the corners together along the folds and pressing them down flat towards the center.

3 This diagram illustrates the previous step more clearly. It is quite complicated.

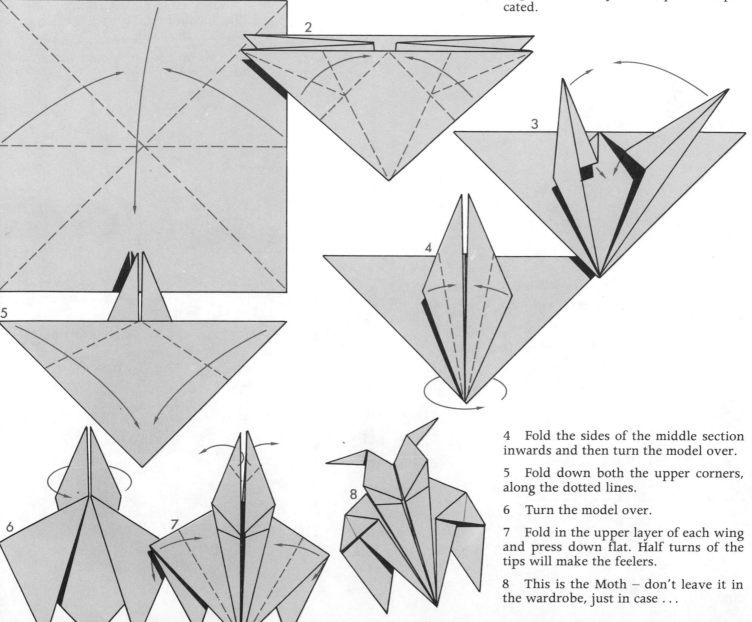

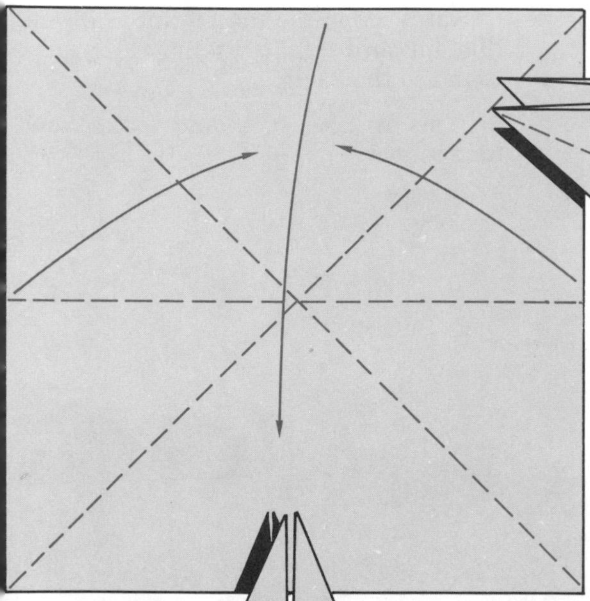

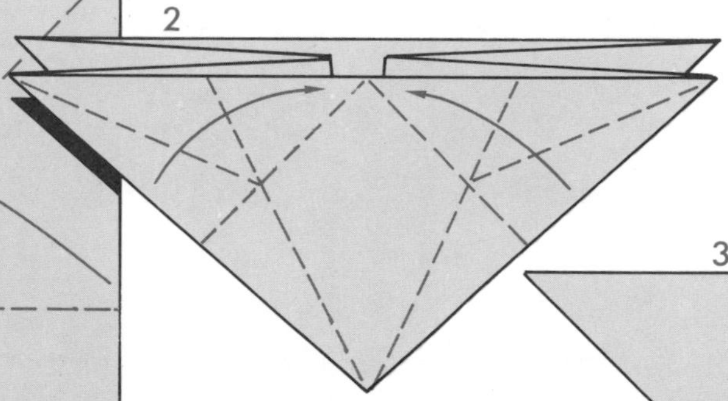

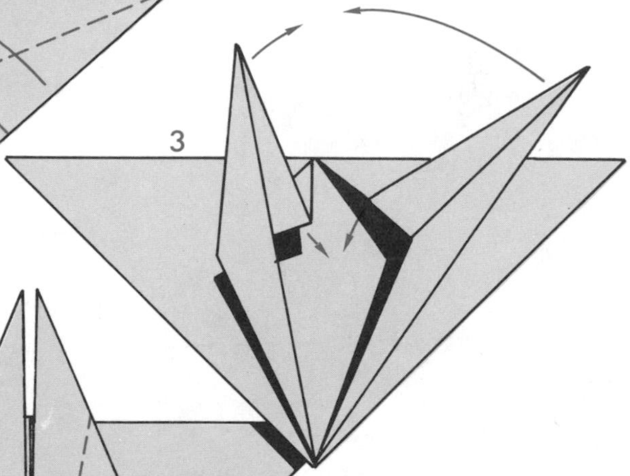

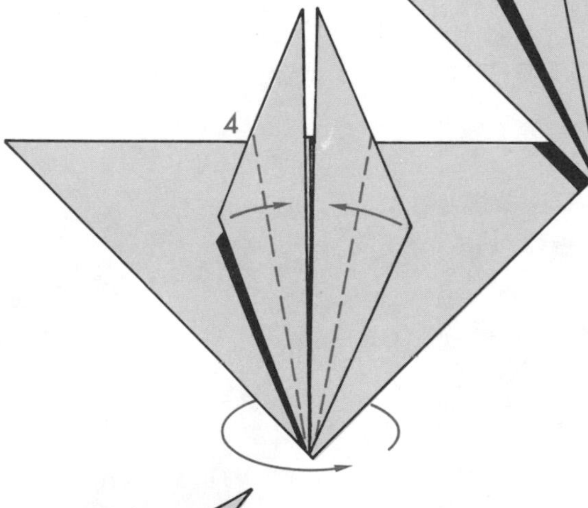

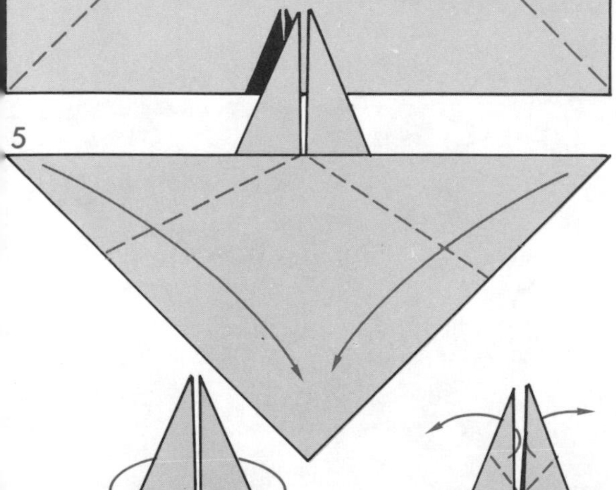

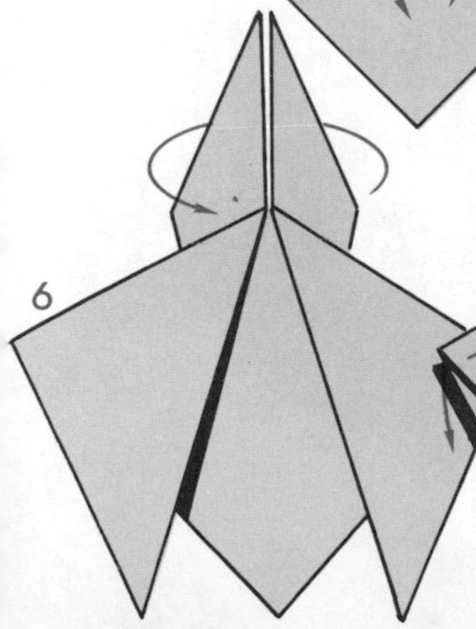

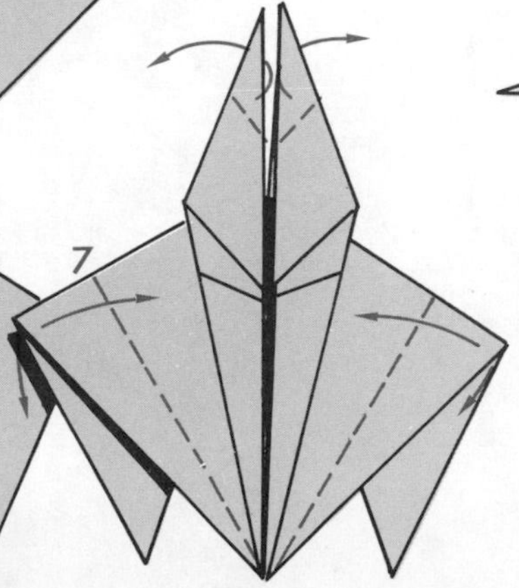

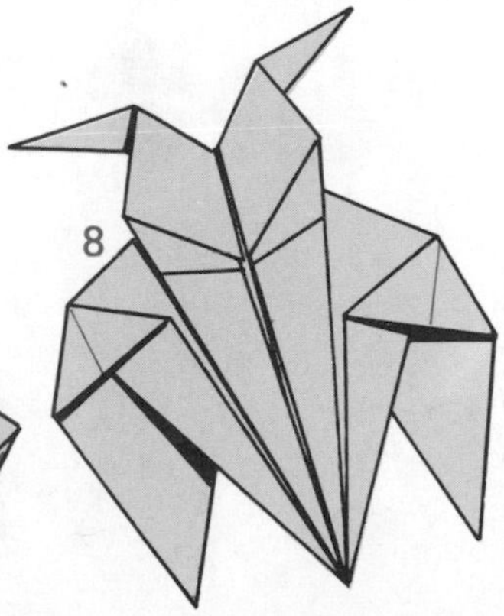

4 Fold the sides of the middle section inwards and then turn the model over.

5 Fold down both the upper corners, along the dotted lines.

6 Turn the model over.

7 Fold in the upper layer of each wing and press down flat. Half turns of the tips will make the feelers.

8 This is the Moth – don't leave it in the wardrobe, just in case . . .

FLIES

These paper flies are much more acceptable than the real thing. While envying their ability to fly, people do everything they can to destroy flies, both by using insecticide aerosol sprays and by simply swatting them with a rolled up newspaper. Flies can succeed in getting on your nerves on hot summer days, prevent you from sleeping at night, contaminate food and spread disease – generally not easily tolerated at all.

For the best results make these harmless Flies out of cigarette papers producing tiny life-like models which should fly very well. To start with it is best to experiment with a larger sheet of paper to perfect the folding method.

1 Take a sheet of paper 20 × 20cm (8 × 8in) and make folds along both diagonals. Fold it in half along one diagonal.

2 Fold up the two bottom corners along the dotted lines.

3 Fold down the two top corners of the upper layer along the dotted lines.

4 Make folds along all dotted lines. Following the direction of the arrows, fold the top section backwards and forwards along the dotted line and pull this forward while folding the sides round to the back.

5 This is how it should look. Now turn it over.

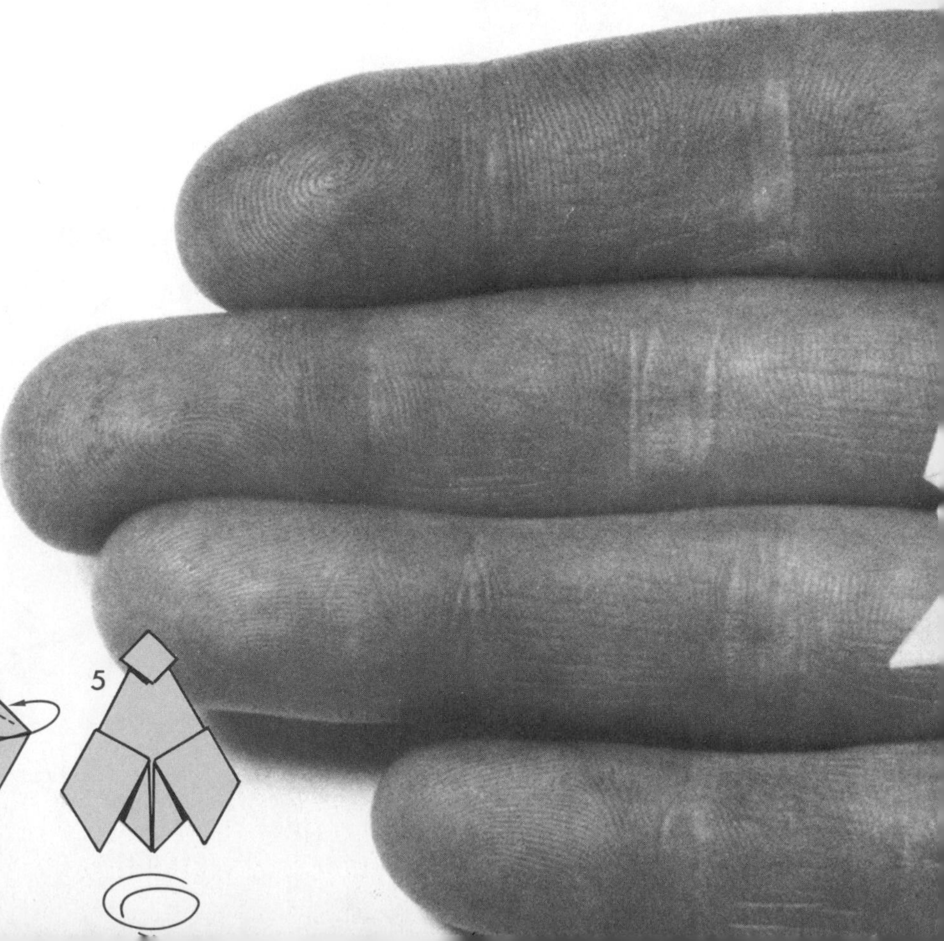

Flies will not bother you as long as they are made of paper . . .

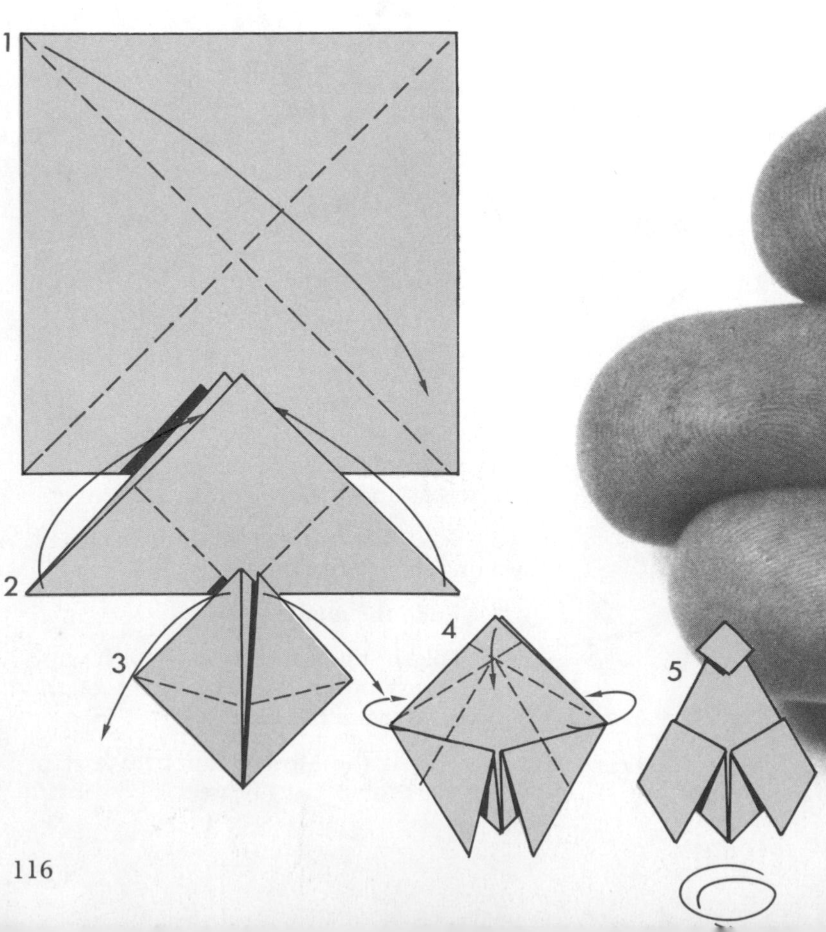

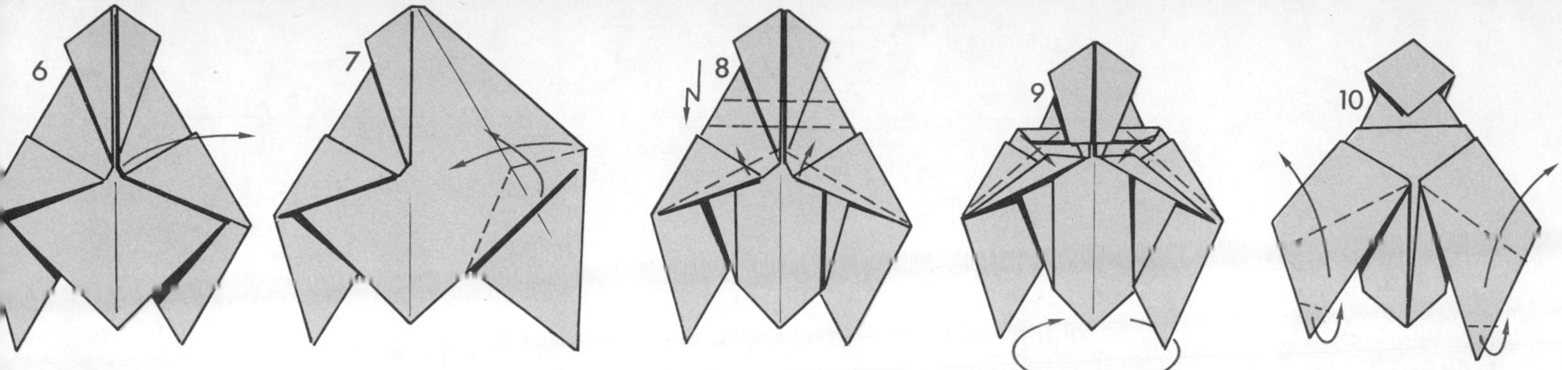

6 Open out one wing, following the arrow.

7 Fold the wing backwards and forwards along the dotted line. Push the fold upwards, press it down flat and repeat the same with the other wing.

8 This is how the model should look. Fold up the inner edges of the wings along the dotted lines and make the neck with a zigzag fold known as the thunderbolt.

9 Fold in the outer edge of the wings as directed by the arrows, then turn the model over.

10 Fold the bottom point of the wings upwards and then bend the wing tips over.

11 That was a good practice run. Now take a cigarette paper and start again from the beginning . . .

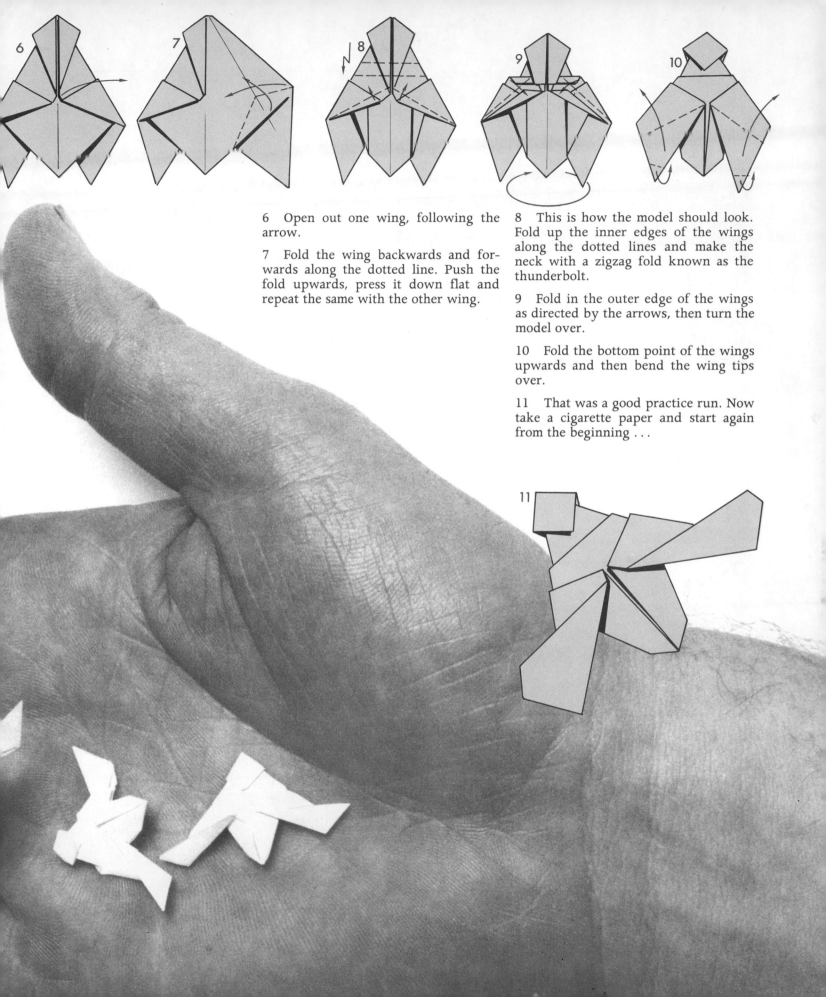

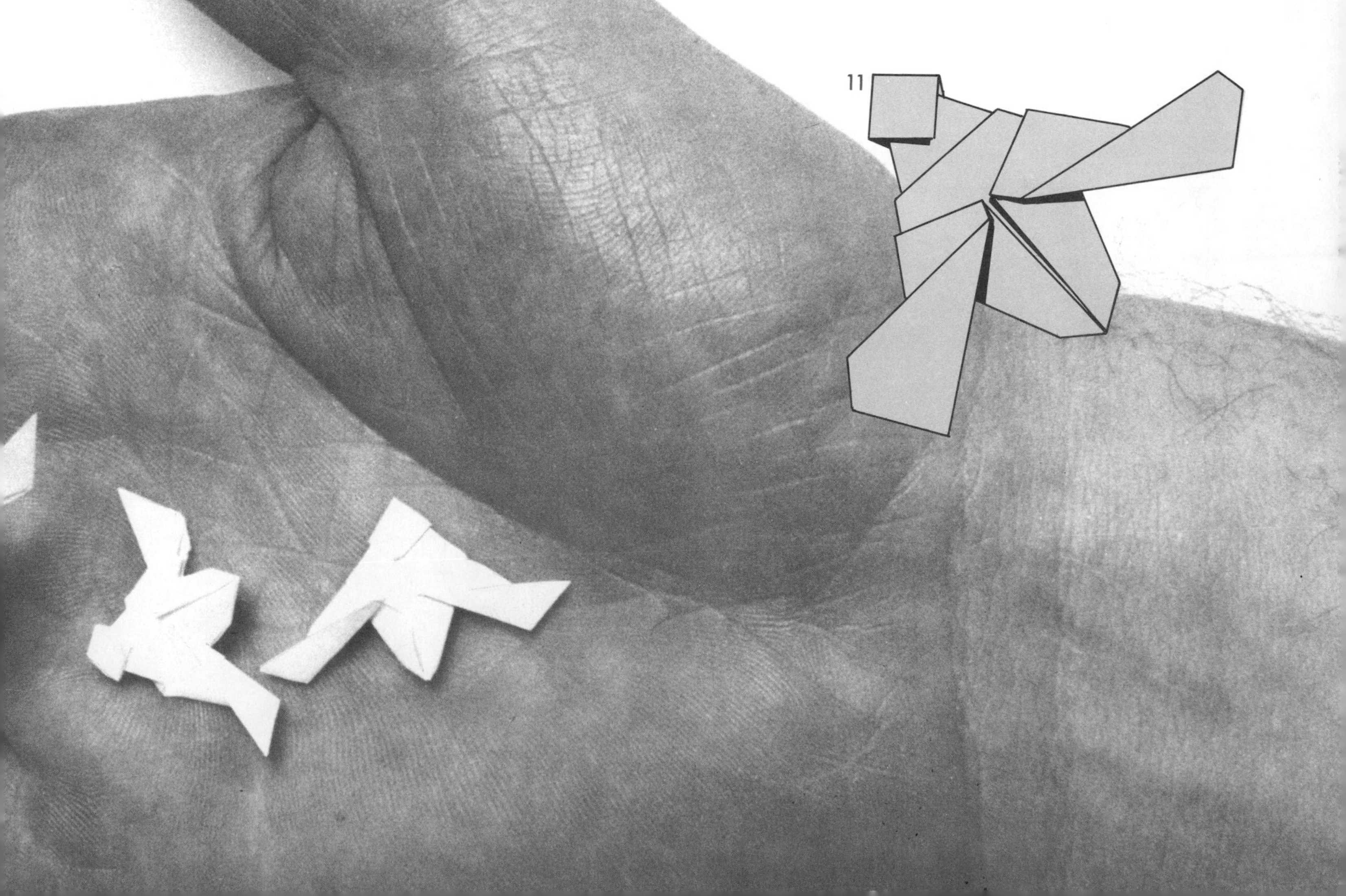

BUTTERFLY

While moths are not always popular and flies are regarded with distaste, butterflies are considered beautiful and romantic. Is it because they flutter to and fro amongst the flowers and remind us of delightful summer days? Lightly flitting around in a carefree way, the butterfly's life is soon over. As the saying goes, 'The butterfly counts not months but moments and has time enough'. It has a fascinating life cycle; first an egg, then a caterpillar, after that a cocoon and, at last, the full glory of the butterfly emerges with only a short time to live. At one time butterflies were frequently caught and pinned to boards in glass display cases, but nowadays people realise that they are best viewed in the wild. You can always make a paper replica at home; it doesn't flutter but otherwise it's a perfect paper copy.

1 Take a sheet of paper 20 × 20cm (8 × 8in) and fold it in half diagonally.

2 Fold in half diagonally again.

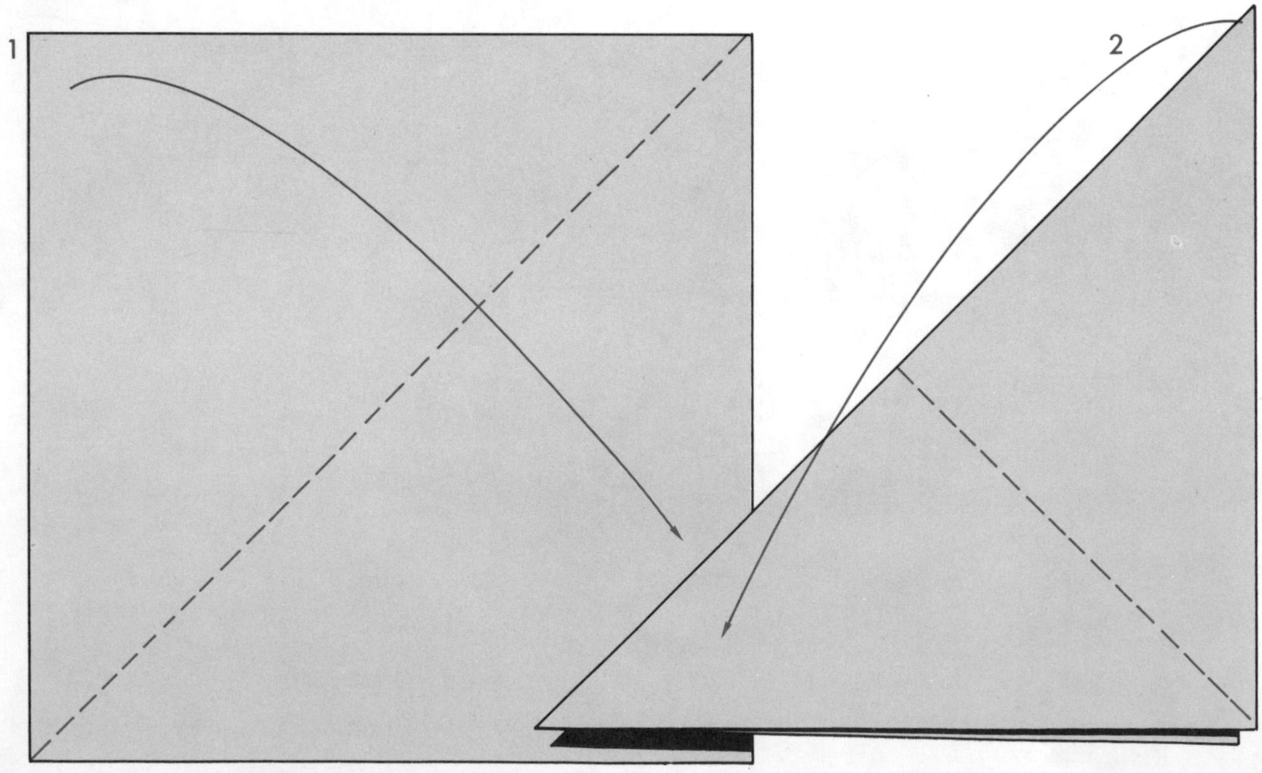

3 Fold the two lefthand corners over to the right – one corner in front, the other behind.

4 This diagram illustrates the result of the previous step.

5 Now fold both the outside flaps back, along the dotted line, one to either side.

6 Cut the outside edge of the righthand triangle, as indicated.

3
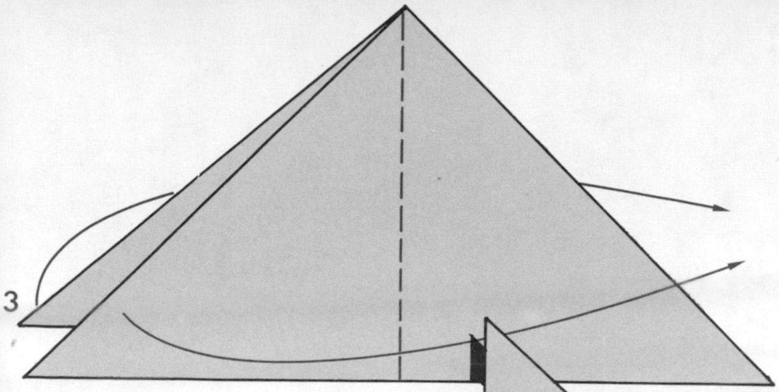

4
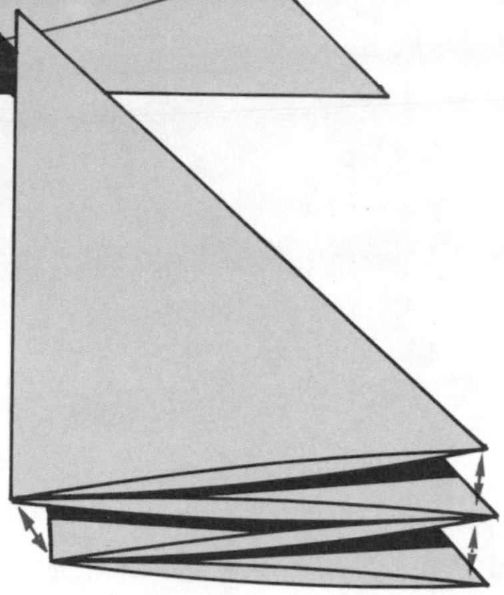

5
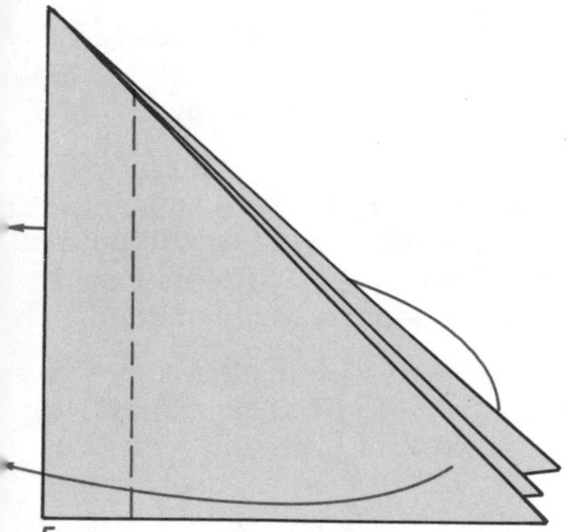

6
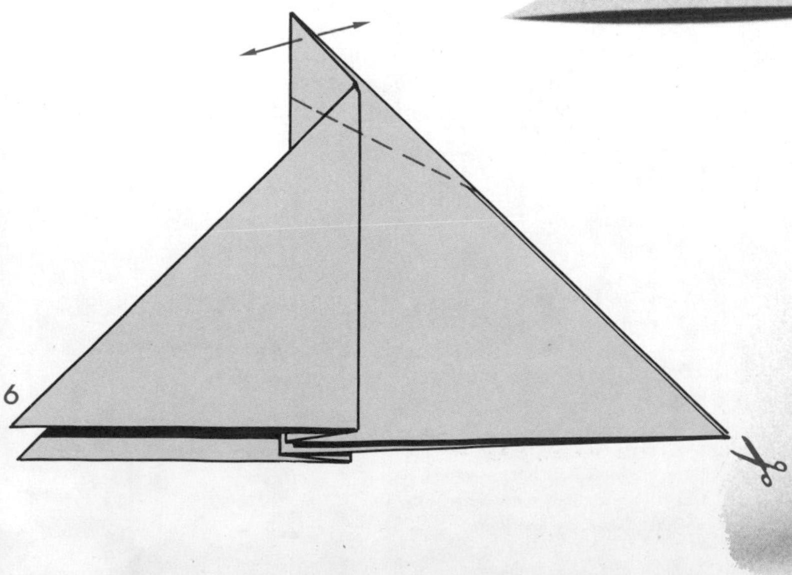

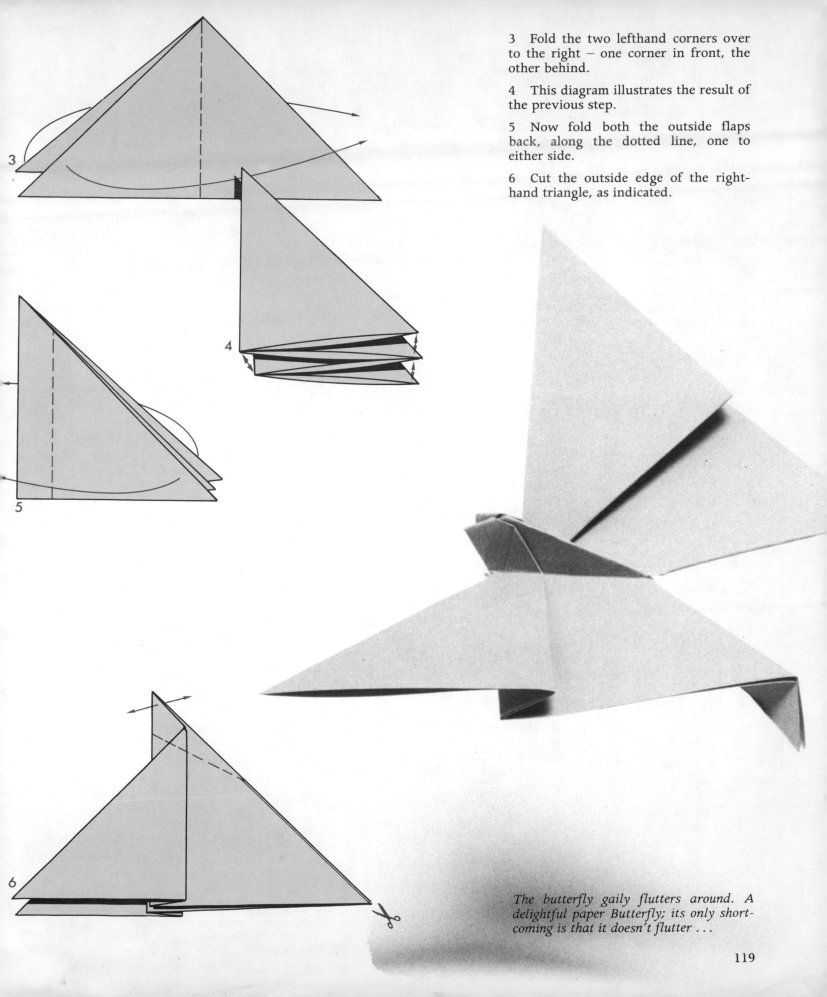

The butterfly gaily flutters around. A delightful paper Butterfly; its only shortcoming is that it doesn't flutter ...

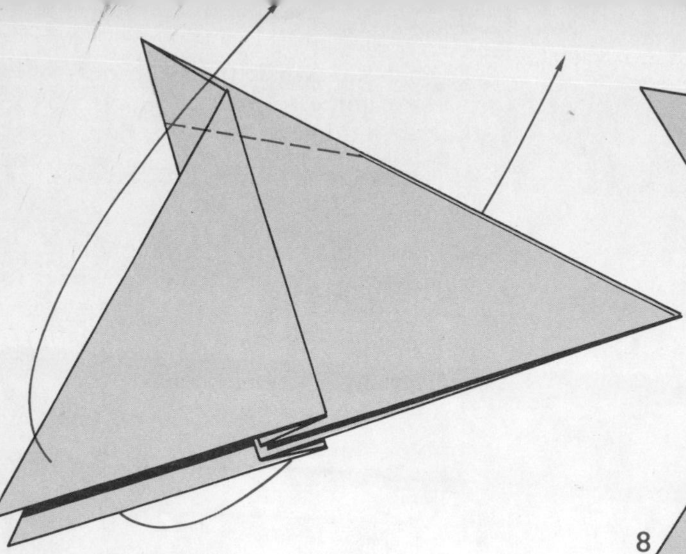

7

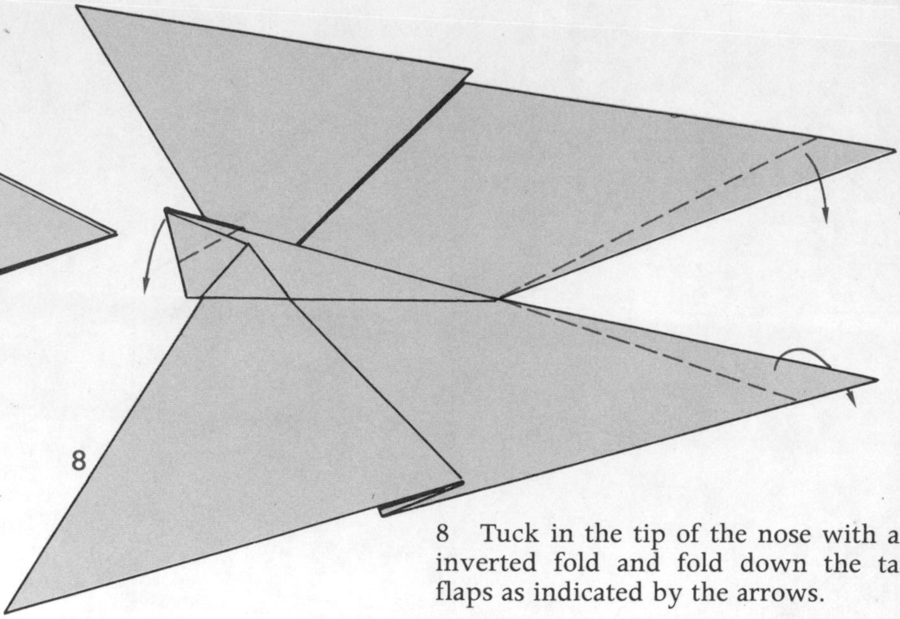

8

7 Make the wings by bringing the two bottom sections together, folding up along the dotted line.

8 Tuck in the tip of the nose with an inverted fold and fold down the tail flaps as indicated by the arrows.

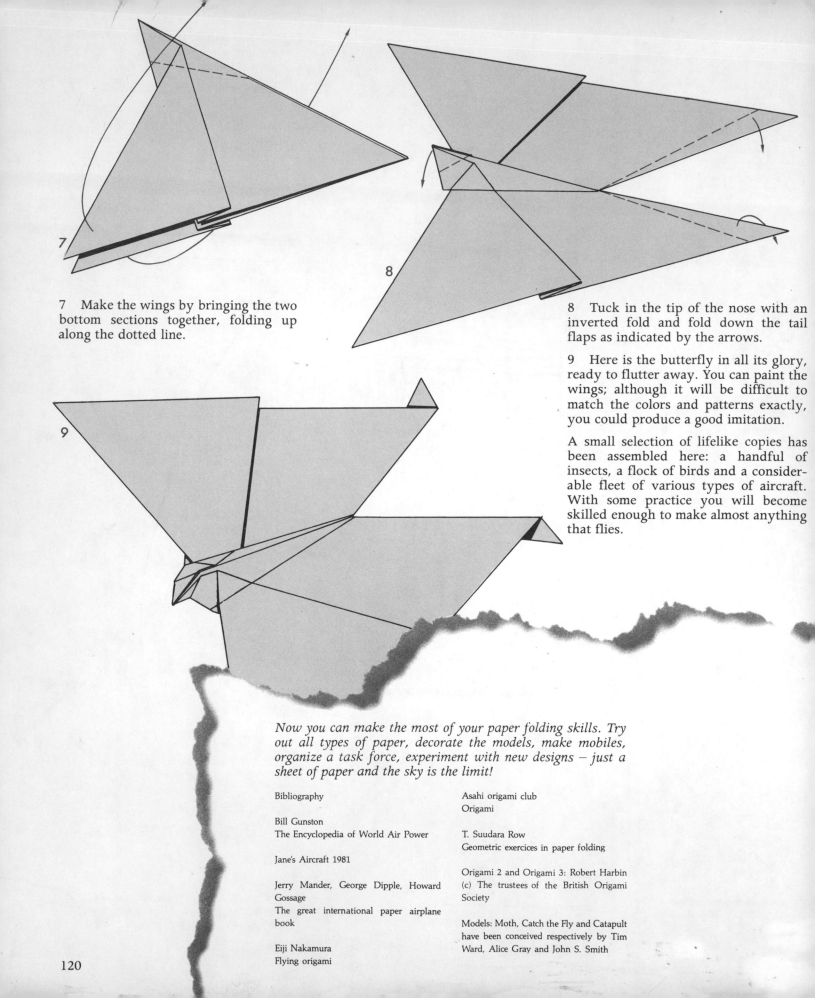

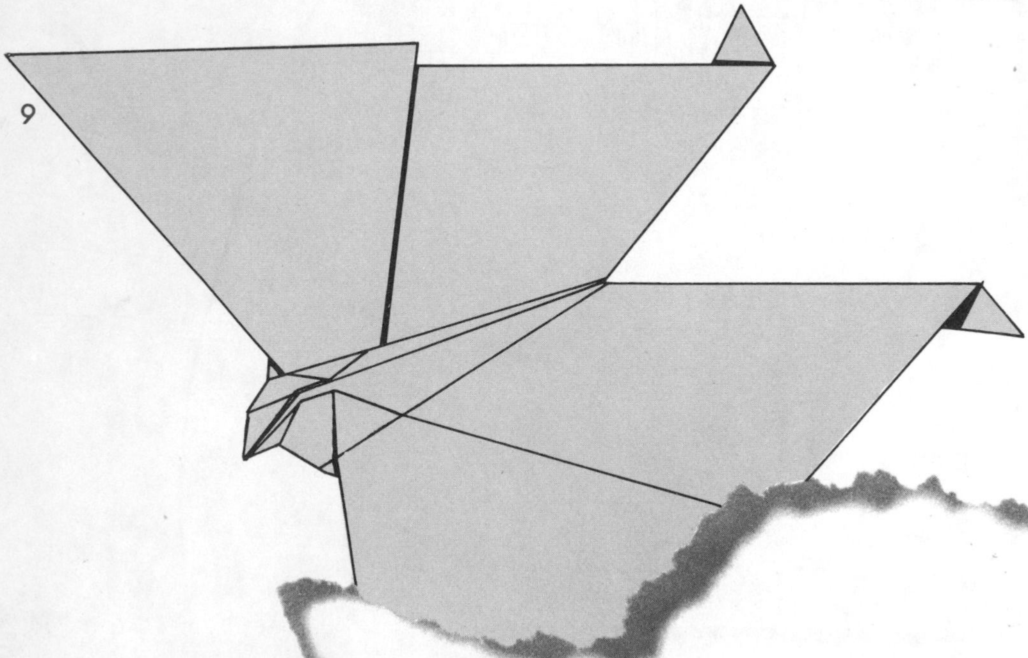

9

9 Here is the butterfly in all its glory, ready to flutter away. You can paint the wings; although it will be difficult to match the colors and patterns exactly, you could produce a good imitation.

A small selection of lifelike copies has been assembled here: a handful of insects, a flock of birds and a considerable fleet of various types of aircraft. With some practice you will become skilled enough to make almost anything that flies.

Now you can make the most of your paper folding skills. Try out all types of paper, decorate the models, make mobiles, organize a task force, experiment with new designs – just a sheet of paper and the sky is the limit!

Bibliography

Bill Gunston
The Encyclopedia of World Air Power

Jane's Aircraft 1981

Jerry Mander, George Dipple, Howard Gossage
The great international paper airplane book

Eiji Nakamura
Flying origami

Asahi origami club
Origami

T. Suudara Row
Geometric exercices in paper folding

Origami 2 and Origami 3: Robert Harbin
(c) The trustees of the British Origami Society

Models: Moth, Catch the Fly and Catapult have been conceived respectively by Tim Ward, Alice Gray and John S. Smith

建築パース・外装

Exteriors: Perspectives in Architectural Design

ビジネス上の要件に合わせたパース画作り

パースは設計者の意図を第三者に最も判りやすくしかも効果的に伝える視覚表現手段ですが，構築物を発注しさらにそれを長期間にわたって使用し続ける側からの要望を，申し上げたいと思います。

ユーザーの立場から今日の日本におけるパースを眺めてみると，一般にはキレイごとに終っていて，甘すぎるといわざるを得ません。

最も大事な着眼点は，そのパースを見て投資決定ができるかどうかです。「よし，これなら何十年間も，わが社の営業道具として，使い続けられる」と，経営の意志決定者に決断させるだけの内容が必要だからです。

美しいとか，カッコよいパースはいっぱいありますが，それだけではインパクトになりません。

第１にどこが他の類似デザインと違った個性なのか。

第２に，その個性は，店舗として，ショッピングセンターとして，あるいは物流加工施設として，斬新な機能を発揮できるものか。

第３に，長期の使用に耐えられるものか。さらにメインテナンスが楽に継続できるものか。

第４に，わが社が描き出したい企業イメージをそれは明確にイメージづけるものか。

第５に，（チェーンストアの場合は）それらの諸要素は標準化できるものなのか。

という５点は，いずれもユーザーにとってはこのうえなく大事な条件です。

いいかえれば，こうしたビジネス上の要件をひとつづつクリアーするノウハウが，このパースにこめられていなければなりません。単に雰囲気を盛りたてるための作図であってはならないのです。

このパース作成のノウハウが，空想と美的感覚だけで形づけられている限り，それは独立した技術ではなくて，単なる設計図の下請けでしかないでしょう。（具体的提案は本書の姉妹書「内装編」に書きました）

日本リテイリングセンター　チーフコンサルタント　渥美俊一

Perspectives that meet business requirements

A perspective conveys the planners idea to the third party in an easily understandable form. It is the stage where the planner's vision is communicated to the third party. Here I would like to discuss the perspective from the standpoint of the client, the individual or group who will be using the planned facility over a continuous, longterm period.

From the viewpoint of the customer recent renderings in Japan are probably aesthetically pleasing, but that is the best that can be said for them. The most important issue is the question of whether a decision to invest or not can be reached. "Yes, this structure will serve our company's needs for the next ten years" is a decision which the perspective must evoke from those responsible. In one sense it is the only thing the perspective must do.

But there are numberless perspectives which are beautiful or well done, yet nonetheless lack this essential strength. Problems are as follows :

1) Is there anything characteristic which separates this design from similar ones?

2) Is that individuality something which is well displayed, and gives the store, shopping center, distribu-

tion center or what have you, some novel capacity?

3) Is this a perspective of a structure which is easily maintained for a extended duration?

4) Does the perspective accurately reflect the stipulations which the client has made?

5) In the case of chain stores, is the design amenable to the various standards of the group?

These five points are of paramount importance to the customer, conditions which must necessarily be met.

To put it another way, a clear understanding of these practical business requisites must be invested into the creation of the draft. A perspective which is created simply to evoke a certain atmosphere will not be acceptable.

When perspective work is limited to an aptitude for ambient work, it cannot be considered technically proficient, and falls into the limited category of subordinate planning. (Concrete details of the proposal are included in the Interiors edition.)

Shunichi Atsumi, Chief Consultant, JAPAN RETAILING CENTER

目　次

まえがき ……………………………………… 2

物販 ……………………………………………… 9

カー・ディーラー　デパート　美容室　集合店舗　電気店
ジーンズ・ショップ　給油所　スーパー　ファッション・
タウン　テナントビル　カルチャー・ショップ　etc.

飲食 ……………………………………………41

レストラン　喫茶店　ファミリーレストラン　活魚炉端焼
ディスコ　ビア・レストラン　大飯店　etc.

レジャー ………………………………………55

リゾートホテル　ペンション　総合クラブ　山荘　野球場
ウェディングプラザ　ホテル　スイミングセンター
ゲスト・ハウス　ヨット・クラブ　博物館　パビリオン　etc.

住宅 ……………………………………………85

学生会館　ナーシングホーム　集合住宅　プレハブ住宅
ビラ　マンション　個人住宅　寮　ハイツ　etc.

事務所ビル……………………………………103

生命保険会社ビル　商社ビル　一般事務所ビル　銀行
共同ビル　etc.

公共施設　その他……………………………131

大学　総合病院　体育館　庁舎　浄化センター　駅前再開発
コミュニケーションセンター　デザイン研究所　牧場看視舎
記念文庫　公園　バス営業所　大橋　etc.

索引……………………………………………145

応募者　146
パース作画者　148

CONTENTS

PREFACE ··4

SALES ···9

Car Dealerships, Markets, Beauty Salons, Malls, Appliance Stores, Clothing Stores, Filling Stations, Fashion Plazas, Culture Shops, etc.

FOOD & DRINK ··41

Family Restaurants, Coffee Shops, I keuo-robatayaki Grills, Discos, Beer Halls, Chinese Restaurants, etc.

LEISURE ··55

Resort Hotels, Pensions, Clubs, Mountain Villas, Wedding Plazas, Hotel Swimming Centers, Guest Houses, Yacht Clubs, Museums, Pavilions, etc.

RESIDENCES ··85

Student Centers, Nursing Homes, Housing Developments, Pre-fabricated Homes, Villas, Mansions, Private Homes, Dormitories, etc.

OFFICE BUILDINGS ··103

Life Insurance Companies, Business Buildings, Tokyo Gas Offices, Banking Partnerships, etc.

PUBLIC FACILITIES ··131

Universities, General Hospitals, Government Office Buildings, Stationfront Re-development, Communication Centers, Purification Plants, Design Research Centers, Veterinary Stables, Memorial Archives, Parks, Bus Stations, Bridges, etc.

INDEX ···145

Applicants 146

Rendering Illustrators 148

凡　例

a.→建築物名称
b.→所在地
c.→設計事務所
d.→パース作画者
e.→作品応募者

EXPLANATORY NOTES

a.→Project Title
b.→Location
c.→Planning Office
d.→Rendering Illustrator
e.→Applicant

EXTERIORS : PERSPECTIVES IN ARCHITECTURAL DESIGN

First Edition April 1987
ISBN4-7661-0425-0

Graphic-sha Publishing Company Ltd.
1-9-12 Kudan-kita Chiyoda-ku Tokyo 102, Japan
Phone 03-263-4310
Fax.03-263-5297
Telex.J29877 Graphic
Printed in Japan

1.物販

カー・ディーラー

デパート

美容室

集合店舗

電気店

ジーンズ・ショップ

給油所

ファッション・タウン

カルチャー・ショップ

etc.

1.SALES

Car Dealerships

Markets

Beauty Salons

Malls

Appliance Stores

Clothing Stores

Filling Stations

Fashion Plazas

Culture Shops

etc.

a. トヨタショウルーム　b. 福岡県福岡市
c. 新和建設大阪営業所　d. 秦曻八　e. 秦曻八

a. TOYOTA SHOWROOM　b. Fukuoka-shi, Fukuoka
c. Shinwa Kensetsu Co., Ltd.　d. Shohachi Hata　e. Shohachi Hata

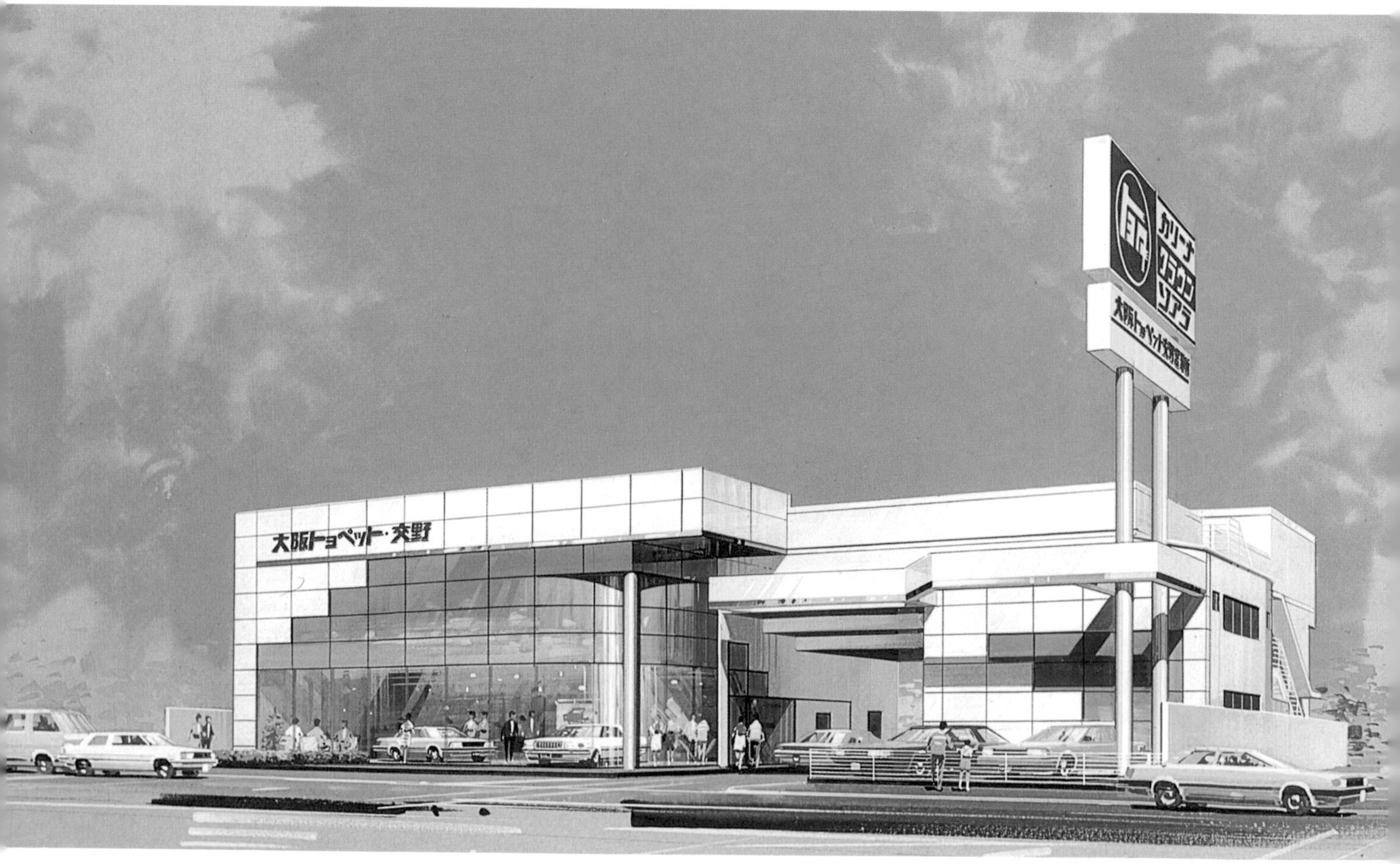

a. 大阪トヨペット交野営業所　b. 大阪府交野市
c. 新和建設　d. レンダリング RIYA　e. レンダリング RIYA

a. KATANO OFFICE, OSAKA TOYOPET　b. Katano-shi, Osaka
c. Shinwa Construction Co.,Ltd.　d. Rendering RIYA Co., Ltd.　e. K. K. Rendering RIYA

a. TOYOTA オート中部　b. 愛知県名古屋市
c. 菱田建築事務所　d. 吉田勝義　e. 吉田勝義

a. TOYOTA AUTO CHUBU　b. Nagoya-shi, Aichi
c. Hishida Architectural Office　d. Katsuyoshi Yoshida　e. Katsuyoshi Yoshida

a. ホンダクリオ西東京　b. 東京都町田市
c. レイデザイン事務所　d. 武藤渥巳　e. 武藤渥巳

a. HONDA CLIO NISHI TOKYO　b. Machida-shi, Tokyo
c. Rey Design Co., Ltd.　d. Atsumi Muto　e. Atsumi Muto

a. 伊南農協中沢給油所　b. 長野県
c. 長野経団連一級建築士事務所　d. 武藤渥巳　e. 武藤渥巳

a. INAN NOKYO NAKAZAWA GS.　b. Nagano
c. Nagano Builders Association Office　d. Atsumi Muto　e. Atsumi Muto

a. 神奈川トヨタショールーム　b. 神奈川県横浜市
c. 中西設計事務所　d. 赤坂孝史　e. 赤坂孝史

a. KANAGAWA TOYOTA SHOWROOM　b. Yokohama-shi, Kanagawa
c. Nakanishi Architectural Design Co., Ltd.　d. Takashi Akasaka　e. Takashi Akasaka

a. 計画案　b. 東京都板橋区
c. 大林組　d. 箕箸純子　e. 箕箸純子

a. PLAN　b. Itabashi-ku, Tokyo
c. Obayashi-gumi　d. Junko Minowa　e. Junko Minowa

a. リバーサイドモールオギノ計画
c. 丹青社　d. 原田剛　e. 丹青社

a. RIVERSIDE MALL OGINO
c. Tanseisha Co., Ltd.　d. Tsuyoshi Harada　e. Tanseisha Co., Ltd.

a. VIA アピタ岡谷　b. 長野県岡谷市
c. 東海興業　d. 吉田勝義　e. 吉田勝義

a. VIA APITA OKAYA b. Okaya-shi, Nagano
c. Tokai Kogyo Co., Ltd. d. Katsuyoshi Yoshida e. Katsuyoshi Yoshida

a. 奈良そごう百貨店計画案　c. 奥村組　d. 堀口憲嗣　e. 堀口憲嗣

a. NARA SOGO DEPARTMENT STORE c. Okumura Co., Ltd. d. Noritsugu Horiguchi e. Noritsugu Horiguchi

a. ユニー　ショップランド　b. 岐阜県可児市
c. 東京スペース　d. 吉田勝義　e. 吉田勝義

a. UNI SHOPLAND　b. Kani-shi, Gifu
c. Tokyo Space Co., Ltd.　d. Katsuyoshi Yoshida　e. Katsuyoshi Yoshida

a. ファニチャー OKAMOTO　b. 三重県津市
c. キャップ　d. 吉田勝義　e. 吉田勝義

a. FURNITURE OKAMOTO　b. Tsu-shi, Mie
c. Cap Ltd.　d. Katsuyoshi Yoshida　e. Katsuyoshi Yoshida

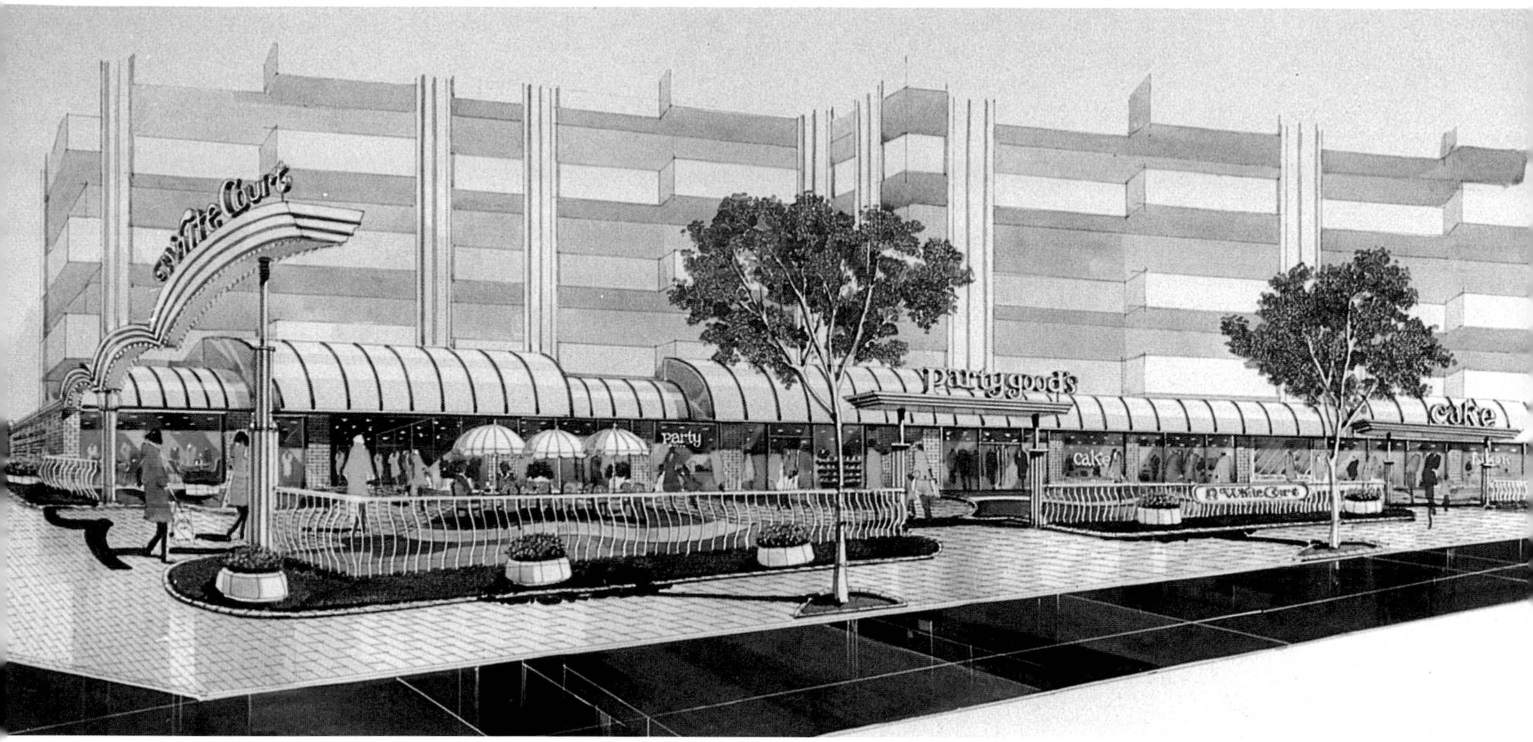

a. 神戸ファッションタウン・ホワイトコート計画　b. 兵庫県神戸市
c. 乃村工藝社　d. 西村昭　e. 乃村工藝社 大阪社

a. KOBE FASHION TOWN WHITE COURT PLAN　b. Kobe-shi, Hyogo
c. Nomura Display Co., Ltd.　d. Akira Nishimura　e. Nomura Display Co., Ltd. Osaka Branch

a. 北長岡ショッピングセンターパルス　b. 新潟県長岡市
c. 丹青社　d. 前島和也　e. 丹青社

a. 原村ショッピングモール計画案　b. 長野県諏訪郡
c. ドーンデザイン研究所　d. 水戸岡鋭治＋ドーンデザイン研究所　e. 水戸岡鋭治

a. PULSE SHOPPING CENTER b. Nagaoka-shi, Niigata
c. Tanseisha Co., Ltd. d. Kazuya Maejima e. Tanseisha Co., Ltd.

a. HARAMURA SHOPPING MALL b. Suwa-gun, Nagano
c. Don Design Associates d. Eiji Mitooka + Don Design Associates e. Eiji Mitooka

a. K計画　c. 丹青社
d. 原田剛　e. 丹青社

a. K PLAN c. Tanseisha Co., Ltd.
d. Tsuyoshi Harada e. Tanseisha Co., Ltd.

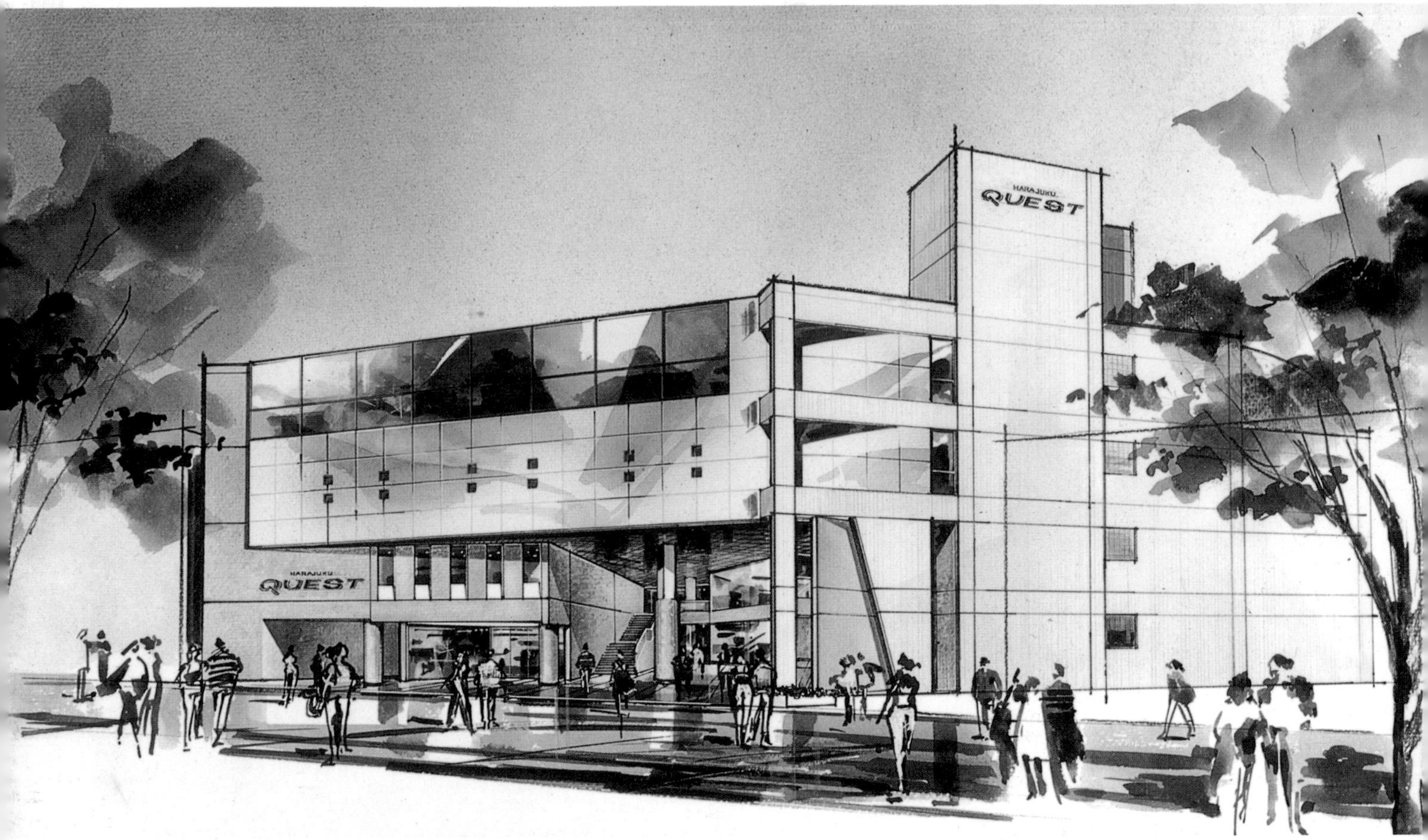

a. 原宿クェスト　b. 東京都渋谷区
c. ＮＴＴ都市開発設計部門　d. アトリエ105　西村弘美　e. 西村弘美

a. HARAJUKU QUEST　b. Shibuya-ku, Tokyo
c. NTT Co., Ltd., Planning Section　d. Atelier 105　Hiromi Nishimura　e. Hiromi Nishimura

a. ＹＳ－３計画　b. 愛知県名古屋市
c. 竹中工務店　d. 竹中工務店　渡辺廣史　e. 竹中工務店

a. YS-3 PROJECT　b. Nagoya-shi, Aichi　c. Takenaka Komuten Co., Ltd.
d. Takenaka Komuten Co., Ltd.　Koji Watanabe　e. Takenaka Komuten Co., Ltd.

a. No.10ミツワビル　b. 愛媛県松山市
c. エス・アイ・ピー　d. 川嶋俊介　e. 川嶋俊介

a. NO.10 MITSUWA BUILD.　b. Matsuyama-shi, Ehime
c. Space Imagination Project Co., Ltd.　d. Shunsuke Kawashima　e. Shunsuke Kawashima

a. ギヤマビル　b. 兵庫県神戸市
c. 竹中工務店　d. 竹中工務店　渡辺廣史　e. 竹中工務店

a. GIYAMA BLDG.　b. Kobe-shi, Hyogo　c. Takenaka Komuten Co., Ltd.
d. Takenaka Komuten Co., Ltd., Koji Watanabe　e. Takenaka Komuten Co., Ltd.

a. サンルートプラザ東京モニュメント　b. 東京都
c. 丹青社　d. 前島和也　e. 丹青社

a. SUN ROUTE PLAZA MONUMENT　b. Tokyo
c. Tanseisha Co., Ltd.　d. Kazuya Maejima　e. Tanseisha Co., Ltd.

a. ラフィーネ007　b. 東京都　c. セスドプランニング／事業企画＝長谷川工務店
d. ヒューマン・ファクター　横山博　e. ヒューマン・ファクター

a. RAFFINE 007　b. Tokyo　c. CESD Enterprise Planning Co., Ltd. Hasegawa Branch Office
d. HUMAN FACTOR, Hiroshi Yokoyama　e. HUMAN FACTOR

a. ナショナルショップ　b. 兵庫県姫路市
d. 四海隼一　e. 四海隼一

a. NATIONAL SHOP　b. Himeji-shi, Hyogo
d. Shunichi Shikai　e. Shunichi Shikai

a. ビューティーサロン　アルルヘアー
b. 愛知県高浜市
c. シンコー
d. 藤城勝範
e. 藤城勝範

a. BEAUTY SALON ALULUHAIR
b. Takahama-shi, Aichi
c. Shinko Co., Ltd.
d. Masanori Fujishiro
e. Masanori Fujishiro

a. フキ美容室　b. 兵庫県氷上郡
c. 有原一級建築設計事務所　d. 四海隼一　e. 四海隼一

a. FUKI BEAUTY SALON　b. Hikami-gun, Hyogo
c. Arihara Ikkyu Planning Office　d. Shunichi Shikai　e. Shunichi Shikai

a. レイ・エ・ルイ
b. 愛知県名古屋市
c. 商業計画＝乃村工藝社／
建築設計＝山下設計名古屋支社
d. 徳永元義
e. 乃村工藝社　大阪社

a. LEI E LUI
b. Nagoya-shi, Aichi
c. Nomura Display Co., Ltd.／
Yamashita Architects and Engineers
Nagoya Branch
d. Motoyoshi Tokunaga
e. Nomura Display Co., Ltd., Osaka Branch

a. 桃山カルチャービル（仮称） b. 京都府京都市
c. 澤設計 d. 森聖一デザイン事務所 森聖一 e. 森聖一

a. THE MOMOYAMA CULTURE BLDG. b. Kyoto-shi, Kyoto
c. Taku Architectural Design Co., Ltd. d. Seiichi Mori Design Office e. Seiichi Mori

a. 光が丘パークタウン中心施設 b. 東京都練馬区
c. ＩＮＡ新建築研究所 d. 箕箸重郎 e. 箕箸重郎

a. HIKARIGAOKA PARKTOWN b. Nerima-ku, Tokyo
c. Institute New Architecture Co., Ltd. d. Juro Mihashi e. Juro Mihashi

a. ホームケアジャパン本社ショールーム　b. 東京都世田谷区
c. 殖産住宅相互　d. 斎藤由美子　e. 殖産住宅相互

a. HOMECARE JAPAN SHOWROOM　b. Setagaya-ku, Tokyo
c. Shokusan Jutaku Sogo Co., Ltd.　d. Yumiko Saito　e. Shokusan Jutaku Sogo Co., Ltd.

a. 鵜方テナントビル　b. 三重県志摩郡
c. 矢内店舗設計事務所　d. 古橋孝之　e. 古橋孝之

a. UGATA TENANT BLDG.　b. Shima-gun, Mie
c. Yanai Design Office　d. Takayuki Furuhashi　e. Takayuki Furuhashi

a. サントノーレ白川
b. 京都府京都市
c. 竹中工務店
d. 竹中工務店　小武内美佐世
e. 竹中工務店

a. SANTONORE SHIRAKAWA
b. Kyoto-shi, Kyoto
c. Takenaka Komuten Co., Ltd.
d. Takenaka Komuten Co., Ltd., Misayo Omunai
e. Takenaka Komuten Co., Ltd.

a. 金山ビューティビル
b. 愛知県名古屋市
c. デザム建築事務所
d. 吉田勝義
e. 吉田勝義

a. KANAYAMA BEAUTY BLDG.
b. Nagoya-shi, Aichi
c. Dezamu Architect Co., Ltd.
d. Katsuyoshi Yoshida
e. Katsuyoshi Yoshida

a. 読売銀座ビル（プランタンデパート） b. 東京都中央区
c. 三菱地所一級建築士事務所 d. 第三建築部（アール・エム＝南几代美） e. 三菱地所

a. YOMIURI GINZA BLDG. b. Chuo-ku, Tokyo
c. Mitsubishi Estate Co., Ltd. d. The Third Architectural and Engineering Dept. e. Mitsubishi Estate Co., Ltd.

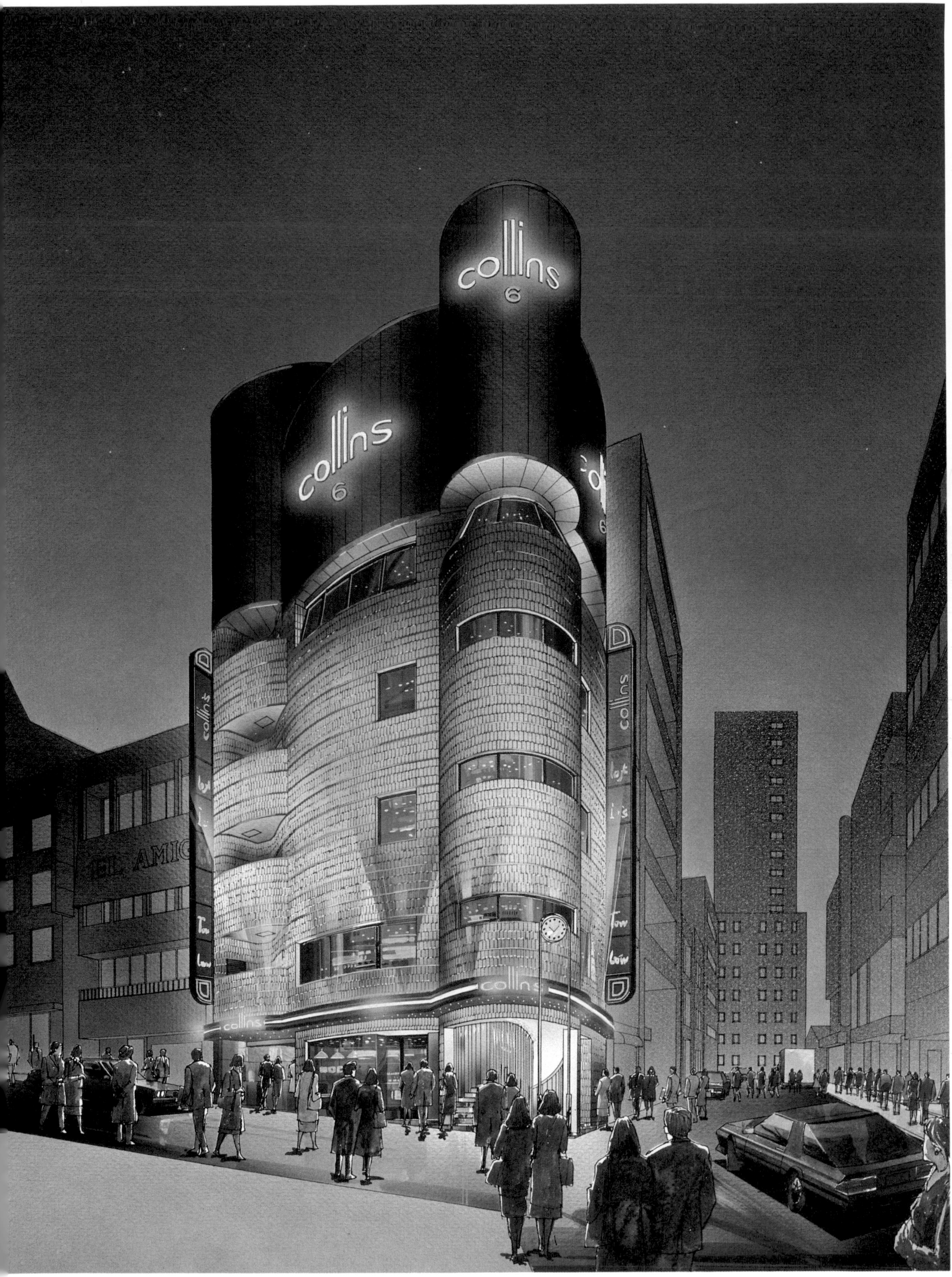

a. コリンズ六本木　b. 東京都港区
c. 石原トータルプランニング　d. 山城義彦　e. 山城デザインスタジオ

a. COLLINS ROPPONGI　b. Minato-ku, Tokyo
c. Ishihara Total Planning　d. Yoshihiko Yamashiro　e. Yamashiro Design Studio

a. 三井ホームファインシリーズ
c. 三井ホーム
d. 福永文昭
e. フクナガレンダリング

a. MITSUI HOME FINE
c. Mitsui Home Co., Ltd.
d. Fumiaki Fukunaga
e. Fukunaga Rendering Co., Ltd.

a. レイトンハウス　b. 北海道札幌市
c. 画工房　d. 髙崎千鶴子　e. 髙橋千鶴子

a. LEYTON HOUSE　b. Sapporo-shi, Hokkaido
c. Kaku Kobo Co., Ltd.　d. Chizuko Takasaki　e. Chizuko Takasaki

a. 集合店舗計画案　b. 静岡県浜松市
c. 矢内店舗設計事務所　d. 古橋孝之　e. 古橋孝之

a. SHOPPING MALL PLAN　b. Hamamatsu-shi, Shizuoka
c. Yanai Design Office Co., Ltd.　d. Takayuki Furuhashi　e. Takayuki Furuhashi

a. 蔦屋書店　b. 大阪府堺市
c. 都市計画　d. 松田邦裕　e. コラムデザインセンター

a. BOOK SHOP TSUTAYA　b. Sakai-shi, Osaka
c. Urban Planning Co., Ltd.　d. Kunihiro Matsuda　e. Koramu Design Center

a. ＩＢジーンズショップ　b. 大阪府
c. 八洋工芸　d. 井内一夫　e. 井内一夫

a. IB JEAN'S SHOP　b. Osaka
c. Hachiyo Kogei Co., Ltd.　d. Kazuo Inouchi　e. Kazuo Inouchi

a. ホーメストショップ
b. 福岡県志摩町
c. 殖産住宅相互
d. 坂本牧子
e. 殖産住宅相互

a. HOMEST SHOP
b. Shima-cho, Fukuoka
c. Shokusan Jutaku Sogo Co., Ltd.
d. Makiko Sakamoto
e. Shokusan Jutaku Sogo Co., Ltd.

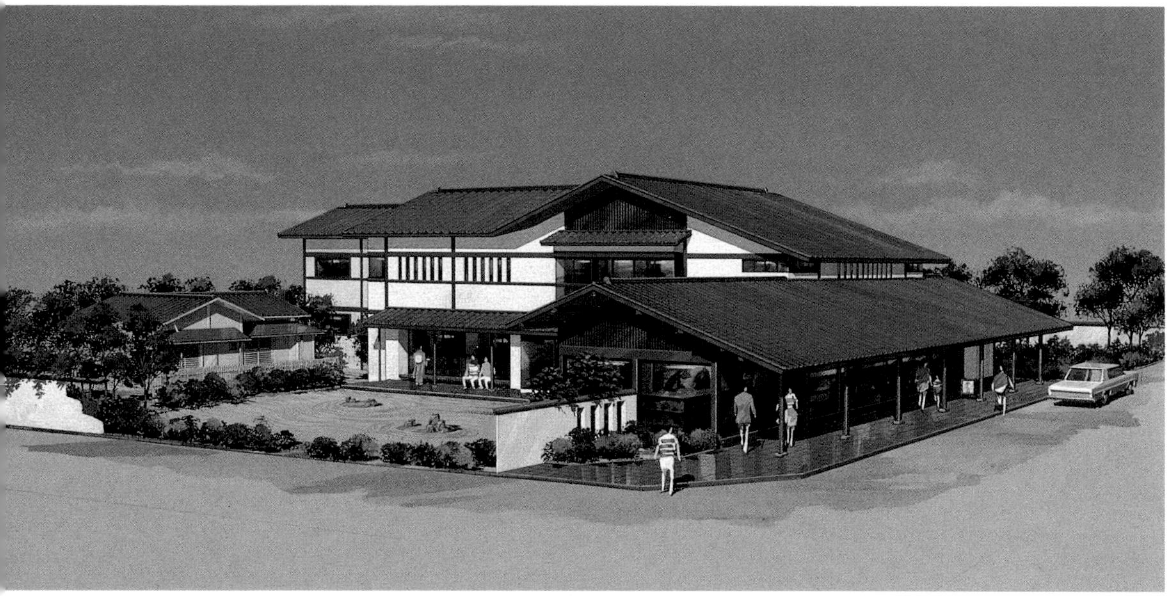

a. 金庄園
b. 千葉県
c. 長建設計
d. 四十澤健文
e. 四十澤健文

a. KINSHOEN
b. Chiba
c. Choken Architects Co., Ltd.
d. Takefumi Yosozawa
e. Takefumi Yosozawa

a. 仏壇中原三法堂（倉敷店）
b. 岡山県倉敷市
c. 矢内店舗設計事務所
d. 古橋孝之
e. 古橋孝之

a. BUTSUDAN NAKAHARASANPODO
b. Kurashiki-shi, Okayama
c. Yanai Design Office Co., Ltd.
d. Takayuki Furuhashi
e. Takayuki Furuhashi

2.飲食

レストラン

喫茶店

ファミリーレストラン

活魚炉端焼

ディスコ

ビア・レストラン

大飯店

etc.

2.FOOD & DRINK

Family Restaurants

Coffee Shops

Ikeuo-robatayaki Grills

Discos

Beer Halls

Chinese Restaurants

etc.

a. ボンジュール　b. 兵庫県姫路市
d. 四海隼一　e. 四海隼一

a. BONJOUR　b. Himeji-shi, Hyogo
d. Shunichi Shikai　e. Shunichi Shikai

a. レストランココス計画　c. 丹青社
d. 菅原律子　e. 丹青社

a. RESTAURANT COCOS PLAN　c. Tanseisha Co., Ltd.
d. Ritsuko Sugawara　e. Tanseisha Co., Ltd.

a. 喫茶スカイ・ライト　b. 岐阜県各務原市
c. 建築造型　d. 小野木司　e. 建築造型

a. COFFEE SHOP SKY LIGHT　b. Kakamigahara-shi, Gifu
c. Architecture Modeling　d. Tsukasa Onogi　e. Architectural Modeling

a. 喫茶サザン・クロス　b. 岐阜県岐阜市
c. 酒井設計　d. 小野木司　e. 建築造型

a. COFFEE SHOP SOUTHERN CROSS　b. Gifu-shi, Gifu
c. Sakai Co., Ltd.　d. Tsukasa Onogi　e. Architecture Modeling

a. レストラン　b. 群馬県桐生市
c. 飯塚建築設計室　d. 津田益司　e. 津田益司

a. RESTAURANT　b. Kiryu-shi, Gunma
c. Iizuka Architectural Design Office　d. Masumori Tsuda　e. Masumori Tsuda

a. スカイラーク足立扇店　b. 東京都足立区
c. 丹青社　d. 前島和也　e. 丹青社

a. SKYLARK ADACHI-OGI-TEN　b. Adachi-ku, Tokyo
c. Tanseisha Co., Ltd.　d. Kazuya Maejima　e. Tanseisha Co., Ltd.

a. あわいさ亭　b. 奈良県王寺町
c. 秦スペースデザイン研究所　d. 秦舁八　e. 秦舁八

a. AWAISA TEI　b. Oji-cho, Nara
c. Hata Space Design Lab.　d. Shohachi Hata　e. Shohachi Hata

a. 活魚炉端 万葉　b. 奈良県奈良市
c. アーバン設計　d. 芳野明　e. 芳野明

a. IKEUO ROBATA MANYO　b. Nara-shi, Nara
c. Urban Planning Co., Ltd.　d. Akira Yoshino　e. Akira Yoshino

a. ディスコＪ　c. ザ・ポイントスタジオ／アヅチ・プランニングスタジオ
d. 安土実　e. アヅチ・プランニングスタジオ

a. DISCO J c. The Point Studio/Azuchi Planning Studio
d. Minoru Azuchi e. Azuchi Planning Studio

a. ラ・フォーレがんこや　b. 大阪府東大阪市
c. 飛田建築設計事務所　d. 芳野明　e. 芳野明

a. LA FOLLET GANKOYA　b. Higashi Osaka-shi,Osaka
c. Tobita Architectural Planning Office　d. Akira Yoshino　e. Akira Yoshino

a. ２Ｍビル　b. 北海道札幌市
c. コラム建築設計事務所　d. 髙崎千鶴子　e. 髙崎千鶴子

a. 2M BLD.　b. Sapporo-shi, Hokkaido
c. Column Architectural Co., Ltd.　d. Chizuko Takasaki　e. Chizuko Takasaki

aレストラン"望月" b. 東京都杉並区
c. 殖産住宅相互 d. 高橋くみ子 e. 殖産住宅相互

a. RESTAURANT MOCHIZUKI b. Suginami-ku, Tokyo
c. Shokusan Jutaku Sogo Co., Ltd. d. Kumiko Takahashi e. Shokusan Jutaku Sogo Co., Ltd.

a. レストラン"バッキンガム" b. 東京都中野区
c. 殖産住宅相互 d. 坂本牧子 e. 殖産住宅相互

a. RESTAURANT BUCKINGHAM b. Nakano-ku, Tokyo
c. Shokusan Jutaku Sogo Co., Ltd. d. Makiko Sakamoto e. Shokusan Jutaku Sogo Co., Ltd.

a. 北京大飯店　藤吉楼
b. 三重県名張市
c. グローバルデザインオフィス
d. 森聖一デザイン事務所　森聖一
e. 森聖一

a. CHINESE RESTAURANT TOKICHIRO
b. Nabari-shi, Mie
c. Global Design Office Co., Ltd.
d. Seiichi Mori Design Office
e. Seiichi Mori

a. フランス料理店
b. 三重県桑名市
c. ポストホーム
d. 川上和子
e. 川上和子

a. FRANCH RESTAURANT
b. Kuwana-shi, Mie
c. Posuto Home Co., Ltd.
d. Kazuko Kawakami
e. Kazuko Kawakami

a. シェ・ハマザキ
b. 徳島県徳島市
c. アタケ河野陽一建築事務所
d. 福永文昭
e. アタケ河野陽一建築事務所

a. CHEZ HAMAZAKI
b. Tokushima-shi, Tokushima
c. Atake Yoichi Kawano Architectural Office
d. Fumiaki Fukunaga
e. Atake Yoichi Kawano Architectural Office

a. ビアレストラン　ミュンヘン　b. 愛媛県砥部町
c. プランニングアクス　関谷正男　d. 川嶋俊介＋花岡徳久　e. 川嶋俊介

a. BEER RESTAURANT MUNCHEN　b. Tobe-cho, Ehime　c. Planning Ax Masao Sekiya
d. Shunsuke Kawashima＋Norihisa Hanaoka　e. Shunsuke Kawashima

a. スパニッシュレストラン（プラン）　b. 愛媛県伊予三島市
c. ＷＡＶＥ　d. 川嶋俊介　e. 川嶋俊介

a. SPANISH RESTAURANT PLAN　b. Iyomishima-shi, Ehime
c. Wave Co., Ltd.　d. Shunsuke Kawashima　e. Shunsuke Kawashima

a. RESTAURANT & COFFEE ま〜くうえい b. 北海道石狩郡
c. 辻野建設工業 d. 鏡デザインプロ e. 辻野建設工業

a. RESTAURANT & COFFEE MARK WAY b. Ishikari-gun, Hokkaido
c. Tsujino Construction Co., Ltd. d. Kagami Design Pro. Co., Ltd. e. Tsujino Construction Co., Ltd.

a. サウスピア'86 b. 広島県
c. デザインハウスひがし d. 金本正 e. 金本正

a. SOUTH PIER '86 b. Hiroshima
c. Design House Higashi Co., Ltd. d. Tadashi Kanemoto e. Tadashi Kanemoto

a. レストラン（プラン） b. 愛媛県松山市
c. 西原由人 d. 川嶋俊介／制作＝ビンデザインオフィス e. 川嶋俊介

a. RESTAURANT PLAN b. Matsuyama-shi, Ehime
c. Yoshihito Nishihara d. Shunsuke Kawashima Bin Design Office e. Shunsuke Kawashima

3. レジャー

山荘

野球場

ウェディングプラザ

ホテル

スイミングセンター

ゲスト・ハウス

ヨット・クラブ

博物館

パビリオン

etc.

3. LEISURE

Mountain Villas

Wedding Plazas

Hotel Swimming Centers

Guest Houses

Yacht Clubs

Museums

Pavilions

etc.

a. リゾート・ホテル清芳閣　b. 岐阜県下呂町
c. 久米建築事務所　d. 吉田勝義　e. 吉田勝義

a. HOTEL SEIHOKAKU　b. Gero-cho, Gifu
c. Kume Architects-Engineers　d. Katsuyoshi Yoshida　e. Katsuyoshi Yoshida

a. サイパン某ホテル計画　b. サイパン
c. 栄建築研究所　d. オズ・アトリエ　e. オズ・アトリエ

a. HOTEL PROJECT IN SAIPAN　b. Saipan
c. Sakae Architects & Engineers　d. Ozu Atorie　e. Ozu Atorie

a. ペンション“仙”　b. 長野県明科町
c. 殖産住宅相互　d. 高橋くみ子　e. 殖産住宅相互

a. PENSION ‘SEN’　b. Akashina-machi, Nagano
c. Shokusan Jutaku Sogo Co., Ltd.　d. Kumiko Takahashi　e. Shokusan Jutaku Sogo Co., Ltd.

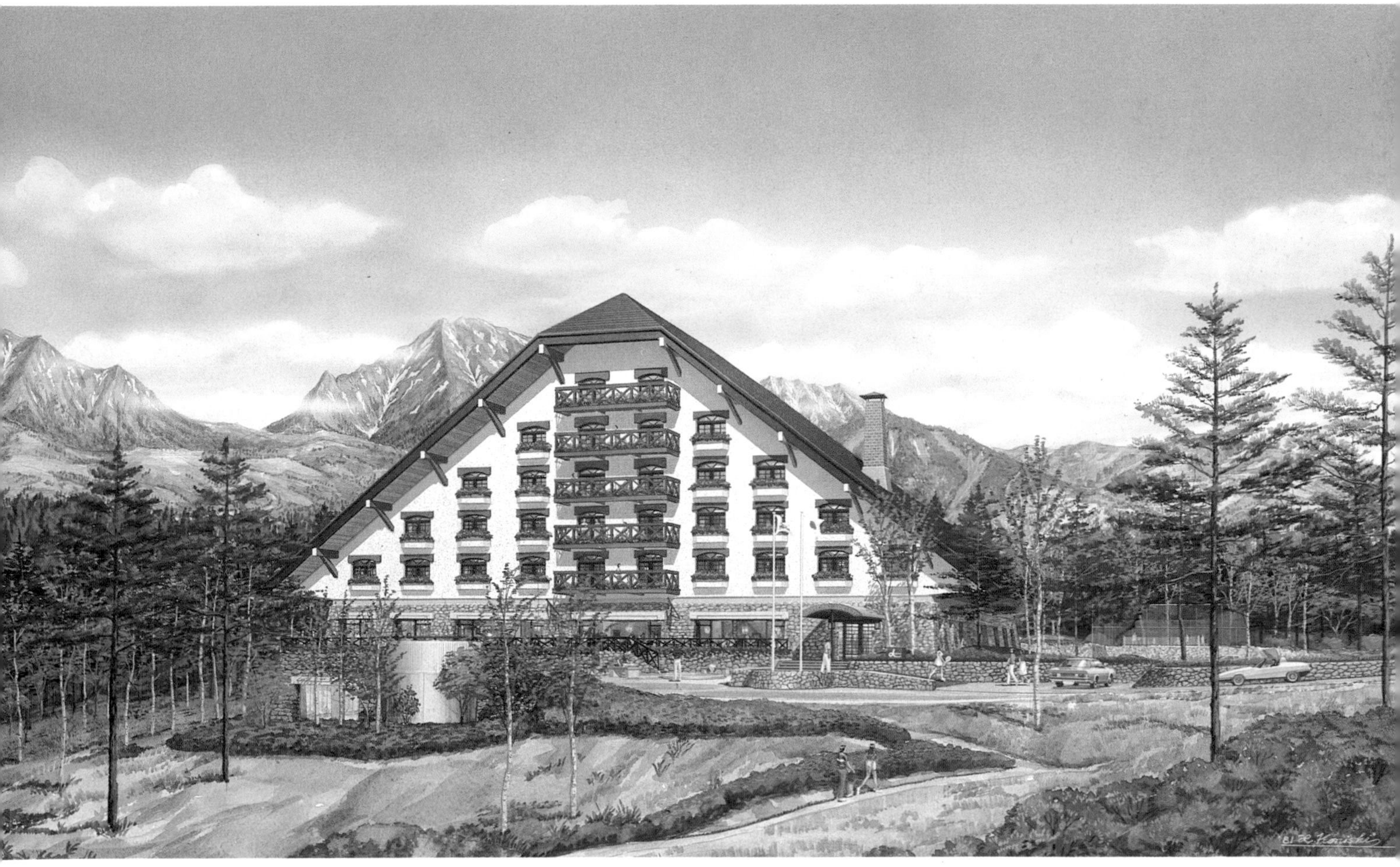

a. 総合経営ダイヤモンドクラブ八ヶ岳ソサイエティ　b. 山梨県北巨摩郡
c. 竹中工務店　d. 小西久雄　e. 小西久雄

a. DIAMOND CLUB Tatsugatake Society　b. Kitakoma-gun, Yamanashi
c. Takenaka Komuten Co., Ltd.　d. Hisao Konishi　e. Hisao Konishi

a. 日本火災海上保険軽井沢山荘　b. 長野県軽井沢町
c. 秋元和雄設計事務所　d. 村崎茂　e. 村崎茂

a. MOUNTAIN LODGE　b. Karuizawa-machi, Nagano
c. Kazuo Akimoto & Partners　d. Shigeru Murasaki　e. Shigeru Murasaki

a. ウェディングプラザ日本閣　b. 愛媛県松山市
c. 富士造型　d. 川嶋俊介＋花岡徳久　e. 川嶋俊介

a. WEDDING PLAZA NIHONKAKU　b. Matsuyama-shi, Ehime
c. Fujizokei Co., Ltd.　d. Shunsuke Kawashima＋Norihisa Hanaoka　e. Shunsuke Kawashima

a. リゾートホテル「モンシャトル北城」　b. 長野県北安曇郡
c. 伊藤建築設計事務所　d. 四十澤健文　e. 四十澤健文

a. THE RESORT HOTEL MON CHATELET HOKUJYO　b. Kitaazumi-gun, Nagano
c. Ito Architects & Associates　d. Takefumi Yosozawa　e. Takefumi Yosozawa

a. 柏平安閣　b. 千葉県柏市
c. 竹中工務店　d. 竹中工務店　松下久美　e. 竹中工務店

a. KASHIWA HEIANKAKU　b. Kashiwa-shi, Chiba　c. Takenaka Komuten Co., Ltd.
d. Takenaka Komuten Co., Ltd., Kumi Matsushita　e. Takenaka Komuten Co., Ltd.

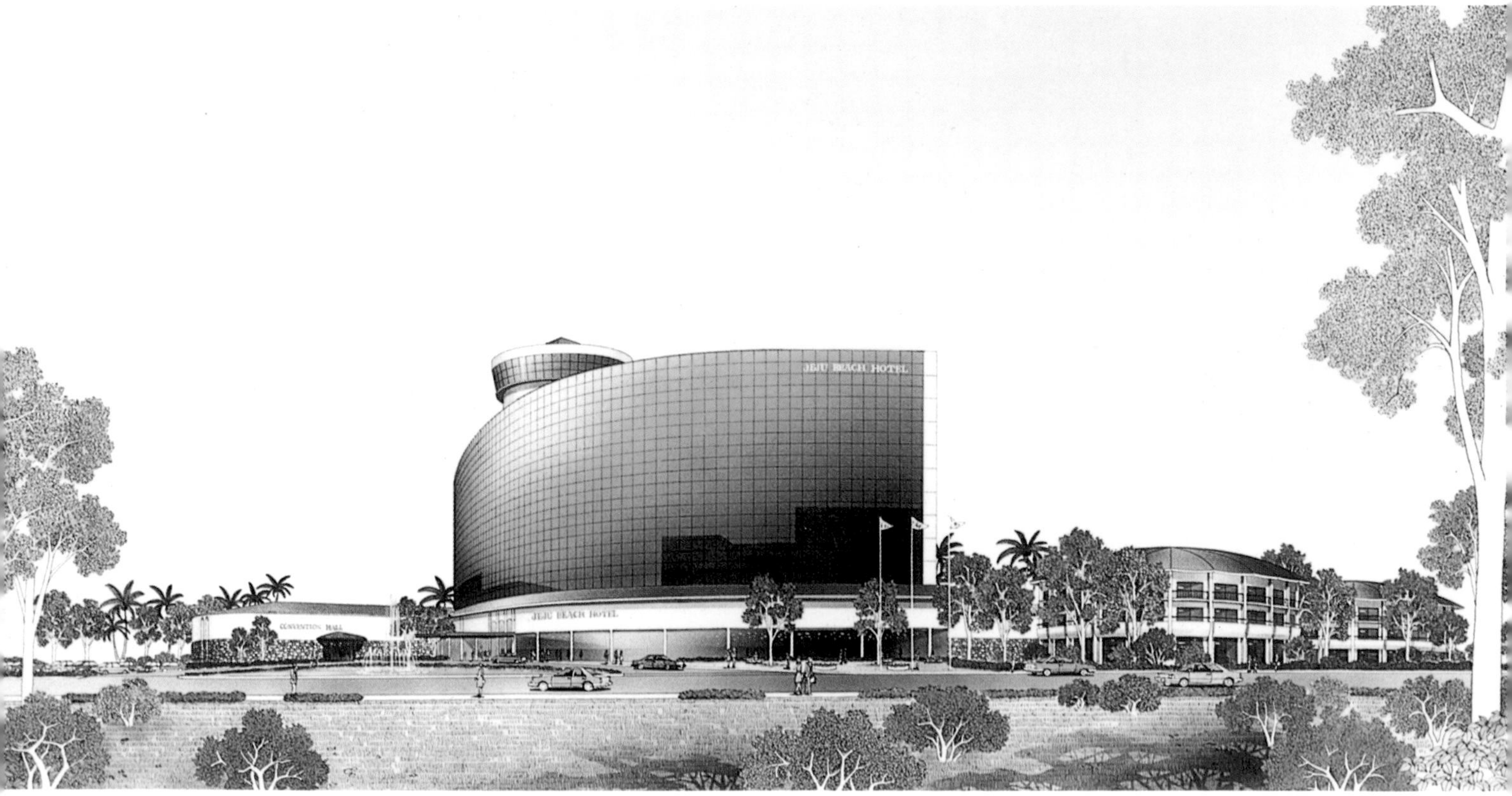

a. D 計画（BEACH HOTEL）　c. 小河建築設計事務所
d. 橋本デザイン事務所　橋本秀章　e. 橋本デザイン事務所

a. D.PLAN（BEACH HOTEL ）　c. Ogawa Kenchiku Sekkei Co., Ltd.
d. Hashimoto Design Office　e. Hashimoto Design Office

a. ホテル　b. 中国
c. 国建　d. 橋本弘徳　e. 橋本弘徳

a. HOTEL　b. China
c. Kuniken Co., Ltd.　d. Hironori Hashimoto　e. Hironori Hashimoto

a. 小松グランドホテル　b. 石川県小松市
c. 設計＝中島建築事務所／デザイン＝辻本デザイン事務所　d. 辻本デザイン事務所　e. 辻本デザイン事務所

a. KOMATSU GRAND HOTEL b. Komatsu-shi, Ishikawa
c. Nakajima Architects Co., Ltd., Tsujimoto Design Office Co., Ltd. d. Tsujimoto Design Office Co., Ltd. e. Tsujimoto Design Office Co., Ltd.

a. 琴平ロイヤルホテル　b. 香川県琴平町
c. 三木建築設計事務所　d. 金本正　e. 金本正

a. KOTOHIRA ROYAL HOTEL　b. Kotohira-machi, Kagawa
c. Miki Architectural Planning Office　d. Tadashi Kanemoto　e. Tadashi Kanemoto

a. 金沢ファーストホテル
b. 石川県金沢市
c. 設計＝中島建築事務所／デザイン＝辻本デザイン事務所
d. 辻本デザイン事務所
e. 辻本デザイン事務所

a. KANAZAWA FIRST HOTEL
b. Kanazawa-shi, Ishikawa
c. Nakajima Architects Office Co., Ltd.
Tsujimoto Design Office Co., Ltd.
d. Tsujimoto Design Office Co., Ltd.
e. Tsujimoto Design Office Co., Ltd.

a. ホテル八木
b. 福井県芦原町
c. 竹中工務店
d. 竹中工務店　右高良樹
e. 竹中工務店

a. HOTEL YAGI
b. Awara-cho, Fukui
c. Takenaka Komuten Co., Ltd.
d. Takenaka Komuten Co., Ltd., Yoshie Migitaka
e. Takenaka Komuten Co., Ltd.

a. ホテル「ウインク」
b. 愛知県名古屋市
c. エーアンドユー建築設計事務所
d. 坂井田優実
e. 坂井田優実

a. HOTEL 'WINK'
b. Nagoya-shi, Aichi
c. A & U Architecture Design Office
d. Yumi Sakaida
e. Yumi Sakaida

a. ホテルニッコーサンフランシスコ b. アメリカ合衆国カリフォルニア州
c. 竹中工務店 d. 竹中工務店 山岸和治 e. 竹中工務店

a. HOTEL NIKKO SAN FRANCISCO b. California, USA c. Takenaka Komuten Co., Ltd.
d. Takenaka Komuten Co., Ltd., Katsuji Yamagishi e. Takenaka Komuten Co., Ltd.

a. ホテル“エス” b. 東京都豊島区
c. 殖産住宅相互 d. 斉木美香子 e. 殖産住宅相互

a. HOTEL 'S' b. Toshima-ku, Tokyo
c. Shokusan Jutaku Sogo Co., Ltd. d. Mikako Saiki e. Shokusan Jutaku Sogo Co., Ltd.

a. 工場の厚生体育館棟新築計画　c. アコン
d. 四十澤健文　e. 四十澤健文

a. A WELFARE HOUSE & GYMNASIUM FOR A FACTORY　c. Acon. Laboratory
d. Takefumi Yosozawa　e. Takefumi Yosozawa

a. 那覇市民体育館　b. 沖縄県那覇市
c. 国建　d. 橋本弘徳　e. 橋本弘徳

a. NAHA CIVIL PHYSICAL CENTER　b. Naha-shi, Okinawa
c. Kuniken Co., Ltd.　d. Hironori Hashimoto　e. Hironori Hashimoto

a. スイミングセンター計画案　b. 長野県木曽郡
c. 佐田建築設計事務所　d. 中根典子　e. 中根典子

a. SWIMMING CENTER　b. Kiso-gun, Nagano
c. Sada Architectural Office　d. Noriko Nakane　e. Noriko Nakane

a. スポーツセンター計画　b. 兵庫県神戸市
c. 浅沼組　d. 森山雅彦　e. コラムデザインセンター

a. SPORTS CENTER　b. Kobe-shi, Hyogo
c. Asanuma-Gumi　d. Masahiko Moriyama　e. Koramu Design Center Co., Ltd.

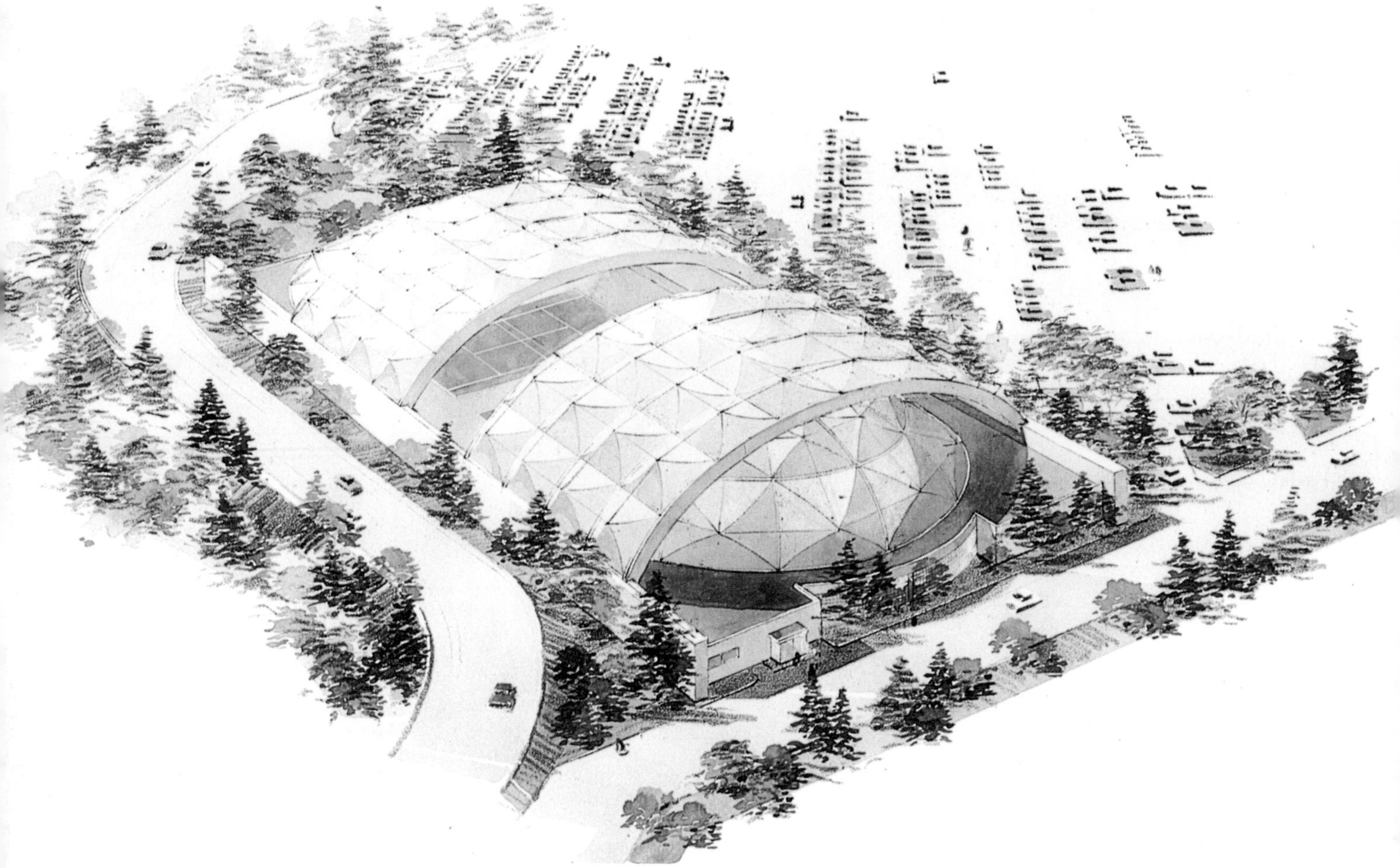

a. F計画　b. 静岡県
c. 清水建設設計本部　d. オズ・アトリエ　e. オズ・アトリエ

a. F PROJECT　b. Shizuoka
c. Shimizu Construction Co., Ltd.　d. Ozu Atorie　e. Ozu Atorie

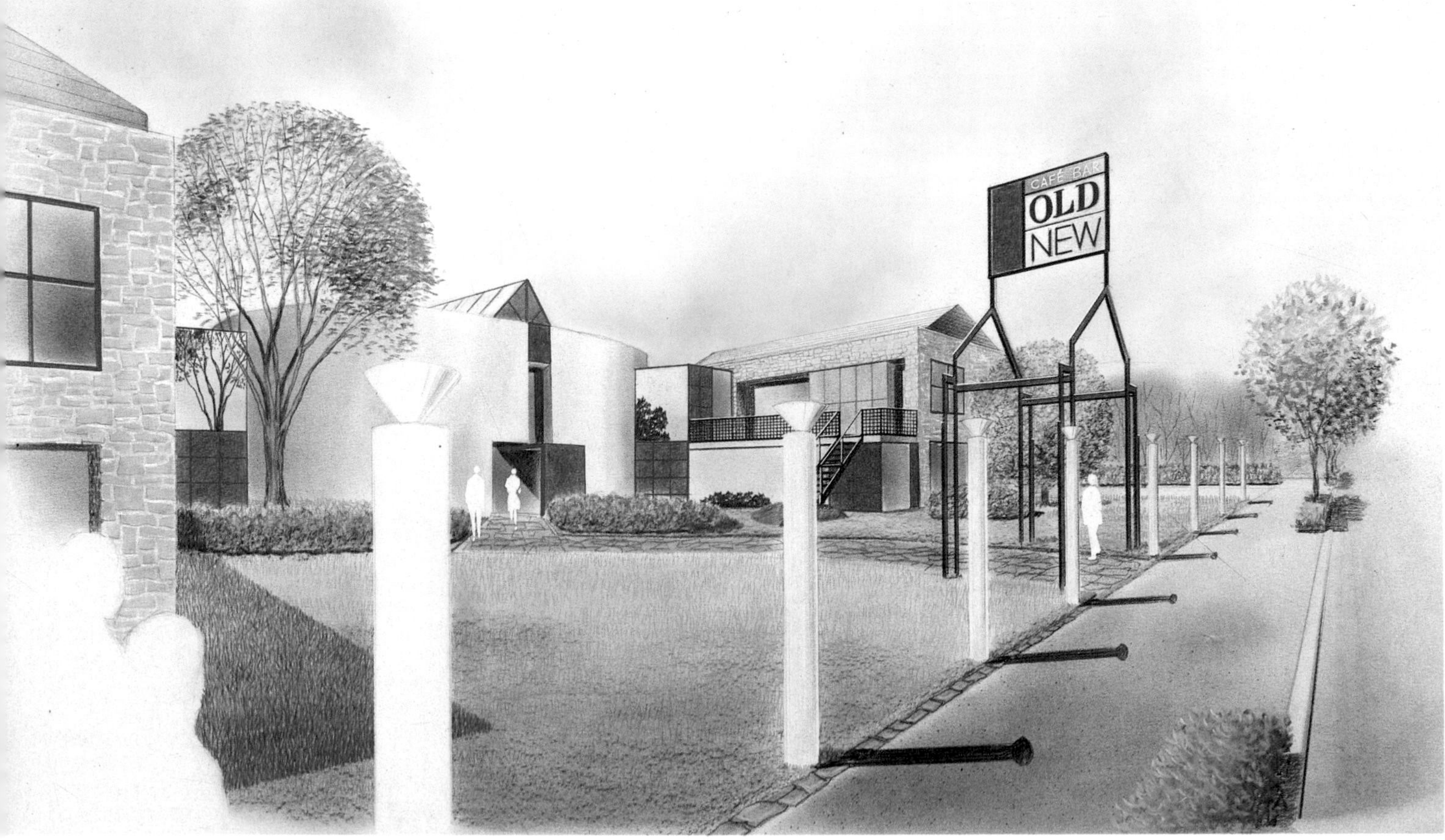

a. ゲストハウス オールドニュー　b. 東京都大田区
c. 竹中工務店　d. 竹中工務店　山岸和治　e. 竹中工務店

a. GUEST HOUSE OLD NEW　b. Ota-ku, Tokyo　c. Takenaka Komuten Co., Ltd.
d. Takenaka Komuten Co., Ltd., Katsuji Yamagishi　e. Takenaka Komuten Co., Ltd.

a. 台北県県立体育場全景　b. 板橋(台湾)
c. 乾隆廣告企業有限公司　d. 葛念台　e. 葛念台

a. TAIPEI SHAIN GYMNASIUM　b. Pan Chyau, Taiwan
c. Chyan Long Advertisement Co.　d. Ger Lain Tai　e. Ger Lain Tai

a. B・B・Cレストハウス　b. 三重県志摩町
c. デザム建築事務所　d. 吉田勝義　e. 吉田勝義

a. B.B.C. REST HOUSE　b. Shima-cho, Mie
c. Dezamu Architect Co., Ltd.　d. Katsuyoshi Yoshida　e. Katsuyoshi Yoshida

a. おのころアイランド　b. 兵庫県津名郡
c. くにうみの祭典実行委員会　d. 浅田能生　e. 浅田能生

a. ISLAND OF ONOKORO b. Tsuna-gun, Hyogo
c. Festival of Kuniumi Practice Committee d. Yoshio Asada e. Yoshio Asada

a. 箕面スパ・ガーデン　b. 大阪府箕面市
c. 坂倉建築研究所　d. 桑野忠　e. コラムデザインセンター

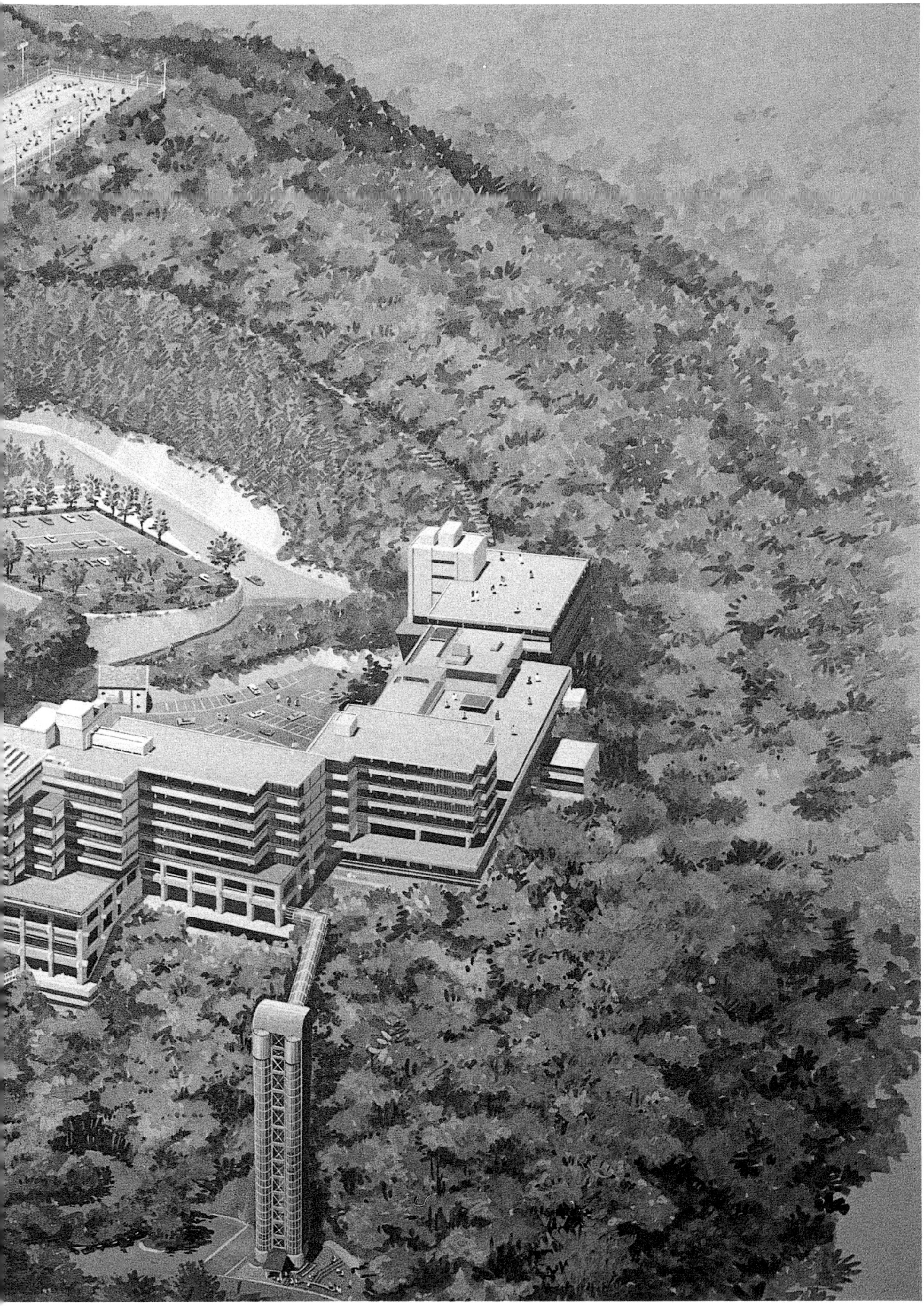

a. MINO SPA GARDEN b. Mino-shi, Osaka
c. Sakakura Associates Architecture & Engineering Co., Ltd. d. Tadashi Kuwano e. Koramu Design Center Co., Ltd.

a. 奥浜名湖ヨットクラブレスト
b. 静岡県浜名郡
c. デザム建築事務所
d. 吉田勝義
e. 吉田勝義

a. OKUHAMANAKO YACHT CLUB REST
b. Hamana-gun, Shizuoka
c. Dezamu Architect Co., Ltd.
d. Katsuyoshi Yoshida
e. Katsuyoshi Yoshida

a. ローベルジュ・デ・ブルーマーリン
b. 静岡県下田市
c. 殖産住宅相互
d. 斉木美香子
e. 殖産住宅相互

a. LAUBERGE DES BLUE MARLINS
b. Shimoda-shi, Shizuoka
c. Shokusan Jutaku Sogo Co., Ltd.
d. Mikako Saiki
e. Shokusan Jutaku Sogo Co., Ltd.

a. E．S．マリーナ　b. 神奈川県
c. 小田急建設　d. 安土実　e. 安土実

a. E.S.MARINA　b. Kanagawa
c. Odakyu Co., Ltd.　d. Minoru Azuchi　e. Minoru Azuchi

a. レストハウス計画案　b. 兵庫県加東郡
c. A & Nデザイン　d. 中根典子　e. 中根典子

a. RESTHOUSE　b. Kato-gun, Hyogo
c. A & N Design　d. Noriko Nakane　e. Noriko Nakane

a. 近鉄藤井寺球場　b. 大阪府藤井寺市
c. メディアート　d. 堀口憲嗣　e. 堀口憲嗣

a. KINTETSU STADIUM　b. Fujiidera-shi, Osaka
c. Mediart Co., Ltd.　d. Noritsugu Horiguchi　e. Noritsugu Horiguchi

a. ツイン21 ＭＩＤシアター　b. 大阪府大阪市
c. 日建設計（大阪）　d. 當山悦司　e. 日建設計（大阪）

a. TWIN 21 MID THEATER　b. Osaka-shi, Osaka
c. Nikken Sekkei Ltd.　d. Etsuji Toyama　e. Nikken Sekkei Ltd.

a. 科学万博ハートピア　自然美のパビリオン　b. 茨城県筑波研究学園都市
c. 清水建設　d. 細川桂子　e. 清水建設

a. TSUKUBA '85 HEART PAVILION　b. Tsukuba-gun Ibaraki
c. Shimizu Construction Co., Ltd.　d. Keiko Hosokawa　e. Shimizu Construction Co., Ltd.

a. 神戸海洋博物館（原案）　b. 兵庫県神戸市
c. 神戸市港湾局／日建設計（大阪）　d. 芳谷勝瀾　e. 日建設計

a. KOBE MARINE MUSEUM (ORIGINAL)　b. Kobe-shi, Hyogo
c. Kobe-shi Port Authority／Nikken Sekkei Ltd.　d. Katsumi Yoshitani　e. Nikken Sekkei Ltd.

a. 第 2 国立劇場設計競技（入賞案） b. 東京都渋谷区
c. 鹿島建設建築設計本部 e. 鹿島建設

a. THE SECOND NATIONAL THEATER DESIGN COMPETITION (PRIZE WINNER) b. Shibuya-ku, Tokyo
c. Kajima Corporation Architectural Design Division e. Kajima Corporation

a. 12ヶ月　b. 東京都渋谷区　c. 松田，平田，坂本　設計事務所
d. 水戸岡鋭治＋ドーンデザイン研究所　e. 水戸岡鋭治

a. TWELVE MONTHS　b. Shibuya-ku, Tokyo　c. Matsuda, Hirata & Sakamoto Architects, Planners & Engineers
d. Eiji Mitooka ＋ Don Design Assoc.　e. Eiji Mitooka

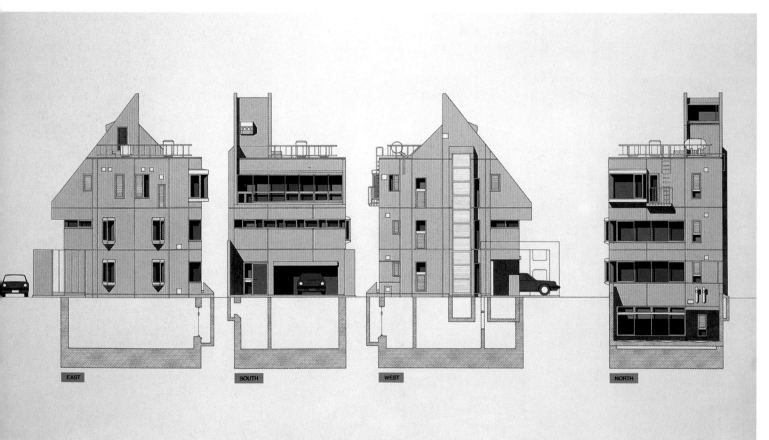

a. マスターズＲＩスタジオ　b. 東京都港区　c. マスターズ建築企画
d. 水戸岡鋭治＋ドーンデザイン研究所　e. 水戸岡鋭治

a. MASTER'S RI STUDIO　b. Minato-ku, Tokyo　c. Master's Planning Co., Ltd.
d. Eiji Mitooka＋Don Design Assoc.　e. Eiji Mitooka

a. パチンコ店
b. 群馬県太田市
c. 糸井設計
d. 津田益司
e. 津田益司

a. PACHINKO
b. Ota-shi, Gunma
c. Itoi Design
d. Masumori Tsuda
e. Masumori Tsuda

a. レジャービルアイオイ
b. 大阪府大阪市
c. 藤田建築設計事務所
d. 小西久雄
e. 小西久雄

a. LEISURE BUILDING AIOI
b. Osaka-shi, Osaka
c. Fujita Architectural & Engineering Firm
d. Hisao Konishi
e. Hisao Konishi

a. パチンコ「ディズニー」(計画案) b. 福岡県
c. 河野建築設計事務所 d. 坂井田優実 e. 坂井田優実

a. PACHINKO 'DISNEY' b. Fukuoka
c. Kono Architecture Design Office d. Yumi Sakaida e. Yumi Sakaida

a. パチンコ「岐阜サミット」 b. 岐阜県
c. 村瀬建築設計事務所 d. 坂井田優実 e. 坂井田優実

a. PACHINKO 'GIFU SUMMIT' b. Gifu
c. Murase Architectural Office d. Yumi Sakaida e. Yumi Sakaida

4.住宅

学生会館

ナーシングホーム

集合住宅

ビラ

マンション

個人住宅

寮

ハイツ

etc.

4.RESIDENCES

Student Centers

Nursing Homes

Housing Developments

Pre-fabricated Homes

Villa Mansions

Private Homes

Dormitories

etc.

a. 環亜門第
b. 台北市南京本路（台湾）
c. 精心設計公司
d. 陳釙贈
e. 陳釙贈

a. ASIAWORLD PLAZA
b. Taipei, Taiwan
c. Deliberate Design Co., Ltd.
d. Chen Paul
e. Chen Paul

a. 初穂グアムコンドミニアム
b. グアム
c. パシフィック設計
d. 山城義彦
e. 山城デザインスタジオ

a. HATSUHO GUAM CONDOMINIUM
b. Guam
c. Pacific Design Co., Ltd.
d. Yoshihiko Yamashiro
e. Yamashiro Design Studio

a. 湘南学生会館（仮称） b. 神奈川県秦野市
c. 殖産住宅相互 d. 坂本牧子 e. 殖産住宅相互

a. SHONAN GAKUSEI KAIKAN b. Hadano-shi, Kanagawa
c. Shokusan Jutaku Sogo Co., Ltd. d. Makiko Sakamoto e. Shokusan Jutaku Sogo Co., Ltd.

a. 新竹科学園区宿舎 b. 新竹科学園区（台湾）
c. 陳其寛建築師事務所 d. 金斯倉 e. 金斯倉

a. SHIN-JWU SCIENCE REGION DORMITORY b. Shin-Jwu Science Region,Taiwan
c. Chern Chyi-kuan Architecture Office d. King S Tsang e. King S Tsang

a. サンハウス野並　b. 愛知県名古屋市
c. 杉本設計　d. 川上和子　e. 川上和子

a. SUN HOUSE NONAMI　b. Nagoya-shi, Aichi
c. Sugimoto Sekkei Co., Ltd.　d. Kazuko Kawakami　e. Kazuko Kawakami

a. エスポワール平針　b. 愛知県名古屋市
c. 名研設計　d. 川上和子　e. 川上和子

a. ESUPOWARU HIRABARI　b. Nagoya-shi, Aichi
c. Meiken Sekkei Co., Ltd.　d. Kazuko Kawakami　e. Kazuko Kawakami

a. シティハイツ土佐堀　b. 大阪府大阪市
c. 関西建設コンサルタント　d. エクステリアパース・吉田　e. エクステリアパース・吉田

a. CITY HEIGHTS TOSABORI　b. Osaka-shi, Osaka　c. Kansai Civil & Architectural Consultants
d. Exterior Pers - Yoshida　e. Exterior Pers - Yoshida

a. ピュアハイツ星ヶ丘　b. 兵庫県神戸市
c. 太平工業広畑支店　d. 四海隼一　e. 四海隼一

a. PURE HEIGHTS HOSHIGAOKA　b. Kobe-shi, Hyogo
c. Taihei Kogyo Co., Ltd. Hirohata Branch　d. Shikai Shunichi　e. Shikai Shunichi

a. 東京都東村山ナーシングホーム（仮称）　b. 東京都東村山市
c. アール・アイ・エー建築綜合研究所　d. 斉藤富子　e. 斉藤富子

a. TOKYO HIGASHIMURAYAMA NURSING HOME　b. Higashimurayama-shi, Tokyo
c. Research Institute of Architecture Co., Ltd.　d. Tomiko Saito　e. Tomiko Saito

a. エスポア「自由ヶ丘」 b. 愛知県名古屋市
c. 東海興業名古屋支店 d. 坂井田優実 e. 坂井田優実

a. ESPOIR JIYUGAOKA b. Nagoya-shi, Aichi
c. Tokai Kogyo Co., Ltd. Nagoya Office d. Yumi Sakaida e. Yumi Sakaida

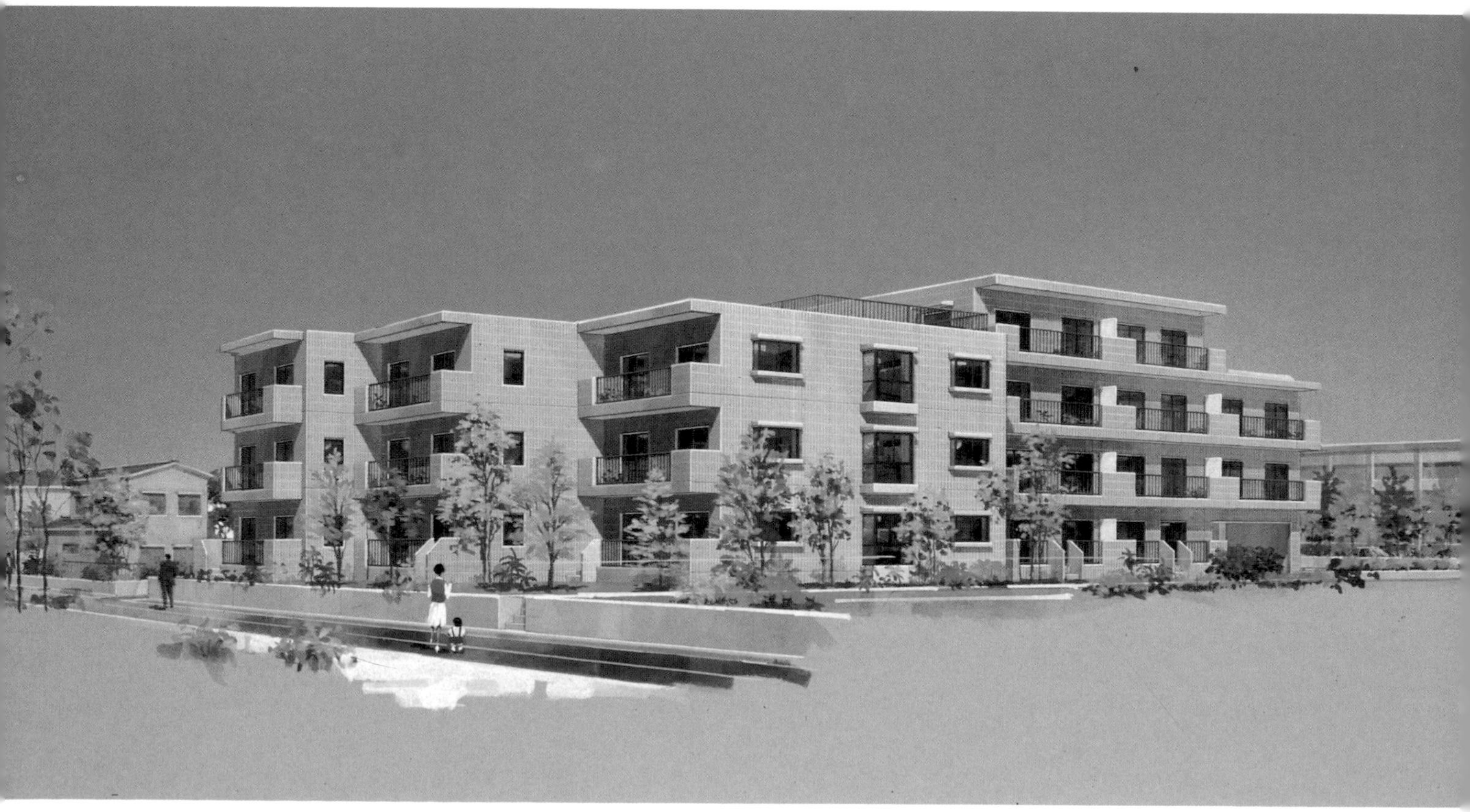

a. キャニオンガーデン豊島園 b. 東京都練馬区
d. 箕箸重郎 e. 箕箸重郎

a. CANYON GARDEN TOSHIMAEN b. Nerima-ku, Tokyo
d. Juro Mihashi e. Juro Mihashi

a. キャニオンマンション常盤台　b. 東京都板橋区
c. 早川綜合設計　d. 箕箸純子　e. 箕箸純子

a. CANYON MANSION TOKIWADAI　b. Itabashi-ku, Tokyo
c. Hayakawa Co., Ltd.　d. Junko Mihashi　e. Junko Mihashi

a. キャニオンマンション西台　b. 東京都板橋区
c. 石川正義建築事務所　d. 清水俊裕　e. 清水俊裕

a. CANYON MANSION NISHIDAI　b. Itabashi-ku, Tokyo
c. Ishikawa　d. Toshihiro Shimizu　e. Toshihiro Shimizu

a. 電通独身寮
b. 東京都
c. 清水建設
d. 中門静子
e. 中門静子

a. DENTSU BACHELOR DORMITORY
b. Tokyo
c. Shimizu Construction Co., Ltd.
d. Shizuko Nakakado
e. Shizuko Nakakado

a. 原マンション(仮称)
b. 東京都調布市
c. 殖産住宅相互
d. 斉木美香子
e. 殖産住宅相互

a. HARA MANSION
b. Chofu-shi, Tokyo
c. Shokusan Jutaku Sogo Co., Ltd.
d. Mikako Saiki
e. Shokusan Jutaku Sogo Co., Ltd.

a. アルファ清心町
b. 岡山県
c. 穴吹工務店一級建築士事務所
d. 金本正
e. 金本正

a. ALPHA SEISHINCHO
b. Okayama
c. Anahuki Komuten
d. Tadashi Kanemoto
e. Tadashi Kanemoto

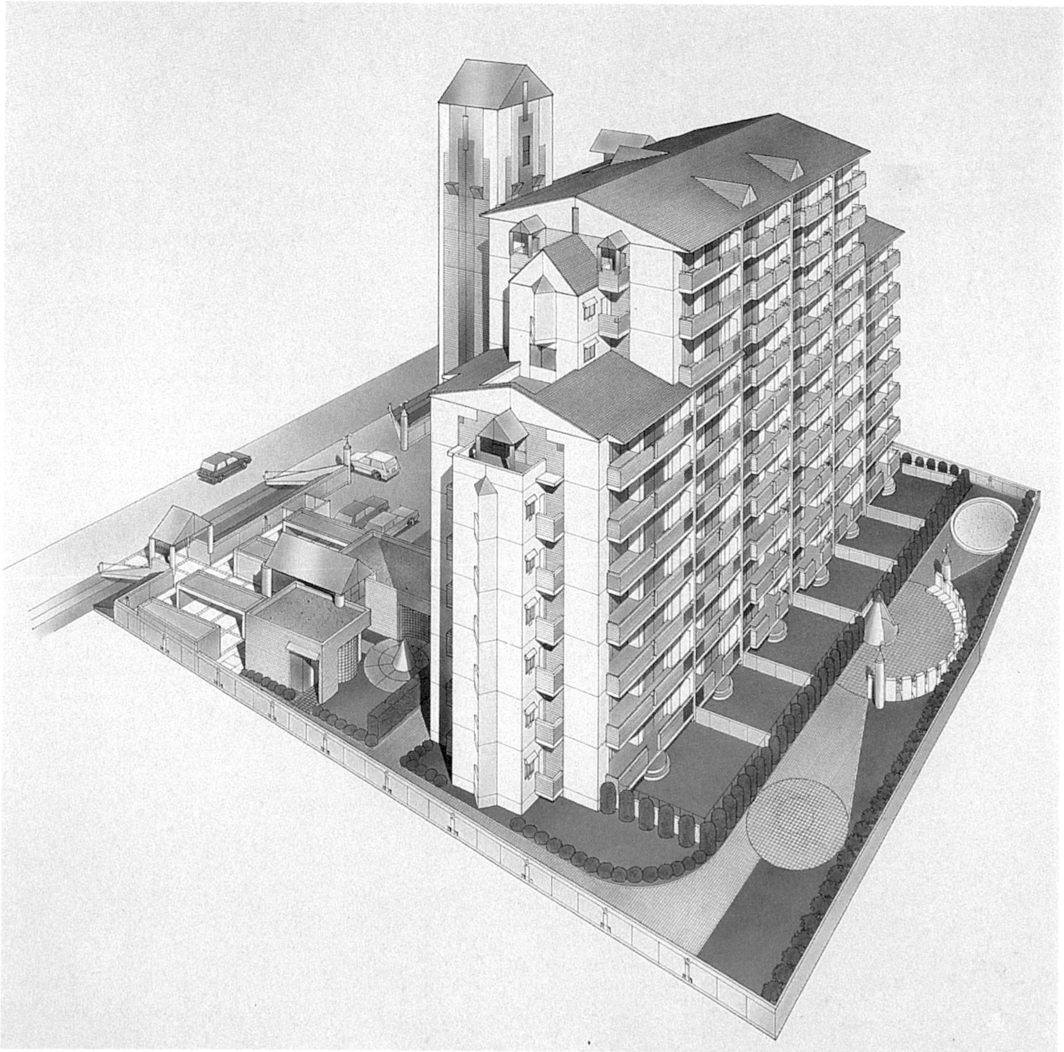

a. サーパス木太
b. 香川県高松市
c. 穴吹工務店一級建築士事務所
d. 金本正
e. 金本正

a. SURPASS KITA
b. Takamatsu-shi, Kagawa
c. Anahuki Komuten
d. Tadashi Kanemoto
e. Tadashi Kanemoto

a. 住宅　b. 福岡県
c. 中村建築設計事務所　d. 中根典子　e. 中根典子

a. HOUSE　b. Fukuoka
c. Nakamura Architectural Office　d. Noriko Nakane　e. Noriko Nakane

a. Y計画
c. 丹青社
d. 前島和也
e. 丹青社

a. Y PLAN
c. Tanseisha Co., Ltd.
d. Kazuya Maejima
e. Tanseisha Co., Ltd.

a. 千氏住宅　b. 慶南三千浦市（韓國）
c. 綜合建築士事務所 建園　d. 金容培　e. 金容培

a. CHUN'S HOUSE　b. Kyoung Nam, Sam Chun Po City
c. Kun Won Institute for Environmental Design & Planning　d. Yong Bae Kim　e. Yong Bae Kim

a. パナハイツ ウィンディア
c. ナショナル住宅産業
d. 津田勉
e. 津田勉

a. PANAHEIGHTS WINDIA
c. National House Industrial Co., Ltd.
d. Tsutomu Tsuda
e. Tsutomu Tsuda

a. グロリアハイツ碑文谷　b. 東京都目黒区
c. 石原トータルプランニング　d. とみあとりえ　e. 斉藤富子

a. GLORIA HEIGHTS HIMONYA　b. Meguro-ku, Tokyo
c. Ishihara Total Planning Co., Ltd.　d. Tomiatorie　e. Tomiko Saito

a. 八王子びら　b. 静岡県浜松市
c. 須山建設　d. 和田宅矛（造研）　e. 和田宅矛

a. HACHIOUJI VILLA　b. Hamamatsu-shi, Shizuoka
c. Suyamakensetsu Co., Ltd.　d. Takumu Wada (Zoken)　e. Takumu Wada

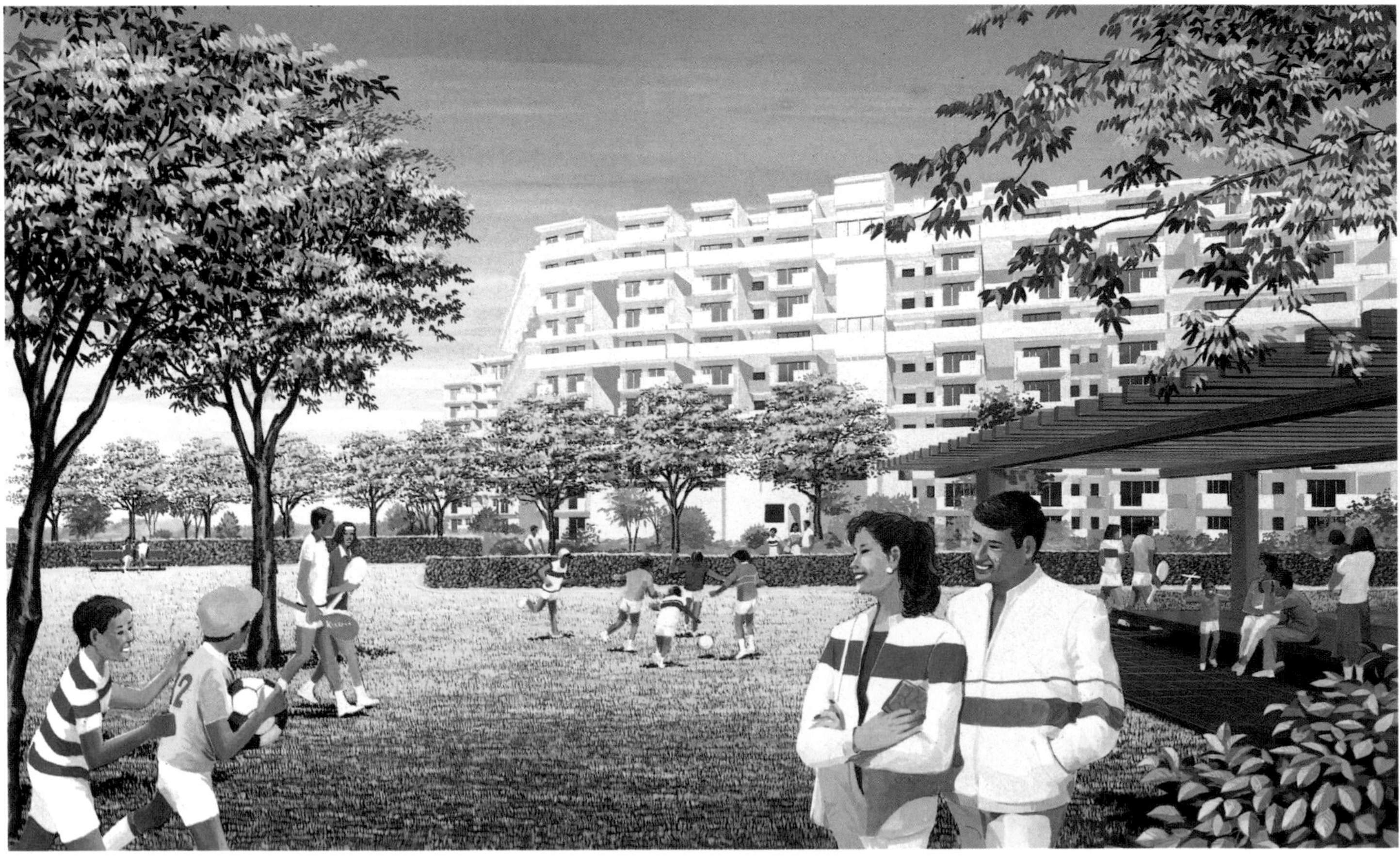

a. ビレッジ船橋　b. 千葉県船橋市
c. 東急不動産　d. 山城義彦　e. 山城デザインスタジオ

a. VILLAGE FUNABASHI　b. Funabashi-shi, Chiba
c. Tokyu Land Corporation　d. Yoshihiko Yamashiro　e. Yamashiro Design Studio

a. 明治薬科大学八ヶ岳寮
b. 山梨県清里
c. 鹿島建設建築設計本部
e. 鹿島建設

a. YATSUGATAKE SEMINAR HOUSE FOR THE MEIJI COLLEGE OF PHARMACY
b. Kiyosato, Yamanashi
c. Kajima Corporation Architectural Design Division
e. Kajima Corporation

a. アトリエ付邸宅
b. 大阪府東大阪市
c. 平山建築事務所
d. エクステリアパース・吉田
e. エクステリアパース・吉田

a. ATELIER & RESIDENCE
b. Higashi Osaka-shi, Osaka
c. Hirayama Associated Architects
d. Exterior Pers-Yoshida
e. Exterior Pers-Yoshida

a. 住宅　c. 積水ハウス
d. いでのよしえ　e. いでのよしえ

a. HOUSE PLAN　c. Sekisui House
d. Yoshie Ideno　e. Yoshie Ideno

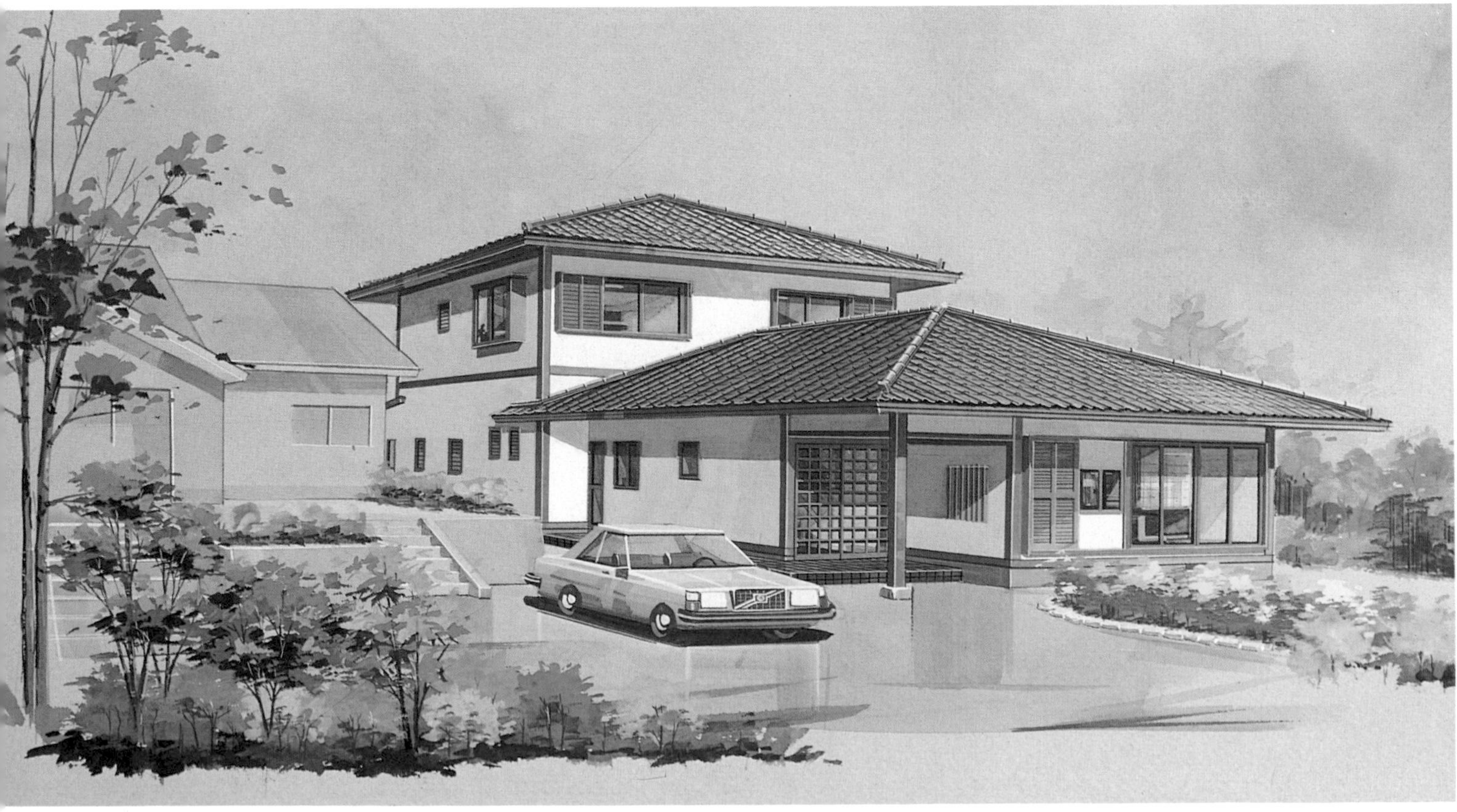

a. 大石邸　b. 静岡県袋井市
c. 智建築設計室　d. 和田宅矛　e. 和田宅矛

a. OISHI TEI　b. Fukuroi-shi, Shizuoka
c. Tomo Architectural Design Room　d. Takumu Wada　e. Takumu Wada

5.事務所ビル

生命保険会社ビル

商社ビル

一般事務所ビル

銀行

共同ビル

etc.

5.OFFICE BUILDINGS

Life Insurance Companies

Business Buildings

Tokyo Gas

Offices

Banking Partnerships

etc.

a. コリンズ計画　b. 東京都新宿区
c. 鹿島建設建築設計本部　e. 鹿島建設

a. OFFICE BLDG. FOR COLLINS CO., LTD.　b. Shinjuku-ku, Tokyo
c. Kajima Corporation Architectural Design Division　e. Kajima Construction Corporation

a. ＳＴ計画　b. 宮城県仙台市
c. 竹中工務店　d. 竹中工務店　佐藤忠明　e. 竹中工務店

a. ST PROJECT　b. Sendai-shi, Miyagi　c. Takenaka Komuten Co., Ltd.
d. Takenaka Komuten Co., Ltd., Tadaaki Sato　e. Takenaka Komuten Co., Ltd.

a. Mビル　b. 大阪府大阪市
c. 総合都市設計　d. 橋本デザイン事務所　橋本秀章　e. 橋本デザイン事務所

a. M. BUILDING　b. Osaka-shi, Osaka　c. Sogotoshi Sekkei Co., Ltd.
d. Hashimoto Design Office, Hideaki Hashimoto　e. Hashimoto Design Office

a. 神戸セントラル開発ビル　b. 兵庫県神戸市
c. 竹中工務店　d. 竹中工務店　絹田貞子　e. 竹中工務店

a. KOBE CENTRAL KAIHATSU BUILDING　b. Kobe-shi, Hyogo　c. Takenaka Komuten Co., Ltd.
d. Takenaka Komuten Co., Ltd., Sadako Kinuta　e. Takenaka Komuten Co., Ltd.

a. ビル　b. 大阪府
c. 環匠社　d. レンダリング RIYA　e. レンダリング RIYA

a. BLDG.　b. Osaka
c. Kanshosha Co., Ltd.　d. Rendering RIYA Co., Ltd.　e. Rendering RIYA Co., Ltd.

a. ＡＳ計画　b. 秋田県秋田市
c. 竹中工務店　d. 竹中工務店　佐藤忠明　e. 竹中工務店

a. AS PROJECT　b. Akita-shi, Akita　c. Takenaka Komuten Co., Ltd.
d. Takenaka Komuten Co., Ltd., Tadaaki Sato　e. Takenaka Komuten Co., Ltd.

a. 東邦生命社屋
b. SEOUL 中区太平路（韓國）
c. BECKET INTERNATIONAL 社（美國）／三友設計（韓國）
d. 安容植
e. 安建社

a. DONG BANG PLAZA
b. Seoul Joong Gu Tae Pyong-Ro, Korea
c. Becket International Co. (USA)／Sam Woo Planning Institute Co. (Korea)
d. An Yong Sik
e. Ankunsa

a. 1996（習作）
d. 津田勉
e. 津田勉

a. 1996
d. Tsutomu Tsuda
e. Tsutomu Tsuda

a. 大阪北野ビル　b. 大阪府大阪市
c. 積水ハウス　d. 喜多照子　e. 積水ハウス大阪綜建営業所

a. OSAKA KITANO BUILDING　b. Osaka-shi, Osaka
c. Sekisui House Ltd.　d. Teruko Kita　e. Sekisui House Ltd. Osaka Soken Office

a. 沼津ビルディング　b. 静岡県沼津市
c. 志村建築設計事務所　d. 西川日出世　e. アトリエ TOKI

a. NUMAZU BLDG.　b. Numazu-shi, Shizuoka
c. Shimura Construction Design Office Co., Ltd.　d. Hideyo Nishikawa　e. Atorie Toki

a. 第百生命高松ビル　b. 香川県高松市
c. 田邊博司　レーモンド設計事務所　d. 塩田純一　e. 塩田純一

a. DAIHYAKU SEIMEI TAKAMATSU BLDG.　b. Takamatsu-shi, Kagawa
c. Hiroshi Tanabe Raymond A.D. Office Inc.　d. Junichi Shiota　e. Junichi Shiota

a. 東京ガスビルディング　b. 東京都港区
c. 三菱地所一級建築士事務所　d. 第三建築部　フクナガレンダリング　e. 三菱地所

a. TOKYO GAS BUILDING　b. Minato-ku, Tokyo　c. Mitsubishi Estate Co., Ltd.
d. The Third Architectural and Engineering Department　e. Mitsubishi Estate

a. 丸紅大阪本社ビル
b. 大阪府東区
c. 三菱地所一級建築士事務所
d. フクナガレンダリング
e. 三菱地所

a. MARUBENI CORPORATION OSAKA OFFICE
b. Higashi-ku, Osaka
c. Mitsubishi Estate Co., Ltd.
d. Fukunaga Rendering Co., Ltd.
e. Mitsubishi Estate Co., Ltd.

a. 服部ビル
b. 北海道札幌市
c. フジタ工業
d. 髙崎千鶴子
e. 髙崎千鶴子

a. HATTORI BLDG.
b. Sapporo-shi, Hokkaido
c. Fujita Industry Co., Ltd.
d. Chizuko Takasaki
e. Chizuko Takasaki

a. 廣-大廈
b. 台北（台湾）
c. 藝洲廣告設計公司
d. 鍾文虎
e. 鍾文虎

a. KAI-YUE BLDG.
b. Taipei, Taiwan
c. Yue-Shou Development Design Co.
d. Jong Wen-Huu
e. Jong Wen-Huu

a. 人形町 I － I ビル
b. 東京都中央区
c. 竹中工務店
d. 竹中工務店　松浦眞巳
e. 竹中工務店

a. NINGYO-CHO I-I BLDG.
b. Chuo-ku, Tokyo
c. Takenaka Komuten Co., Ltd.
d. Takenaka Komuten Co., Ltd., Masami Matsuura
e. Takenaka Komuten Co., Ltd.

a. ゴールドタワー　b. 兵庫県神戸市
c. 設計工房ゼロ　d. 森山雅彦　e. コラムデザインセンター

a. GOLD TOWER　b. Kobe-shi, Hyogo
c. Creative Room Zero　d. Masahiko Moriyama　e. Koramu Design Center Co., Ltd.

a. I．D．A．九段下ビル　b. 東京都千代田区
c. 都市建築設計　d. 赤坂孝史　e. アカサカレンダリング

a. I.D.A. KUDAN-SHITA BLDG.　b. Chiyoda-ku, Tokyo
c. International Design Architect Co., Ltd.　d. Takashi Akasaka　e. Akasaka Rendering

a. 匯泰台大華厦
b. 羅斯福路与辛亥路交叉口（台湾）
c. 三門建築師事務所
d. 金斯倉
e. 金斯倉

a. TAI-DAN BLDG.
b. Taipei, Taiwan
c. San-men Building Company
d. King S Tsang
e. King S Tsang

a. 山京商事本館，別館
b. 東京都千代田区
c. 幸和建築設計事務所
d. 成瀬英揮
e. 成瀬英揮

a. SANKYO SHOJI
b. Chiyoda-ku, Tokyo
c. Kowa Associated Architects and Engineers Co., Ltd.
d. Hideki Naruse
e. Hideki Naruse

a. 川崎信用金庫　b. 神奈川県川崎市
c. 乃村工藝社　d. 柳川敏行　e. 柳川敏行

a. KAWASAKI SHINYO KINKO　b. Kawasaki-shi, Kanagawa
c. Nomura Display Co., Ltd.　d. Toshiyuki Yanagawa　e. Toshiyuki Yanagawa

a. 香山ビル
b. 東京都新宿区
c. 三衛建築設計事務所
d. 清水俊裕
e. 清水俊裕

a. KAYAMA BLDG.
b. Shinjuku-ku, Tokyo
c. Sanei Associated Architects and Engineers Co., Ltd.
d. Toshihiro Shimizu
e. Toshihiro Shimizu

a. 平和台クリスタル２１７　b. 東京都練馬区
c. 三栄建築事務所　d. 成瀬英揮　e. 成瀬英揮

a. HEIWADAI CRYSTAL 217　b. Nerima-ku, Tokyo
c. Sanei Associated Architects and Engineers Co., Ltd.　d. Hideki Naruse　e. Hideki Naruse

a. 伊藤園ビル　b. 沖縄県浦添市
c. 大浜設計　d. 橋本弘徳　e. 橋本弘徳

a. ITOEN BUILDING　b. Urasoe-shi, Okinawa
c. Ohama Architectural Office　d. Hironori Hashimoto　e. Hironori Hashimoto

a. 樂華黃金城
b. 台北（台湾）
c. 輝鴻廣告事業有限公司
d. 吳長鴻
e. 吳長鴻

a. LEH-HWA GOLDEN TOWN
b. Taipei, Taiwan
c. Whain Hong Advertisement Co.
d. Wu Chang-Hong
e. Wu Chang-Hong

a. 出水センタービル
b. 鹿児島県出水市
c. 岡田設計
d. 春田信行
e. 現代画房

a. IZUMI CENTER BUILDING
b. Izumi-shi, Kagoshima
c. Okada Planning Co., Ltd.
d. Nobuyuki Haruta
e. Gendai Gabo Co., Ltd.

a. 日本銀行大阪支店
b. 大阪府大阪市
c. 日建設計（大阪）
d. 芳谷勝濔
e. 日建設計

a. NIHONGINKO OSAKA SHITEN
b. Osaka-shi, Osaka
c. Nikken Sekkei Ltd.
d. Katsumi Yoshitani
e. Nikken Sekkei Ltd.

a. 栃木相互銀行東越谷支店
b. 埼玉県越谷市
c. ATO 綜合設計
d. 斉藤富子
e. 斉藤富子

a. TOCHIGI SOGO BANK
b. Koshigaya-shi, Saitama
c. ATO Architects & Engineers Co.
d. Tomiko Saito
e. Tomiko Saito

K.YOSHITANI

栃木相互銀行

a. クリーニング・ツネトミヤビル
b. 岐阜県羽島郡
c. 聖設計事務所
d. 小野木司
e. 建築造型

a. CLEANING TSUNETOMIYA
b. Hashima-gun, Gifu
c. Hijiri Planning Office Co., Ltd.
d. Tsukasa Onogi
e. Kenchiku Zokei

a. オフィス・ビル
b. 大阪府大阪市
c. マセ建築設計事務所
d. 中根典子
e. 中根典子

a. OFFICE BUILDING
b. Osaka-shi, Osaka
c. Mase Architectural Office
d. Noriko Nakane
e. Noriko Nakane

a. N社N町支店再開発計画　b. 東京都中央区
c. 鹿島建設建築設計本部　e. 鹿島建設

a. OFFICE BLDG. FOR N CO., LTD.　b. Chuo-ku, Tokyo
c. Kajima Corporation Architectural Design Division　e. Kajima Construction Corporation

a. 安田生命仙台第4ビル　b. 宮城県仙台市
c. 鹿島建設建築設計本部　e. 鹿島建設

a. SENDAI DAIYON BLDG. FOR THE YASUDA MUTUAL LIFE INSURANCE CO.　b. Sendai-shi, Miyagi
c. Kajima Corporation Architectural Design Division　e. Kajima Construction Corporation

a. 共栄火災徳島ビル　b. 徳島県徳島市
c. 旭栄建築設計　d. 赤坂孝史　e. 赤坂孝史

a. KYOEI KASAI TOKUSHIMA　b. Tokushima-shi, Tokushima
c. Kyokuei Architect Design Co., Ltd.　d. Takashi Akasaka　e. Takashi Akasaka

a. 烏丸プラザ（仮称） b. 京都府京都市
c. 一粒社ヴォーリズ建築事務所 d. 浅田能生 e. 浅田能生

a. KARASUMA PLAZA b. Kyoto-shi, Kyoto
c. Ichiryusha Vories Architectural Office Inc. d. Yoshio Asada e. Yoshio Asada

a. かくやビル
b. 奈良県奈良市
c. 積水ハウス
d. 西村正純
e. 積水ハウス大阪綜建営業所

a. KAKUYA BLDG.
b. Nara-shi, Nara
c. Sekisui House Ltd.
d. Masazumi Nishimura
e. Sekisui House Ltd. Osaka Soken Office

a. ビル計画案
b. 兵庫県神戸市
c. 村上工務店
d. 森聖一デザイン事務所　森聖一
e. 森聖一

a. BUILDING PLAN
b. Kobe-shi, Hyogo
c. Murakami Komuten Co., Ltd.
d. Seiichi Mori Design Office
e. Seiichi Mori

a. 日本橋浜町Ｍビル
b. 東京都中央区
c. 殖産住宅相互
d. 坂本牧子
e. 殖産住宅相互

a. NIHONBASHI HAMACHO M. BLDG.
b. Chuo-ku, Tokyo
c. Shokusan Jutaku Sogo Co., Ltd.
d. Makiko Sakamoto
e. Shokusan Jutaku Sogo Co., Ltd.

a. ＭＧビル
b. 大阪府大阪市
c. 積水ハウス
d. 西村正純
e. 積水ハウス大阪綜建営業所

a. MG BUILDING
b. Osaka-shi, Osaka
c. Sekisui House Ltd.
d. Masazumi Nishimura
e. Sekisui House Ltd. Osaka Soken Office

a. 新宿西口共同ビル「ＦＦビル」
b. 東京都新宿区
c. 日本設計事務所／タス
d. 深谷彪
e. 深谷彪

a. SHINJUKU 'FF' BLDG.
b. Shinjuku-ku, Tokyo
c. Nihon Architects & Consultants Inc./TAS
d. Akira Fukaya
e. Akira Fukaya

a. 鹿児島錦江湾ビル（計画案） b. 鹿児島県鹿児島市
c. アトリエ・ヒロシ・フクナガ d. 春田信行 e. 現代画房

a. KAGOSHIMA KINKO WAN BLDG. b. Kagoshima-shi, Kagoshima
c. Atelier Hiroshi Fukunaga d. Nobuyuki Haruta e. Gendai Gabo

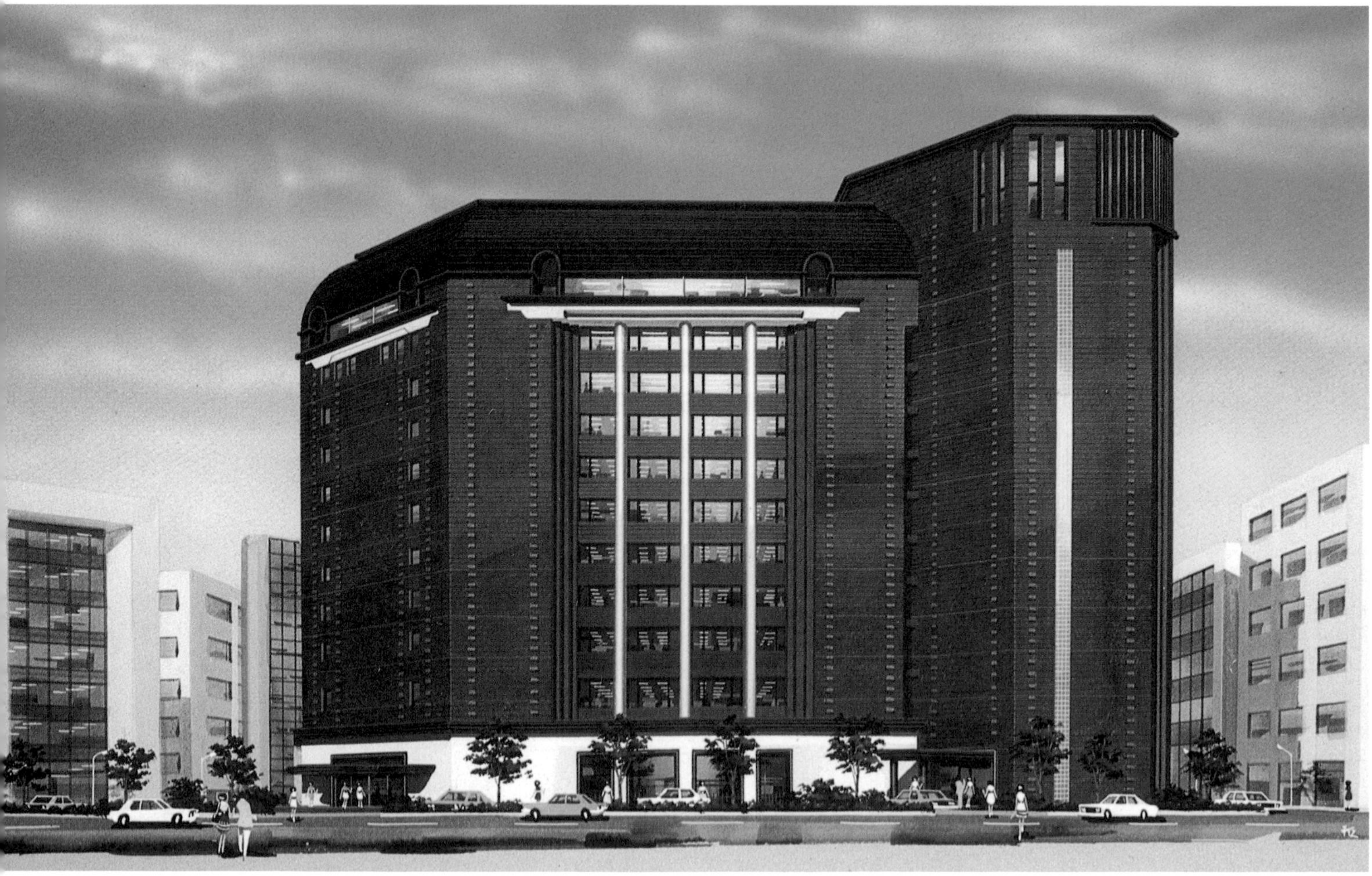

a. 台北Aビル計画 b. 台北市（台湾）
c. 丹青社 d. 前島和也 e. 丹青社

a. TAIPEI A BLDG. PLAN b. Taipei, Taiwan
c. Tanseisha Co., Ltd. d. Kazuya Maejima e. Tanseisha Co., Ltd.

6. 公共施設　その他

大学

総合病院

体育館

庁舎

駅前再開発

コミュニケーションセンター

デザイン研究所

記念文庫

etc.

6. PUBLIC FACILITIES

Universities

General Hospitals

Government Office Buildings

Stationfront Re-development

Communication Centers

Purification Plants

Design Research Centers

Memorial Archives

etc.

a. 東海大学湘南校舎12号館　b. 神奈川県
c. 大成建設　d. 西川日出世　e. アトリエ TOKI

a. TOKAI UNIVERSITY SHONAN SCHOOL BUILDING NO.12　b. Kanagawa
c. Taisei Construction Co., Ltd.　d. Hideyo Nishikawa　e. Atorie Toki

a. いわき明星大学　b. 福島県いわき市
c. 白川建築設計事務所　d. テツ・デザイン　伊藤鉄平　e. 伊藤鉄平

a. IWAKI MEISEI UNIVERSITY　b. Iwaki-shi, Fukushima
c. Shirakawa Kenchiku Sekkei Co., Ltd.　d. Tetsu Design Teppei Ito　e. Teppei Ito

a. 中國廟宇
b. 鹿苑（台湾）
c. 乾隆廣告企業有限公司
d. 葛念台
e. 葛念台

a. CHINA TEMPLE
b. Luh Yuann, Taiwan
c. Chyan Long Advertisement Co.
d. Ger Lain Tai
e. Ger Lain Tai

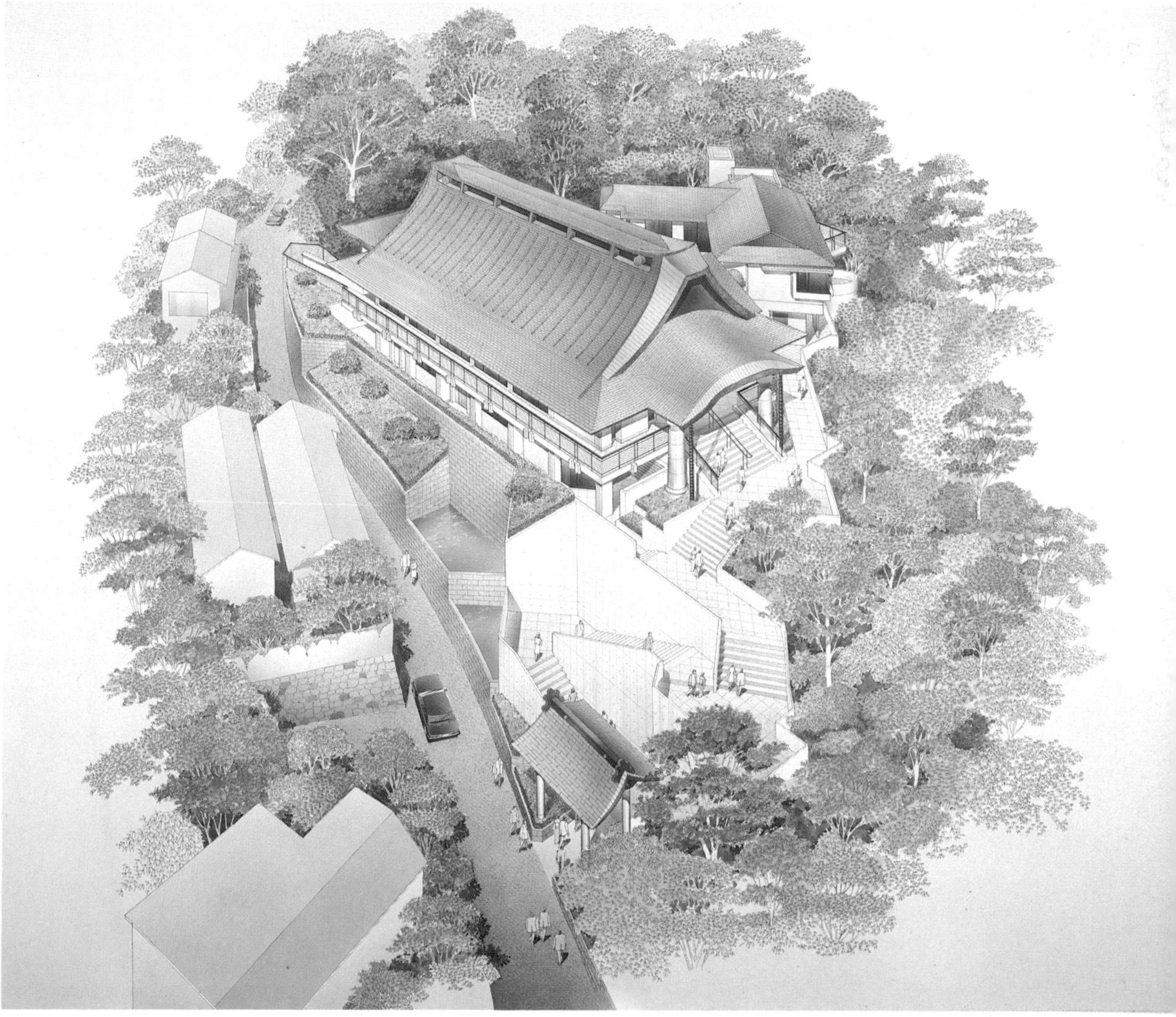

a. 法照寺寺院
b. 静岡県
c. 勝又由紀夫建築事務所
d. 山城義彦
e. 山城デザインスタジオ

a. HOSHOJI TEMPLE
b. Shizuoka
c. Katsumata Yukio Architectural Office
d. Yoshihiko Yamashiro
e. Yamashiro Design Studio

a. 神戸市庁舎　b. 兵庫県神戸市
c. 日建設計　d. 柳谷隆　e. 日建設計

a. KOBE CITY HALL　b. Kobe-shi, Hyogo
c. Nikken Sekkei Ltd.　d. Takashi Yanagitani　e. Nikken Sekkei Ltd.

a. 具志川市庁舎　b. 沖縄県具志川市
c. 国建　d. 橋本弘徳　e. 橋本弘徳

a. GUSHIKAWA CITY OFFICE　b. Gushikawa-shi, Okinawa
c. Kuniken Co., Ltd.　d. Hironori Hashimoto　e. Hironori Hashimoto

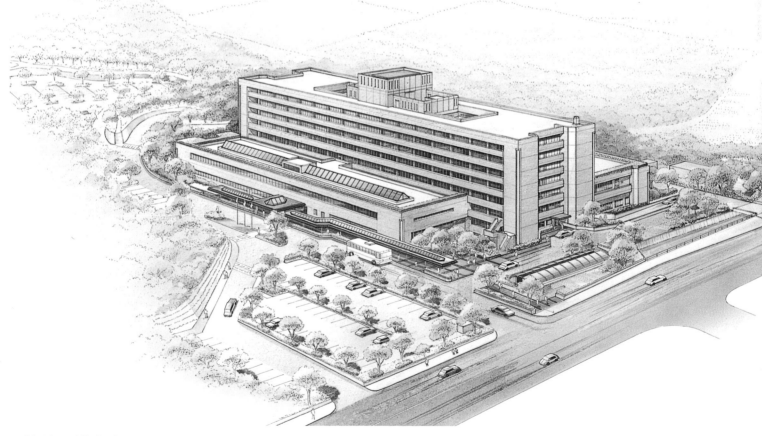

a. 清水市立総合病院（仮称）　b. 静岡県清水市
c. 田中建築事務所　d. とみあとりえ　斉藤富子　e. 斉藤富子

a. SHIMIZU CITY HOSPITAL　b. Shimizu-shi, Shizuoka
c. Tanaka Architectural Office　d. Tomiatorie　Tomiko Saito　e. Tomiko Saito

a. 八反丸病院　b. 鹿児島県鹿児島市
c. 設計事務所九州ゲンプラン　d. 春田信行　e. 現代画房

a. HATTANMARU HOSPITAL　b. Kagoshima-shi, Kagoshima
c. Kyushu Genplan Co., Ltd.　d. Nobuyuki Haruta　e. Gendai Gabo

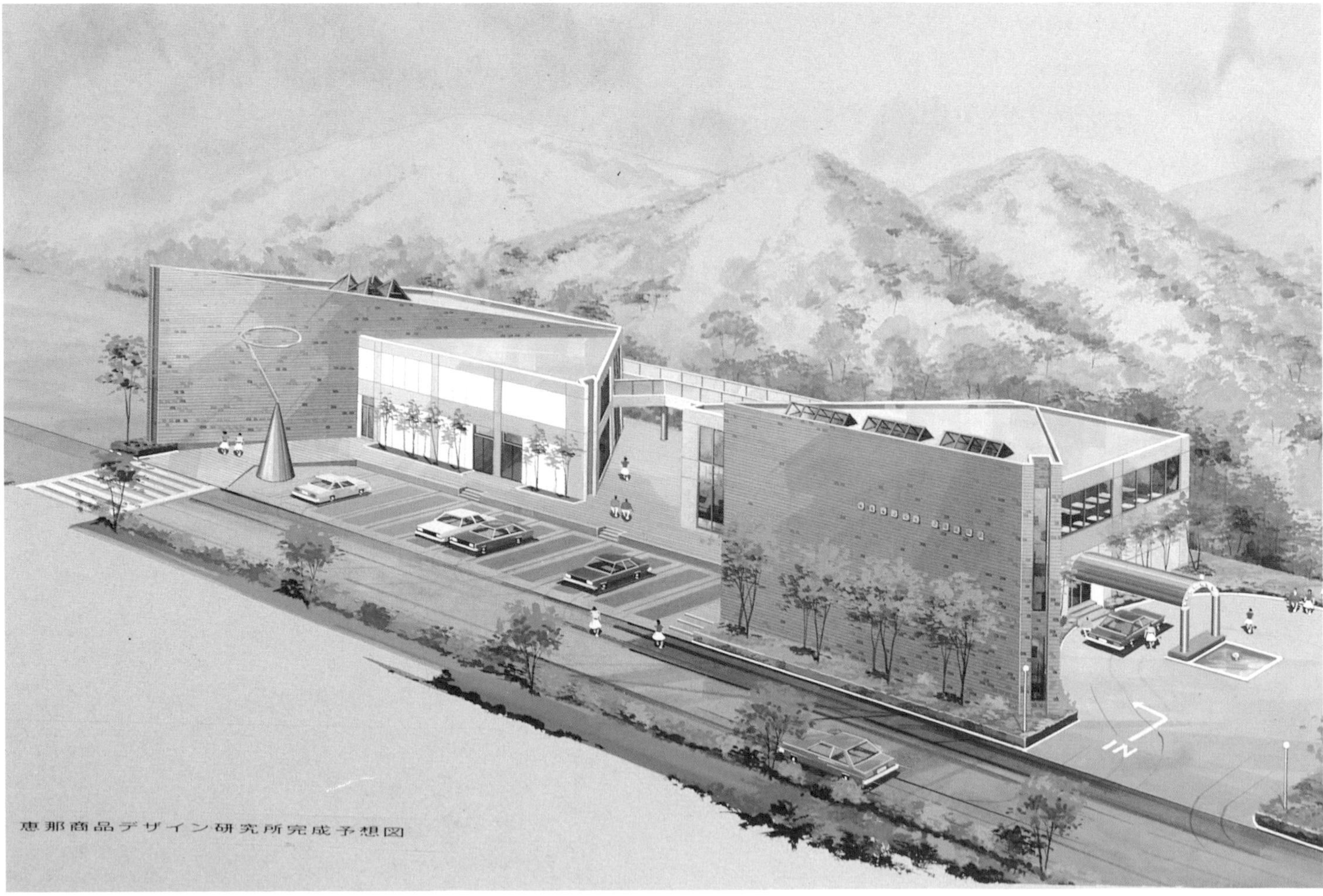

a. 恵那商品デザイン研究所　b. 岐阜県恵那市
c. 渋谷仁絵設計室＋加藤誠　d. 和田宅矛（造研）　e. 和田宅矛

a. ENA DESIGN INSTITUTE　b. Ena-shi, Gifu
c. Hitoe Shibuya & Makoto Kato　d. Takumu Wada (Zoken)　e. Takumu Wada

a. 郡山町庁舎（コンペ当選案） b. 鹿児島県郡山町
c. AOI 美建 d. 春田信行 e. 現代画房

a. KORIYAMA-CHO CHOSHA b. Koriyama-cho, Kagoshima
c. AOI Biken Co., Ltd. d. Nobuyuki Haruta e. Gendai Gabo

a. 徳山東部浄化センター b. 山口県徳山市
c. 東京設計事務所・大阪支社 d. 中根典子 e. 中根典子

a. TOKUYAMA CLEANUP CENTER b. Tokuyama-shi, Yamaguchi
c. Tokyo Architectural Office d. Noriko Nakane e. Noriko Nakane

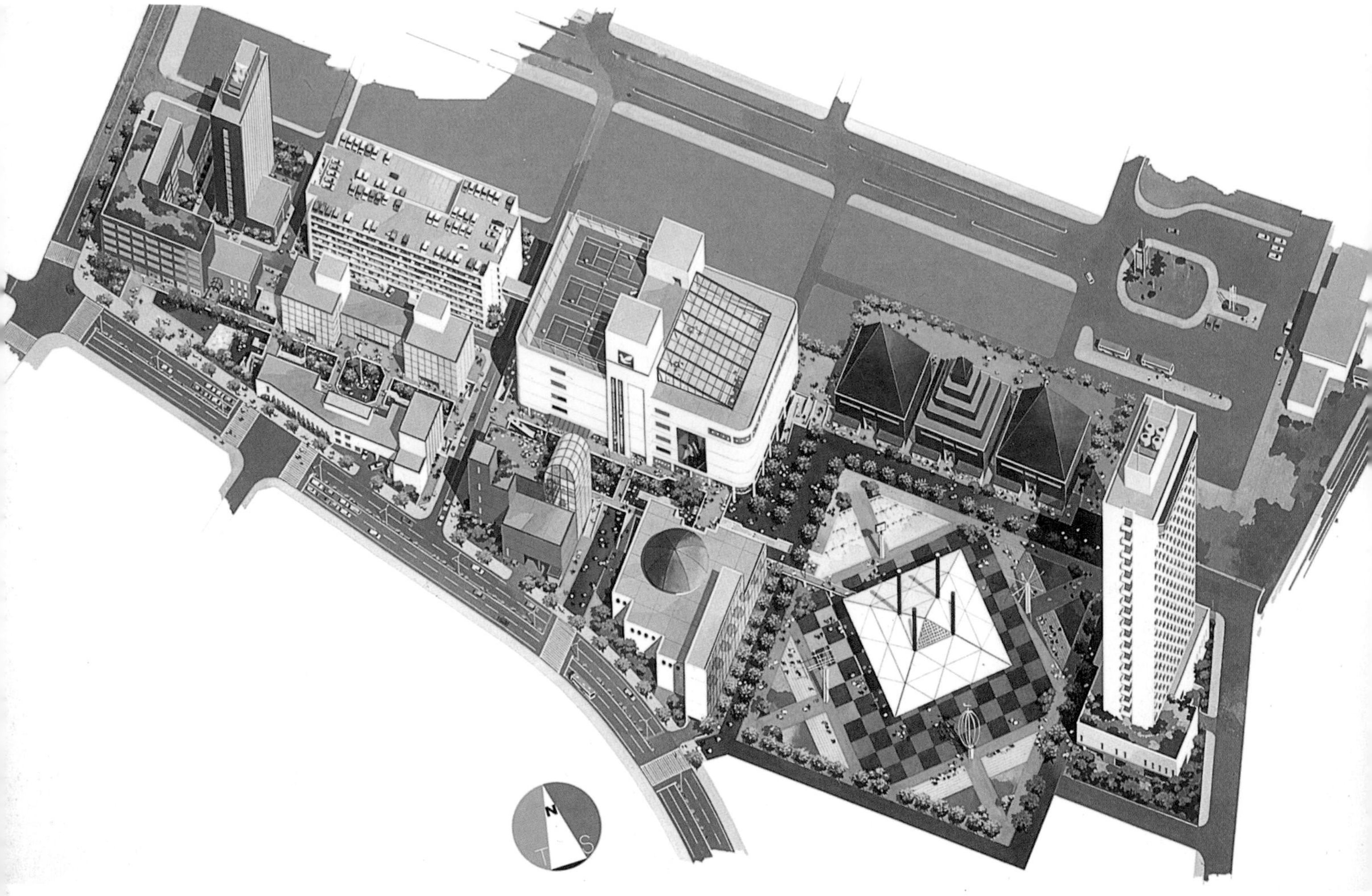

a. 日立駅前再開発計画　b. 茨城県日立市
c. 日本商業企画研究所／タス　d. 深谷彪　e. 深谷彪

a. HITACHI STATION DEVELOPMENT PLAN　b. Hitachi-shi, Ibaraki
c. Architectural Design Office of the Institute for Non-merchandising Development in Japan／TAS
d. Akira Fukaya　e. Akira Fukaya

a. 琉球医科大学　b. 沖縄県
c. 伊藤喜三郎建築研究所　d. 四十澤健文　e. 四十澤健文

a. RYUKYU MEDICAL COLLEGE　b. Okinawa
c. Kisaburo Ito Architects and Engineers Inc.　d. Takefumi Yosozawa　e. Takefumi Yosozawa

a. 鹿島田地区再開発　c. 八千代エンジニヤリング
d. いでのよしえ　e. いでのよしえ

a. KASHIMADA DEVELOPMENT　c. Yachiyo Engineering
d. Yoshie Ideno　e. Yoshie Ideno

a. 牧場看視舎　b. 北海道上士幌町
c. 小野設計　d. 鏡好雄　e. 鏡好雄

a. BOKUJOKANSHISHA　b. Kamishihoro-machi, Hokkaido
c. Ono Sekkei Co., Ltd.　d. Yoshio Kagami　e. Yoshio Kagami

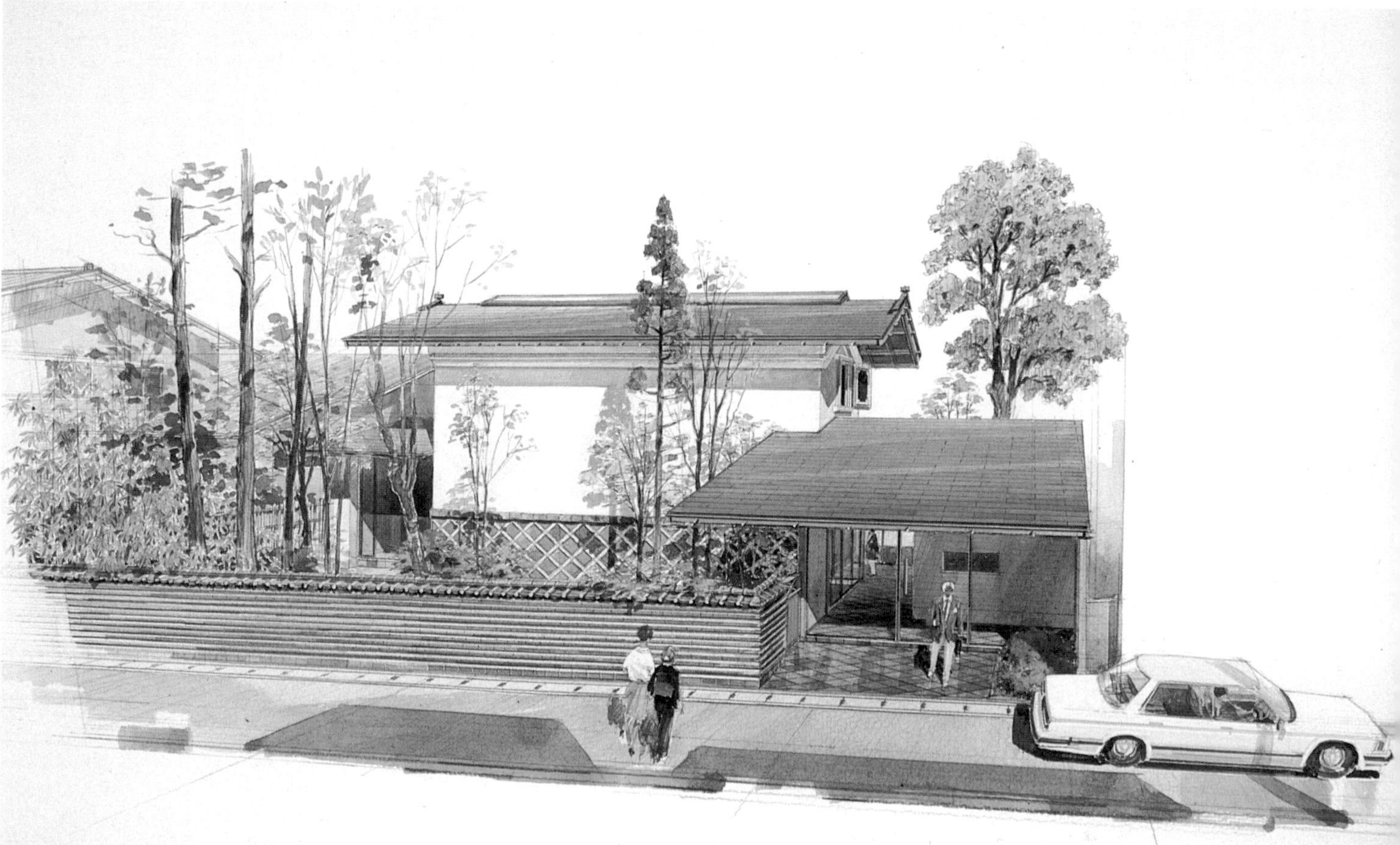

a. 生方記念文庫　b. 群馬県沼田市
c. 林・山田・中原 設計同人　d. 福永文昭　e. フクナガレンダリング

a. UBUKATA MEMORIAL ARCHIVE　b. Numata-shi, Gunma
c. Hayashi, Yamada, Nakahara Sekkei Dojin　d. Fumiaki Fukunaga　e. Fukunaga Rendering Co., Ltd.

a. 新宿駅南口計画
b. 東京都新宿区
c. 小田急建設／アヅチ・プランニングスタジオ
d. 安土実
e. 安土実

a. SHINJUKU STATION SOUTH ENTRANCE PLAN
b. Shinjuku-ku, Tokyo
c. Odakyu Kensetsu Co., Ltd./Azuchi Planning Studio
d. Minoru Azuchi
e. Minoru Azuchi

a. カリヨンの丘
b. 大分県別府市
c. ワープクリエイティブ
d. 松田邦裕
e. コラムデザインセンター

a. CALLION HILL
b. Beppu-shi, Oita
c. Warp Creative Co., Ltd.
d. Kunihiro Matsuda
e. Koramu Design Center Co., Ltd.

a. 東山公園タワー　b. 愛知県名古屋市
c. 日本総合建築設計事務所　d. ヒューマン・ファクター　奥村一也　e. 奥村一也

a. HIGASHIYAMA PARK TOWER　b. Nagoya-shi, Aichi
c. Nihon Sogo Architectural Planning Office　d. Kazuya Okumura　Human Factor Ltd.
e. Kazuya Okumura

a. 猿島コミュニティーセンター　c. 三橋建築設計事務所
d. 西川日出世　e. アトリエ TOKI

a. SASHIMA COMMUNITY CENTER　c. Mitsuhashi Construction Design Office Co., Ltd.
d. Hideyo Nishikawa　e. Atorie Toki

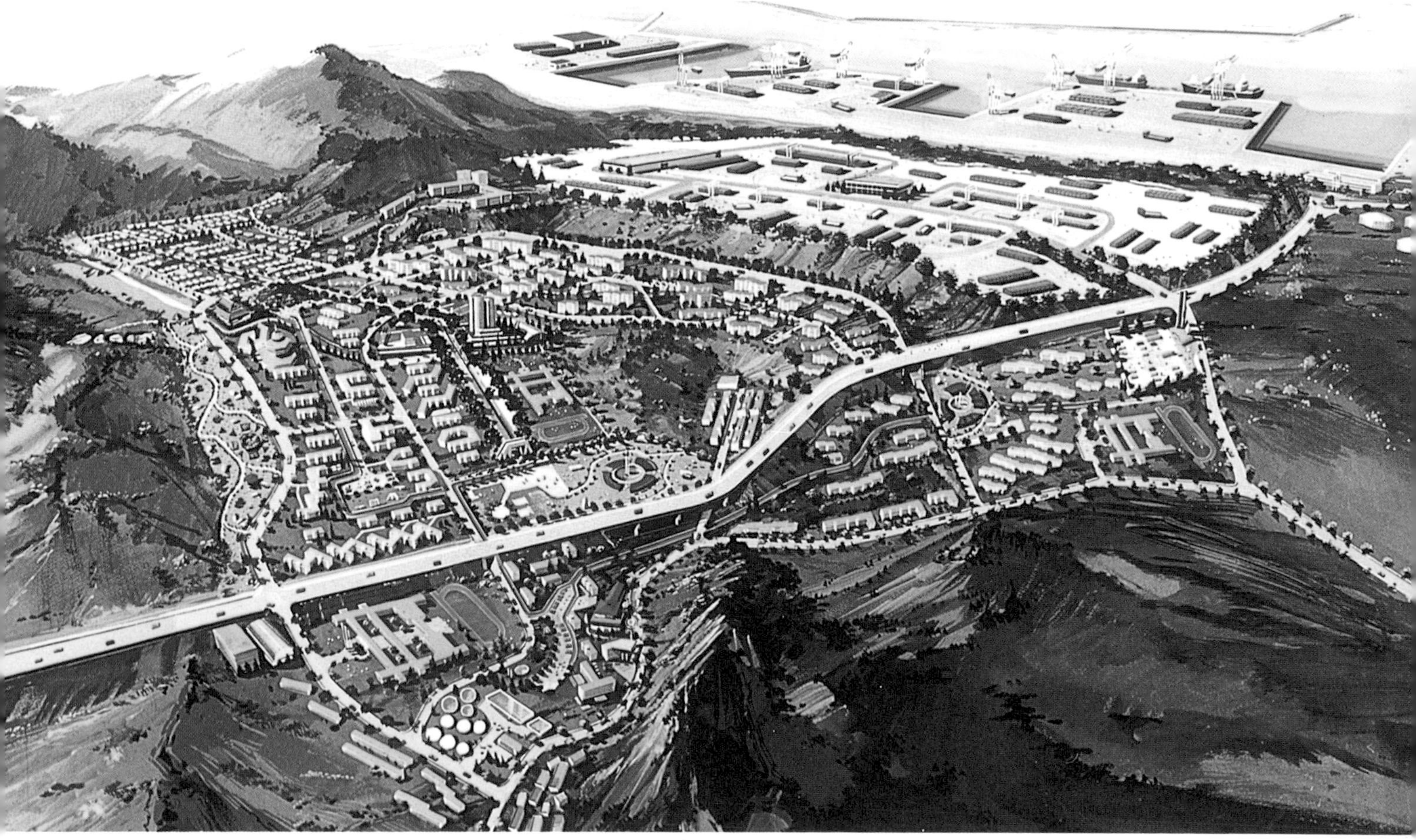

a. 基隆港新都市計画　b. 基隆（台湾）
c. 中華工程顧問公司　d. 王健　e. 王健

a. NEW CITY PLAN IN KEELUNG SPORT　b. Keelung, Taiwan
c. China Engineering Advisor Co.　d. Wang King　e. Wang King

a. 神姫バス西神営業所
b. 兵庫県神戸市
c. 二神建築事務所
d. 四海隼一
e. 四海隼一

a. SHINKI BUS SEISHIN OFFICE
b. Kobe-shi, Hyogo
c. Futagami Architectural Office
d. Shunichi Shikai
e. Shunichi Shikai

a. 新登別大橋完成予想図
b. 北海道登別市
c. 北海道開発コンサルタント
d. 五十嵐茂樹
e. 五十嵐茂樹

a. NEW NOBORIBETSU OHASHI
b. Noboribetsu-shi, Hokkaido
c. Hokkaido Engineering Consultants Co., Ltd.
d. Shigeki Igarashi
e. Shigeki Igarashi

a. 旭川花咲大橋完成予想図
b. 北海道旭川市
c. 北海道土木設計
d. 五十嵐茂樹
e. 五十嵐茂樹

a. ASAHIKAWA HANASAKI OHASHI
b. Asahikawa-shi, Hokkaido
c. Hokkaido Public Works Planning Co., Ltd.
d. Shigeki Igarashi
e. Shigeki Igarashi

索　引

応募者

パース作画者

INDEX

Applicants

Rendering Illustrators

作品応募者一覧

赤坂孝史	〒153	東京都目黒区上目黒1-24-1　玉川ビル301　アカサカレンダリング	☎03-793-1497
アカサカレンダリング	〒153	東京都目黒区上目黒1-24-1　玉川ビル301	☎03-793-1497
浅田能生	〒601	京都府京都市南区上鳥羽塔ノ森東向町84-1	☎075-671-6150
安土　実	〒151	東京都渋谷区本町6-2-21　メゾンヒロ201　アヅチ・プランニングスタジオ	☎03-378-6126
	〒981-11	宮城県仙台市西中田5-3-14　アヅチ・プランニングスタジオ	☎022-241-0877
アヅチ・プランニングスタジオ	〒151	東京都渋谷区本町6-2-21　メゾンヒロ201	☎03-378-6126
	〒981-11	宮城県仙台市西中田5-3-14	☎022-241-0877
㈲アタケ河野陽一建築事務所	〒770	徳島県徳島市安宅町2-5-16	☎0886-53-5272
アトリエ TOKI	〒160	東京都新宿区須賀町11　パープルマンション2F	☎03-357-8495
安建社		SEOUL 鍾路区新榮洞240番地　韓國	☎352・6573
五十嵐茂樹	〒063	北海道札幌市西区発寒12条5-7-26　五十嵐工学パース事務所	☎011-662-5286
いでのよしえ	〒102	東京都千代田区三番町7-10　NK 麹町コータース707　㈱パーススタジオ	☎03-263-4813
伊藤鉄平	〒101	東京都千代田区神田司町2-10　栄ビル3F　テツデザイン	☎03-252-9046
井内一夫	〒662	兵庫県西宮市川添町14-12　㈲スタジオゼロ	☎0798-36-0287
呉長鴻		台北市撫遠街15号　台湾	
エクステリアパース・吉田	〒533	大阪府大阪市東淀川区瑞光4-7-11　本多ビル301号	☎06-327-4947
奥村一也	〒150	東京都渋谷区神宮前2-4-20　外苑アスペイア　㈲ヒューマン・ファクター	☎03-402-2683
㈱オズ・アトリエ	〒107	東京都港区南青山2-29-9　南青山リハイム	☎03-408-4766
鏡　好雄	〒001	北海道札幌市北区新琴似10条1-4-10　㈱鏡デザインプロ	☎011-757-7579
鹿島建設㈱	〒163	東京都新宿区西新宿2-1-1　新宿三井ビル29F	☎03-344-2111
金本　正	〒760	香川県高松市藤塚町3-4-6　㈲金本デザイン事務所	☎0878-34-1765
川上和子	〒465	愛知県名古屋市名東区高社1-157　ロレックス一社305　パースルーム α	☎052-776-8950
川嶋俊介	〒791-31	愛媛県伊予郡松前町北黒田520-2 川嶋レンダリングオフィス㈲	☎0899-84-8498
金容培		SEOUL 江南区論峴洞89-1 (三進 BLDG.301號) 金容培透視図研究所　韓国	
金斯倉		台北市民生東路530巷４号４Ｆ之三　台湾	
建築造型	〒500	岐阜県岐阜市瑞雲町3-26　瑞雲ビル25号室	☎0582-45-3008
㈲現代画房	〒890	鹿児島県鹿児島市下伊敷町561-1　米丸ビル105	☎0992-29-1039
小西久雄	〒604	京都府京都市中京区岩上通六角下ル岩上町741番地リライブ堀川ビル908 エー・アール・ジー 建築画工房	☎075-802-2291
㈱コラムデザインセンター	〒542	大阪府大阪市南区南船場4-13-15　コラムビル	☎06-245-4631
斉藤富子	〒176	東京都練馬区中村南1-30-15　とみあとりえ	☎03-998-7349
坂井田優実	〒451	愛知県名古屋市西区新道1-15-23　ELFA ARCHITECT	☎052-581-0976
塩田純一	〒151	東京都渋谷区代々木5-58-1　㈱レーモンド設計事務所	☎03-460-1171
四海隼一	〒671-12	兵庫県姫路市勝原区山戸22　四海店舗	☎0792-73-6616
清水俊裕	〒102	東京都千代田区飯田橋1-7-10　山京ビル　㈱フクナガレンダリング	☎03-263-5445
清水建設㈱	〒104	東京都中央区京橋2-16-1	☎03-535-4111
殖産住宅相互㈱	〒104	東京都中央区銀座1-9-5	☎03-563-6291
葛念台		台北市安居街84巷３号２Ｆ　台湾	
積水ハウス㈱大阪綜建営業所	〒530	大阪府大阪市北区梅田1-1-3-2800	☎06-344-0731

髙崎千鶴子	〒060	北海道札幌市中央区南3条西12丁目ダイアパレス南3条401　髙崎デザイン事務所	☎011-281-2738
㈱竹中工務店	〒541	大阪府大阪市東区本町4-27	☎06-252-1201
㈱丹青社	〒110	東京都台東区上野5-2-2	☎03-836-7221
陳釙贈		台北市光復南路290巷66号5Ｆ　台湾	
辻野建設工業㈱	〒061-02	北海道石狩郡当別町字西小川通380	☎01332-3-2408
㈱辻本デザイン事務所	〒542	大阪府大阪市南区大宝寺町中之丁22　横山ビル	☎06-252-3478
津田　勉	〒541	大阪府大阪市東区瓦町2-7　フジカワ画廊ビル3Ｆ　デザインルーム　アップル	☎06-231-7128
津田益司	〒374	群馬県館林市本町1-5-18	
中門静子	〒180	東京都武蔵野市吉祥寺北町4-12-9-2A	☎0422-55-1145
成瀬英揮	〒102	東京都千代田区飯田橋1-7-10　山京ビル　㈱フクナガレンダリング	☎03-263-5445
西村弘美	〒107	東京都港区南青山5-12-12　アトリエ105	☎03-407-5669
㈱日建設計	〒541	大阪府大阪市東区高麗橋5-21-1	☎06-203-2361
㈱乃村工藝社　大阪社	〒556	大阪府大阪市浪速区元町1-2-6	☎06-633-3331
橋本弘徳	〒901-21	沖縄県浦添市仲間1482　橋本パース設計事務所	☎0988-78-6531
橋本デザイン事務所	〒540	大阪府大阪市東区内本町橋詰町36-1　第7松屋ビル　11F	☎06-944-0333
秦　昇八	〒546	大阪府大阪市東住吉区湯里2-19-16 秦スペースデザイン研究所	☎06-702-0389
㈲ヒューマン・ファクター	〒150	東京都渋谷区神宮前2-4-20　外苑アスペイア	☎03-402-2683
深谷　彪	〒248	神奈川県鎌倉市材木座3-17-8	☎0467-25-2850
㈱フクナガレンダリング	〒102	東京都千代田区飯田橋1-7-10　山京ビル　㈱フクナガレンダリング	☎03-263-5445
藤城勝範	〒440	愛知県豊橋市柱八番町68	
古橋孝之	〒430	静岡県浜松市田町224-23　㈱矢内店舗設計事務所	☎0534-54-8416
堀口憲嗣	〒543	大阪府大阪市天王寺区生玉町11-29-815	☎06-772-5253
三菱地所㈱	〒100	東京都千代田区丸の内2-4-1	☎03-287-5610
水戸岡鋭治	〒150	東京都渋谷区神南1-13-15　神南ペアシティ301　ドーンデザイン研究所	☎03-463-7029
箕箸純子	〒102	東京都千代田区飯田橋1-7-10　山京ビル　㈱フクナガレンダリング	☎03-263-5445
箕箸重郎	〒102	東京都千代田区飯田橋1-7-10　山京ビル　㈱フクナガレンダリング	☎03-263-5445
武藤渥巳	〒194	東京都町田市南成瀬1-2-1 (2-502)	☎0427-28-7068
村崎　茂	〒272-01	千葉県市川市塩焼2-2-20　1-922	☎0473-96-7595
森　聖一	〒560	大阪府豊中市北緑丘3-1-10-202　森聖一デザイン事務所	☎06-854-4392
柳川敏行	〒194	東京都町田市南大谷838-32　柳川デザイン設計事務所	☎0427-28-7766
山城デザインスタジオ	〒150	東京都渋谷区恵比寿西2-3-15　エビスエイトビル	☎03-770-1501
吉田勝義	〒460	愛知県名古屋市中区葵1-27-37　新栄シティハイツ606　キャップ	☎052-937-7616
芳野　明	〒532	大阪府大阪市淀川区西中島4-8-20-102 よしのデザイン事務所	☎06-303-5448
四十澤健文	〒100	東京都千代田区永田町2-17-5　ローレル永田町412　アートスタジオ画楽	☎03-592-0810
鍾文虎		台北県永和市福和路76巷2号　台湾	
K.K.レンダリングRIYA	〒540	大阪府大阪市東区島町2-17　トキワビル	☎06-941-4906
和田宅矛	〒430	静岡県浜松市野口町501　造研	☎0534-63-7637
王　健		台北市忠孝東路四段250号9楼之三　台湾	☎7712633

パース作画者一覧

あ		頁
赤坂孝史	神奈川トヨタショールーム	12
赤坂孝史	I・D・A 九段下ビル	117
赤坂孝史	共栄火災　徳島ビル	126
浅田能生	おのころアイランド	72
浅田能生	烏丸プラザ（仮称）	127
安土　実	ディスコ　J	46
安土　実	E.S.マリーナ	77
安土　実	新宿駅南口計画	141
安容植	東邦生命社屋	110
五十嵐茂樹	新登別大橋完成予想図	144
五十嵐茂樹	旭川花咲大橋完成予想図	144
いでのよしえ	住宅	102
いでのよしえ	鹿島田地区再開発	139
伊藤鉄平	いわき明星大学	132
井内一夫	IB ジーンズショップ	39
呉長鴻	樂華黃金城	121
エクステリアパース・吉田	シティーハイツ土佐堀	90
エクステリアパース・吉田	アトリエ付邸宅	101
奥村一也	東山公園タワー	142
オズ・アトリエ	サイパン某ホテル計画	56
オズ・アトリエ	F 計画	70
小野木司	喫茶スカイ・ライト	43
小野木司	喫茶サザンクロス	43
小野木司	クリーニング　ツネトミヤビル	124
小武内美佐世	サントノーレ白川	32

か		頁
鏡デザインプロ	RESTAURANT & COFFEE ま～くうえい	52
鏡　好雄	牧場看視舎	140
金本　正	サウスピア'86	53
金本　正	琴平ロイヤルホテル	64
金本　正	アルファ清心町	95
金本　正	サーパス木太	95
川上和子	フランス料理店	51
川上和子	サンハウス野並	89
川上和子	エスポワール平針	89
川嶋俊介	No.10ミツワビル	25
川嶋俊介	スパニッシュレストラン(プラン)	52
川嶋俊介	レストラン（プラン）	54
川嶋俊介＋花岡徳久	ビアレストランミュンヘン	52
川嶋俊介＋花岡徳久	ウェディングプラザ日本閣	59
喜多照子	大阪北野ビル	111
絹田貞子	神戸セントラル開発ビル	107
金容培	千氏住宅	97
金斯倉	新竹科学園区宿舎	88
金斯倉	匯泰台大華厦	118
桑野　忠	箕面スパ・ガーデン	74
小西久雄	総合経営ダイヤモンドクラブ	57
小西久雄	レジャービル　アイオイ	83

さ		頁
斉木美香子	ホテル“エス”	67
斉木美香子	ローベルジュ・デ・ブルーマーリン	76
斉木美香子	原マンション（仮称）	94
斉藤富子	東京都東村山ナーシングホーム(仮称)	91
斉藤富子	栃木相互銀行東越谷支店	122
斉藤富子	清水市立総合病院（仮称）	135
斎藤由美子	ホームケアジャパン本社ショールーム	31
坂井田優実	ホテル「ウインク」	65
坂井田優実	パチンコ「ディズニー」計画案	84
坂井田優実	パチンコ「岐阜」サミット	84
坂井田優実	エスポア「自由ケ丘」	92
坂本牧子	ホーメストショップ	40
坂本牧子	レストラン“バッキンガム”	50
坂本牧子	湘南学生会館（仮称）	88
坂本牧子	日本橋浜町Ｍビル	129
佐藤忠明	ST 計画	105
佐藤忠明	AS 計画	109
塩田純一	第百生命高松ビル	113
四海隼一	ナショナルショップ	28
四海隼一	フキ美容室	29
四海隼一	ボンジュール	42
四海隼一	ピュアハイツ星ケ丘	91
四海隼一	神姫バス西神営業所	144
清水俊裕	キャニオンマンション西台	93
清水俊裕	香山ビル	119
葛念台	台北縣縣立体育場全景	71
葛念台	中國廟宇	133
菅原律子	レストランココス計画	42

た		頁
髙崎千鶴子	レイトンハウス	38
髙崎千鶴子	２Ｍビル	49
髙崎千鶴子	服部ビル	114
高橋くみ子	レストラン“望月”	50
高橋くみ子	ペンション“仙”	57
陳釙贈	環亜門第	86
辻本デザイン事務所	小松グランドホテル	62
辻本デザイン事務所	金沢ファーストホテル	64
津田　勉	パナハイツ ウィンディア	98
津田　勉	1996（習作）	110
津田益司	レストラン	44
津田益司	パチンコ店	83
當山悦司	ツイン21　MID シアター	78
徳永元義	レイ・エ・ルイ	29
とみあとりえ	グロリアハイツ碑文谷	99

パース作画者一覧

な		頁
中門静子	電通独身寮	94
中根典子	スイミングセンター計画案	69
中根典子	レストハウス計画案	77
中根典子	住宅	96
中根典子	オフィス・ビル	124
中根典子	徳山東部浄化センター	137
成瀬英揮	平和台クリスタル217	120
成瀬英揮	山京商事本館　別館	118
西川日出世	沼津ビルディング	112
西川日出世	東海大学湘南校舎12号館	132
西川日出世	猿島コミュニティーセンター	143
西村　昭	神戸ファッションタウン・ホワイトコート計画	19
西村弘美	原宿クエスト	24
西村正純	かくやビル	128
西村正純	MG ビル	129

は		頁
橋本弘徳	ホテル	61
橋本弘徳	那覇市民体育館	68
橋本弘徳	伊藤園ビル	120
橋本弘徳	具志川支庁舎	135
橋本秀章	D 計画(BEACH HOTEL)	60
橋本秀章	M ビル	106
秦　昇八	トヨタショールーム	10
秦　昇八	あわいさ亭	45
原田　剛	リバーサイドモール・オギノ計画	13
原田　剛	K 計画	22
春田信行	出水センタービル	121
春田信行	鹿児島錦江湾ビル(計画案)	130
春田信行	八反丸病院	136
春田信行	郡山町庁舎(コンペ当選案)	137
深谷　彪	新宿西口共同ビル「FF ビル」	129
深谷　彪	日立駅前再開発計画	138
福永文昭	三井ホームファインシリーズ	37
福永文昭	シェ・ハマザキ	51
福永文昭	生方記念文庫	140
フクナガレンダリング	丸紅大阪本社ビル	114
藤城勝範	ビューティーサロンアルルヘアー	28
古橋孝之	鵜方テナントビル	31
古橋孝之	集合店舗計画案	38
古橋孝之	仏壇中原三法堂(倉敷店)	40
細川桂子	科学万博ハートピア自然美のパビリオン	79
堀口憲嗣	奈良そごう百貨店計画案	16
堀口憲嗣	近鉄藤井寺球場	78

ま		頁
前島和也	北長岡ショッピングセンターパレア	30
前島和也	サンルートプラザ東京モニュメント	27
前島和也	スカイラーク足立扇店	44
前島和也	Y 計画	97
前島和也	台北 A ビル計画	130
松浦眞巳	人形町1-1ビル	115
松下久美	柏平安閣	60
松田邦裕	蔦屋書店	39
松田邦裕	カリヨンの丘	141
右高良樹	ホテル八木	65
三菱地所第三建築部(アール・エム南几代美)	読売銀座ビル(プランタンデパート)	34
三菱地所第三建築部+フクナガレンダリング	東京ガスビルディング	113
水戸岡鋭治+ドーンデザイン研究所	原村ショッピングモール計画案	20
水戸岡鋭治+ドーンデザイン研究所	12ケ月	82
水戸岡鋭治+ドーンデザイン研究所	マスターズ R1スタジオ	82
箕箸重郎	光が丘パークタウン中心施設	30
箕箸重郎	キャニオンガーデン豊島園	92
箕箸純子	計画案	13
箕箸純子	キャニオンマンション常盤台	93
武藤渥巳	ホンダクリオ西東京	11
武藤渥巳	伊南農協中沢給油所	12
村崎　茂	日本火災海上保険軽井沢山荘	58
森　聖一	桃山カルチャービル（仮称）	30
森　聖一	北京大飯店　藤吉楼	51
森　聖一	ビル計画案	128
森山雅彦	スポーツセンター計画	69
森山雅彦	ゴールドタワー	116

や・ら・わ		頁
柳川敏行	川崎信用金庫	119
柳谷　隆	神戸市庁舎	134
山岸和治	ホテルニッコーサンフランシスコ	66
山岸和治	ゲストハウス　オールドニュー	70
山城義彦	コリンズ六本木	36
山城義彦	初穂グアムコンドミニアム	87
山城義彦	ビレッジ船橋	100
山城義彦	法照寺寺院	133
横山　博	ラフィーネ007	27
芳谷勝瀰	神戸海洋博物館（原案）	79
芳谷勝瀰	日本銀行大阪支店	122
吉田勝義	TOYOTA オート中部	11
吉田勝義	VIA アピタ岡谷	14
吉田勝義	ユニーショップランド	18
吉田勝義	ファニチャー OKAMOTO	18
吉田勝義	金山ビューティビル	33
吉田勝義	リゾート・ホテル清芳閣	56
吉田勝義	B・B・C レストハウス	71
吉田勝義	奥浜名湖ヨットクラブレスト	76
芳野　明	活魚炉端　万葉	45
芳野　明	ラ・フォーレがんこや	48
四十澤健文	金庄園	40
四十澤健文	リゾートホテル「モンシャトル北城」	59
四十澤健文	工場の厚生体育館棟新築計画	68
四十澤健文	琉球医科大学	138
鍾文虎	廣一大厦	115
レンダリング RIYA	大阪トヨペット交野営業所	10
レンダリング RIYA	ビル	108
渡辺廣史	YS-3計画	24
渡辺廣史	ギヤマビル	26
和田宅矛	八王子びら	99
和田宅矛	大石邸	102
和田宅矛	恵那商品デザイン研究所	136
王　　健	基隆港新都市計画	143

建築パース・外装

初版第1刷発行　1987年4月25日
第10刷発行　1993年6月25日

編集
グラフィック社編集部

発行者
久世利郎

装幀・レイアウト
(株)田村祐介デザイン事務所

印刷
錦明印刷(株)

写植・版下
三和写真工芸(株)

発行
株式会社グラフィック社
〒102 東京都千代田区九段北1-9-12
☎03-3263-4318 振替東京3-114345

乱丁・落丁はお取替え致します。

ISBN4-7661-0425-0 C3052